EIGHTH EDITION

Thinking for Yourself

Developing Critical Thinking Skills
Through Reading and Writing

Marlys Mayfield
College of Alameda

WADSWORTH
CENGAGE Learning

Australia · Brazil · Japan · Korea · Mexico · Singapore · Spain · United Kingdom · United States

WADSWORTH
CENGAGE Learning

Thinking for Yourself: Developing Critical Thinking Skills Through Reading and Writing, Eighth Edition

Marlys Mayfield

Director, Developmental English: Annie Todd

Development Editor: Cate Richard Dodson

Associate Editor: Janine Tangney

Editorial Assistant: Melanie Opacki

Associate Media Editor: Emily Ryan

Marketing Manager: Kirsten Stoller

Marketing Coordinator: Ryan Ahern

Marketing Communications Manager: Martha Pfeiffer

Associate Content Project Manager: Sara Abbott, Anne Finley

Senior Art Director: Jill Ort

Print Buyer: Susan Carroll

Senior Rights Acquisition Account Manager, Text: Margaret Chamberlain-Gaston

Production Service: Elm Street Publishing Services

Rights Acquisition Account Manager, Image: Don Schlotman

Photo Researcher: Jennifer Lim

Cover Designer: Liz Harasymczuk

Cover Image: Getty Images

Compositor: Integra Software Services Pvt. Ltd.

For product information and technology assistance, contact us at **Cengage Learning Customer & Sales Support, 1-800-354-9706**

For permission to use material from this text or product, submit all requests online at **www.cengage.com/permissions.** Further permissions questions can be emailed to **permissionrequest@cengage.com.**

Library of Congress Control Number: 2009922079

ISBN-13: 978-1-4282-3144-3
ISBN-10: 1-4282-3144-7

Wadsworth
20 Channel Center Street
Boston, MA 02210
USA

Cengage Learning products are represented in Canada by Nelson Education, Ltd.

For your course and learning solutions, visit **www.cengage.com.**

Purchase any of our products at your local college store or at our preferred online store **www.ichapters.com.**

Printed in the United States of America
1 2 3 4 5 6 7 13 12 11 10 09

CONTENTS

P R E F A C E

This opening cartoon of the eighth edition of *Thinking for Yourself* offers a metaphor for our present human condition. Collectively, we have come to a place where there are no visible markers or maps to assure our safe passage. We now encounter problems of unprecedented complexity and magnitude: a global financial meltdown, mass unemployment, climate change, and involvement in wars that seem futile. In truth, we can often feel lost.

All that we know for certain is that *we are here*. And all that we can rely upon is our ability to think, to perceive, and to feel our way forward. We need not only to think critically about the ideas, assumptions, and values that led us into this state of crisis, but also to think in new and creative ways through its challenges.

Thus, for us now, sound education in critical thinking is not a fad or an option; it is crucial for our very survival. Now more than ever, we need many people who can think clearly and skillfully for themselves as well as collectively with one another. More than ever, we need to be able to approach our problems and settle our conflicts through a common reference to the arbiter of critical thinking standards.

About the Text

This book originated in 1980 through a series of awakenings. They began with a focus on the nagging dissatisfaction I had felt over fifteen years about teaching English composition. I could help my students edit their writing, but I could not help them improve what generated their writing: their thinking and perceiving. Nor, for that matter, did I know how to do that for myself.

As I set out to investigate this problem, I learned that other educators were beginning to talk about the possibility of teaching thinking; some were saying that thinking was a trainable skill, just like reading and writing. At that time we did not realize that we were on the edge of a high-spirited educational reform movement, one that would generate multiple conferences, academic debates, manifold research, new teacher training programs, new educational requirements, courses, and textbooks.

In 1982 I started teaching a Critical Thinking/Composition course at the College of Alameda, undeterred by the lack of suitable texts then available for this purpose. I prepared handouts of exercises and assignments, kept a class log, and wrote new materials each week in answer to student questions. My students' problems surprised me: they could not write argumentation because they did not know the differences between facts and inferences, between facts and opinions, facts and evaluations, reasons and conclusions. I discovered, moreover, that they had real difficulties understanding assumptions and could not identify political viewpoints. Gradually a text evolved based on what my students wanted and needed to know rather than on my own preconceptions about what they should already know. It took three years of writing, field-testing, and revising for me to produce the first edition that was released in 1986. The text was unique in that it served two purposes:

- To teach English composition by focusing on the perceiving-thinking process
- To teach critical thinking through exercises in writing

More than twenty years later, this book continues to flourish and evolve. My enthusiasm for this work has not diminished although the time required for growing each new edition can feel as burdensome as a mother elephant's pregnancy. Aside from writing, I do all of my own research in order to update the text. The most complex challenge met in preparing each edition has been that of intuiting what topics and examples would remain timely over the next four years. Making those determinations for this eighth edition has been extraordinarily difficult. In the fall of 2008 both presidential candidates were promising to initiate changes at the same time that exterior events were cascading changes. I had to keep my focus on what would endure: what we need to know in order to make best use of our minds; what values and principles; tools, insights, and resources.

New to This Edition

For this edition, twenty new readings were selected and ten retained. It contains eighteen new cartoons to reinforce the learning of chapter concepts and ten photographs for writing exercises. Many of the new readings are short. Some readings were chosen for their currency, and others for their timelessness. Each illustrates a chapter concept and provides another step on a gradient of intellectual/ethical/motivational learning. The whole text has been updated, with the chapters on Assumptions and Viewpoints revised to make them easier to teach and understand. Chapter 9 on Argument has been completely re-written around the theme of illegal immigration, and a complete student essay appears in the Appendix based on an analysis of two arguments on illegal immigration, found in Chapter 9. Chapter 11, Inductive Reasoning, has been divided in half to place the Fallacies of Inductive Reasoning in its own Chapter 12.

Entirely new for this edition is its availability for purchase in digital form. Expanded are also two innovations from the last edition: the instructor's resources and student self-study websites.

Approach and Coverage

1. The text offers the simplicity of an organization based on concepts: concepts that are familiar, yet often misunderstood; concepts that, when correctly understood, make critical thinking possible.

2. This text teaches both critical thinking and composition by emphasizing awareness of the personal thinking process. From the training of personal awareness, it moves to the more advanced stages of analyzing the thinking of others.

3. This book begins on a more fundamental level than most other critical thinking books, yet proceeds to a more advanced level than most, leading students to develop some highly sophisticated analytical skills applied to reading and writing.

4. The first half of the text works extensively with critical thinking in non-verbal problems, using photographs, cartoons, descriptive assignments, and report assignments. The second half moves into more traditional applications of critical thinking through verbal problems, analyses, and arguments.

5. The text constantly provokes its readers to think; indeed, they are obliged to think in order to work their way through the materials. Its problem and writing assignments require personal confrontations with thinking habits that might otherwise remain elusive.

6. In its style and pedagogy, the text consistently shows concern for the interaction of the cognitive and affective domains of learning. It also addresses directly the problems of distinguishing between feelings that clarify thinking and those that hinder thinking.

7. The text uses practical, everyday examples, connecting the concepts learned about thinking to everyday problems. Direct quotations concerning current political and social issues are used extensively to illustrate the ubiquity and influence of arguments in our lives. They also show our need for standards by which to judge them.

8. The text uses every means possible to ensure student success. Discovery exercises encourage students to assess their own knowledge and discover key principles for themselves. The learning of new concepts is continuously reinforced through the use of summaries, quizzes, and application assignments. Directions for writing assignments are designed to prevent confusion, while the scoring boxes clarify expectations and standards for grading.

Special Features

1. A study of the Contents shows that Parts I and II cover basic material not usually presented in such depth in critical thinking texts, whereas Part III offers extensive treatment of the more traditional topics of critical thinking, such as argument, fallacies, inductive reasoning, and deductive reasoning.

2. Multiple tools for evaluating student progress appear in this edition. Each chapter ends with a summary and true-false chapter quiz for the purposes of oral review or written exams. Reviews of learning objectives appear at the end of each major section, and scoring boxes provide an opportunity for peer scoring of most composition assignments. The *Instructor's Manual* contains tests for Parts I and II. It also includes content questions and essay questions for each chapter; tests on dictionary skills; additional tests on fallacies, reasons, and conclusions; additional in-class final exams; a list of media resources; and a bibliography on teaching thinking skills. This manual is now available both in print and at the Instructor's Resource website.

3. This text offers three types of composition assignments. The Composition Writing Applications follow a progression of rhetorical complexity

from description and narration through the longer research papers. The Core Discovery Writing Applications offer experiential understanding of the concepts and skills taught through the text. Each core application is designed to mirror thinking through the writing process, heighten self-awareness, and bring skill deficiencies to the surface. English instructors will want to focus on the core discovery applications as well as draw from the composition series and advanced composition assignments; those using this text for a critical thinking course may want to use only the core discovery applications. The Advanced Composition Series are designed for students who may need more challenging assignments. Writing assignments also may be selected from the questions that follow readings and Internet research exercises.

4. Multicultural viewpoints appear in the text's essays, short stories, and the boxed series on argument. Each reading selection expands on the concepts introduced in each chapter. Whether they appear in the form of fiction or essays, all are designed to stimulate thinking.

5. Internet research exercises have been removed from the text and placed in the *Instructor's Manual*.

6. Argument building and analysis are the most complex skills taught in the text. For this reason, they are introduced through the Building Arguments series in each chapter, both preceding and following Chapter 9, Argument. The first assignment requiring the writing of a short argument appears in Chapter 6, Opinions. The culmination of the whole series appears in Appendix One with two optional research assignments.

7. Appendix Two: Media Literacy may be assigned at any time during the course or left for optional student reading. The information that it provides on source evaluation can also be used to supplement Chapter 8, Viewpoints, or in the preparation for writing research papers.

Acknowledgments

From all those who contributed to this new edition as it grew from 2007 to 2008, I wish to single out for dedication Allen Shulakoff and his students at Laney and Solano colleges. The ongoing dialogue that occurred between us was of immeasurable help and joy to me. I wish to add Raquel Wanzo, also of Laney College, whose creation of a class blog based on my text was a marvel and a revelation.

Among my closest working colleagues, my greatest appreciation goes to Annie Todd, Director of Developmental English at Cengage, and to Cate R. Dodson, Developmental Editor, and Kristin Jobe, Project Editor at Elm Street Publishing Services. My heartfelt thanks goes to the whole staff!

In terms of reviewers, my thanks go first to those of the eighth edition: James Braden, *City University of Seattle*; Amanda Corcoran, *American River College*; Cathy Franklin, *Cypress College*; Mark Hall, *Central Carolina Community College*; Marilyn Hope, *Community Christian College*; Henry McClintock, *Cape Cod Community College*; Deona McEnery, *North Dakota State University*; Anita Pal and Linda Peloquin, *Diablo Valley College*; and Julia Raybould-Rodgers, *Allan Hancock College*.

Then I must give thanks to the reviewers of the first three editions. They include Gary Christensen, *Macomb County Community College*; Robert Dees, *Orange Coast College*; Yvonne Frye, *Community College of Denver*; Helen Gordon, *Bakersfield College*; Patricia Grignon, *Saddleback College*; Elizabeth Hanson-Smith, *California State University, Sacramento*; Ralph Jenkins, *Temple University*; Shelby Kipplen, *Michael J. Owens Technical College*; Eileen Lundy, *University of Texas, San Antonio*; Daniel Lynch, *La Guardia Community College*; L. J. McDoniel, *St. Louis Community College, Meramec*; Paul Olubas, *Southern Ohio College*; Sue Sixberry, *Mesabi Community College*; Patricia Smittle, *Santa Fe Community College*; Fran Bahr, *North Idaho College*; Charlene Doyon, *University of Lowell*; Carol Enns, *College of the Sequoias*; Jon Ford, *College of Alameda*; Nancy Glock, *California Community Colleges*; James Haule, *University of Texas, Pan American*; Jerry Herman, *Laney College*; Becky Patterson, *University of Alaska*; Suzette Schlapkohl, *Scottsdale Community College*; Pamela Spoto, *Shasta College*; and Mark Weinstein, *Montclair State College*.

Reviewers I wish to thank for the fourth edition include C. George Fry, *Lutheran College of Health Professions*; Adrienne Gosselin, *Cleveland State University*; Marilyn Hill, *American River College*; Susan A. Injejikian, *Glendale Community College*; Henry Nardone, *King's College*; Ronn Talbot Pelley, *City University*; and Edith Wollin, *North Seattle Community College*.

Reviewers for the fifth edition included Sandra G. Brown, *Ocean County College, Tom's River, New Jersey*; Dan Clurman, *Golden Gate University, San Francisco*; Maureen Girard, *Monterey Peninsula College, Monterey*; Elizabeth Nelson, *Tidewater Community College, Chesapeake*; Alice K. Perrey, *St. Charles County Community College, St. Peters, Missouri*; Jim Wallace, *King's College, Northeastern Pennsylvania*.

Reviewers for the sixth edition included Michael Berberich, *Galveston College*; Sandra Blakeman, *Hood College*; Maureen Girard, *Monterey Peninsula College*; David Lambert, *City College*; Kerri Morris, *University of Alaska, Anchorage*; and Bruce Suttle, *Parkland College*.

Reviewers for the seventh edition were Alice Adams, *Glendale Community College*; Jerry Herman, *Laney College*; Deborah Jones, *High-Tech Institute*; Carmen Seppa, *Mesabi Community College*; and Cisley Stewart, *State University of New York*.

Marlys Mayfield

Introduction to Critical Thinking

Learning How You Think

This is a book about thinking that will constantly require you to think. Sometimes you will be asked to think out problems for yourself before they are discussed either in the text or in class. In addition, you will always be asked to *observe the way you think* as you go. Discovery Exercises that introduce each chapter in this text will show you *how* you think. They will also help you discover some principles about thinking on your own.

Even this Introduction will begin with a Discovery Exercise. All students should complete it at the same time together in class before continuing to read in this book. After the whole class shares and discusses this exercise, you might each better appreciate the remainder of this Introduction, which discusses the attitudes needed to study critical thinking, a definition of critical thinking, and the habits and values of a critical thinker.

1

© David Lok/SuperStock

DISCOVERY EXERCISE

▩ *Experiencing How We Actually Think:*
An Exercise for the Whole Class to Complete Together

This is an exercise designed for thinking in two stages: first quietly alone and then only afterwards with others. Look at the photograph. Based on what you see there, rate each of the following statements as either *true, false,* or *can't answer.* Write your answers without discussing either the questions or your replies with anyone else.

__T__ 1. This is graduation day for the Johnson family.

__T__ 2. The parents are proud of their daughter.

__T__ 3. The little brother is also proud.

___l___ 4. This is a prosperous family.

___c___ 5. This photo was taken on campus right after the ceremony.

When you have finished this quiz, wait, without talking to anyone else about your choices. Sharing too soon could spoil the results of this experiment. When all have finished, the instructor will poll your answers to each statement. Then you will be asked to break up into two or more groups to defend your answers. Each group will try to arrive at a consensus, functioning somewhat like a jury.

■ After the Discussion

Review the following questions through discussion or writing. You will notice that some of these questions will already have been raised in your groups.

1. What are your definitions of the following terms?
   True   *False*   *Can't Answer*

2. Can a statement be rated *true* if it contains an assumption?

3. Is it possible to determine whether a written statement is *true* if it contains ambiguous words or phrases?

4. Should a statement be rated *true* if it is highly probable?

5. What makes a statement *true* or *false?*

6. Did you find yourself reluctant to choose the option of *can't answer?* Why or why not?

7. How can we know whether or not something is *true?*

8. What did this exercise teach you?

Learning from Sharing How We Think

A surprise can lead us to more learning.

Your work on this last assignment took you from thinking alone to thinking with others. You may have been surprised to discover that there were such different perceptions of a simple photograph.

If your discussion moved your thinking from certainty into uncertainty, you may feel somewhat confused or unsettled at this time. The term we will use for this unsettled state is *disequilibrium.* We feel this kind of discomfort when we need more time to integrate something unfamiliar. Moreover, we feel vulnerable when our thinking is exposed. Even in school, where we are committed to learning, it is not always easy to say,

"I don't know," "I am confused," or "I was wrong." We have to ascertain first if it is safe to be so honest.

Yet if we want to learn new skills, we have to be willing to feel awkward at times. We have to expose our thinking before we can review it. Such a process requires humility, sensitivity, kindness, and humor from everyone involved—from instructors as well as from students. Indeed, if we are not feeling awkward, we may not be really learning.

In review, this assignment was meant to remind you

- What occurs when you think on your own
- How we can further our thinking together in groups
- How such a process can teach us more about thinking

What Is Critical Thinking?

Critical thinking brings conscious awareness, skills, and standards to the process of observing, analyzing, reasoning, evaluating, reading, and communicating.

Thinking is purposeful mental activity.

Critical means to take something apart and analyze it on the basis of standards. The word *critical* comes from *skeri* (Anglo-Saxon) = to cut, separate, sift; and *kriterion* (Greek) = a standard for judging.

Standards of Critical Thinking			
Clarity	Precision	Accuracy	Relevance
Completeness	Soundness	Reliability	Fairness

When we look up the word *thinking* in a dictionary, we find it covers nineteen different mental operations. These range from reasoning to solving problems, to conceiving and discovering ideas, to remembering, to daydreaming. Some of these forms are conscious and directed, whereas others seem to operate on their own without control or awareness. When we need to solve a math problem, we focus and concentrate. When we relax, thoughts and fantasies can come and go without direction. In this book, we will be using the word *thinking* in the sense of *purposeful mental activity.*

What, then, is critical thinking? Most of us associate the word *critical* with negativity or habitual fault-finding. Yet if we look at the history of the word, we can see that connotation was not in its original meaning.

The root of *critical* comes from *skeri,* which means to cut, separate, or sift; thus, its original idea was to take something apart or to analyze it. Moreover, *critical* is also related to the Greek word *kriterion,* which means a standard for judging. Putting together these two original ideas, we see that the word *critical* means *analyzing on the basis of a standard.* When we are critical in the negative sense of blaming and fault-finding, our standards may not be clear, nor our intent constructive.

At present there is not one common definition of critical thinking agreed upon by all teachers in this field. The *Instructor's Manual* that accompanies this text lists more than 20 different definitions. Some come from authors of critical thinking textbooks, some from philosophy professors, and a few from dictionary lexicographers. These definitions differ mainly in the skills, actions, and traits they choose to emphasize. Most would agree that critical thinking is a constructive and deliberate mental activity used to analyze and assess thought and experience. All would also agree that critical thinking hinges upon the ability to understand and apply certain **standards**.

Now, what are the standards of critical thinking? They are the same intellectual standards scientists and scholars have used for centuries to evaluate the reliability of reasoning and information. They include clarity, accuracy, precision, consistency, relevance, reliability, soundness, completeness, and fairness. All these standards help us to aim for truth or to come as close to truth as we can.

When we study critical thinking, we gain **knowledge** of norms and rules for clear and effective thinking. The **norms** embody the standards; the **rules** help us measure them. Each chapter of this text explains norms through rules and examples that compare skilled to unskilled forms of thinking.

What is most difficult about learning critical thinking, however, is that it cannot be mastered through knowledge of norms and rules alone.

Critical thinking is an active skill-building process, not a subject for passive academic study. We need to learn how to apply these standards to our own thinking and help others do the same. And when we accept the challenge of such learning, we go through a process of *unlearning* old habits while also acquiring better ones. Then gradually as we develop these new skills and habits, our knowledge of critical thinking becomes integrated into our lives.

As we work our way through this text, we will be learning both knowledge and skills in spirals of repetition and expansion. What we learn about knowledge and standards will better help us understand the skills required. And developing these skills will help us better appreciate the knowledge and standards required. Thus, we will progress through this text not like mountain climbers, but more like surfers. We will move forward by sometimes rising with the waves, sometimes falling, and sometimes balancing in wondrous new spirals.

> Critical thinking brings conscious awareness, skills, and standards to the process of observing, analyzing, reasoning, evaluating, reading, and communicating.

Relationship to Creative Thinking

Critical thinking analyzes and evaluates given material; creative thinking invents something new.

It is beyond the scope of this book to teach creative thinking, but a brief comparison can help us understand critical thinking better. In brief, whereas critical thinking analyzes and evaluates ideas, creative thinking invents new ideas. To engage in critical thinking, we depend more on the brain's verbal, linear, logical, and analytical functions. Creative thinking also includes these functions but can rely even more on our intuitive-holistic-visual ways of knowing. In the past, these different functions were described as stemming from either the left or right hemispheres of the brain. Recent discoveries in neuroscience have called the simplicity of this distinction into question. Nonetheless, no matter how complex our brains may be, most of us would agree that we experience very different mental states when playing tennis, singing a song, writing a letter, or doing math. Moreover, some of us learn how to enhance our performance in these different activities through **heuristics**, or techniques that help us access the appropriate mental state.

In writing, for instance, we can draw from hidden reserves of creativity by using free writing or clustering. In order to do this, we need to maintain a more relaxed, nonjudgmental state of mind willing to *receive* whatever feelings, symbols, memories, or images may emerge. As we relate to this material, new patterns and insights may arise that would not have resulted from many hours of "hard thinking."

We think critically when we organize, edit, or outline the raw material gained from such a process. Yet we may need to return to a more creative mode of thinking, called **imagination**, should we sense the need to develop new ideas, spot assumptions, assume unfamiliar points of view, formulate multiple inferences, make predictions, and see consequences and implications. Afterwards we may return to analytical thinking again. Bit by bit through such a process, a final work may emerge from this synthesis of critical and creative thinking skills.

We learn to make more conscious use of our critical and creative thinking abilities as we respect their different ways of functioning. If we need to analyze a situation, we sit down in the posture of Rodin's statue *The Thinker,* remain still, and concentrate. When we need to think creatively, we maintain a quality of concentration while also listening to, and following, impulses from within ourselves that we might otherwise censor. Even when we stop concentrating—in deep sleep or while taking a walk—our minds can continue to work creatively on a problem. Once the process is complete, a fresh solution to a complex problem can occur in a sudden flash of insight; it can surprise us while we are doing something entirely mundane and unrelated, such as washing the car, patting a dog, or opening the refrigerator door.

While working with our creative and critical abilities, we need to remember that different standards apply. Critical thinking is concerned mainly with truth, while creative thinking also loves beauty; it wants its designs, ideas, or solutions to be not just adequate, but elegant. Albert Einstein was the model of a scientist who worked quite consciously with his capacities for both creative and critical thinking. He conceived theorems with a simplicity that proved to be both practical and beautiful. Einstein himself valued the creative process so highly that he once said, "Imagination is more important than knowledge."

If you are interested in learning more about the traits and skills of creative thinking, many good books are available, such as *Thinkertoys* by Michael Michalko, *A Whack on the Side of the Head* by Roger von Oech, *Creating Minds* by Howard Gardner, *Sparks of Genius* by Robert and Michele Root-Bernstein, and *Uncommon Genius* by Denise Shekerjian. In addition, Edward de Bono (whom you will meet in Chapter 5) has written dozens of books about creative thinking.

In this text you will also meet a number of authors who demonstrate well-integrated critical and creative thinking abilities. Such authors are able to develop original and complex ideas, yet present them with a simplicity that results from many hours of thinking and writing; such work can inspire their readers to think more deeply as well. Finally, most illustrate the virtues, values, and habits of critical thinkers as listed in Table 1.1 on the last page of this Introduction.

Why Learn Critical Thinking?

We already know how to do many complex kinds of thinking, for many purposes. All of us have developed our own way of solving problems, using "street smarts" and common sense or even trial and error. Yet what we already know can be substantially strengthened by conscious attention, just as those who already know how to walk or fight can greatly improve their abilities by studying dance or karate. This improvement comes from paying closer attention to what we already do, finding the right labels, and finding ways to do it better.

Critical thinking isn't the only form of clear thinking, nor is it always appropriate. If you are just hanging out, swapping stories, sharing feelings, and speculating, the killjoy who demands that every term be defined, every fact be supported, and every speculation be qualified is completely out of place. You don't use an electric saw to slice a roast, but when you do need an electric saw, it is invaluable.

Critical thinking skills are powerful tools. They can empower those who use them more than anything else you learn in college. They can't be picked up on the run; they require careful, disciplined, systematic study. But such study will pay off not only in the short run by improving performance in every single course, but also in the long run by

- Providing protection from manipulation and propaganda
- Helping you exercise more awareness and self-control
- Lessening the likelihood of making serious mistakes
- Helping you make better decisions
- Contributing to better decision making in groups

Although the study of critical thinking leads to mental independence, it is also a path to more productive work with others. It helps people to openly share the workings of their minds: to recognize and direct inner processes for understanding issues, to express ideas and beliefs, to make decisions, and to analyze and solve problems. Critical thinking allows us to welcome life's problems as challenges to be solved. And it gives us the confidence that we can make sense and harmony out of a confusing world.

The Habits of a Critical Thinker

Many of the habits depicted in Table 1.1 may already be part of your life; others may be as yet undeveloped. Because this book is about learning through your own discoveries, these habits will not be fully explained at this time. As you grow in your ability to recognize, monitor, and reshape your own critical thinking habits, you will begin to assimilate your own list. Once you have finished studying this book, you might return to the habits listed here in order to see how far you have come.

The goal is now clear; the time has come to start down its path.

TABLE 1.1 Habits of a Critical Thinker

Awareness	Self-Control	Skills
• Observes self and others in the process of perceiving, thinking, and feeling • Observes and monitors own level of concentration and relative states of confusion or clarity	**Restrains impulses** • To stereotype, to jump to premature judgments and conclusions • To glance instead of observe • To hurry rather than stay present to what is needed • To not ask questions, take too much for granted, not verify information • To cover up mistakes and avoid what can feel difficult to confront **Stands by values** • To discover and express what is true • To be fair, reliable, respectful, and responsible • To seek truth before rightness • To be willing to admit mistakes • To be willing to concede to a better argument • To exercise courage	• Suspends judgment when appropriate • Listens and observes • Uses writing to improve thinking and get ideas across • Reads critically • Persists in gathering and understanding information, getting ideas across, and solving problems • Methodically separates facts from inferences, opinions, and evaluations • Checks for evidence and valid reasoning • Recognizes assumptions • Views content and viewpoint in terms of frame of reference • Uses words with precision and sensitivity to word definitions, connotations, slant, ambiguity • Can prepare a persuasive argument based on sound reasoning • Recognizes fallacies of reasoning • Recognizes unfair persuasion and propaganda

PART I

Basics of Critical Thinking

CHAPTER 1

Observation Skills:
What's Out There?

Not only are we in the wrong parking lot, this isn't the mall we were shopping in.

If we base our thinking on poor observations, then no matter how many strategies we devise, or how well we reason, that thinking will be faulty. This chapter consists mainly of exercises that require observing. The opening Discovery Exercises are designed to show you how *you* observe and how that may be different from the way others observe. Additional exercises are intended to help improve your ability to observe.

DISCOVERY EXERCISES

■ *Comparing Our Perceptions*

In class, write a one-paragraph description of the photograph below. Try to describe what you see in such a way that your readers will be able to visualize it without having the picture before them. Do not discuss your work with anyone else in class while you observe and write.

Used with permission of Mark Townsend.

When you have finished, form small groups to read your descriptions aloud to one another. As you listen, notice in what details your descriptions are similar or different. When your group has finished, signal to the instructor that you are ready for a full class discussion of the following questions.

1. How can our differences be explained?
2. How can we know what is correct and what is not?

In completing this exercise, you may have discovered that what we first see from a glance can be quite different from what we learn when we actually *see*. You may have also discovered that we look for what is familiar, and if we can't find the familiar, we can even distort the unfamiliar to make it seem familiar. Thus, some telling details deemed irrelevant by some will seem highly relevant to others.

▪ What Is Observing?

> To **observe** means to hold something in front of us.
>   *ob* (Latin prefix) = in front of
>   *servare* (Latin) = to keep, hold, watch, pay attention
> To **watch** is to stay awake.
>   *waeccan* (Old English derived from Indo-European *weg*, meaning to stay strong) When we watch, therefore, we stay strong and awake.

The word **observe**, like other words that are the subjects of future chapters, is one that we hear and use every day. Therefore you might wonder why it needs defining at all. Let's hold that question until the following exercises are completed.

▪ Observing a Cube

In this exercise, look at Figure 1.1. Observe the cube by watching it, looking at it intently, and staying "strong and awake" in your concentration. Then write down your answers to the following questions:

1. What happens to the cube as you observe it?
2. How does observing feel as you do it?

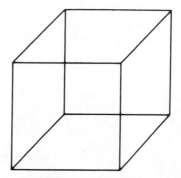

FIGURE 1.1 Observing a Cube

■ *Observation and Insight*

Carefully study the cartoons that appear in this chapter. For each one, notice and write down (1) what you have to notice in order to decode its meaning; (2) how you react when you "get it"; and (3) how you feel when you can't be sure what it is about.

"Could you pass the peanuts?"

Using Observation Skills to Develop New Knowledge

The beginning of science is the ability to be amazed by apparently simple things. (Noam Chomsky)

It is more convenient to assume that reality is similar to our preconceived ideas than to freshly observe what we have before our eyes. (Robert Fritz)

Those of you who discovered something new from these exercises learned because you observed in the true sense of staying awake and being closely attentive. Therefore you became aware of details, which a sweeping

glance would have missed, that revealed significance about the whole. The following reading illustrates this process of learning. It is the story of a trial that a student went through that tested his capacity to do graduate research in science. Samuel H. Scudder (1837–1911) was an American naturalist who attended Lawrence Scientific School at Harvard, where he studied under the great biologist (then called a naturalist) Professor Jean Louis R. Agassiz. Read carefully, for at the end you will be asked some questions followed by a writing exercise.

● R E A D I N G ●

Look at Your Fish

Samuel H. Scudder

It was more than fifteen years ago that I entered the laboratory of Professor Agassiz and told him I had enrolled my name in the Scientific School as a student of natural history. He asked me a few questions about my object in coming, my antecedents generally, the mode in which I afterwards proposed to use the knowledge I might acquire, and, finally, whether I wished to study any special branch. To the latter I replied that, while I wished to be well grounded in all departments of zoology, I purposed to devote myself specially to insects.

"When do you wish to begin?" he asked.

"Now," I replied.

This seemed to please him, and with an energetic "Very well!" he reached from a shelf a huge jar of specimens in yellow alcohol. "Take this fish," he said, "and look at it; we call it a haemulon; by and by I will ask what you have seen."

5　　With that he left me, but in a moment returned with explicit instructions as to the care of the object entrusted to me.

"No man is fit to be a naturalist," he said, "who does not know how to take care of specimens."

I was to keep the fish before me in a tin tray and occasionally moisten the surface with alcohol from the jar, always taking care to replace the stopper tightly. These were not the days of ground-glass stoppers and elegantly shaped exhibition jars; all the old students will recall the huge neckless glass bottles with their leaky, wax-besmeared corks, half-eaten by insects and begrimed with cellar dust. Entomology was a cleaner science than ichthyology, but the example of the Professor, who had unhesitatingly plunged to the bottom of the jar to produce the fish, was infectious, and though this alcohol had a "very ancient and fishlike smell," I really dared not to show any aversion within these sacred precincts and treated the alcohol as though it were pure water. Still I was conscious of a passing feeling of disappointment, for gazing at a fish did not commend itself to an ardent entomologist. My friends at home, too, were annoyed when they discovered that no amount of eau-de-Cologne would drown the perfume that haunted me like a shadow.

In ten minutes I had seen all that could be seen in that fish, and started in search of the Professor—who had, however, left the Museum; and when I returned, after lingering over some of the odd animals stored in the upper apartment, my specimen was dry all over. I dashed the fluid over the fish as if to resuscitate the beast from a fainting fit and looked with anxiety for a return of the normal sloppy appearance. This little excitement over, nothing was to be done but to return to a steadfast gaze at my mute companion. Half an hour passed—an hour—another hour; the fish began to look loathsome. I turned it over and around, looked it in the face—ghastly; from behind, beneath, above, sideways, at a three-quarters' view—just as ghastly. I was in despair; at an early hour I concluded that lunch was necessary; so, with infinite relief, the fish was carefully replaced in the jar, and for an hour I was free.

On my return, I learned that Professor Agassiz had been at the Museum but had gone and would not return for several hours. My fellow students were too busy to be disturbed by continued conversation. Slowly I drew forth that hideous fish, and with a feeling of desperation again looked at it. I might not use a magnifying glass; instruments of all kinds were interdicted. My two hands, my two eyes, and the fish: it seemed a most limited field. I pushed my finger down its throat to feel how sharp the teeth were. I began to count the scales in the different rows, until I was convinced that that was nonsense. At last a happy thought struck me—I would draw the fish; and now with surprise I began to discover new features in the creature. Just then the Professor returned.

10   "That is right," said he; "a pencil is one of the best of eyes. I am glad to notice, too, that you keep your specimen wet and your bottle corked."

With these encouraging words, he added:

"Well, what is it like?"

He listened attentively to my brief rehearsal of the structure of parts whose names were still unknown to me; the fringed gill-arches and movable operculum; the pores of the head, fleshy lips and lidless eyes; the lateral line, the spinous fins and forked tail; the compressed and arched body. When I finished, he waited as if expecting more, and then, with an air of disappointment:

"You have not looked very carefully; why," he continued more earnestly, "you haven't even seen one of the most conspicuous features of the animal, which is as plainly before your eyes as the fish itself; look again, look again!" and he left me to my misery.

15   I was piqued; I was mortified. Still more of that wretched fish! But now I set myself to my task with a will and discovered one new thing after another, until I saw how just the Professor's criticism had been. The afternoon passed quickly; and when, toward its close, the Professor inquired:

"Do you see it yet?"

"No," I replied, "I am certain I do not, but I see how little I saw before."

"That is next best," said he, earnestly, "but I won't hear you now; put away your fish and go home; perhaps you will be ready with a better answer in the morning. I will examine you before you look at the fish."

This was disconcerting. Not only must I think of my fish all night, studying, without the object before me, what this unknown but most visible feature might be; but also, without reviewing my discoveries, I must give an exact account of them the next day. I had a bad memory; so I walked home by the Charles River in a distracted state, with my two perplexities.

20   The cordial greeting from the Professor the next morning was reassuring; here was a man who seemed to be quite as anxious as I that I should see for myself what he saw.

"Do you perhaps mean," I asked, "that the fish has symmetrical sides with paired organs?"

His thoroughly pleased "Of course! of course!" repaid the wakeful hours of the previous night. After he had discoursed most happily and enthusiastically— as he always did—upon the importance of this point, I ventured to ask what I should do next.

"Oh, look at your fish!" he said, and left me again to my own devices. In a little more than an hour he returned and heard my new catalogue.

"That is good, that is good," he repeated; "but that is not all; go on"; and so for three long days he placed that fish before my eyes, forbidding me to look at anything else, or to use any artificial aid. "Look, look, look," was his repeated injunction.

25   This was the best entomological lesson I ever had—a lesson whose influence has extended to the details of every subsequent study; a legacy the Professor had left to me, as he has left it to many others, of inestimable value, which we could not buy, with which we cannot part.

A year afterward, some of us were amusing ourselves with chalking outlandish beasts on the Museum blackboard. We drew prancing starfishes; frogs in mortal combat; hydra-headed worms; stately crawfishes, standing on their tails and bearing aloft umbrellas; and grotesque fishes with gaping mouths and staring eyes. The Professor came in shortly after and was as amused as any at our experiments. He looked at the fishes.

"Haemulons, every one of them," he said; "Mr. _____ drew them."

True; and to this day, if I attempt a fish, I can draw nothing but haemulons.

The fourth day, a second fish of the same group was placed beside the first, and I was bidden to point out the resemblances and differences between the two; another and another followed, until the entire family lay before me, and a whole legion of jars covered the table and surrounding shelves; the odor had become a pleasant perfume; and even now, the sight of an old, six-inch, worm-eaten cork brings fragrant memories.

30   The whole group of haemulons was thus brought in review; and whether engaged upon the dissection of the internal organs, the preparation and examination of the bony framework, or the description of the various parts, Agassiz's training in the method of observing facts and their orderly arrangement was ever accompanied by the urgent exhortation not to be content with them.

"Facts are stupid things," he would say, "until brought into connection with some general law."

At the end of eight months, it was almost with reluctance that I left these friends and turned to insects; but what I had gained by this outside experience has been of greater value than years of later investigation in my favorite groups.

• • •

Study/Writing/Discussion Questions

1. Why did Agassiz keep saying "Look at your fish!"? What was he trying to teach Scudder?
2. How would you describe the stages in Scudder's process of looking? What happened at each stage?
3. How did Scudder change personally in the course of his "trial"?
4. Explain why you think Agassiz's method of teaching was either effective or wasteful.

Core Discovery Writing Application

Creativity is piercing the mundane to find the marvelous. (Bill Moyers)

■ *Observing the Familiar: Vegetable or Fruit*

This is not an easy assignment. Its purpose is to show you how your descriptive writing can improve when you deepen your capacity to observe. It will require that you struggle with some old habits, such as relying more upon memory, imagination, and clichés of thought. The directions are designed to steer you away from these habits. If you follow them exactly, once you have finished you might realize that it provided an initiation experience comparable to that described by Scudder. There is only one prerequisite: *a willingness to stretch your limits by spending at least one hour in the process of observing and recording.* If you resolve to remain primarily "interest*ed*" in the fruit or vegetable, rather than trying to produce an "interest*ing*" piece of writing, the hour will go by very quickly and the results may astonish even you.

You might have sufficient time to complete this assignment in class. However, it is more likely that your instructor will make this a home assignment. If that is the case, be sure to set up a place to work at home where you will not be distracted or interrupted.

■ *Assignment Directions*

1. First of all, set up your note sheets by drawing a line down the center of several pages to create two columns with these two headings:

Physical Details (what I observe and discover about the object)	Inner Process Details (what I observe and discover happening within myself as I work: my moods, reactions, associations, and thoughts)

2. Select as your subject one vegetable or fruit that you have seen and handled many times, such as a sweet potato, an onion, a tomato, or an apple. Whatever you can find in your neighborhood grocery store or home refrigerator will do. It does not have to be an exotic mango or persimmon. Consider your selection to be your specimen for study just as Scudder worked with one fish.

3. Set up your workplace on your desk or a kitchen table. Perhaps you will want to have a knife and cutting board handy as well as some drawing paper for sketching.

4. Begin by really taking your time to explore this object. Let yourself become absorbed in the task like either a curious child or a dedicated scientist. As your mind slows down, your sensations will tell you more, and you will make more and more discoveries. Remember to notice not only parts but also wholes, not only see but also touch, hear, smell, and taste. Whenever you become aware of a characteristic that you can articulate, write that down in the left column under "Physical Details."

5. Do not forget to use the right column for noting your personal reactions as you work. At what points did you become bored? Excited? Angry? Impatient? Lost in daydreams? Acknowledge these distractions by writing them down as you bring your attention back to the task of observing your object.

6. See how many times you need to renew your commitment to keep observing. Note all the stages of interest and concentration that you pass through: the plateaus, valleys, and peaks.

7. When you know for certain that you have finished, assemble your notes and prepare to write up a complete description of your fruit or vegetable.

8. Your final description may take one of two forms: (1) a report that describes the object completely with the addition of a final paragraph describing your own inner personal process, or (2) a narrative—or story of your observing process—that describes your object, the stages you went through, the progression of your discoveries, insights, and reactions.

9. Type up your final draft as a double-spaced paper. Suggested length is *at least two pages.*

● STUDENT WRITING EXAMPLE

This example is not offered as a model for you to imitate like a recipe. Rather, it is meant to demonstrate how one student became absorbed in her work and solved the problem of staying sensitive to her subject and herself at the same time. Read it as a reminder of what the assignment is asking you to do, then forget it and create your own paper by being true to your own experience. Remember that one purpose of this exercise is to help you discover your own observation style and biases.

TOMATO CALIFORNIA FRESH #4798
Jessi Thompson

I made fajitas last week for my roommates, so I had a few leftover vegetables as options for my observation assignment. At first I thought I would describe the most unusual of these to make the assignment more interesting. I had to remind myself

Physical Details	Inner Process Details
→ Green in Color → tiny brown marks → Soft on one side → Hard on the rest of the side → Has deep hole with a stem coming out → Smells sweet → When you shake it, it makes no noise → Shallow on the bottom with some soft leaves. → 2 stickers labeled as "Granny Smith #4139" and USA.	I felt hungry and felt the need to bite it and taste it.

- Green in color
- tiny brown marks
- Soft on one side
- Hard on the ___ of the side.
- Has deep hole with a stem comming out
- smells sweet
- When you shake it, it makes no noise.
- Shallow on the bottom with some soft leaves

- I felt hungry and felt the need to bite it and taste it.

that the intent of the essay was to write in depth about something seemingly simple and ordinary; reconsidering, I opted for the most everyday, commonplace vegetable I could find.

I opened the refrigerator and chose a tomato. Although I felt certain this was as uncomplicated a choice as I could make, I realized I didn't know the simplest detail: Is a tomato a fruit or a vegetable? My dictionary answered that a tomato is a *red or yellowish fruit with a juicy pulp; used as a vegetable*. The entry further noted that botanically, a tomato is actually a berry. Immediately, I imagined the tomato as the subject of some kind of fruit and vegetable controversy, complete with paparazzi and sleazy talk shows.

Taking the tomato out of the container, I felt its cold, plastic-like skin. It even looked plastic, and it felt hard and dense in my hand. If I didn't know from experience, I would not have guessed the tomato was juicy inside. A sticker on the top of one side labeled it "California Fresh #4798"; the top of the tomato dipped down towards the center where the stem and five little wiry leaves were the only other break from the red color, at least at first glance. It was apparent, though, that the shape of my tomato was not perfectly round. It had a soft, almost cubed shape, with rounded corners, and it seemed like it had molded its shape to the container in which it had been stored, making this wobbly, semi-round shape.

Holding the tomato closer to my face, I noticed that the bright red color and the smoothness of the skin were not as consistent and even as they had first appeared. There were blotches of yellow spattered along the top surface, as if tiny particles of paint had been sprayed there. I ran my fingers along the skin, feeling peaks and valleys now along the surface with scars and other imperfections. When I held the tomato up to the light, the peaks reflected light more brightly than the softer divots of the skin. I was reminded of the brilliance of a diamond when it is cut, and how the shine from those many facets is so pleasing to the eye. My tomato beamed at me, and I smiled back.

Finally I turned my fruit over, seeing that the underside was significantly smoother than the top half had been, with one exception. The skin looked as if it had been pinched off in the middle, similar to how the skin on top had dipped and puckered at the stem. The shape came to a soft point at the center where a tiny green "x" marked the bottom of the tomato.

Turning my attention to other senses now, I held the tomato next to my ear and tapped at the skin, listening. I could actually hear how ready-to-burst it was; the sound was not hollow, but also not as dense as a solid object would have sounded. The tomato absorbed much of the sound, bringing to mind how explosively juicy it must be inside. I saw an image of Fozzie Bear from The Muppets getting battered by tomatoes after delivering a terrible joke which he had undoubtedly finished with "Waka-waka-waka!" Along with the familiar picture of a bombing comic came a reminder about the negative connotation of tomatoes as being the disgruntled audience member's weapon of choice.

I brought myself back from the Fozzie distraction, trying to regain my unbiased perspective. I sniffed the skin, and a combination of smells overwhelmed my nostrils. There was a sharp, astringently citrus smell, followed by a muskiness, and then back to sour again. It was hard to pinpoint any one smell that stood out above the rest, giving weight to the idea of a tomato being identified as both a fruit and vegetable. I licked the skin, too, feeling again a hard, plastic texture but noticing no flavor. I inhaled one more time; and despite the fact that I don't like tomatoes, I felt the urge to take a big bite out of it, and my mouth watered when I thought about the juice dripping into my mouth and down my chin.

Finally I closed my eyes, hoping to hone in on anything I might have missed with my eyes open. Beyond the scars and what had been visible landscape, I could feel softer spots where the fruit had been bruised and the skin was now more vulnerable. I knew what was rolling around in my hand, but I still found myself wanting to treat the object like a baseball. My grip changed instinctively to grip tighter, and I wanted to toss it in the air. I also noticed that the sticker, stem and leaves were uncomfortable to touch now, interrupting the smooth quality of texture. I wanted to feel a more infallible shape, and I avoided running my fingers along the blemishes.

I felt like I had a grasp of the tomato's nooks and crannies now, so although I couldn't bring myself to take a bite out of it, I cut it in half to look at the meat of the fruit. Before I had cut even a third of the way through, tomato juice began to drip down my hand and onto my cutting board. The very center of the fruit, or what would have been the core of an apple, was a light yellowish-green color which ran from the stem through to the bottom "x." More flecks of this color sprouted out from the center, each one leading to a seed. I could see now what made the skin seem so solid: a thick, dense meat surrounded the juicy center, and I knew this was what had felt so solid and impenetrable when I had squeezed it like a ball. Now, without the protective casing, I was able to squeeze the skin and watch juice almost *pour* from the exposed side of the half I held. My mouth watered for a second time.

As I finished up my notes and thoughts about this assignment, I remembered the lengthy discussion in class about how to appropriately acknowledge boredom and distraction, and then to draw focus back to the task of observation. I realized this hadn't been my challenge at all; my challenge was curbing my imagination and preventing myself from falling into the natural desire to write creatively. I had indulged to a point with each of these detours in my thought process, and this had kept me entertained. I had felt oppositely distracted each time I reminded myself to stay objective, and I had resented the "rules" of the assignment a little as I resisted my imagination and got back on track.

Writing without bias—while at the same time avoiding the mundane sound of an instruction manual—proved difficult enough for me to have almost been two mutually exclusive ideas. I felt humbled when I realized this type of writing would not come as easily or flow as smoothly as I had hoped. On the other hand, I feel I have opened the door to a fresh perspective on nuances around me, and I understand this process to have been that of self-discovery which fostered a deepened understanding of observation itself.

Used with permission of Jessi Thompson.

Evaluating Your Work by Using the Scoring Boxes

The scoring box offers a simple, consistent checklist for reviewing the assignment's objectives, for understanding its priorities, and for clarifying standards for peer feedback, draft revision, and quite possibly, instructor grading.

A scoring box, like the one on the following page, follows each Writing Application Assignment in this book. The scoring box is intended to remind you of what thinking skills the assignment is intended to foster. For instance, you will notice that you are given 20 points for completing at least two full typed pages for this first assignment. In other words, if you only skim through this assignment, you will not have much to say, certainly not enough to fill two typed pages. Thus, these 20 points represent a reward for persevering in your observing long enough to produce that much material; it shows to what extent you stretched your capacities to observe.

If your typed draft comes to less than two pages, this could mean that you will need to return to your subject for another round of observing with note taking. Or it could mean that you only need to go over your notes again and reconsider what you discovered but did not fully explain.

Thus, the scoring boxes can serve first as a checklist to help you determine the strengths and weaknesses of your first draft. Second, they can be used in class to guide you and your classmates in assessing one another's work. If your peers give you some useful feedback in the form of low ratings in some areas, and if your instructor agrees, you might want to give your draft another revision before submitting it for a grade. Finally, if your instructor so chooses, the boxes may serve as standards for the final grading of your paper. In summary, the scoring boxes have the following purposes:

1. To clarify each assignment's skill-building components
2. To clarify priorities and criteria
3. To clarify standards for a peer critical analysis that will take place in class
4. To enable you to turn in your best work for a grade

It needs to be emphasized that this evaluation technique is not intended to set up an arbitrary point grading system. Its most important purpose is to take more of the stress out of writing—for both students and instructors. The scoring boxes accomplish this by

1. Reminding you of the instructions' components
2. Keeping your attention on all of the instructions
3. Preventing wasted time from going off on the wrong track
4. Clarifying what priorities and standards you are expected to meet
5. Making it easy for your peers and instructor to judge your work with focus and fairness

Scoring for Description of Fruit or Vegetable
1. Minimum of two full pages. *20 points*
2. All senses used. *24 points* (3 points each)
Touch/texture	Sound
Taste	Color
Smell	Shape
Temperature	Changes that occur during description
3. Physical description (at least 2/3 of paper). *10 points*
4. Language accuracy. *10 points*
5. Crucial aspects not omitted (skin, seeds, interior aspects, and design). *10 points*
6. Inner process described. *10 points*
7. No distracting errors of spelling, punctuation, or sentence structure. *16 points*

Alternate Core Discovery
Writing Application

■ *Observing the Unfamiliar: A Tool*

Bring to class some household tool whose function may be unfamiliar or difficult for most people to identify. This could be a cooking implement, a highly specialized tool for some craft, a cosmetic tool, or any interesting item from your kitchen drawer or tool chest. Do not select anything that has sharp points or blades. Carry this object to class in a paper sack so that no one else can see it. Do not discuss with anyone else what you have brought.

Step 1 The instructor will ask you to exchange your bag with someone else. Sitting at your desk with your eyes closed, put the bag on your lap under your desk and take the object out of the bag quietly. Spend at least fifteen minutes exploring your subject with your hands, getting to know its shape and texture by touch. Set aside your concerns about how to label it. Your perceiving mind will want to categorize it immediately according to some mental stereotype. "Oh," it will say, "that is just a can opener. All can openers are the same. I know what this looks like already." When this happens, just notice what your mind is doing and go on exploring the object as though you were a child, enjoying its touch, its smell, temperature, and taste (if you dare!). *Remember, this is not a guessing game whose purpose is to label an object, but an exercise in gaining information about an object through your senses.* Get all the data you can without looking. Try to guess its color. Take notes as you go along.

Step 2 When the instructor gives the signal, put the tool on top of your desk and open your eyes. Notice and write down your first reaction. Now spend at least fifteen minutes observing the visual details of your object and taking more notes. Gather all the information you can now from seeing.

Step 3 After class, put all your information together and write at least a one-page typed description that enables readers to imagine the object. (You can also provide a drawing.) Organize your information so that the reader can follow your process of exploration. In a final paragraph, or as you go along, describe what it felt like for you as you worked. Were there different stages in your process? Did you feel frustrated and anxious if you couldn't label your object?

Scoring for the Tool Exercise

1. One full page minimum. *15 points*
2. Exploration of the following elements. *40 points* (5 points each)
   Temperature
   Texture
   Weight
   Smell
   General shape and parts
   Colors
   Sounds
   Visual design elements such as scratches, trademarks, thumbprints
3. Inferences or guesses regarding its function. *15 points*
4. Physical description complete. *10 points*
5. No distracting errors of spelling, punctuation, or sentence structure. *10 points*
6. Personal process described. *10 points*

● STUDENT WRITING EXAMPLE

UNDERCOVER TOOL

Kenneth Wong

My partner handed me the brown paper bag that contained some unidentified tool. I placed the bag under my desk and reached inside, took it out, and dropped the bag to the floor. I immediately knew that what I was holding was a plastic disposable spoon. I was extremely disappointed that my partner did not take the time and effort to look for something more challenging. In my mind I imagined that she forgot to bring her tool and ran down to the cafeteria to see what she could scrounge up. Although I was displeased with my object, I decided to make the best of the situation. I began my investigation through touch. My first observation was that the tool felt smooth and concave. I thought it resembled the shape of a half lemon without all the pulp. Judging from the smoothness of the object, I imagined it to be as clean and glossy as glass. As I felt my way up the object, I noticed it had a stem extending from its head. The extension was also relatively smooth except for what appeared to be a border about 2 mm thick along its edges. I could also feel a rough surface on the hind side of the stem. I assumed it was an imprint of the manufacturer's name. I identified a "D" in the writing and continued to survey the rest of this new terrain. In a valiant attempt to entertain myself, I attempted to decipher the rest of the writing. However, I failed miserably. After exploring the head and stem, my mind went blank. I assumed that was all there was to know about this typical plastic spoon.

After sitting still for about a minute, I decided to continue my investigation. I began examining the object with greater precision and concentration. I tried flicking the object and noticed it made a peculiar "click." Then I tried flicking it harder and harder. The noise would get louder but the tone and pitch of the click remained constant. My action of flicking the spoon then made me notice its flexibility, which led me to conclude that it was definitely not made of metal. I also began feeling for warmth. The object wasn't cold; however, it wasn't exactly warm either. I knew then for sure that the object was made of flexible plastic.

My mind went numb again until I had another great idea. I began playing catch with the tool, still keeping it under the table, of course. I realized it was very light in weight, almost weightless. It had a very airy sensation. The tool landed in my palms gently and with great ease. Then I tried bending the object and realized it was not as flexible as I first had imagined. After a certain point the object felt suddenly stiffer as though it were about to snap: so I let go. I realized that this spoon was not as flexible as ones I had used before. It was much stronger and more solid. However, the longer I played with it, the more flexible it became. It also seemed to get warmer. I placed my thumb in the concave head of the spoon and left it there while I continued to examine the object with my other hand. When I released my thumb, I could feel that the tool was much warmer in that area. Then I remembered to smell the tool. I couldn't detect any scent I could describe, either of plastic or of food.

The fifteen-minute examination time was finally over, thank God. I was about to go out of my mind with boredom. I brought my spoon up to my eyes and immediately a rush of images flooded my head. Though I wasn't exactly surprised by the identity of my object, little things like the reflection that came off the shine of the spoon captured my attention. I was stunned by the piercing glow of its white plastic: its shimmering whiteness resembled strong sunlight reflecting off fresh snow. I now also saw small dents and scratches that my fingertips had not detected. The curves of the spoon were also more detailed than I had pictured. Next I flipped the spoon on its backside to see what had been written there. I read "DIXIE."

5   I took the object home for a closer examination, but I didn't notice any other features I had overlooked. However, I did use the plastic spoon to shoot roasted peanuts at my brother. The spoon later snapped when I tried shooting a peanut across my living room.

I realized afterwards that even though I didn't need my vision to discover the identity of my object, there was a lot in that tool that I would have overlooked if I had used my vision first. After spending so much time first depending on touch, the final use of my vision brought me into a heightened relationship to the tool. Truly then I was seeing the tool with my own eyes.

Reprinted with permission of Kenneth Wong.

The Observation Process:
Sensing, Perceiving, Thinking

> When you can slow down sufficiently to experience the operation of your own sensing, perceiving, and thinking, then you can begin to use each faculty with more skill.

When you worked with your fruit, vegetable, or tool, you went through a process of collecting data, seeing patterns, and drawing conclusions. You used a process called **inductive reasoning.** If you observed your own mental processes as you proceeded in this simple task, you might have noticed that you went through different stages, using different skills.

So what are the parts of this process? When we take in data without preconceptions we are **sensing;** when we focus on particular sensations and categorize them according to our memory system, we are **perceiving;** and when we draw conclusions about their patterns and meaning, we are **thinking.**

Thinking

Thinking comes from the root Indo-European word *thong,* a word related to *thing.* When we think, we *thing-a-fy;* we make "things" of nature and events from our perceptions of them.

Perceive comes from the Latin word *percipere—per,* meaning thoroughly, and *capere,* meaning to catch, seize, or hold. When we perceive something, we catch and hold it in consciousness until we recognize patterns and find meaning.

Sensing comes from the Latin *sentire,* to feel.

Sensing occurs through sense organs such as the eyes and skin. When our sense organs become activated by stimuli—such as by a bright, warm light—they send this information through the nervous system to the brain. When we sense something, we *feel* it; we feel certain about the presence of something. As we sense, we may not yet have the words to identify or explain what is happening, because in order to find words, we have to think. *Yet, when we begin to think, we risk cutting ourselves off from our sensations.* We cannot fully sense and think at the same time. If we open the front door in the morning to sense how warm the day is, we have to stop thinking in order to sense the temperature of air on face and skin. If we want to truly hear music, we can't be absorbed in our thoughts.

In everyday speech, the word *perceiving* is often used loosely as a synonym for sensing, although there are distinct differences. Perception is both passive and active; it holds sensations in consciousness long enough to interpret them. This holding allows the time needed to find patterns, to organize, and to interpret the sensations. A study of Figure 1.2 will show you how your own perception operates to interpret space, dimension, and shape.

Perception helps us move through the physical world. When we are walking, we use perception to tell us the level of the surface below our feet; without perception, we would fall over curbs. Perception also helps us detect dimensions, telling us the difference between a lamp and its shadow. It enables us to identify sounds and estimate their location.

All of us sense, perceive, and think continually. But what is *thinking?* Philosopher Alan Watts uses the etymology of the word to show us how the earlier peoples (who gave us our language) explained thinking. The root word *thong* tells us that thinking is used to make "things" of nature and of events. We give a name to what we perceive, thus making it into a thing we can move around in our heads. A psychologist, Jean Piaget, defined thinking as "an active process whereby people organize their

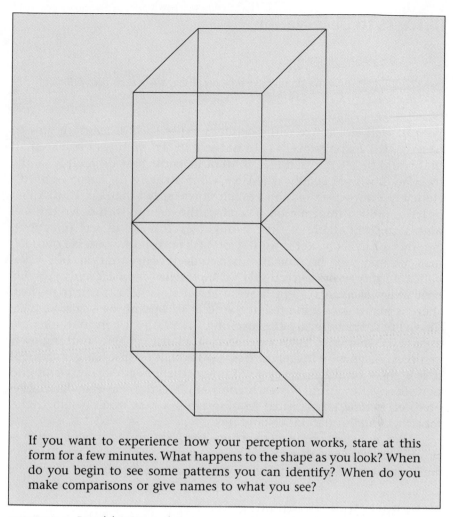

If you want to experience how your perception works, stare at this form for a few minutes. What happens to the shape as you look? When do you begin to see some patterns you can identify? When do you make comparisons or give names to what you see?

FIGURE 1.2 Perceiving Perception

perceptions of the world." Both these definitions explain thinking in terms of what people do with their perceptions.

Our intention in studying these definitions has been to help us become more aware of the observing process. When we can match precise words to inner experience, we can better observe and think about that experience. We can monitor and direct what was previously unidentified and invisible. Its stages can be consciously directed as we

- Take in data (sensing)
- Interpret the data (perceiving)
- Draw conclusions and communicate (thinking)

Barriers to Observation

The barriers lie inside us.

Thinking is an active process whereby people organize their perceptions of the world. (Jean Piaget)

We can well empathize with Scudder's experience in learning how to observe. His first mistake was to hurry. ("In ten minutes I had seen all that could be seen in that fish.") All of us know how difficult it can be to slow down, especially when we value striving for speed and efficiency. Yet our senses require a much slower speed than our thinking in order to process information. Therefore the need to shift down can feel highly uncomfortable at first. It might even make us feel impatient, anxious, or irritable. Yet if we stay on task and simply observe our feelings, we may soon become absorbed in deep concentration. *One explanation for this phenomenon is that we have moved from left brain over into right brain dominance.* Here concern about time is lost; words are lost; there is just silence and presence. And at this point, we begin to make discoveries. Yet typically this exciting interval will continue for only about six minutes. Then we reach a plateau where nothing new emerges. Again we will feel restless. However, if we just hang in there or take a short break, a new cycle of interest will begin again, leading to new discoveries—until we reach another plateau. Yet as Scudder discovered, each time he returned to observing, a new cycle would begin, leading to additional understandings.

Like Scudder, our experiencing—even suffering through—such a process can teach us that we have a far greater capacity to discover than we knew; it can show us that we *can* rely more on ourselves.

Short Break Study Questions

1. Did you ever feel uncomfortable while working on either or both of these assignments? How did you handle your discomfort?
2. Discuss other examples taken from your own life, or those of others, where persistence in overcoming inner obstacles led to breakthroughs.

How Discomfort Leads Us to Think

In our daily lives, when we are presented with a problem, our first reaction may be one of denial and inertia. We may try first to explain this situation in a way that will not require any change or effort from us. Let's take the case of a young man who tries one job after another, only to always find himself bored or fired. He attributes his problem to bad luck.

As time goes by, if he continues to fail, he may begin to review his situation all over again. In short, he may really begin to think about it. Perhaps he might consider that more training or college would get him a better job. Should returning to school work for him, he will find himself feeling better. His thinking will have taken him out of a problem that was causing him more and more discomfort.

Let's look again at Jean Piaget's definition of thinking as "an active process whereby people organize their perceptions of the world." At one point, Piaget described this process as involving both **assimilation** (or easily inserting new data into an existing mental folder) and **accommodation** (or having to create a new folder). When we cannot grasp a new idea or make it fit with what we already know, we feel discomfort, or what Piaget called "disequilibrium." We may not even realize that this discomfort stems from our inability to assimilate that new idea. Indeed, we may blame something or someone else for our discomfort. But if we can create a new file drawer to rightly accommodate this new idea, we will then feel immediately better. Our equilibrium has been restored.

Should we run away from the problem, our discomfort will still remain there on a suppressed level. Basically, we human beings feel good when we can make sense of things, but uncomfortable when we don't (see Figure 1.3). And that discomfort can push us to think.

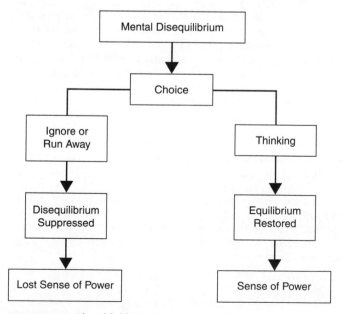

FIGURE 1.3 The Thinking Process

Building Arguments
Observation Skills

This is the first of a series called Building Arguments that runs through each chapter. Each is designed to show you how that chapter's concept applies to the construction of an argument. This chapter will help prepare you for Chapter 9 when you will need to integrate all you have learned from each chapter into the analysis and writing of arguments.

Here are some key terms related to arguments that you will need to understand:

Parts of an argument—An argument consists of two parts: the **conclusion** and the **reasons.** The **conclusion** is the idea that the argument wants you to accept. **Reasons** support, defend, or justify the conclusion. Observation skills furnish us with one form of evidence in the form of witness accounts. Reasons can also be based on historical records, statistics, testimony, and scientific studies.

Hypotheses—When we observe, we collect data and form tentative ideas or *hypotheses* about the data's meaning. Notice how Christopher Columbus draws hypotheses from his journal observations made below.

They came swimming to the ships' boats, where we were, and brought us parrots and cotton thread in balls, and spears and many other things. They all go naked as their mothers bore them . . . they were very well built, with very handsome bodies and very good faces. Their hair is coarse almost like the hairs of a horse's tail and short; they wear their hair down over their eyebrows, except for a few strands behind, which they wear long and never cut. Some of them are painted black, and they are the colour of the people of the Canaries, neither black nor white, and some of them are painted white and some red and some in any colour they can find. . . . They do not bear arms or know them, for I showed to them swords and they took them by the blade and cut themselves through ignorance. (So far all these sentences are claims presented as evidence gained from observation.) They should be good servants and of quick intelligence, since I see that they very soon say all that is said to them, and I believe that they would easily be made Christians, for it appeared to me that they had no creed (summary conclusions/hypotheses).

From the *Journal of Christopher Columbus,* October 12, 1492.

Exercise
1. Give your reaction to Columbus's conclusion. What were the historical consequences?
2. What other possible hypotheses would have taken history in a totally different direction?

The Rewards of Skilled Observation

Sensitive, accurate observing is an essential skill of both scientists and artists. The following reading, "The Innocent Eye," is taken from a book on art design. This book consists of exercises for developing design perception and control. Dorr Bothwell, the painter who wrote this essay, was still exhibiting her works and winning national awards until her death at the age of 98. Her essay serves as a reminder of what you may have already discovered—that although observing may require self-control and patience, it nevertheless can lead to the rapture, power, and wonder we feel when immersed in the creative process.

● R E A D I N G ●

The Innocent Eye

Dorr Bothwell

Creative observation of our surroundings revives in us a sense of the wonder of life. Much of this discovery involves the recovery of something that we all once had in childhood. When we were very young we were all artists. We all came into this world with the doors of perception wide open. Everything was a delightful surprise. Everything, at first, required the slow, loving touch of our tongues and our hands. Long before we could speak we knew the comfort of our mother's warm body, the delightful feel of a furry toy. Smooth and rough surfaces, things cold and hot, surprised and enchanted us. Touch by touch we built up our store of tactile impressions, keenly sensed in minute detail.

Later on, this tactile sensing was transferred to our eyes, and we were able to "feel" through the sense of vision things beyond the grasp of our hands. This kind of seeing was not the rapid sophisticated eye sweep of the well informed. This kind of seeing was a slow, uncritical examination in depth. The more we looked the more lovely and surprising things appeared, until we were pervaded by that wordless thrill which is the sense of wonder.

None of us has lost our store of tactile memories. Nor have we lost our sense of wonder. All that has happened is that we have substituted identifying and labeling, which can be done very rapidly, for the tactile sort of feel-seeing which requires much more time and concentration. For example, if you were asked to look at the edge of your desk and estimate its length, it would only take you a few seconds to flick your eyes back and forth and say it is so many inches long. But suppose you were asked to run the tip of your finger along the edge of the desk and count every tiny nick? You would press your finger along the edge and move it very, very slowly, and your eye would move no faster than your finger. This slow, concentrated way of feeling and seeing is the first step towards regaining our sense of wonder.

There was a time when man moved no faster than his feet or the feet of some animal that could carry him. During that period the artistic or creative spirit seemed to have free expression. Today, in order to be creative and yet move smoothly and efficiently through our fast-paced world, we must be able to function on two different speed levels. The mistake we have made, often with tragic results, is to try to do *all* our living at the speed our machines have imposed upon us.

5   In order to live at this speed we must scan the surface of things, pick out salient aspects, disregard secondary features; and there is certainly nothing wrong in this if we are driving on a busy freeway. But when we allow this pressure to invade every aspect of our life, we begin to "lose touch," to have a feeling that we are missing something, and we are hungry for we don't know what. When that happens, we have begun to suffer from aesthetic malnutrition. Fortunately, the cure for this condition is very pleasant, and although it takes a little self-discipline at the beginning, the results are worth the effort.

When we see as design artists, we become especially aware of the interaction between positive and negative space. In architecture we are suddenly aware of the spaces between the windows, at the ballet we notice how the spaces between the dancers open and close, and in music we realize that rhythm is made by the shapes of silence between the notes.

Everywhere we look we see this principle in action. Trees are not silhouetted against blank air, but hold blue spangles between their leaves while branches frame living shapes of sky. Space seems to be pulled between the leaves of a fern. We delight in the openings between petals of a flower or the spokes of a wheel. This endless exchange between form and space excites us. Once more we feel in touch with our world; our aesthetic sense is being fed and we are comforted.

We may have been taught that butterflies are lovely and toads are ugly, so we admire the butterfly and shrink away from the toad without really examining it to find out if what we had been taught is true. Or we are taught that flowers are good and weeds are bad, so we pull up the latter without a glance. To the artist's eye there is no good or bad. There is just the inappropriate. In the garden, weeds are not appropriate, but in the vacant lot they offer a world of enchantment. And after we have learned to see the beauty in weeds, even though we have to pull them out of the garden, we can first admire their design.

When no preconceived ideas keep us from looking and we take all the time we need to really "feel" what we see—when we are able to do that—the universe opens up and we catch our breath in awe at the incredible complexity of design in the humblest things. It is only when this happens that we regain our sense of wonder.

From Dorr Bothwell and Marlys Mayfield, *Notan: The Dark Light Principle of Design.* New York: Dover, 1991. Used with permission of Dorr Bothwell.

● ● ●

FIGURE 1.4 Can you see in this design the interaction between positive and negative space described in "The Innocent Eye?" Is either less important than the other?

Study/Writing/Discussion Questions

1. Explain the statement, "When we were very young we were all artists."
2. Explain what the author means by the expression "aesthetic malnutrition" that comes from high-speed living.
3. Describe what is meant by the "interaction of positive and negative space." (See Figure 1.4.)
4. Explain what is meant by the statement, "To the artist's eye there is no good or bad. There is just the inappropriate." When you were writing your descriptions of objects, was there a feeling of dislike for the object that kept you from making contact with it fully? Did your attitude change as you continued to work?

Chapter Summary

1. If we want to develop more conscious thinking habits, we have to first observe our own thinking processes so we can recognize our strengths and weaknesses.
2. Careful observation can help us see details that contain the key to unlocking problems or arriving at insights. It can also help us discover new knowledge.
3. Observation is a process of sensing, perceiving, and thinking. Sensing is collecting data through the sense organs. Perceiving is holding sense data in consciousness until we can categorize and interpret it. Thinking organizes our perceptions.
4. Careful observation requires us to stay awake, take our time, give full attention, and suspend thinking in an attitude of listening.
5. The rewards of cultivating observation skills are self-understanding, creativity, rapture, power, and wonder.

Chapter Quiz

Rate each of the following statements as *true* or *false*. Justify your answer with an example or explanation to prove and illustrate your understanding. *Do not omit this part of the test.* True/false answers can be guessed. But when you defend your answer by example or explanation, you demonstrate not only your memory and understanding but also that you can apply what you have learned. The first question is answered for you.

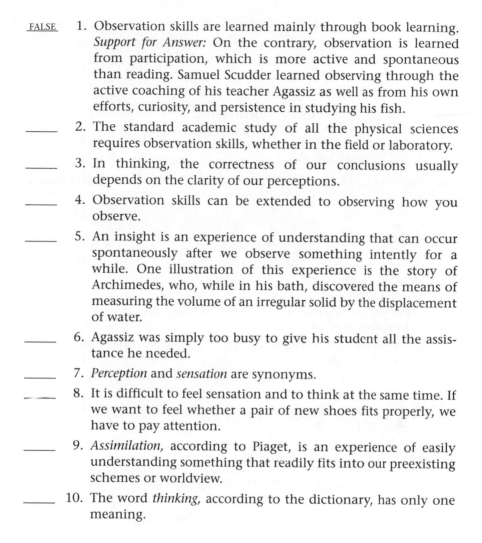

FALSE 1. Observation skills are learned mainly through book learning. *Support for Answer:* On the contrary, observation is learned from participation, which is more active and spontaneous than reading. Samuel Scudder learned observing through the active coaching of his teacher Agassiz as well as from his own efforts, curiosity, and persistence in studying his fish.

_____ 2. The standard academic study of all the physical sciences requires observation skills, whether in the field or laboratory.

_____ 3. In thinking, the correctness of our conclusions usually depends on the clarity of our perceptions.

_____ 4. Observation skills can be extended to observing how you observe.

_____ 5. An insight is an experience of understanding that can occur spontaneously after we observe something intently for a while. One illustration of this experience is the story of Archimedes, who, while in his bath, discovered the means of measuring the volume of an irregular solid by the displacement of water.

_____ 6. Agassiz was simply too busy to give his student all the assistance he needed.

_____ 7. *Perception* and *sensation* are synonyms.

_____ 8. It is difficult to feel sensation and to think at the same time. If we want to feel whether a pair of new shoes fits properly, we have to pay attention.

_____ 9. *Assimilation,* according to Piaget, is an experience of easily understanding something that readily fits into our preexisting schemes or worldview.

_____ 10. The word *thinking,* according to the dictionary, has only one meaning.

Composition Writing Application

■ *Survival as a Result of Observing: A Descriptive Narrative Essay*

Describe an experience in which your safety, welfare, comfort, or survival depended upon your ability to observe a situation or problem clearly. This could involve a danger in city life, in camping, or in sports, or perhaps a life decision where observation skills were crucial. Write from three to five pages, telling your story as a narrative. Remember that the theme that should tie your story together is the theme of observation. Be sure to emphasize in your story where you observed and where you did not and what the consequences were.

■ Review of Assignment Guidelines

1. *Form:* A story or narrative
2. *Theme:* How observation skills helped you survive
3. *Length:* Three to five typed pages or until you feel the story is complete

Scoring for Narrative Essay

1. Minimum of three typed pages. *20 points*
2. Story offers enough specifics to enable the reader to go through the experience. *20 points*
3. Story flows; the reader can follow it without difficulty. *10 points*
4. The language is accurate, appropriate, and appears carefully chosen. *10 points*
5. The use of observation skills is clearly a theme in the story. *25 points*
6. Free of errors in spelling, sentence structure, and punctuation. *15 points*

• R E A D I N G S •

Three Authors, Three Perceivers

Three descriptive readings appear in this section that are all descriptions of nighttime events. Note as you read (1) how each author's observation process enters into the plot of their stories and (2) how all these stories were created from the memories or recordings of observations.

God Grew Tired of Us

John Bul Dau

John Bul Dau was one of three central figures in a documentary film called God Grew Tired of Us; the film is about the thousands of Sudanese boys who fled their homes during the 1983–2005 civil war and wandered for years in search of refuge. John

Bul Dau chose the same title, God Grew Tired of Us *for his autobiography from which this excerpt is taken. His story begins with an attack on his village in 1987. Notice as you read how he uses the revelations of his senses to develop his story.*

The night the djellabas came to Duk Payuel,* I remember that I had been feeling tense all over, as if my body were trying to tell me something. I could not sleep.

It was a dark night, with no moon to reflect off the standing water that pooled beside our huts. My parents and the other adults were sleeping outside, so the children and elderly could all be inside, away from the clouds of biting insects. My brothers and sisters and I, as well as about a dozen refugees from other villages in southern Sudan, stretched out on the ground inside a hut that had been built especially for kids. I lay in the sticky heat, tossing and turning on a dried cowhide, while others tried to sleep on mats of *aguot,* a hollow, grasslike plant from the wetlands that women of my Dinka tribe stitch together. Our crowded bodies seemed to form their own patchwork quilt, filling every square foot with arms and legs.

I opened my eyes and stared toward the grass ceiling and the sticks that supported it, but I could see nothing. Inside the hut it was as dark as the bottom of a well. All was silent except for the whine of the occasional mosquito that penetrated the defenses of the double door, a two-foot-high opening filled with twin plugs of grass that were designed, with obviously limited success, to keep pests outside.

Silence. It must have been around 2 a.m.

5   Silence.

Then, a whistle. It started low and soft at first, then grew louder as it came closer. Other whistles joined the chorus. Next came a sound like the cracking of some giant limb in the forest. Again, the same sound, louder and in short bursts. I wondered if I were dreaming. As deafening explosions made the earth vibrate beneath me and hysterical voices penetrated the walls of the hut, I realized what was happening.

My village was being shelled.

I sprang up, fully awake. In my panic, I tried to run, but the hut's interior was so impenetrably black I slammed headfirst into something hard. The impact knocked me backward, and I fell onto the bodies of the other children. I could not see even the outline of the door. But I could hear the voices of my brothers and sisters, loud and crying as the shells began exploding, punctuated by the occasional burst of automatic gunfire.

"Is this the end of the world?" a woman screamed in panic somewhere outside the hut. There was a pause, and other voices repeated the question. I did not know the answer. Then I heard my mother calling my name. "Dhieu! Dhieu!" she screamed. Try as I might, I could not figure out where the voice came from. I strained to listen, but recumbent bodies had come alive all over the floor and children inside the hut started to scream, too. My mother shrieked the names of my brothers and sisters, who were in the hut with me, and cried, "*Mith! Mith!*" ("Children! Children!"). The village cattle joined in, mooing and urinating loudly, like a rainstorm, in their fright.

*The name of the village as it appears on English-language maps is often shown as Duk Fawil, a variation from the Arabic.

10   My whole being focused on the single thought of finding the door. I scrambled around the darkened interior of the hut, bumping into a mass of suddenly upright bodies. A group of us, a tangle of arms and legs, flailed around the room, trying to find the way out. We ran into each other, and all of us fell, a jumble of bodies on the ground. The hut seemed not to have a door, and in the chaos and darkness I felt as if I were suffocating. It was a living nightmare.

Suddenly, I felt a hint of a breeze. It had to be from an opening in the exterior wall. I stumbled, let out a cry, and strained toward the puff of fresh air. I found myself on top of somebody, but I could see the door's faint outline. I crawled through the two layers of grass that formed the door of the hut and emerged into the outside world.

I stood and watched the strangely red dawn of a world gone mad. The undergrowth in our village is as thick as a curtain in the rainy season, the eight-foot-tall grasses blocking the view of the horizon. On this night, though, fires had burned away some of the brush. I could see neighbors' huts normally hidden to me, ablaze like fireworks. A big *luak*—cowshed—in the distance, its squat brown, conical roof awash in crimson, resembled a miniature volcano. Shells landed in showers of dirt, smoke, and thunder. Bullets zipped through the air like angry bees, but I could not see who fired them.

I started to run but did not know where to go. Suddenly, my father ran from right to left in front of me. I pivoted and followed him. He ran between the huts, and I tried to catch up with him, but, after about a hundred yards, he halted and knelt, disappearing into the grass at the edge of a footpath. I kept running. As I started to pass him in the darkness, my father reached up, grabbed my shoulder, and pulled me down beside him.

He motioned me to be quiet, and we knelt together in the grass at the edge of the path. I crumpled awkwardly. My weight pressed on my right leg, which had folded beneath me. I half-rose and tried to shift my body to get comfortable, but I had moved only a fraction when my father gestured to me to freeze.

15   Within seconds a line of shadowy forms, carrying automatic rifles, ran along the path toward the hut I had just left. There were perhaps nine men, dressed in dark clothes. They did not see us. They passed close enough for me to spit on them, if I had been so inclined. As they vanished beyond a curve in the path, I could hear them fire their guns. The shooting seemed to ring inside my head, and I clapped my hands to my ears. A bitter taste flooded my mouth. Perhaps the sourness of my tense stomach had overflowed. It's odd to remember such a small detail now, but the events of that night are cut into my memory as if etched by acid.

My father dropped low to the ground and seized me with one hand. With the other hand, he pulled himself deeper into the bush, dragging me behind him like a sack of millet. I started to crawl. We moved through the muck, smearing our knees and hands, until we reached the sanctuary of the forest. Inside the shelter of the trees, where the djellabas could not see us, we rested. My father did not speak, and I did not press him to do so.

The light grew. It was not daybreak, but the dance of fire on the huts and surrounding trees made it seem so. I heard more gunshots and more crying. I knew nobody in the village had a gun, so each report of the automatic rifles could only mean more death for those I loved. I recall having two thoughts. First, I convinced myself that the women in the village had been right: It really was the end of the world. Second, I wondered what had happened to my mother and my siblings.

After two hours, the sounds of attack faded. I took stock of my situation. I had just turned 13. I was naked. I carried no food or water. My village had been destroyed. I had become separated from my mother and siblings. Armed men who spoke a foreign tongue combed the forests and grasslands, and if they found me, they most likely would kill me. The only good thing I could imagine was that I might be safe for a while.

It was then that I realized the man who sat beside me was not my father.

20   In the 19 years since that August night, as one of the "lost boys" of Sudan, I have witnessed my share of death and despair. I have seen the hyenas come at dusk to feed on the bodies of my friends. I have been so hungry and thirsty in the dusty plains of Africa that I consumed things I would rather forget. I have crossed a crocodile-infested river while being shelled and shot at. I have walked until I thought I could walk no more. I have wondered, more times than I can count, if my friends or I would live to see a new day. Those were the times I thought God had grown tired of us.

In some ways, my story is like those of tens of thousands of boys who lost their homes, their families, and in many cases their lives in a civil war between north and south that raged in Sudan from 1983 to 2005. In some ways, I represent the nearly 4,000 Sudanese refugees who found haven in the United States. But in other ways, my story is my own. I have a job, an apartment, a new family, and a wonderful new country to call home. I am studying public policy and world affairs at a university, and I plan to use my education to make life better in Africa and in America. I know I have been blessed and that I have been kept alive for a purpose.

They call me a Lost Boy, but let me assure you, God has found me.

Used with the permission of the National Geographic Society.

● ● ●

Study/Writing/Discussion Questions

1. Explain how John Bul Dau tells his story through what his senses gradually revealed to his awareness.
2. What do his senses reveal that enables him to escape?
3. How do his senses protect him?
4. What do his senses reveal that surprises him?
5. Why were these events "etched in his memory like acid?"

"Walking" from *Seeing Nature*
Paul Krafel

Paul Krafel is founder and administrator of the Chrysalis Charter School located near Redding, California. Notice as you read how his story centers on his resolve to improve his observation skills and how these skills bring him new discoveries about nature.

As a beginning hiker, I had to carry a flashlight when I went walking at night. I pointed the beam of light down around my feet and stared into its bright pool. My eyes adjusted to this brightness, so that when I glanced away, the unlit night appeared dark and impenetrable—which confirmed my need for a flashlight. I became fixated like a moth on light. But a spiral of learning freed my feet to walk without a flashlight. In the darkness, my eyes dilated wide open and saw the mysterious, alluring world of night.

The night world looks different because I see it with different parts of my eyes and brain. Colors dominate my daytime sight, but the color-sensitive part of the eye requires abundant light; it cannot operate in night's dim light. I see the night's light with a part of my eye more sensitive to shapes and bulks. The land takes on an almost palpable weight at night, almost as if my eyes feel the world more than see it.

Dusky owls fly silently low over the ground, back and forth in long hunting swaths. Twice owls have come upon this unilluminated human staring right at them and have swerved away in surprise and then circled several times, observing me.

Night is a quieter world, quiet enough to hear the scurrying of a mouse. In the desert moonlight, a mouse went about its business, staying under overhangs and in the shadows as much as possible. The mouse dashed across the moonlight only when there was no other way to reach another shadow. The mouse never paused in the light. As the moon moves through the night, the shadows will move and the mouse will have to change its path. Perhaps by staying within the shifting shadows, the mouse can forage over most of the ground in the course of the night.

5   Walking at night opens new areas of learning. Once, I went to a beach to watch the grunion mate. Grunion are small fish that wriggle out of the surf during the night's high tide to mate and lay their eggs in the beach. Other people had flashlights with which they watched individual fish. Not having a flashlight, I walked to a deserted, dark section of the beach. In the calm between the crashing of invisible breakers, I heard the grunion slithering and wriggling. The grunion flashed with a ghostly pale luminescence. I don't know whether the luminescence was caused by the grunion disturbing phosphorescence in the water or if the grunions themselves have luminescence, perhaps so the females can attract the males. This luminescence was as invisible in a flashlight beam as the stars are invisible in the sunlight.

Used with the permission of Chelsea Green Publishing.

●   ●   ●

Study/Writing/Discussion Questions

1. In the first two paragraphs, what does he observe about how his perceptions differ when he walks at night with a flashlight and without one?
2. What did walking in the dark without a flashlight enable him to see and learn about owls, mice, and grunions?

Spanish Harlem at Night

Ernesto Quiñonez

This short description is taken from Bodega Dreams, *a novel set in New York City's Spanish Harlem. This is a district that Quiñonez knew well from the years he spent growing up there. At present he teaches creative writing at Cornell University.*

". . . it was a hot spring night and El Barrio had turned into a maraca and all the people had come out transformed as seeds. Like all ghettos, Spanish Harlem looks better in the dark when everything broken and dirty is hidden by darkness and the moonlight makes everything else glow like pearls. That night the people were jamming, shaking, moving. Hydrants were opened, women were dancing to salsa blaring from a boom box on the cement. They danced with one eye on their partner and one eye on their children playing hopscotch, cullies with bottle caps, or skipping rope. Teenage girls in tight jeans flirted with guys who showed them their jewelry and tattoos. Old men played dominoes as they drank Budweisers wrapped in brown bags. I walked home happy. I even said hello to a rat that crossed my path, running from one garbage heap to another. "Hey, dusty guy. Where you going, eh?" I said when it poked its head from a plastic bag. I was happy . . ."

Used with the permission of Random House, Watkins-Loomis Agency, and Profile Books, London.

●　●　●

Study/Writing/Discussion Questions

1. Name four ways that this description of a nighttime scene differs from the other two readings.
2. Why does the author find Spanish Harlem's nighttime preferable to its daytime?
3. Mention some of the images that he offers that enable you to see the scene.
4. What is the mood of the scene? Can you feel it?

CHAPTER 2

Word Precision:

How Do I Describe It?

dé·jà vu

WENDELL HAS A STRANGE FEELING THAT HE HAS SEEN THIS WORD BEFORE.

In order to share our experiences with others through writing, we need to give much thought to our choice of words. This chapter takes a close look at that process of translation. It will describe how

- Words interconnect with thinking and perceiving
- A good dictionary helps thinking
- Words are defined
- Words convey feelings
- Concepts abstract thought
- Critical reading works
- Critical reading has two distinct phases

This chapter cannot cover everything a college student needs to know about words. But when you have finished this chapter, you should know more about how well you actually work with words, how word confusion and word clarity affect your thinking, and how word precision can satisfy the spirit.

On Finding the Right Word

The search to find the right match between words and experience can lead to the learning of new words. Moreover, each new word that we master enables us to see even more of the world.

Looking back at your descriptive writing in the last chapter, you may have noticed that there were also different stages involved in your word search. The first was probably one of silent absorption. If words came to you at that time, they could have interfered with your sensing process. Nevertheless—once you were ready to write down your experiences— you may have been surprised to find yourself at a loss for words. You knew what you had seen or touched or felt, but you also realized that any word choices were only *translations* into another medium that might never fully duplicate your silent experience. It took persistence to continue searching for the words that would make your translation as true as possible to your experience. If you were describing an orange, you might have found that although you had held hundreds of oranges, you still could not describe its color, texture, smell, and taste. For instance, if you wrote down, "It tastes like an orange," you knew already that the word *orange* was inadequate. To erase this and write down "citrus flavor" would have been still more abstract, including the taste of lemons, grapefruit, and tangerines. You could have picked up the orange to taste it again, giving more studied awareness to your senses. This round of savoring could have summoned up such words as *sticky-sweet, tangy-flesh, spicy-warm.* If you still were not satisfied, you could have gone to *Random House Word Menu* or *Roget's International Thesaurus* and looked under the lists of words for *sweetness* and *sourness,* finding choices like *pungent, acidic,* and *fermented.* Here you would have also discovered more words to describe the colors in the orange's rind: *reddish-yellow, ocher, pumpkin, gold, apricot, carrot, yellow-orange, gilt, canary, beige, saffron, topaz-yellow, green, emerald, olive, chartreuse, nut-brown, fawn, rusty, bronze,* and *chestnut.*

Keeping an experience in mind as a constant, while searching both through word memory and thesaurus to find appropriate word correspondences, is a complex mental operation. Writing challenges you to stretch your abilities to use the words you know and to find new ones. Through this process you will move in time toward greater word mastery. Nevertheless, learning more words enables you to actually *see* more. To learn the words for things, you have to pay more attention to them. And once you recognize by name a Washington navel orange and a Valencia orange, you also perceive more of their details: the navels' shapes, the rinds' different textures, the subtleties of their shades of color. When someone offers you an orange, you enjoy appreciating its characteristics and talking about them; for your perception, together with your vocabulary, has enabled you to make finer differentiations. *The advantage of having a precise vocabulary to describe your experience is that it enables you to learn and experience even more.*

DISCOVERY EXERCISE

■ Taking an Interest in Dictionaries

Rate each of the following statements as *true* or *false.* Be prepared to defend your answers in writing or in a class discussion.

1. Dictionaries are like phone books; basically, they all offer the same information.

2. If a dictionary is named Webster's, that means it is one of the best.

3. Experts who decide how we should speak English write dictionaries.

4. Small pocket dictionaries are the best kind to use for in-depth word study because they eliminate unnecessary, confusing information and make understanding easier.

5. Because a dictionary can confuse us with so many definitions for any single word, it is better to try to figure out a word's meaning from its context or ask someone else.

6. Dictionaries are like cookbooks; a family needs to buy only one for the family's lifetime.

7. Dictionaries give us information about spelling and definitions, but that is about all they offer.

8. An online dictionary is just as good for understanding and using a new word as a printed dictionary.

Here is a discussion of the correct answers. Read this only *after* you've completed the quiz.

1. *False.* A comparative study of several dictionaries—for instance, *The American Heritage Dictionary, Merriam-Webster's Collegiate Dictionary,* and *Webster's New World Dictionary*—will make this apparent.

2. *False.* Noah Webster was a nineteenth-century American lexicographer. The Merriam Company purchased the rights to his book and has continued, under the name Merriam-Webster, to publish and revise the large *Webster's New International Dictionary.* However, because the name Webster's is not protected by a copyright, many other companies have used it to put out both excellent and inferior products. The most prestigious and scientifically researched dictionary is the *Oxford English Dictionary,* bound in versions that range from two to twenty volumes.

3. *False.* Dictionaries serve as authoritative reference sources; however, they are not authoritative in the sense of being infallible but in the sense of offering reliable historical information about words and their use. In the case of *The American Heritage Dictionary,* this information is based on the opinions of a panel of lexicographers, linguists, writers, and scientists. Dictionaries are not written to dictate dogma but only to reflect agreements and standards about how people use their language, in both popular speech and formal writing.

4. *False.* Pocket dictionaries may be more convenient to carry and use for understanding simpler words or spellings, but they are too condensed for use in the more serious study of word ideas, concepts, and usage. Moreover, their definitions can sometimes be oversimplified to the point of being misleading. Finally, and more obviously, a pocket dictionary containing 30,000 words cannot offer you as much as an unabridged dictionary with 600,000 words or a college desk-sized one with 60,000 words.

5. *False.* Although most study skill texts suggest this, and most English composition-reading texts select the vocabulary for you, a guess based on your view of the context may be mistaken, and your friend may be even more confused than you. The result may be the need to "unlearn" a misunderstood word later.

6. *False.* If your dictionary is more than fifteen years old, it is time to buy a new one. The English language acquires or invents thousands of new words each year, and our customs about word usage change also.

7. *False.* It's worth spending a little time just browsing through your dictionary to find out all it has to offer. You'll find a concise history of the English language, for one thing.

8. *True and False.* Some online dictionaries have all the limitations of pocket dictionaries. For completeness, Merriam-Webster Online is one of the best; it even includes etymological information. One drawback to online dictionaries is that because you can only search for one word at a time, you cannot learn from browsing. On the other hand, if you need to define a concept, a Google search can produce the miracle of pages of short definitions of that word extracted from sources across the Web.

How Well Do You Use Your Dictionary?

Bring to class a college desk-sized dictionary. If you need to buy one, choose a hardcover dictionary that is comprehensive, easy to read, and recently published or updated. Here are two recommendations:

- *The American Heritage College Dictionary*, Fourth Edition (Houghton Mifflin, 2002) Updated 2007.
- *Webster's New World Dictionary*, Fourth Edition (John Wiley & Sons, 1999) Updated 2004.

Working with a partner, take turns finding three random entries to discuss. Explain to your partner every piece of information that you find there, including every symbol and every abbreviation. If you do not understand something, take the time to look it up. (If, for instance, you do not understand what is meant by the abbreviation *OF,* find out where your dictionary explains its abbreviations.) Work together to understand *all* the information given, and do not let one another off the hook until you sense everything interpreted is fully understood.

Finally, one of you should write down your answers to the following questions:

1. State the name of the dictionary you own and its date of publication. How many pages does it have? How many entries are there? Is it a desk-sized dictionary?

2. Test your knowledge of the history of the English language by explaining what your dictionary means when it refers to a word as *Anglo-Saxon* or *Middle English, Late Latin,* and *Indo-European.*

3. Look up *Pago Pago.* Write down how it is pronounced. Pronounce it for your partner.

4. Have you ever discovered that you had misunderstood a familiar word and were misusing it? Give an example and explain how you found out.

5. How does the word *plan* differ from the words *design, project,* and *scheme*? The *Webster's New World Dictionary* will explain how they differ in connotation. What are word connotations, and why are they important to consider when you make your selection?

6. Describe the mental signals that show you, in dictionary study, that you have fully understood a new word. Do you usually persist in word study until you have these signals?

7. If you can't find a word or clear definition of a word in one dictionary, do you usually consult another dictionary? Explain why or why not.

8. Describe situations in which you might use a thesaurus.

9. Compare the advantages of using an electronic handheld dictionary to a pocket print dictionary. What are the advantages of online dictionaries? Explain why you might prefer electronic to print media, or vice versa.

Clear Thinking Depends on Clear Word Definitions

Confusion about words affects not only our communications but also our alertness and consciousness. We can be confused about not only unfamiliar words but also familiar ones.

Clear thinking and expression depend on clear word understanding. Yet, as obvious as this idea may seem, word clarity is not necessarily common. It takes dedication and some effort to truly understand all the words that pass through your day. Yet the effort need not be so great if you can establish two simple habits:

1. Pay attention to the inner discomfort that indicates you have not fully understood a word.

2. Take the time to clear things up.

Word confusion stands out more in conversation than in reading. If a friend were to say you were *contumacious,* you would have to ask what that word meant before you could respond. However, in reading it can be easier to ride over word confusion, just as it is in listening to radio or television. Moreover, a person can be just as confused about familiar words as unfamiliar ones. Unfamiliar words are easier to recognize, such as when we first hear the word *factoid;* however, we may not realize that there's more to learn about the meaning of the word *fact.* This text is organized, in terms of its chapter headings, around words that describe the thinking process; although these are ordinary words, they are, nevertheless, subject to much confusion. In the previous chapter much attention was given to defining such words as *observing, perceiving, sensing,* and *thinking.*

Dictionaries are your most reliable resources for the study of words. Yet the habit of using them needs to be cultivated. Of course it can feel like an annoying interruption to stop your reading and look up a word. You might tell yourself that if you keep going, you would eventually understand it from the context. Indeed, reading study guides often advise just that. However, should understanding not occur, you will find yourself soon becoming drowsy. Often it's not the need for sleep that is occurring but a gradual loss of consciousness. The knack here is to recognize the early signs of word confusion before drowsiness takes over when it is easier to exert sufficient willpower to grab a dictionary for word study. Although this special effort is needed, once the meaning is clarified, the perceptible sense of relief makes the effort worthwhile. You may need to refer to more than one dictionary, diagram the word, or use it in sentences. But when you have finished you will find yourself more alert, with a renewed energy for continuing your work.

The definitions of key concepts in every chapter of this text are designed to emphasize the importance of gaining better word-understanding habits. However, you will also come across many unfamiliar words as you read this textbook. *It will remain your responsibility to use the dictionary to understand any unfamiliar words that you may find while reading this textbook and thus to reinforce this important critical thinking habit. Your instructor might even require that you keep a vocabulary notebook for this purpose.*

What Makes a Definition?

Definitions clarify words through boundaries.

The etymology, or history, of the word **definition** shows us something interesting. It comes from the Latin roots *de,* meaning off or away from, and *finis,* meaning end or boundary; the Latin word *definire* means to set

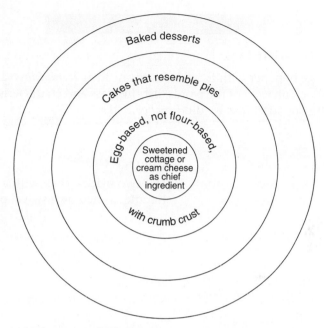

FIGURE 2.1 Definition Boundaries

bounds to. So when we *define* something, we discover or establish its boundaries. When we learn a new word, the definition shows us what boundaries separate it from every other word. For example, let's take the word *cheesecake.* If we only go for its meaning as a dessert, we see (Figure 2.1) how it can be defined through four boundaries that classify the word:

Baked desserts

Cakes that resemble pies

Egg-based, not flour-based, with crumb crust

Sweetened cottage or cream cheese as chief ingredient

In a definition, the word to be defined is called a **term.** Every term can be included in a **class,** or the largest family to which it is related within this particular boundary. Thus the term *cake* belongs in the class of baked desserts whose boundaries also include baked custard or baked Alaska. In addition, cheesecake has three other distinguishing characteristics, which create smaller boundaries that gradually separate it from every other kind of baked dessert. Thus, when we define a thing, we methodically set it apart from everything else.

Word Boundaries

Set up a piece of paper with three columns headed *Term, Class,* and *Characteristics.* Look up each of the words, list the class and characteristics, and diagram the boundaries as we did for *cheesecake.*

Example

Term	Class	Characteristics
1. Scissors	A cutting tool	Has two blades, each with a loop handle, joined by a swivel pin

2. Mailbag

3. Moppet

4. November

5. Pneumonia

6. Cat

Kinds of Definitions

Not all definitions are dictionary definitions.

When you looked up the word *cat,* you probably found it described as a mammal of the family felidae, or of the genus and species *Felis catus.* This taxonomic description indicates the boundaries that differentiate cats from all other animals. The cat family includes lions and tigers as well as house cats, while a particular breed name distinguishes a Siamese from a Persian cat. The rules that govern this system of classification are based on a science called **taxonomy.** This science, established by an international commission, enables us to know what agreements have been made to identify all plants and animals so that no two can be confused. Just as taxonomy helps us distinguish one living thing from another, **dictionary definitions** describe terms according to the boundaries established by shared and separate characteristics. Both taxonomy and dictionary definitions owe their value to agreements that everyone can refer to.

This is especially important for **scientific definitions,** which remain more fixed than other kinds of definitions because they are specific and technical. Nurses or medical students who study the heart have to learn definitions of words such as *aorta, atrium, diastole,* and *endocardium.* Indeed, a large part of scientific training is word training in a vocabulary handed down from one decade to the next.

At the other extreme are **stipulative definitions** based on individual or group agreements. The term *middle class* does not have a commonly agreed-upon meaning in the United States. Most Americans call themselves middle class whether they live in a mansion or a trailer. In 2008, when pressed to make a *stipulative* definition of the middle class, presidential candidate Barack Obama defined it as an income of $150,000 or less a year. When considering a tax cut in 1995, Democrats defined the middle class as making $75,000 a year, whereas Republicans set the amount at $200,000. Other commentators have preferred to define the middle class in terms of financial stability rather than income. And thus the debate continues. Other terms with more stable stipulative definitions include *functional illiteracy, disability,* and *sexual harassment.* In all these cases, such definitions are useful for legal, research, or policy purposes. In such cases, dictionary definitions would not be of much use.

Definitions can also be **inventive**, describing previously unrecognized ideas, categories, or concepts. A new term *neuromarketing,* for instance, refers to new marketing methods based on laboratory studies of human brain responses to ads, brands, and cultural messages. Another inventive term is *echo boomers*, coined to describe the children of the "baby boomers" born in the 1980s and 1990s. Carl Jensen, a journalism professor at Sonoma State University, invented the term *junk-food news* to describe "sensationalized, personalized, and homogenized inconsequential trivia that is served up to the public on a daily basis." He gives examples of show business and celebrity stories, the stock market's ups and downs, fads, crazes and murders, anniversaries of events, and news about people in sports and politics.

People can also take familiar concepts and give them **personal definitions.** The artist Andy Warhol defined art as "what you can get away with." The poet Robert Frost defined love as "an irresistible desire to be irresistibly desired."

Definitions may also be **poetic** and **whimsical**, like "Happiness is a commute before the rush hour," or **philosophical**, like "Death is the invisible companion of life." Below this level are **eccentric** definitions that disregard the kind of agreements that make communication possible.

A final category of definitions might be called **persuasive definitions.** These are definitions that advocate an opinion. Examples of these would be such statements as the following: "A state lottery is a form of voluntary taxation." "A state lottery is stealing from the poor." "Abortion is murder." "Women deserve the right to choose." All these equations are opinions offered as though they were given truths in order to win others over to the same opinion. Obviously, they are far removed from dictionary definitions.

From "Through the Looking Glass" by Lewis Carroll.

"I don't know what you mean by 'glory,'" Alice said.

Humpty Dumpty smiled contemptuously. "Of course you don't—till I tell you. I meant 'there's a nice knock-down argument for you!'"

"But 'glory' doesn't mean 'a nice knock-down argument,'" Alice objected.

"When *I* use a word," Humpty Dumpty said in rather a scornful tone, "it means just what I choose it to mean—neither more nor less."

"The question is," said Alice, "whether you *can* make words mean so many different things."

"The question is," said Humpty Dumpty, "which is to be master—that's all."

(Lewis Carroll, *Through the Looking Glass*)

The Connotations of Words

Word connotations are about feelings.

An important aspect of definitions is the **connotations** of words or the *associations* that they suggest to us. These associations can evoke reactions, images, emotions, or thoughts. For instance, let's take the word *snake*. The *denotation* of this word, or its literal meaning, is a reptile without legs. There it is: simply a "thing," nothing to get excited about. But for many people the word *snake* carries many negative connotations, such as being slimy, treacherous, poisonous, or evil. These common reactions can nevertheless be overcome through conscious familiarity with snakes.

Do dictionaries explain connotations? Not in the case of the snake, where such connotations are universally understood. A few, but not all, dictionaries help us understand the connotations a defined word carries by discussing subtle differences among its synonyms. For instance, if you look up the word *lying* in *Webster's New World Dictionary of the American Language,* you will find explanations of the connotative differences among *lie, prevaricate, equivocate,* and *fib.* If you were to arrange these synonyms on a scale of their potential for emotional impact, *lying* would be at the top and *fibbing* at the bottom.

Class Discussion

1. Explain the meaning of and connotative differences among *disinformation, misspeaking,* and *falsifying.*
2. Make a list of synonyms for *cheating,* and rank their connotations as negative, positive, neutral, or phony neutral (a euphemism that hides a true negative meaning).
3. Repeat the procedure for the word *stealing.*

In later chapters of this book we will look at how connotations show our judgments of things and how they can be used to manipulate others to accept the same evaluations. But for now, simply consider connotations in your word choices and reading by asking questions or by dictionary study.

> "*Miscegenation.* The word is humpbacked, ugly, portending a monstrous outcome: like *antebellum* or *octoroon,* it evokes images of another era, a distant world of horsewhips and flames, dead magnolias and crumbling porticos . . . In 1960, the year that my parents were married, *miscegenation* still described a felony in over half the states in the Union." (Barack Obama, *Dreams from My Father: A Story of Race and Inheritance,* (New York: Random House, 2004, 11–12.)

The Importance of Defining Key Ideas

Both study and debate need to begin with clear definitions.

The French philosopher Voltaire once said, "If you would argue with me, first define your terms." What he was talking about was not arguing in the sense of quarreling but in the sense of persuasive reasoning. He did not say *how* terms should be defined but that one should be very clear about what one has decided that key ideas mean.

For example, if you want to argue in defense of *health care reform,* you would first need to define what you mean by *health care* as well as by the word *reform*. How you define these three words affects what you will include within your boundaries to consider as well as what will remain outside. In order to create a sound and effective argument, time and thought has to be given to the defining of all key terms because an argument based on undefined words will collapse when challenged.

Clear definitions are an essential part of all fields of learning. For example, in law, definitions help juries decide the difference between crimes and misdemeanors, between sanity and insanity. In public affairs, debates over definitions can generate controversy, as has become the case with the meaning of the word *torture*. In addition, definitions comprise a large part of any subject of learning. If you study political science, you have to begin by asking what the familiar word *political* really means. From that point, you can move into learning more unfamiliar words like *plebiscite*. In order to study our terms, we must study more than one dictionary and use each well, beginning always with a good desk-sized college dictionary. Unfortunately, many students have already formed the habit of only using pocket dictionaries that are helpful for spelling, but not always helpful for understanding a word's meaning. However, not all full-sized dictionaries are equally well written. Therefore it is desirable to have some knowledge about what kinds of dictionaries there are, including electronic versions, as well as having the skills to explore and evaluate each one.

Word Concepts

Concepts abstract experience.

> **Concept:** A word that organizes and abstracts a body of related experience; a general idea. From the Latin *conceptus*, meaning a thing conceived.

The study of critical thinking begins with a review of many concepts. Each chapter of this book is titled by a concept. The word *concept* comes from the Latin *conceptus*, a thing conceived, suggesting a mental creation. Concepts convey abstractions of experience from the past such as *pluralism, aristocracy*, and *hegemony*, or they convey new ideas such as *sustainability, postmodern*, and *ergonomics*. Learning the key concepts from any field of learning comprises an important part of higher education. If we want to study economics, we begin by learning the difference between microeconomics and macroeconomics. Concepts help us make distinctions, as between a *heuristic* and an *algorithm* in problem solving.

Concept learning not only conveys complex ideas but also enables us to talk about them.

If we want to truly understand new concepts, it can be helpful to begin with the word's etymology or history, with its earliest root idea. This idea can give us a concrete sense of the word's original conception. Traditional aids for concept study are encyclopedias, textbooks, and books written by leading thinkers in their special fields of knowledge. Yet even scholars cannot always agree on the definition of a term. *Critical thinking,* as mentioned earlier, has as many definitions as people who write on the subject or teach it. Yet each definition contributes to a dialogue that eventually will reach consensus as to which boundaries this new field of study should include or exclude.

Defining terms is a dynamic process in any field of learning. And there are some words that challenge each new generation. Two of these words, *truth* and *reality,* are discussed in boxes on these pages. They are both ordinary but profound words; they both remain elusive, yet they are the standards for measuring our ways of knowing and proceeding in the world and for thinking critically about the world. However, before going on to these terms, one example will serve to show how the grasp of a concept can totally change a person's life. In the *Narrative of the Life of Frederick Douglass,* first published in 1845, its author tells the story of how he was born into bondage on an American plantation. As a young man, he secretly taught himself to read and write (a crime punishable by death), then gradually made his escape into freedom and a life of renown.

> I often found myself regretting my own existence and wishing myself dead; and but for the hope of being free, I have no doubt but that I should have killed myself, or done something for which I should have been killed. While in this state of mind, I was eager to hear any one speak of slavery. I was a ready listener. Every little while, I could hear something about the abolitionists. It was some time before I found what the word meant. If a slave ran away and succeeded in getting clear, or if a slave killed his master, set fire to a barn, or did anything very wrong in the mind of a slaveholder, it was spoken of as the fruit of *abolition.* Hearing the word in this connection very often, I set about learning what it meant. The dictionary afforded me little or no help. I found it was "the act of abolishing;" but then I did not know what was to be abolished. Here I was perplexed. I did not dare to ask anyone about its meaning, for I was satisfied that it was something they wanted me to know very little about. After a patient waiting, I got one of our city papers, containing an account of the number of petitions from the north, praying for the abolition of slavery in the District of Columbia, and of the slave trade between the States. From this time I understood the words abolition and abolitionist, and always drew near when that word was spoken, expecting to hear something of importance to myself and fellow-slaves. The light broke in upon me by degrees.

Defining Reality

Reality comes from the Latin word *res,* which means thing, property, or possession. Related to *res* is *reri,* which means to reason and from which we derive the words *reason, ratio,* and *realize.* The past participle of *reri* is *ratus,* which means fixed by calculation or established for certain. The ideas etymologically involved in the word *reality* therefore involve reasoning and certainty. Here is what other noted thinkers have said about reality:

> *Everything flows.* (Heraclitus, Greek philosopher)

> *The world was created by the word of God so that what is seen was made out of things which do not appear.* (St. Paul)

> *Reality is what we bump against.* (William James, American psychologist)

> *Reality is something as it actually is, independent of our thoughts about how it is.* (Mortimer J. Adler, American philosopher)

> *Reality is an unknown and undefinable totality of flux that is the ground of all things and of the process of thought itself, as well as the movement of intelligent perception.* (David Bohm, philosopher and physicist)

Defining Truth

The word *true* comes from the Old English form *troewe,* which means loyal or trustworthy, which in turn comes from the Indo-European base *deru,* meaning firm, solid, or steadfast. Related to the base word *deru* is *dru,* meaning firm as a tree or hard as wood. This etymology suggests that *truth* is something as hard and firm and as steadfast as a tree or its wood. Here are some definitions and descriptions of truth:

> *Truth suggests conformity with the facts or with reality, either as an idealized abstraction ("What is truth?" said jesting Pilate) or in actual application to statements, ideas, acts, etc. ("There is no truth in that rumor.")* (The American Heritage Dictionary)

> *Truth is a correspondence or agreement between our minds and reality.* (Mortimer J. Adler)

> *The ordinary mode of language is very unsuitable for discussing questions of truth and falsity, because it tends to treat each truth as a separate fragment that is essentially fixed and static in its nature. . . . However, truth and falsity have to be seen from moment to moment, in an act of perception of a very high order.* (David Bohm)

> *Truth is what stands the test of experience.* (Albert Einstein)

What Is Critical Reading?

Critical reading begins with a resolve to aim for a neutral and accurate comprehension of the material.

When we read a detective story, we enjoy getting lost in another world; when we read a training manual, we follow and memorize. In both cases, we rarely question what we read. Such reading is like boarding a bus; we get on and we get off. However, if we were to apply this attitude to newspaper reading (or watching TV news), we would always believe—or doubt—the last thing we read or heard. A critical reader does not soak up information like a sponge but interacts and asks questions based on clear standards that assess information reliability.

Yet critical reading cannot *begin* with these questions but rather with making sure that our reading has been accurate—that we have not substituted words and ideas not there, nor misunderstood ideas that were there. This first phase then requires an *attitude of receptivity.* The problem is that remaining receptive is not easy when the topic goes against our own experiences, opinions, and beliefs. If we strongly disagree with what we read—or hear—it can actually feel painful to remain attentive or true to the goal of faithfully recording the message, regardless of our opinions. Yet we cannot adequately respond to any material that we have not correctly understood. Thus the *critical reading phase* of challenging and questioning has to wait until we have achieved a faithful reconstruction of the information given. And achieving accurate comprehension can take more than one reading and include the use of a dictionary.

In reading this book you will not always feel receptive to the different viewpoints it presents. When an argument goes against our beliefs and values, we cannot help reacting. Many psychological studies have shown that in reading we tend to accept the views we already hold and minimize those we do not. Thus exercising control over our biases in order to maintain neutrality, even on issues we favor, can be a struggle. It may help to remember that perfect neutrality is rarely achieved. At best, we might only be able to admit to our biases and restrain our habitual personal reactions. Objectivity need not mean that we have changed what we feel; it does mean that we can set aside our prior convictions in order to make the effort to hear, read, and understand exactly what is being told to us. Thus, only when the material has been accurately understood can the critical reading phase truly begin. This second stage also cannot be hurried; it is a slow and careful process led by questions. Again we return to the definition of critical, whose original idea was to sift and separate. When one reads critically, one studies and reflects in order to sift words and ideas. When we become critical too soon, we lose the focus needed to make an accurate reading. And a criticism of information or arguments based on an inaccurate reading is a waste of time.

As you study each chapter of this book, you will be considering some key questions designed to help you critically assess information. The content of this Word Skills chapter can be summed up in four questions:

- Am I making the best word choice?
- Do I fully understand this word or concept?
- Is this word well defined?
- What are the connotations of this word?

The reading selections offered in this text are intended to stimulate critical thinking. You are encouraged to read each selection at least twice—once for comprehension and once for critical interaction. The study/writing/discussion questions are intended to take you to deeper stages of critical analysis. Remember also to consult your dictionary regularly as you read, and write down your questions. As you follow these steps, you will find that your reading has become an active thinking endeavor.

Building Arguments
Word Choices

When we make a **claim**, each word appearing in the claim needs careful thought and definition. (*"If you would argue with me, first define your terms."* Voltaire) Word choices vary according to the values and purposes of the speaker. Notice how this author uses his definition of *Indians* to sway others to accept his beliefs.

Mr. Baily:

With the narrative enclosed, I subjoin some observations with regard to the animals, vulgarly called Indians. (definition of key term)

In the United States Magazine in the year 1777, I published a dissertation denying them to have a right in the soil. (conclusion)

The whole of this earth was given to man, and all descendants of Adam have a right to share it equally. There is no right of primogeniture in the laws of nature and of nations. (moral reasoning made through further claims to back principal claim)

What use do these ringed, streaked, spotted and speckled cattle make of the soil? Do they till it? Revelation said to man, "Thou shalt till the ground." . . . I would as soon admit a right in the buffalo to grant lands, as in Killbuck, the Big Cat, the Big Dog, or any of the ragged wretches that are called chiefs. . . . What would you think of going to a big lick or place where the beasts collect to lick saline nitrous earth and water, and addressing yourself to a great buffalo to grant you land? (analogy used to support conclusion) (H. H. Brackenridge, 1782)

Exercise

1. The issue here is whether Indians should have the right to their land. What is the author's claim on this issue?

2. How does the author use his definition of Indians to help his argument?

3. What reasoning does he offer to prove Indians are not human?

4. What is *primogeniture?*

5. What is unfair about this argument?

6. Write a one-paragraph argument in which you make a claim about anything. Give either a neutral or a controversial definition of your key term or subject. Then offer two reasons to support your definition.

Chapter Summary

1. An accurate use of words improves our thinking. Words give form to our thoughts so that we can make use of them. Words enable us to communicate with others and ourselves. Knowing the words for things and experiences helps us see and perceive more.

2. Writing helps us learn more about words and how to use them. When we struggle to select words that will describe our experiences, we realize that words are only *translations* of experience and not the experience itself.

3. Clear thinking depends on a clear understanding of the words we use. Word confusion leads to less consciousness, or disequilibrium, which can only be restored through word clarification.

4. We need to understand what dictionaries can and cannot offer us; we need to use them skillfully and frequently.

5. The thesaurus helps us when we are writing and translating nonverbal experiences and ideas into words; the dictionary helps us when we are reading and interpreting the words of others.

6. Definitions set boundaries for word ideas and show us their specific and general characteristics and how they are related to or distinguished from one another.

7. Dictionary definitions show us the agreements that society has made about a word's meaning. But we may also compose our own personal or stipulative definitions of experiences or compose persuasive definitions to sway the opinions of others. In critical thinking it is important not to confuse these different kinds of definitions, or to believe that personal, persuasive, or stipulative definitions carry the same agreements as those found in a dictionary.

8. The test of our understanding of a word is our ability to define it. This ability is particularly important for words representing key ideas that we wish to explain or defend. Taking the time to define the words we use is an essential preliminary to genuine communication.

9. A study of a word's etymology can help us trace a word back to its earliest root idea and can give us an image that conveys a more concrete sense of the word's logic. Learning a word's etymology can also help us recognize its relationship to other words with the same root meanings.

10. The connotations of a word are its associative meanings, which can be positive, negative, or neutral. These associations can take the form of feelings, ideas, images, or thoughts. Thus, although politicians might rarely admit to *lying* or being *confused,* it is quite acceptable for them to admit they *misspoke.*

11. The first stage of critical reading is objective receptivity to the material; this means having the technical ability as well as the willingness to accurately reproduce its content without alterations or distortions. If we question and interact with material that we have not accurately interpreted, our criticisms will not be fair or worthwhile.

Chapter Quiz

Rate each of the following statements as *true* or *false.* To answer some of these questions, you will need to consult your dictionary.

_____ 1. When Frederick Douglass grasped the concept of abolition, he understood it was possible for him to become free.

_____ 2. Words can be used to do a better or worse job of describing experiences but can never be more than translations of the experiences themselves.

_____ 3. A dictionary can help us think better when we use it to clear up word confusion.

_____ 4. Definitions of a word show the word's boundaries.

_____ 5. Knowing the words for things helps us see them better.

_____ 6. We do not fully understand a word unless we can define it.

_____ 7. When people debate a topic, understanding is greatly helped by their taking the time to define the key terms.

_____ 8. Etymology gives us word histories.

_____ 9. Pocket dictionaries are sufficient guides for a critical study of word meanings.

_____ 10. The word *ohm* comes from the Sanskrit language and means the sound of creation.

_____ 11. According to most dictionaries, there is more than one acceptable spelling of the word *cooperate.*

_____ 12. The term *French leave* means to say good-bye with a big kiss.

_____ 13. The prefix *in* in the words *insignificant* and *inflammable* means *not* in Latin.

_____ 14. The following words all contain the sound called a *schwa: mass, polite, placement, bogus, visible.*

_____ 15. The word *nausea* can be pronounced at least three different ways.

_____ 16. The word *round* can function as six different parts of speech: adjective, noun, transitive and intransitive verb, adverb, and preposition.

_____ 17. *Egregious* comes from a Latin word meaning standing out from the herd.

_____ 18. The word *nadir* in the phrase "the nadir of politics" means the highest point.

_____ 19. A *cogent* argument is a convincing one.

_____ 20. The word *decimate* means to dice something up into pieces.

Composition Writing Application

■ A Short Essay of Definition

Write an essay based on an extended definition or full discussion of a word or phrase supported by examples. It should also be an **essay of exposition,** which is a form of writing that explains something. In this case you will want to explain your definition fully through stories, examples, or specific information.

Clustering

To begin **clustering**, place an oval in the center of a page and write your key word inside that oval. Focus on that word. As thoughts, symbols, memories, or new word associations come, draw lines to new ovals that contain these new words. As words stimulate still further associations, draw lines to these. In time you will have a number of new clusters, all radiating from the key word. Notice how this is done with the word *family*.

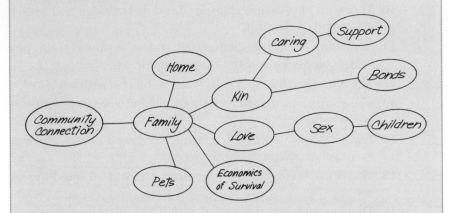

Clustering allows us to use both of our brain hemispheres at once. This method can feel more natural than restricting ourselves to the left brain by making an outline first. When we list or outline thoughts, we use our left brain to force our thinking into a sequence before we know all we could think about the subject. In clustering, we invite input from the right brain as well as from the left at the beginning of our work and thus achieve a visual sense of the whole picture. Clustering is a free-association method that is best done without censorship, allowing discoveries and surprises at the results.

The thinking tasks of making definitions followed by explanations play a frequent part in our daily conversations. If you are having a conversation with a friend and say, "She just isn't mature," your friend may reply, "What do you mean by *mature?*" Thus, you are challenged to respond with a definition together with an explanation of how you use that term.

The directions for this assignment, and for all the other writing assignments in this book, are designed to make you conscious of the thinking elements involved in solving it as a given problem, much like a problem in mathematics. However, you must follow the instructions exactly as they define its parameters.

Summary of Instructions for This Assignment

1. *Objective:* To give your own definition of a word and to explain that word's meaning through your own experience.
2. *Form and length:* At least one typed page.
3. *Structure:* Begin with a topic sentence and end with a conclusion.

Step 1 Suppose you choose as your topic defining *adult*. Think of what the word has come to mean to you in your own life. Think about how you have heard others use this word. Look up its definition in several dictionaries. Now turn back to the diagram of the word *cheesecake*. Draw and define the boundaries for the word *adult* using dictionary definitions or whatever you can add in terms of your own experience.

Step 2 Now try *clustering* with the word *adult*. Clustering (or mapping) is a warm-up exercise that invites both hemispheres of the brain to work with an idea. It can be a magical way to quickly release all the ideas, memories, and associations you have on a particular subject.

Step 3 Next, take the information you discovered from your cluster and begin to write a good paragraph about the various meanings and boundaries of the word *adult*. Contrast what you feel to be the true meaning of the word with some false meanings. Bring together your findings into one sentence that announces all you want to say about the definitions and boundaries of *adult*. This is a *topic sentence*, which generalizes your findings into a kind of conclusion. The rest of the sentences in the paragraph should support, or provide examples that support, the topic sentence. In this paragraph you can see how well you think about words while also working on the college level in expository writing.

■ Peer Review

In class, read your essays of definition to one another in small groups. For each paper, write a critique that answers these questions:

1. Was each of the parameters observed?
2. Did you understand all that was said? Did anything need to be explained more?
3. Did you honestly find the writing interesting?

■ STUDENT WRITING EXAMPLE

COOL
Claire Frey

Cool. It's arguably what everyone should have. For me, born in the 80's and raised by TV, being cool was what mattered most. What does it really mean to be cool, where does it come from and how can one get it? Can coolness be taught or bought? Can it be earned like little, gold stars beside one's name?

"What's cool?" I asked the 16-year-old daughter of a friend of mine. She began to rattle off a seemingly endless list of the "uncool":

". . . buying CDs, bell bottoms, tattoos of butterflies, the GAP, Britney Spears, hanging out with your parents . . ."

"Wait," I interrupt her, "what's *cool*, though?"

She looks at me questioningly, as though I'm from another planet. She's lost patience.

"You're either cool or you're not. If you're cool then you don't care about being cool." And with that her attention snapped back to her iPhone, her fingers resuming a million-word-a-minute texting frenzy.

I know I've gotten all I can from this one. I guess by her logic I'm most definitely uncool in my search for cool.

One definition of *cool* that I found through a Google search is "an aesthetic of attitude, behavior, comportment, appearance, style and zeitgeist." This definition coincides with my own idea of cool as being reflective of the spirit of the popular culture from the inside out. Coolness is a reaction, a form of expression. It's a word for the young and each generation creates its own representation of cool. There was the swing era with cool cat jazz musicians and flapper girls, young couples sneaking around in bad neighborhoods, with only those cool enough to know where to find the speakeasies. This was sort of like the treasure hunt maps to hidden raves in the 90's. You had to be in the "know" to find the right warehouse parties. When I was little, the Fonz was cool in his black motorcycle jacket and his comb in greasy pomped hair. Then there were boys with Lucky Strike cigarettes rolled up in the sleeve of a tight white T and the girls with bright peroxide blond hair, red red lips and blue jeans. Cool was about being a rebel. It was for those driven to push society's strict limitations on what it meant to have a good time.

For my generation being cool means a rebellious form or detachment. Our parents rebelled by confronting authority, protesting and yelling until their voices were heard. My generation has distanced itself from authority. Coolness is apathy, depressed maybe? It wasn't exactly cool when Sid killed Nancy or when Kurt Cobain offed himself, but it was definitely cool to wear all black and write suicidal poetry. What's next? I guess as someone nearing my thirties I'm out of the loop, but I do have a whole new outlook now on my idea of cool. Cool is just being myself. It's being content to do what I like and be the person I am without trying to conform. For me that part of the meaning of cool will always stay the same.

Used with permission of Claire Frey.

● R E A D I N G S ●

Rankism: What Divides Americans

Robert W. Fuller

Robert W. Fuller, PhD, is a physicist who became president of Oberlin College at the age of 33. He has created many careers for himself including service as a citizen diplomat to the Soviet Union during the Cold War years. In 2003 he published Somebodies and Nobodies: Overcoming the Abuse of Rank. *This excerpt is taken from a 2003 essay that appears on his website.*

What underlies *all* forms of discrimination is something less conspicuous than race or gender, but no less profound in its consequences. It is rank—in particular, low rank signifying a lack of power.

The primary rift dividing America today is not one of race, gender, age, or religion. Rather, it is between the "somebodies"—the relatively powerful and successful—and the "nobodies"—the relatively weak and vulnerable. Ah, another special interest group, you're probably thinking. But there's something different about this one, because each and every one of us can be a member, just as all of us have at some point nominated someone for inclusion.

It happens everyday. A boss harasses an employee; a customer demeans a waiter; a coach bullies a player; a doctor disparages a nurse; a teacher humiliates a student; a parent belittles a child. Somebodies with higher rank and more power in a particular setting can maintain an environment that is hostile and demeaning to nobodies with lower rank and less power in that setting, much as most everywhere whites used to be at liberty to mistreat blacks.

Although 35 years of affirmative action have put racists and sexists on notice, this does not mean that abuse and discrimination have disappeared. It is rather that they now occur more blatantly *within* a race or gender than across racial or gender lines. Blacks insult and exploit other blacks of lower rank, whites do the same to whites, and women to women, all with confidence that it will pass as business as usual.

5   We don't have a ready name for abuse and discrimination based on rank, but it deserves one. When discrimination and injustice are race-based, we call it racism; when they're gender-based, we call it sexism. By analogy, rank-based abuse and exploitation can be called "rankism." Naming rankism, putting it in the spotlight, is half the battle.

Rankism occurs when rank-holders use the power of their position to secure unwarranted advantages or benefits for themselves. It typically takes the form of self-aggrandizement and exploitation of subordinates. It is the opposite of service. Good leaders eschew rankism; bad ones indulge in it. It can be found in government, business, families, the workplace, schools and universities, and religious, nonprofit, and healthcare organizations. It distorts personal relationships, erodes the will to learn, fosters disease, taxes productivity, undermines public trust, stokes ethnic hatred, and incites revenge. Recent front-page examples of rankism include corporate and philanthropic corruption, sexual abuse by clergy, school hazing, and abuse of elders.

At the societal level, rank-based discrimination afflicts none more inescapably than those lacking the protections of social rank—the working poor. Two recent books chronicle this widening fissure. In *Nickel and Dimed: On (Not) Getting By in America*, Barbara Ehrenreich makes a compelling case that the working poor are in effect unacknowledged benefactors whose labor subsidizes the more advantaged. In *Wealth and Democracy: A Political History of the American Rich*, Kevin Phillips explores how the rich and politically powerful create and perpetuate privilege, at the expense of the middle and lower classes.

Don't conclude that I am proposing we do away with rank. This would make about as much sense as doing away with race or gender. When earned and exercised appropriately, rank is a legitimate, virtually indispensable tool of organization. But when the high-ranking abuse their authority, those of lower rank experience discrimination and injustice not different in their material and psychological effects from the discrimination and injustice we now disallow when their victims belong to the familiar identity groups.

To achieve a just society, we have to decide what it means to be a nation of equals. Indeed, at first glance, such a goal might seem absurd. How can we be equals when we are obviously unequal in skill, talent, beauty, strength, health, and wealth—in any commonly recognized trait for that matter? The answer is that people are equal in a sense they have always considered fundamental to being human. They are equal in dignity.

10   This is not some utopian ideal. As Vartan Gregorian has put it, "Dignity is not negotiable." Rankism is invariably an insult to the dignity of an individual or group. If the aggrieved party dare not protest, it will nurse its wounds until a time when it can exact revenge. The twentieth century has seen numerous demagogues who have promised to restore the pride and dignity of a people who felt they'd been "nobodied." The long-term and most horrific consequences of rankism between peoples range from sabotage and terrorism to genocide and war.

It's natural at first to wonder whether rankism is part of human nature. Not so long ago, it was widely believed that racism and sexism were, but now they are generally regarded as learned. While the impulse to exploit a power advantage for personal gain is hardly uncommon in our species, history shows it is equally in our nature to detest such abuses and to act together to circumscribe the authority of rank-holders. To this end, we have overthrown kings and tyrants and placed political power in the hands of the people. We have reined in monopolies with antitrust legislation. We have limited the power of employers through unionization. Blacks, women, homosexuals, and people with disabilities have all built effective movements that succeeded in replacing a once-sacrosanct social consensus with another that repudiated it.

People acquiesce in rankism because they fear the consequences of resisting: demerit, demotion, ridicule, and ostracism. The muffled complaints, occasional whistle-blowing, and sporadic outbursts we do hear echo those of blacks and women who resisted in solitary protest before popular movements made it impossible to ignore their demands.

The identity group movements succeeded by creating the safety in numbers that persuaded millions of oppressed individuals to stop putting up with discrimination. As the costs of rankism are exposed and it loses social sanction, its victims will likewise join forces and make themselves heard. A striking example is the recently founded lay Catholic organization "Voice of the Faithful," whose goal is to limit the absolute authority of clerics.

Today's n-word is "nobody." The successes of affirmative action have brought us to a time in which victims of indignity, injustice, and inequity are as apt to be white as black, male as female, or straight as gay. What primarily marks people for mistreatment and exploitation now is low rank and the powerlessness it signifies. Overcoming rankism is democracy's next step. In taking it we will have the opportunity to honor the dual commitment to both freedom *and* justice that our nation's founders imprinted on the American psyche.

● ● ●

Study/Writing/Discussion Questions

1. How does the author define *rankism*?

2. How is *rankism* a word concept? Did the understanding of this expression offer you a new way of looking at many situations and experiences?

3. What does the author mean when he says "naming *rankism*, putting it in the spotlight, is half the battle?"

4. Explain why you would agree or disagree with his opinion that "overcoming *rankism* is democracy's next step."

Saved

Malcolm X

Interest in the life and work of Malcolm X continues to grow. The recognition he achieved during his lifetime as a provocative thinker and public speaker was short; he died, at age 40, the victim of a political assassination. In this selection, now a classic, Malcolm X describes how he managed through self-education to pull himself out of a life of street hustling and prison into literacy and power.

It was because of my letters that I happened to stumble upon starting to acquire some kind of a homemade education.

I became increasingly frustrated at not being able to express what I wanted to convey in letters that I wrote, especially those to Mr. Elijah Muhammad. In the street, I had been the most articulate hustler out there—I had commanded attention when I said something. But now, trying to write simple English, I not only wasn't articulate, I wasn't even functional. How would I sound writing in slang, the way I would *say* it, something such as, "Look, daddy, let me pull your coat about a cat, Elijah Muhammad."

Many who today hear me somewhere in person, or on television, or those who read something I've said, will think I went to school far beyond the eighth grade. This impression is due entirely to my prison studies.

It had really begun back in the Charlestown Prison, when Bimbi first made me feel envy of his stock of knowledge. Bimbi had always taken charge of any conversation he was in, and I had tried to emulate him. But every book I picked up had few sentences which didn't contain anywhere from one to nearly all of the words that might as well have been in Chinese. When I just skipped those words, of course, I really ended up with little idea of what the book said. So I had come to the Norfolk Prison Colony still going through only book-reading motions. Pretty soon, I would have quit even these motions, unless I had received the motivation that I did.

5   I saw that the best thing I could do was get hold of a dictionary—to study, to learn some words. I was lucky enough to reason also that I should try to

improve my penmanship. It was sad. I couldn't even write in a straight line. It was both ideas together that moved me to request a dictionary along with some tablets and pencils from the Norfolk Prison Colony school.

I spent two days just riffling uncertainly through the dictionary's pages. I'd never realized so many words existed! I didn't know *which* words I needed to learn. Finally, just to start some kind of action, I began copying.

In my slow, painstaking, ragged handwriting, I copied into my tablet everything printed on that first page, down to the punctuation marks.

I believe it took me a day. Then, aloud, I read back, to myself, everything I'd written on the tablet. Over and over, aloud, to myself, I read my own hand-writing.

I woke up the next morning, thinking about those words—immensely proud to realize that not only had I written so much at one time, but I'd written words that I never knew were in the world. Moreover, with a little effort, I also could remember what many of these words meant. I reviewed the words whose meanings I didn't remember. Funny thing, from the dictionary first page right now, that "aardvark" springs to my mind. The dictionary had a picture of it, a long-tailed, long-eared, burrowing African mammal, which lives off termites caught by sticking out its tongue as an anteater does for ants.

10   I was so fascinated that I went on—I copied the dictionary's next page. And the same experience came when I studied that. With every succeeding page, I also learned of people and places and events from history. Actually the dictionary is like a miniature encyclopedia. Finally the dictionary's A section had filled a whole tablet—and I went on into the B's. That was the way I started copying what eventually became the entire dictionary. It went a lot faster after so much practice helped me to pick up handwriting speed. Between what I wrote in my tablet, and writing letters, during the rest of my time in prison I would guess I wrote a million words.

I suppose it was inevitable that as my word-base broadened, I could for the first time pick up a book and read and now begin to understand what the book was saying. Anyone who has read a great deal can imagine the new world that opened. Let me tell you something: from then until I left that prison, in every free moment I had, if I was not reading in the library, I was reading on my bunk. You couldn't have gotten me out of books with a wedge. Between Mr. Muhammad's teachings, my correspondence, my visitors—usu-ally Ella and Reginald—and my reading of books, months passed without my even thinking about being imprisoned. In fact, up to then, I never had been so truly free in my life.

The Norfolk Prison Colony's library was in the school building. A variety of classes was taught there by instructors who came from such places as Harvard and Boston universities. The weekly debates between inmate teams were also held in the school building. You would be astonished to know how worked up convict debaters and audiences would get over subjects like "Should Babies Be Fed Milk?"

Available on the prison library's shelves were books on just about every general subject. Much of the big private collection that Parkhurst had willed to the prison was still in crates and boxes in the back of the library—thousands of old books. Some of them looked ancient: covers faded, old-time parchment-looking binding. Parkhurst, I've mentioned, seemed to have been principally interested in history and religion. He had the money and the special interest to have a lot of books that you wouldn't have in general circulation. Any college library would have been lucky to get that collection.

As you can imagine, especially in a prison where there was heavy emphasis on rehabilitation, an inmate was smiled upon if he demonstrated an unusually intense interest in books. There was a sizable number of well-read inmates, especially the popular debaters. Some were said by many to be practically walking encyclopedias. They were almost celebrities. No university would ask any student to devour literature as I did when this new world opened to me, of being able to read and *understand*.

15   I read more in my room than in the library itself. An inmate who was known to read a lot could check out more than the permitted maximum number of books. I preferred reading in the total isolation of my own room.

When I had progressed to really serious reading, every night at about ten P.M. I would be outraged with the "lights out." It always seemed to catch me right in the middle of something engrossing.

Fortunately, right outside my door was a corridor light that cast a glow into my room. The glow was enough to read by, once my eyes adjusted to it. So when "lights out" came, I would sit on the floor where I could continue reading in that glow.

At one-hour intervals the night guards paced past every room. Each time I heard the approaching footsteps, I jumped into bed and feigned sleep. And as soon as the guard passed, I got back out of bed onto the floor area of that light-glow, where I would read for another fifty-eight minutes—until the guard approached again. That went on until three or four every morning. Three or four hours of sleep a night was enough for me. Often in the years in the streets I had slept less than that.

● ● ●

Study/Writing/Discussion Questions

1. Why do you think Malcolm X could be so confident and articulate as a hustler, yet have so much difficulty writing "simple English?"

2. What do you think of his practice of copying out every word in a dictionary?

3. Why did Malcolm X find it so empowering to learn new words?
4. What motivated him to read in his cell in semidarkness late through the night?
5. Why do you think Malcolm X wanted others to hear this story?

Advanced Optional Writing Assignment

Write an essay of about three typed pages in which you describe a significant learning experience in your life that involved your use of language. What was easy for you? What was difficult? Explain how your sense of self and personal power changed through a greater or lesser mastery of language.

3. List five facts about the room you are in right now. Do not just name objects or events (such as lights, door), but make statements describing what you see in its context. For instance, do not say "Four windows" but "There are four open windows on the south wall of this room."

4. Which of the following are statements of facts?

   a. Human blood is grouped into four types: A, B, AB, and O.

   b. One centimeter is the equivalent of 0.3937 inch.

   c. The major religion in Mexico is Roman Catholicism.

   d. The food is awful in the cafeteria.

   e. Amelia Earhart was the first woman to fly solo around the world.

   f. Everybody should have health insurance.

   g. He must have forgotten his keys; they are on the table.

   h. Advertisement: Big 6 offers you the best buys in camping equipment.

5. Explain why items 4d through 4h are not facts.

■ Verifying Facts

One characteristic of facts is that they can be objectively verified—proven to be true—through the testimony of witnesses, through observations, or through records or documentation. Read the following list of facts. Select three to study. Aside from using the Internet, how would you go about verifying that each is indeed a fact?

1. One tablespoon is the equivalent of three teaspoons.

2. The composer Amadeus Mozart died at the age of 36.

3. Until 1893 lynching was legal in the United States.

4. A rainbow can only be seen in morning or late afternoon.

5. Eritrea was once the northernmost province of Ethiopia.

6. The highest mountain peak in the world is Mt. Everest at 29,035 feet.

7. In 2006 the population of Alaska was 670,053. That is less than the population of Memphis, Tennessee.

8. All snow crystals are hexagonal.

9. The word *bible* comes from the Greek word *biblia*, meaning a collection of writings.

10. There is a job available as a receptionist in the college president's office.

Facts and Reality

What we call facts do not necessarily represent what is real and true.

If you were to stand on a street corner and ask each passerby to tell you what a **fact** is, most people would tell you that a fact is what is real and true. However, this common notion is mistaken. Facts are our *interpretations* of what is real and true. Yet the problem with interpretations is that they can be dead wrong. Human history provides us with many examples.

Every schoolchild knows that the long-accepted "fact" that the earth was flat was an error based on limited perception. In every century mistaken notions taken for fact come and go, such as the idea that bathing is unhealthy, that blood-letting cures the sick, that women are inferior to men, that some races are inferior to others. Toward the end of the twentieth century, science and government assured us that pesticides would not harm human beings, nor would lead paint, nor buried toxic wastes. Such false notions remind us that what we call facts are the creations of human minds and, for this reason, subject to error. Most of us grew up believing that 98.6 degrees Fahrenheit represented normal body temperature. This medical "fact" was commonly accepted until 1992, when new investigations revealed that 98.6 wasn't normal at all; indeed, it was downright unusual. Indeed, it was found that healthy people thrive between 96.0 and 99.9, depending on the individual, time of day, sex, and race. Science moved forward in this case because facts long assumed to be true were reexamined. We need to continually reevaluate our "facts" in light of the feedback received from their tests against reality.

What, then, is reality?

Reality is another term that we all use every day, yet few of us can define. It remains a mystery elusive of a definition that can be agreed upon. In the previous chapter, you were offered a number of very different definitions, some by philosophers who have long debated the nature of reality. Philosophers have divided themselves into two camps: those who consider reality to be relative and those who view reality as absolute. In other words, some say the observer determines what reality is, while others say that reality is what it is—regardless of what people may think about it. Yet, no matter what side we may lean toward ourselves, we must concede that our judgments do change about the truth of some facts.

In summary, facts are not the equivalent of truths or reality; they are, at best, only our decisions about what seems to be most real. Human beings need facts because they need certainties in order to proceed through the world. But we should not forget that human beings are fallible.

Discussion Break Questions

1. State two facts that you are certain are true.
2. State two facts that you are certain will never change.
3. State two facts that you are certain will change.

Facts Are Not Absolutes

> The most we can say about any fact is that its certainty is higher or lower in probability.

Facts that are most useful to us are those that have been repeatedly verified by many sources over time. Our lives and welfare depend on these certainties. On this planet we know that the fact of gravity limits what we can do and not do safely; we know that we can plan our daily schedules around the rising and the setting of the sun. But none can say that the orbit of this planet or its condition of gravity will always remain the same. We live in a physical universe that is eternally changing—from the invisible-to-the-eye subatomic level to obvious levels of wrinkles in our skin, the courses of rivers, the growth of children, and the motion of the sun and stars. Furthermore, modern technology is accelerating all kinds of unexpected environmental changes.

The sciences have their own way of coming to terms with the problem of certainties. Many statements that most of us would call facts are considered *probability* statements by the sciences. If a thermometer says the temperature is 65 degrees, a scientist would say that there is a 99 percent chance that the temperature is between 62.5 and 67.5 degrees. This would take into account any inaccuracies of the instrument. *Certainty* in science is usually considered to be a probability that is approaching certainty. In our human social history, beliefs that have often been mistaken for facts sometimes change as human knowledge evolves. In the eighteenth century and earlier, the belief that witches existed and caused malevolent harm to others was assumed to be fact. In nineteenth-century England, parents believed it necessary to "break the wills" of their children and beat them regularly in order to "civilize" them. Today neither of these beliefs is commonly considered true. Thus, many of our present cultural assumptions, thought to represent facts, may also be discovered mistaken over time. It is because of this human tendency to confuse beliefs with facts that a healthy society needs to preserve the freedom to debate, the right to disagree, the right to investigate one another's claims about facts, truths, and realities. Indeed, this is the only kind of environment in which critical thinking can flourish.

© Richard Sandler

A government that seeks absolute power over its citizens suppresses every stimulus to critical thinking. It buys out the media, censors a dissident press, discourages public protests, closes down schools, and imprisons those who dissent. Critical thinking is a fragile product of civilizations that value the freedom to search for truth. For the advancement of human knowledge and welfare, we need to value the right to continually reexamine whatever equations are made between reality, truth, and "facts."

Discussion Break Questions

1. Discuss a belief that you feel absolutely certain about. Discuss a belief that you are uncertain about.
2. Give an example of some methods used to suppress critical thinking.

Distinguishing Facts from Fiction

Surprisingly enough, we can sometimes be led to believe that the difference between fact and fiction doesn't really matter.

Commercial advertising uses a lot of sophisticated knowledge about how to get consumers to accept fakery. Actors in television commercials have to convince us that they are not actors: they should look "real"—like one of us.

© Rita Bernstein

They have to persuade us that it is natural for two homemakers doing aerobics together to share advice on laundry detergents or that a celebrity is sincere in making a product testimonial. The blurring of fact and fiction extends beyond commercials, sometimes with little concern for the distinction. We watch documentaries that alternate between actual news footage and reenactments. We watch adventure stories that use news footage with pseudo-newsreels. Consider the following instances of fact mixed with fiction.

1. Ronald Reagan was known for his "presidency by photo ops." When he went to the demilitarized zone in Korea, his video managers wanted to get footage of Reagan at the most exposed American bunker, Guardpost Collier, which overlooked North Korea. However, the Secret Service vetoed the idea for fear of sharpshooters or infiltrators. After several days of negotiation, protection was provided for the president by erecting posts strong enough to hold 30,000 yards of camouflage netting in front of the bunker. Then, to get the most dramatic shots, the army built camera platforms on the hill beyond the guardpost so Reagan could be snapped standing there at the front. In the final shot, he was to be seen surrounded by sandbags, peering with his binoculars toward North Korea, evoking the memory of General Douglas MacArthur (from "The Storybook Presidency," *Power Game: How Washington Works,* by Hedrick Smith, 1988).

2. In a newspaper cartoon a father is changing a flat tire in the rain while his two children complain from the car window. The father says, "Don't you understand? This is *life;* this is what is happening. We *can't* switch to another channel."

3. Some TV stations regularly reenact true local crime events for the news, using actors to play the parts on the exact locations. They claim this is done as a public service.

4. A film star who regularly played the surgeon Colonel Potter on the TV series *M*A*S*H* appeared, wearing a doctor's white coat, in an aspirin commercial to endorse the product.

5. Sears has entered into a first-ever deal with the United States military to market a new line of officially sanctioned, military-styled clothing to men, women and boys. The military has officially licensed a "soldier chic" line of clothing to Sears called the "All American Army Brand First Infantry Division" collection. The garb . . . consists of "authentic lifestyle reinterpretations" of regulation uniforms and military-issued gear like T-shirts, hooded sweatshirts, denim, and other outerwear. The partnership is part of a marketing strategy to raise the public profile of the U.S. military. (*Spin of the Day,* September 2, 2008. Source: Advertising Age.)

6. In August of 2008, the opening sale of iPhone 36 drew long lines of waiting customers in the United States as well as in Poland. However, as it was later confessed, the eager Polish customers were paid actors. The Polish subsidiary of the French firm France Telecom admitted that they had staged the event as a marketing strategy. (PCIN pact, August 24, 2008)

Feelings Can Be Facts

Feelings can deceive as well as illuminate.

We often hear that we should be objective and not subjective in order to determine facts. This warning is needed to remind us that anger, fear, envy, and prejudice can distort our perceptions and keep us from seeing things fairly as they really are. However, many interpret this familiar advice to mean that all feelings are "subjective"—and therefore irrational and unreliable—or that they invariably keep us from knowing what is true. This is a false assumption. There are times when feelings lead us to make a more careful investigation of a situation, such as when we feel mistrust. Therefore, it would seem wiser not to deny or suppress our feelings but instead to examine our *attitude* toward an issue. Is it objective or subjective? We can hate the taste of a bitter medication, yet

© Eve Arnold/Magnum Photos

decide to take it because our health depends on it. This would be assuming an objective attitude in spite of our feelings. A subjective attitude, on the other hand, would only choose what feels most comfortable despite long-term consequences. Thus, attitude can be objective, in the sense of being under conscious control, or subjective, in terms of remaining under unconscious influence. Ambulance attendants, police officers, or firefighters may flinch when they see a maimed or burned person, but nevertheless carry on with their work. Personal reactions of aversion cannot be allowed to interfere with such professional duty. Yet this does not mean that professionals need to deny what they are feeling in order to function well.

There are many circumstances in which a careful consideration of our feelings offers vital information. We need this sensitivity in human relationships, and we need sensitivity to interpret art. Look for instance at the photo on this page.

Suppose that you first react to the photo by feeling startled, then amused and curious. Such feelings might draw you to look more closely in order to learn more. You might even wonder if the photographer intended to lure your interest in this way.

When we are studying art, we give attention to our feeling reactions, because they can lead us to better understand a work's meaning. Artists, like the photographers whose pictures appear in this book, intentionally try to provoke reactions. Indeed, you cannot come into objective contact with a work unless you first assess how it affects you. When we listen to salsa, our mood is affected and we feel enticed to dance. The release of joy we feel inside, when recognized, becomes a fact. Such experiences, when shared with others, can be especially powerful. We have all attended public performances where we laughed and cried together in an audience that was sharing the same feeling response. Here the feelings became a shared reality, a fact.

Let's now go back to the terms *objective* and *subjective*. Some believe that in order to be objective, a person must deny or suppress any feelings, because feelings keep one from being coolly rational and observant. Certainly this belief expresses an ideal. But, without faking, can it be achieved? Let us then consider how we might proceed with more honest realism about our feelings. We can learn how to observe, rather than react to, our feelings—to observe while feeling them at the same time. This means simply allowing feelings to be present without ignoring, denying, or suppressing them. When we are subjective about feelings, we are driven by them, we are unaware of how they are influencing our thoughts and decisions, and we react blindly to their directives. Unrecognized feelings can distort our reasoning and lead us to deceive others and ourselves. When subjectivity rules us, we cannot clearly discern what is real and true. However, when we take our feelings into account, staying present both with them and in what lies before us, we come closer to that ideal of objectivity.

Facts and Social Pressure

> Our need to have our perceptions verified by others also makes us susceptible to manipulation.

We only need to use our senses and perceptions to determine some facts. However, to be sure of their accuracy, we need confirmation from other sources.

1. JOHN: "Tell me, am I asleep or awake?"
   MARY: "You are awake."
2. BILL: "Did that woman make a pass at me or did I imagine it?"
   JANE: "She made a pass, alright."
3. EMILY: "I think this suit is too large for me. What do you think?"
   MAY: "Much too large."

4. VERNA: "My checking account balances."

   NORMA: "My figures show you are correct."

In each of these examples, a personal examination alone could not determine what was real. To test the perception accuracy, confirmation was needed from others. Confirmation takes us out of disequilibrium and restores us to equilibrium. The reverse side of this principle is that someone who contradicts perceptions we feel certain about can make us feel uncomfortable, angry, even crazy.

5. JOSE: "I didn't have too much to drink last night."

   WANDA: "Yes, you did! You were drunk!"

6. CHILD: "I don't want to eat my carrots. They taste icky."

   PARENT: "Yes, you do want to eat them. You are just imagining things. They taste good."

As these examples illustrate, disagreements about perceptions result in conflicts. Sometimes conflicts can be settled by arbiters: an umpire in a game, a speedometer in a car, or a thermometer on the wall. But without an arbiter, we can be left feeling off balance and unsettled.

This human need for confirmation leaves us vulnerable to manipulation. The truth of this principle was demonstrated by American psychologist Solomon Asch, who conducted some simple experiments to test how a group could affect the perceptions of an individual. He found that in a small group, people are willing to deny the evidence of their own senses if the other members of the group interpret reality differently. In one experiment, Asch assembled groups of seven to nine college students in what was described as a test of visual judgment. In each group, only one of the students was actually a subject in the experiment; the others were the researcher's secret accomplices. The researcher informed the students that they would be comparing the lengths of lines. He showed them two white cards. On the first was a single vertical black line—the standard—whose length was to be matched. On the second white card were vertical lines of various lengths. The subjects were to choose the one line of the same length as the standard line (see Figure 3.1).

A series of eighteen trials was conducted. When the first pair of cards was presented, the group gave a unanimous judgment. The same thing happened on the second trial. In twelve of the remaining sixteen trials, however, all of Asch's accomplices agreed on what was clearly an incorrect answer. The real subject of the experiment was left to react. In about a third of the cases, the subject yielded to the majority and

Standard   Comparison

FIGURE 3.1 Standard and Comparison Lines
in the Asch Experiment

conformed to its decision. In separate experiments with a control group
consisting of only genuine subjects, Asch found that people made mistakes less than one percent of the time. Subsequent interviews with
those who yielded to the majority revealed that only a few of them had
actually believed that the majority choice was correct. They admitted
that they thought they had judged the length of the lines correctly but
did not want to "rock the boat" or "spoil the results" by giving the right
answer. And then there were those who had doubted their own perceptions and had concluded that they had better hide this from the others.
The test provided a significant demonstration of the power of consensus
to bring about conformity and to make a person invalidate his or her
own perception.*

Class Discussion

1. Why did a third of the subjects in Asch's experiments conform to
   the incorrect majority even when their perceptions told them they
   were correct?

2. Did these subjects have any other means of judging the correctness
   of their perceptions than from the others in the group?

3. If group pressure can affect us this much in such a simple problem
   as determining the relative length of a line, what do you think are
   the implications in more complex problems such as public opinion
   on controversial issues?

4. If you are familiar with the story "The Emperor's New Clothes,"
   what parallels do you see between its theme and Asch's experiment?

*Figure and text adapted from Solomon Asch, "Effects of Group Pressure upon Modifica-
tion and Distortion of Judgments," in H. Proshansky and B. Seidenberg (Eds.), *Basic Studies in Social Psychology* (New York: Holt, Rinehart & Winston, 1965), pp. 393–401. Used
with permission of CBS College Publishing.

Facts and Our Limited Senses

> Both science and wisdom are needed to help us compensate for the
> limitations of our senses.

We have seen how consensus and conformity influence perception and thus
limit our ability to know the facts. But even aside from the influence of
social pressure, we are limited in our ability to know the facts because of the
limits of our senses. We now know that dogs can hear levels of pitch that we
cannot and that butterflies can see colors invisible to us. If we look at a chart
of the electromagnetic spectrum, the portion visible to us is only a tiny slit
in the whole band. We have to use instruments—X rays, radar, the seismo-
graph, smoke detectors—to compensate for our sense limitations.

But aside from all this, our senses are affected by many other variables such as mental preoccupations, distractions, or our varying degrees
of alertness in different circumstances. How much do you actually see on
your commute route? How much attention do you pay to background
sounds when you live in the city? Has a friend ever complained you
didn't notice when he shaved off his beard?

Another human failing is that we interpret what we perceive on the
basis of our experience. Moreover, this experience may be too narrow and
limited to embrace what lies before us. The Buddha once succinctly
illustrated this point and more in the following wise parable.

● R E A D I N G ●

The Blind Men and the Elephant

Once upon a time a king gathered some blind men about an elephant and
asked them to tell him what an elephant was like. The first man felt a tusk and
said an elephant was like a giant carrot; another happened to touch an ear
and said it was like a big fan; another touched its trunk and said it was like a
pestle; still another, who happened to feel its leg, said it was like a mortar; and
another, who grasped its tail, said it was like a rope. Not one of them was
able to tell the king the elephant's real form.

● ● ●

Study Questions

1. What do you think the elephant represents?
2. Why did each of the blind men think in terms of comparisons?

3. What was wrong with their comparisons?

4. Can you think of examples in your life where you could not experience something new because you were comparing it to something familiar?

Statements of Fact

How we state a fact makes all the difference.

As the preceding sections have demonstrated, it is not always easy to determine some facts. Moreover, facts depend on the language used to express them. When we make statements of fact, our language needs to be quite specific and guarded against assumptions. This does not mean we must use tentative language all the time. But if we are stating facts, our language has to reflect the limits of our data as well as the measure of our certainty.

Study the photograph on page 90. Then read the following statements; notice how those in italics differ from those in regular type.

1. *A puppy has jumped up onto a car's running board.*

   In the near center of this rectangular black-and-white photo, a small white-spotted furry animal stands with four feet resting on two horizontal lines, one dark and one light. The head, ears, and legs of this little creature suggest those of a young dog. Behind and above him are two rectangular planes that share the same gray metallic-smooth reflecting surface. In front of his head a dark vertical hollow-seeming line extends to the top of the photo, leading the eye to two shiny overlapping disks that resemble a car's door lock and lock cover as well as to a shiny arc that suggests a car door handle. Below the horizontal lines that could comprise a car's running board, there appears a wide dark surface area such as one finds beneath a standing car. This darkest area becomes lighter as it moves into a speckled foreground of a rougher texture reminiscent of a dirt road surface.

2. *Someone put the puppy up there as a joke. He could not have jumped up there on his own.*

   The distance between the running board and the ground cannot be measured, but in this photo the distance appears to be almost twice the height of the dog. The width of the running board also cannot be seen, but it accommodates the four feet of the puppy. No people appear in the picture, nor do any human shapes appear in reflection.

From Anonymous by Robert Flynn Johnson, Thames & Hudson, London and New York. Used with permission of Thames & Hudson, Ltd.

3. *Although he can't jump down, the puppy does not appear terrified; some-one outside the photo could be reassuring him.*

   We see the small dog in profile with his head and body facing the photo's left border. He stands with his back feet together and his front feet apart. His gaze and stance suggest curiosity but not tension.

4. *Trees and clouds are reflected in the car door.*

   The medium grey metallic planes behind the puppy appear overlaid with darker shaded images consisting of wispy, smoky shapes forming a pyramid and two columns. Horizontal cloudlike formations rest suspended between these shapes.

5. *This is an old photo, probably from the 1920s or 1930s.*

   Wide running boards were featured on motor car sedans during the 1920s and 1930s. The craftsmanship of the car's door fixtures and sculptured door also suggest the elegance of that era. Moreover, during that time, dirt roads and rural scenes were more common.

As you probably have guessed, the italicized sentences are hasty interpretations of the photo, whereas the statements appearing in regular type offer objective descriptions derived from a careful study of the photo. The interpretations are *inferences* that may or may not be carefully drawn, whereas the objective *descriptions* offer perceptions and information that can be verified—that is, tested for factual accuracy. You yourself will be engaging in verification when you compare your own visual study of the photo to these statements. Moreover, you will be questioning whether they support such inferences. All in all, however, no study of the photo alone will be able to tell you with certainty how or why the puppy got on the running board, how the puppy is reacting, or where or when the picture was taken.

   In preparation for writing your own description of different photos, it can be useful to pause in order to study some of the characteristics of factual statements.

1. Factual statements show an awareness of context and limitations. If a photo is being described, the writer does not pretend it is a life situation in which one can see all angles and ask questions.

   "In the near center of this black-and-white photo a small white-spotted furry animal stands with four feet resting on two horizontal lines, one dark and one light."

2. Factual statements use appropriate qualifiers to indicate uncertainties.

   "two shining overlapping disks that resemble . . ."

   "below the horizontal lines that could comprise . . ."

3. Factual statements state the obvious.

   "We see the small dog in profile."

4. Factual statements show a disciplined effort to describe what is present while restraining the impulse to jump to conclusions.

   "darker shaded images consisting of wispy, smoky shapes . . ."

5. Factual statements are not inappropriately cautious, such as to say,

   "The dog appears to have legs."

6. Factual statements are *not* guesses.

   "Someone outside the photo could be reassuring him."

7. Factual statements provide specific details that others can verify.

"In this photo the distance appears to be almost twice the height of the dog."

Class Discussion

1. How do the detailed statements resemble police reports? Why are police taught to write like this?
2. If you were on a jury, how could it be useful to know the difference between factual statements and claims that are interpretations of data?
3. Why would it be important to know the difference if you were an attorney, a judge, a witness, or a defendant?
4. Why would a reporter be concerned with the difference between facts and interpretations?
5. Why would the difference matter to (a) a doctor, (b) a car mechanic, (c) a biologist, (d) a pharmacist?

Core Discovery Writing Application

■ Using a List of Facts to Describe a Photograph

This is an exercise that challenges your mental and verbal awareness. Its task seems simple: to describe a photograph by making a list of at least ten factual statements about it. This exercise is best done first by the whole class working together on one photograph. Then small groups can work with other photographs.

1. Choose one photograph from this book for your group to study that has not already been described by the author. Each person should work quietly alone, then discuss his or her effort when everyone is finished. Spend some time absorbing the photograph, then take notes. Imagine that you are writing for someone who cannot see the photograph. Be as specific and detailed as you can, even about the picture's most obvious aspects. Be on guard against jumping to conclusions. Stay with your evidence. Arrange your list in some kind of logical order. (Don't jump around from the background to a person's clothes to another's hair.)

2. Write out your list of ten or more factual statements. Then compare your list to others in your group who worked on the same picture. How do you agree or differ about the facts you found? Star the facts you can agree upon.

Scoring for Using a List of Facts to Describe a Photograph
1. Obvious details not ignored. *20 points*
2. Things are described, not just labeled. (To say "bus" is not to describe the evidence of the clues you actually see; besides, this label could be a mistaken inference.) *20 points*
3. Facts are stated in at least 10 sentences. *10 points*
4. Inferences are not stated. *30 points*
5. Systematic presentation of data. *10 points*
6. No distracting errors of spelling, punctuation, or sentence structure. *10 points*

Standards We Use to Determine Facts: *Verifiability, Reliability, Plausibility, Probability*

In any situation, when we need to think critically, the first thing we have to determine is what the facts are. We solve practical problems through facts, such as proving the payment of a bill; we seek facts in every form of investigation, whether in a court of law or a geographical survey. This primary need for facts has led to the development of standards for determining both their existence and their reliability. When we think critically, we fully understand and use these standards, many of which have already been suggested in this chapter. Let's now look directly at four of them: verifiability, reliability, plausibility, and probability.

Verifiability means the data can be confirmed by another source. This source can be a reference source (such as a dictionary), a record (such as a marriage license), or a standard (such as Greenwich mean time). Another source could be the testimony of a witness or an expert. Data can be verified by the senses, by agreements, by measurements, or by documentation.

A second standard for determining facts is **reliability**. When we obtain agreements or disagreements about facts, we have to consider their degree of dependability. To do this we have to ask some critical questions. Is the witness biased? Do we need a larger survey? Were the senses used carefully and consciously? Were they adequate to the task? Were the measurements accurate? Were the documents genuine?

Probability, as tested through time and repetition, represents another standard used to determine the reliability of a fact. If the weather pattern in one region alters radically over a period of several years, this phenomenon of change becomes a fact. If over a ten-year period, the prices of homes in your neighborhood have risen 10 percent a year, this is a fact.

However, that rate of increase may not hold true next year. Thus, facts depend on our observation of the recurrence of things over time as well as on our assessment of the probability of their continuation.

Plausibility is a fourth standard for facts, meaning they undergo the test of credibility. If a friend tells you that he "totaled" the car you loaned him, you would want to ask a lot more questions. The same might be said for a car insurance salesperson who offers you a special $100-per-year deal on your new car. In both these cases, since neither claim seems totally plausible, you might well decide that you would have to check out what they told you. Should you find contradictions, such as spotting your car parked on the street without a dent, then you would know for certain that you had not been given the facts. Likewise, you might learn that the insurance person is not employed by the company she claims to represent. In both of these cases, you could also have been conned by more plausible arguments. Nevertheless, for facts to be accepted, they have to be plausible, make sense, or seem to be the most likely possibility.

In conclusion, these four standards suggest a few useful rules to follow:

1. Don't believe any facts given to you unless sufficient information is provided about their source to allow verification.
2. Don't totally accept—or take action on the basis of—facts given to you until you verify them for yourself.
3. Don't accept facts that appear implausible, that contain discrepancies or contradictions. (You will read more on the subject in Chapter 9.)
4. When you have an important decision to make, verify all the facts given to you even if they come from someone you trust.

Chapter Summary

1. By definition, a fact is something known with certainty through experience, observation, or measurement. A fact can be objectively demonstrated and verified. A fact is something that people agree corresponds to reality.
2. It is not easy for us to determine whether facts correspond to reality. This can only be determined over time with repeated feedback and testing.
3. The difference between facts and fiction does matter.
4. Feelings are facts; they can distort or enhance our perceptions, depending on how conscious we are of their presence.
5. Facts are not absolutes but statements of probability.
6. Because we are dependent on confirmation from others in our search for facts, social pressures can lead us to distrust or distort our own perceptions.

7. Our senses are limited both in range and capacity and are affected by many factors, such as selective focus and mental preoccupations.

8. Facts must be expressed in carefully formulated statements that have the following characteristics:

   a. They define their own limitations.

   b. They are objectively stated.

   c. They use appropriate qualifiers.

   d. They state the obvious.

   e. They are not inappropriately cautious.

   f. They do not include guesses or inferences.

   g. They are specific and offer their evidence for others to verify.

9. The standards traditionally used to determine facts are verifiability, reliability, probability, and plausibility. Facts have to undergo the test of time and repetition and not contradict other known facts.

Chapter Quiz

Rate each of the following statements as *true* or *false*. In class discussion or in writing, give an example to substantiate your answer in each case.

_T_ 1. Some facts can be determined by measurement.

_____ 2. Some facts can be confirmed by the senses, others by records.

_T_ 3. The most reliable facts are those that have been repeatedly confirmed by tests over time.

_F_ 4. Facts often consist of obvious details that are seen but not consciously recognized.

_____ 5. Sometimes what we claim to be facts are untrue because the human perceptions used to determine them are limited and fallible.

_____ 6. A person educated in critical thinking qualifies statements to reflect probabilities and uncertainties using provisional phrases such as "it appears that. . . ."

_____ 7. The only standards we use to determine facts are verifiability, reliability, plausibility, and credibility.

_____ 8. The study of many subjects consists of memorizing facts, because they are the nearest things we have to certainties.

_____ 9. All newspapers can be depended upon as reliable sources of facts about world events.

_____ 10. An atmosphere that permits disagreements about widely accepted perceptions and beliefs helps critical thinking to flourish.

Composition Writing Application

■ Writing a Short Fact-Finding Report

Think of a problem that you might solve by getting whatever facts you may need to make a decision or take effective action. This could involve buying a used car, selecting a college, agreeing to a date, getting insurance, finding affordable housing, or making a complaint before the city council. Write a simple report on the subject. Here is a summary of the parameters:

1. *Objective:* Write a report concerning a problem that could be solved through knowing or verifying more facts. Also describe how determining and verifying these facts helped you make a better decision or take more effective action.

2. *Structure:* Begin with a topic sentence and end with a summary statement. Your content should include three parts:

   a. Describe the problem.

   b. Describe what facts you needed, where you found them, and how you interpreted them.

Scoring for the Fact-Finding Report

1. The problem is clearly explained. *10 points*
2. There is a systematic assessment of the missing or needed facts. *20 points*
3. There is a description of how the facts were found, what information was discovered, and how these facts were verified and interpreted. *20 points*
4. A conclusion shows how these facts aided understanding, made a decision or action possible, or solved the problem. *20 points*
5. The report is from one to four typed pages in length. *20 points*
6. There are no distracting errors of spelling, punctuation, or sentence structure. *10 points*

    c. Describe the final outcome. Explain how getting these facts affected your perspective of the problem and helped you make a decision or take action toward solving the problem.

3. *Length:* The length of your report will be from one to four typed pages.

▦ STUDENT WRITING EXAMPLE

A PROBLEM SOLVED BY FACTS
Anthony Choy

I am an auto mechanic; a large part of my job requires skills in observing, investigating, and determining facts. Often people bring in cars with problems they can't identify, much less repair. In such cases, they hire me to get the facts. And the final test of whether or not I got the facts right is a car that runs right. Let me illustrate this with a story.

One day a customer brought in a 1977 Ford Pinto. His complaint was about the awful noise in his V-6 engine, which was louder when it revved high and quieter when it revved low. I began my inspection by locating the noise at the front of the engine area. I checked the alternator, water pump, valve adjustment, cam gears. Nothing was out of the ordinary. I was stumped.

I then removed the timing chain cover. I noticed there was a gear-to-gear system that is known to make a racket, but nothing comparable to the sound this engine was producing. Again the gears checked out okay. I was stumped again.

Then I started looking at the obvious. I retraced my diagnosing steps to study the engine some more. I noticed an excessive amount of silicone on the oil pan gasket where the bottom of the timing chain cover meets the oil pan. I noticed some broken gears inside the oil pan. I wondered: "Why didn't the last mechanic take care of this?" I examined the gears again and noticed how hard it was to remove the crank gear. The only way to remove that gear would be to remove the oil pan by lifting the engine off its mounts first. I realized then that the last mechanic who replaced the cam and crank gears did not do the job correctly: if the mechanic had removed the gears, there would not have been an excessive amount of silicone on the oil pan gasket. The gasket had not been replaced, otherwise the broken pieces in the oil pan would have been cleaned out. Why did the mechanic omit doing this? I realized it was probably because he or she could not figure out how to remove the oil pan.

5   Well, I replaced the parts and proceeded to repair the vehicle the way I was taught. I started up the engine, checked for leaks, and there were none. Then I revved the engine high for a moment and left it at idle, and the noise was completely gone. It purred like a kitten. I felt good to have corrected the problem. When my customer returned, he shook my hand and gave me a bonus.

Used with permission of Anthony Choy.

• R E A D I N G •

Our Daily Meds

Melody Peterson

Melody Peterson specialized in writing articles on the pharmaceutical industry for the New York Times for four years and was winner of the Gerald Loeb Award, the highest honor for business journalism. This excerpt is taken from the Introduction to her book with the full title of Our Daily Meds: How the Pharmaceutical Companies Transformed Themselves into Slick Marketing Machines and Hooked the Nation on Prescription Drugs. *(2008)*

This is a book about a great transformation in the prescription drug industry over the last twenty-five years. Once the most successful pharmaceutical companies were those with the brightest scientists searching for cures. Now the most profitable and powerful drugmakers are those with the most creative and aggressive marketers. The drug companies have become marketing machines, selling antidepressants like Paxil, pain pills like Celebrex, and heart medications like Lipitor with the same methods that Coca-Cola uses to sell Sprite and Procter & Gamble uses to sell Tide.

Selling prescription drugs—rather than *discovering* them—has become the pharmaceutical industry's obsession.

Prescription drug marketing now permeates every corner of American society—from *Sesame Street* to nursing homes to the nightly news. Medicine ads sprout from billboards, scoreboards, the hoods of race cars, and the back covers of magazines—all once venues of the similarly ubiquitous cigarette ads of the 1960s and 1970s. Imitating neighborhood grocers, the drugmakers offer coupons, free gifts, and deals to buy six prescriptions and get one free. They hold sweepstakes and scholarship contests. They pay to sponsor rock concerts, movie premieres, and baseball's major leagues.

The marketers make the use of their dangerous medicines look attractive and easy. Fentanyl, an addictive narcotic eighty times more potent than morphine, comes in a berry-flavored lollipop. Syringes used to inject children with growth hormone look like kaleidoscope-colored writing pens and PlaySkool toys. In 2006 drug companies gained approval to coat their pills with "pearlescent pigments" to enhance them with a shimmery satin luster and make them look as precious as their price.

5   During New York's 2003 Fashion Week, swimsuit models shimmied down the catwalk, showing off Johnson & Johnson's new contraceptive, a white-colored patch that was glued to the skin. By wearing the drug as a fashion accessory, one company executive explained, women "can look beautiful and feel confident."

Men attending professional golf tournaments in 2004 heard a different pitch. Step right up for free tips on your golf game, offered marketers working in a tent promoting Cialis, a drug for erectile dysfunction. Step right up for a free video lesson from a sports psychologist, the salesmen invited. By the way, they added, do we have the perfect drug for you!

America has become the world's greatest medicine show.

The marketing works. Never have Americans taken so many prescription drugs.

Americans spent $250 billion in 2005 on prescription drugs, more than the combined gross domestic product of Argentina and Peru. Americans spent more on prescription drugs in 2004 than they did on gasoline or fast food. They paid *twice* as much for their prescription medicines that year as they spent on either higher education or new automobiles.

10   The American prescription drug market is so lucrative that many foreign drug companies have moved in and now depend on Americans for most of their profits. For foreign executives, the math is simple. Americans spend more on medicines than do all the people of Japan, Germany, France, Italy, Spain, the United Kingdom, Australia, New Zealand, Canada, Mexico, Brazil, and Argentina *combined*.

As the medicine merchants have poured billions of dollars into selling their wares, they have become America's most powerful industry. In the process, they have transformed American life. The small white-capped whiskey-colored bottles that once took up a corner of the bathroom cabinet now play a role in lives that few products can match. Almost 65 percent of the nation now takes a drug available only by prescription. Children line up in the dining hall of their summer camps to get their daily doses. Pharmacies stay open twenty-four hours to meet America's demand. Even the dogs get Prozac if they howl too much at the moon.

The pharmaceutical companies build their laboratories on the campuses of public universities. They recruit patients for clinical trials at shopping malls and county fairs. On network television, the plots of prime-time shows revolve around brand name prescription drugs, at times at the suggestion of marketers at a pharmaceutical company.

The medicine promoters have turned what were once normal life events—menopause, despair from a divorce, anxiety caused by a workaholic boss—into maladies that can be treated with a pill. After all, when patients are customers and medicines are commodities, the industry thrives when people are ill—or believe they are.

The companies have found the United States, with its consumer-driven culture, a perfect medicine market. We expect instant gratification of our desires and a quick fix for whatever bothers or distracts. Americans are eager to believe in the panaceas offered in the six drug commercials that regularly accompany each evening's news. We are told—and want to believe—that we can swallow a pill and soon be dancing on a dinner cruise, running on the beach, or playing football like John Elway, the former NFL quarterback and promoter of Prevacid, a heartburn pill. If we eat too many cheeseburgers and fries, there is comfort knowing one pill will settle our stomachs while another brings our cholesterol back down.

15   In the condos of Palm Beach, the bungalows of Los Angeles, and the farm-
houses of Iowa, people are taking more and more pills. The average American
collected more than twelve prescriptions from his pharmacy in 2006, up from
eight prescriptions in 1994. Older Americans take home even more—an average of thirty prescriptions each year.

        In 2003 Secretary of State Colin Powell explained the nation's new pre-
scription habit to a journalist for the Arabic newspaper *Asharq Al-Awsat*.

        "So do you use sleeping tablets to organize yourself?" asked the writer,
Abdul Rahman Al-Rashed.

        "Yes. Well, I wouldn't call them that," Powell replied. "They're a wonderful
medication—not medication. How would you call it? They're called Ambien,
which is very good. You don't use Ambien? Everybody here uses Ambien."

        There is a problem, however, with the new American way, one that
the drug companies and doctors prescribing the medicines do not like to
talk about. Experts estimate that more than a hundred thousand Americans
die each year not from illness but from their prescription drugs. Those
deaths, occurring quietly, almost without notice in hospitals, emergency
rooms, and homes, make medicines one of the leading causes of death in
the United States.

Used with permission of Farrar, Straus & Giroux and the Karpfinger Agency.

Footnotes

1 **transformation in the . . . industry over the last twenty-five years:** This is described in
   detail in chapters 4 and 5. Also see comments by pharmaceutical executives about how
   the industry has entered an era of marketing and me-too drugs in "Viewpoint: In Your
   Own Words," *Pharmaceutical Executive,* Aug. 2006.

4 **"pearlescent pigments":** Andrew Bridges, "FDA OKs Pearly Pigments to Color Pills," The
   Associated Press, July 20, 2006.

5 **"can look beautiful":** "Ortho Evra Joins Rosa Cha by Amir Slama for Mercedes-Benz Fashion Week Spring 2004," Press release from Johnson & Johnson, Sept. 2003.

6 **free tips on your golf game:** "New PGA Tour Partner Cialis Debuts Consumer Golf Plans
   at the Honda Classic," Press release from Lilly ICOS, March 11, 2004.

9 **Americans spent more on prescription drugs in 2004:** According to IMS Health, a
   consulting firm, Americans spent $251.8 billion on prescription drugs in 2005 and $238.9
   billion in 2004. See IMS National Sales Perspectives, Jan. 2006. Gross domestic product in
   2005 in U.S. dollars for Argentina ($172.1 billion) and Peru ($72.9 billion) is from *World
   Economic Outlook Database,* Apr. 2005. Accessed from International Monetary Fund website
   (imf.org) in Apr. 2006. Year 2004 consumer spending figures are from U.S. Department of
   Commerce's Bureau of Economic Analysis "Table 2.4.5U. Personal Consumption Expendi-
   tures by Type of Product." In 2004, Americans spent $227.2 billion on gasoline and other
   motor fuel, $200 billion on "meals at limited service eating places," $117.7 billion on

higher education, and $97.5 billion on new automobiles. Americans spent $213.7 billion on prescription drugs in 2004, according to Table 2.4.5U, but this amount does not include drugs used in hospitals and other such facilities.

10 **Americans spend more on medicines than do all the people of Japan:** According to statistics from IMS Health's "Retail Drug Monitor: 12 months to Feb. 2005." Available at imshealth.com.

11 **65 percent of the nation now takes:** "Outpatient Prescription Drug Expenses in the U.S. Community Population, 2003," Medical Expenditure Panel Survey Chartbook No. 16. Available at meps.ahrq.gov.

12 **build their laboratories on . . . public universities:** For example, Eli Lilly operated a clinical research lab in 2004 on the campus of Indiana University School of Medicine.

15 **average American collected more than twelve prescriptions . . . in 2006:** "Prescription Drug Trends," Kaiser Family Foundation, May 2007.

15 **Older Americans take . . . an average of thirty prescriptions:** See "Cost Overdose: Growth in Drug Spending for the Elderly," a report by Families USA, July 2000.

17 **"do you use sleeping tablets":** Transcript of interview of Secretary Powell by Abdul Rahman al-Rashed, Nov. 5, 2003. Accessed from state.gov in July 2006.

19 **hundred thousand Americans die each year:** Lazarou et al., "Incidence of Adverse Drug Reactions in Hospitalized Patients," *JAMA*, Apr. 15, 1998.

● ● ●

Study/Writing/Discussion Questions

1. Notice in this reading how, in writing about facts, Melody Peterson keeps your attention both through her many vivid examples as well as from her rather startling generalizations. Write down two facts that she offered that informed and/or surprised you.

2. In the first five paragraphs, what examples does she provide in support of her claim that "America has become the world's greatest medicine show?" Taking two of these examples, how would you know if they were accurate and true?

3. Why does she conclude that so much marketing is harmful?

4. For the author, why is the fact that Americans spent $250 billion in 2005 on prescription drugs so significant?

5. How would you verify that this statistic is true and accurate?

6. In the concluding paragraphs she states, "Experts estimate that more than a hundred thousand Americans die each year . . . from their prescription drugs." She also states, "On a daily basis prescription pills are estimated to kill more than 270 Americans." How would you know that these claims were accurate and true?

Building Arguments
Facts

One powerful form of argument is to simply state the facts, allowing the facts to support an inevitable but implied conclusion. (This is generally known as "letting the facts speak for themselves.") Notice how this is accomplished in the reading given below. It offers the words of a Blackfoot woman from the year 1835, who offers only (her version of) the facts to explain why she left her husband to live with a white trapper.

I was the wife of a Blackfoot warrior, and I served him faithfully. (conclusion) I brought wood in the morning, and placed water always at hand. I watched for his coming; and he found his food cooked and waiting. If he rose to go forth there was nothing to delay him. I searched the thought that was in his heart, to save him the trouble of speaking. When I went abroad on errands for him, the chiefs and warriors smiled upon me, the braves spoke soft things, in secret; but my feet were in the straight path, and my eyes could see nothing but him.

  When he went out to hunt, or to war, who aided to equip him but I? When he returned I met him at the door; I took his gun; and he entered without further thought. When he sat and smoked, I unloaded his horses; tied them to stakes, brought in their loads, and was quickly at his feet. If his moccasins were wet I took them off and put on others which were warm and dry. I dressed all the skins that were taken in the chase. . . . I served him faithfully; and what was my reward? A cloud was always on his brow, and sharp lightning on his tongue. I was his dog; and not his wife. Who was it scarred and bruised me? It was he.

Exercise

1. Put into words the final conclusion the Blackfoot woman leads you to draw from her story. (This is called an **implicit conclusion.**) What reasons does she present as fact in order to support this conclusion?

2. Compose an argument in which you state two paragraphs of facts that give compelling support to a conclusion.

Advanced Optional Writing Assignment

Write an essay of about four typed pages in which you describe an event in your own life or family life that involved facing and dealing with "hard facts." Were the facts subject to different interpretations? Did you go through different stages before you could come to acceptance? What changes resulted in your life because of these facts?

CHAPTER 4

Inferences:

What Follows?

Used with permission of Mark Stivers.

Are women all the same, even in a bobble-headed world? We might infer that from what we can see in a cartoon that depicts a silent inference.

This chapter offers a new look at inferences, their hazards, and complexities. When you finish studying this chapter, you might conclude that giving more conscious attention to inferences, both your own and those of others, will result in more skillful thinking.

I think I know why your liquid diet isn't working.

EVAN4SH.com

THE TOOTHPASTE PERSONALITY TEST

TOOTHPASTE

OOTHPASTE

TOOTHPASTE

TOOTHPASTE

IMPULSIVE, LIFE OF THE PARTY

THRIFTY, PRONE TO DEPRESSION

STUBBORN, SLOW WITTED

ANTISOCIAL, BAD BREATH

EVAN4SH.com

DISCOVERY EXERCISES

■ Recognizing Inferential Thinking

Study the cartoons on the preceding pages. What kind of thinking is going on in the cartoons? How does the humor relate to this kind of thinking?

■ Defining Infer

After consulting a dictionary, write down your own definitions of the following words:

1. Reasoning
2. Conclusion
3. Guess
4. Explanation
5. Imagine
6. Infer
7. Inference
8. Interpret

Understanding the Words *Infer* and *Inference*

When we infer, we imagine, reason, guess, surmise, speculate, estimate, predict, and conclude.

> **Infer** The word *infer* comes from the Latin root *inferre,* meaning to bring in or to carry.
>
> When we infer, we bring in our imaginations to fill in for missing facts. We make guesses to form a bridge between what we know and don't know. We connect the dots.

We use inferences every hour of our lives in all its forms of imagining, guessing, estimating, predicting, and concluding. Inferences govern our simplest actions. If we see dark clouds (it must be going to rain), we take out our umbrellas. We devise complex chains of inferences in order to make decisions: what products to buy, apartments to rent, jobs to take, people to trust. Sometimes we connect the dots correctly, and sometimes we don't. The following two discovery exercises are designed to make this inference-making process more aware and conscious.

DISCOVERY EXERCISES

▨ Drawing Inferences from Evidence

Read the following scenarios and think of three inferences you could make to explain each situation:

1. Your neighbors have regular habits and spend a lot of time at home. One day you notice that no lights have appeared in their house in the evenings for at least a week.

2. In an airport waiting room, you sit down next to a nun wearing a dark blue dress, starched white collar, and starched white headdress. You notice she is reading *Playboy* magazine.

3. Your child, age four, usually has a good appetite. However, she says no this morning when you offer her a dish of applesauce.

4. You are on a Greyhound bus. A man gets on and sits beside you. He is carrying an expensive briefcase, although he is shabbily dressed, unshaven, and perspiring heavily. When you suggest he place his briefcase on the rack overhead, he refuses, saying he doesn't mind holding it in his lap.

5. You are looking in your wife's closet for your missing shoe, and you notice a new and expensive man's sports jacket hanging there.

6. After a class you go to see your professor about an error in addition on your test score. You explain to him respectfully that 100 minus 18 is 82, not 79. He tells you to get the hell out of his office.

7. You are driving through a valley on a spring morning in a heavy rainstorm. You are on a two-lane highway, and you notice that only about half the cars that pass you head-on have their lights on.

▨ Drawing Inferences from Facts

When we interpret the meaning of facts, we draw inferences about them. How many inferences can you draw from the facts in Tables 4.1, 4.2, and 4.3?

TABLE 4.1 Biggest Global Employers in 2007

1. Wal-Mart Stores	2,055,000 employees
2. State Grid (China's largest power distributor)	1,486,000
3. China National Petroleum (China's largest oil and gas company)	1,117,345
4. U.S. Postal Service	785,929

Fortune Global 500 Listing. *Fortune* Magazine, July 21, 2008.

TABLE 4.2 US POPClock Projection

The resident population of the United States, projected to 09/04/08 at 22:35 GMT is 305,061,288.

Component Settings

One birth every 7 seconds

One death every 13 seconds

One immigrant every 29 seconds

Net gain of one person every 9 seconds

Source: U.S. Bureau of Census, Population Division, September, 2008.

TABLE 4.3 World Vital Events, 2008

Births during year: 135,330,281
Deaths during year: 55,205,782
Natural increase: 80,124,499

The world population increased from 3 billion in 1959 to 6 billion by 1999. The world population is projected to grow from 6 billion in 1999 to 9 billion by 2040.

Source: International Data Base of the U.S. Bureau of Census, 2008.

Distinguishing Inferences from Facts

Good writing distinguishes inferences from facts, description from interpretation.

Inferences are very often confused with facts, as you may well have discovered from doing the Discovery Exercise on the mythical Johnson family in the Introduction.

Moreover, as you learned when you described a photograph in the last chapter, the work of identifying the facts by stating details instead of substituting inferences made about these details is the primary challenge of descriptive writing. Usually, specific details are the most conspicuous and obvious information we can see; indeed, they can be so obvious that we do not even realize we are seeing them. One of the most difficult things about learning how to write descriptive reports is to remember to give the details and let them speak for themselves as much as possible instead of substituting our inferences or interpretations of what they mean.

ADEK BERRY/AFP/Getty Images

To review the difference between statements of fact and inferences, suppose three people were asked to describe what they saw when they looked at a photograph of a man wearing overalls and lying with his eyes closed under a tree. Suppose each person just gave you one statement:

- This is a picture of a man who is dead drunk.
- This is a farmer resting during his lunch hour.
- This is a picture of a man who just had a car crash.

Although each person might think that he or she has sized up the situation correctly, none has carefully examined or described the evidence. Instead, only final *interpretations* are offered. Each statement might seem to be a plausible explanation of why the man is lying under the tree, but none of these conclusions can be verified. Therefore, we have to present our evidence carefully, which is what we do in description. Our facts are our evidence. And facts can often lie in the *obvious*—the ordinary details that we take for granted. When we describe, we need to set forth our perceptions without assuming that others see or interpret things as we do.

The practice of stating the obvious also helps the writer draw better inferences. When we review our evidence, we may discover that we had rushed to hasty conclusions such as those offered previously. A man dressed in overalls lying under a tree is just a man dressed in overalls lying under a tree; he is not a drunk, not a lunchtime loafer, and not a car wreck victim. Such labels are not facts, only interpretations. However, this does not mean we should never make interpretations. It is just that we need to draw only those that our facts can support. Yet such a practice goes contrary to human inclinations, or to the preference to rush to interpretations.

Thus, descriptive writing can become a discipline for the mind; it stretches our capacities to state our facts and think about them with care. And it requires slowing down and taking our time. Nevertheless, the results are worth it, for descriptive writing that presents its facts with responsible clarity is also *interesting* writing. When we clearly describe what we observe and think, our work naturally becomes concrete and specific, and therefore more alive and interesting to ourselves and to others.

Short Break Study Questions

Which of the following statements are descriptive statements and which are interpretations? Translate the latter into descriptive.

a. She is a strange person.

b. When you don't pass the ketchup when I ask, I wonder why.

c. Whenever I see him, I feel angry inside.

d. Instead of listening to me, she tore out of the room on a rampage.

How Inferences Can Go Right and Wrong

We make inferences to help us fill in for missing facts and in order to make sense of the facts we have. As we make inferences, we have to keep checking them against our facts; otherwise we can build one faulty inference on top of another.

We solve problems by asking questions, gathering facts, making inferences from them, and then letting these inferences suggest strategies for finding new facts, which in turn lead to new inferences. Each inference directs us toward our objective. When we use inferences consciously and imaginatively, they give us the certainties we need to move forward. Inferences are *essential* mental operations in the search for knowledge. But we have to learn how to make them soundly. The greatest difficulties occur when inferences are confused with facts or acted upon as though they were facts. Inferences used with conscious skill lead us to knowledge. When used without conscious awareness, they lead us to confusion and illusion.

Let us now consider contrasting examples of how inferences can create either knowledge or confusion. Let's begin with a reading

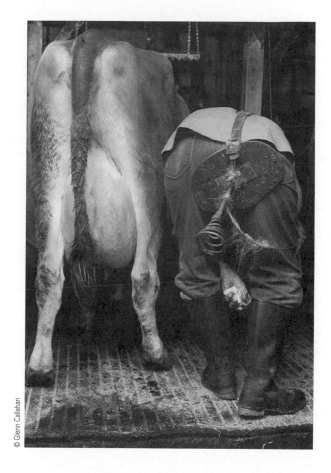

© Glenn Callahan

selection showing the thinking of that master of skillful inference, Sherlock Holmes.

● R E A D I N G ●

The Adventure of the Speckled Band (1892)

Sir Arthur Conan Doyle (1859–1930)

"Good-morning, madam," said Holmes cheerily. "My name is Sherlock Holmes. This is my intimate friend and associate, Dr. Watson, before whom you can speak as freely as before myself. Ha! I am glad to see that Mrs. Hudson has had the good sense to light the fire. Pray draw up to it, and I shall order you a cup of hot coffee, for I observe that you are shivering."

"It is not cold which makes me shiver," said the woman in a low voice, changing her seat as requested.

"What, then?"

"It is fear, Mr. Holmes. It is terror." She raised her veil as she spoke, and we could see that she was indeed in a pitiable state of agitation, her face all drawn and gray, with restless frightened eyes, like those of some hunted animal. Her features and figure were those of a woman of thirty, but her hair was shot with premature gray, and her expression was weary and haggard. Sherlock Holmes ran her over with one of his quick, all-comprehensive glances.

5   "You must not fear," said he soothingly, bending forward and patting her forearm. "We shall soon set matters right, I have no doubt. You have come in by train this morning, I see."

"You know me, then?"

"No, but I observe the second half of a return ticket in the palm of your left glove. You must have started early, and yet you had a good drive in a dog-cart, along heavy roads, before you reached the station."

The lady gave a violent start and stared in bewilderment at my companion.

"There is no mystery, my dear madam," said he, smiling. "The left arm of your jacket is spattered with mud in no less than seven places. The marks are perfectly fresh. There is no vehicle save a dog-cart which throws up mud in that way, and then only when you sit on the left-hand side of the driver."

10   "Whatever your reasons may be, you are perfectly correct," said she. "I started from home before six, reached Leatherhead at twenty past, and came in by the first train to Waterloo. Sir, I can stand this strain no longer; I . . . ."

Excerpt from Sir Arthur Conan Doyle, "The Adventure of the Speckled Band," 1892.

● ● ●

Study/Writing/Discussion Questions

1. In this short excerpt, what three inferences does Sherlock Holmes make about the visiting lady? Are all three correct?

2. On what observations (clues) does he base these inferences?

3. Describe a situation in which one of the following individuals would need to make skillful inferences:

   a. A physician   d. A cook

   b. A salesperson   e. An antique appraiser

   c. A car mechanic

The fascination that Holmes holds for us lies in his uncanny ability to draw correct inferences. He is a fictional hero, not of physical but of mental prowess. His appeal endures because we all know that wrong inferences can hurt us, whereas correct inferences give us power, vision, and speed. The danger is that even one faulty inference can get us into trouble. Moreover, we can build a wobbly leaning tower of inferences on the foundation of one mistaken one. Let's look at a simple example of how two different people confronted this challenge.

CUSTOMER 1

Standing in line while waiting to pay for some small items in a computer store, I see a man pick up a laptop computer on display and carry it out the door.

Chain of inferences

1. He is a thief.
2. He should be caught.
3. I must tell the cashier.
4. He will go after the man or call the police.

New chain of inferences

1. If he is caught, I will be thanked.
2. I might get a reward if I caught him.

Next chain of inferences

1. I will go out and make a citizen's arrest.
2. He might be armed and shoot me.
3. Come to think of it, the cashier, who didn't notice anything, could be an accomplice.

Conclusion

I had better not say anything.

CUSTOMER 2

Standing in line while waiting to pay for some small items in a computer store, I see a man pick up a laptop computer on display and carry it out the door.

Chain of inferences

1. He could be a thief.
2. He could have already paid.
3. It could be his own computer that he brought in for repairs.
4. He could be the owner of the store.

Conclusion

I will quietly tell the cashier since he will know enough to decide what to do.

© Rita Bernstein

Class Discussion

1. Why do the inferences of these two customers go in such different directions?

2. Give an example of a time when you jumped to a conclusion or made a wrong and hasty inference, then went way off course by continuing to reason from this wrong inference?

Drawing Inferences from Careful Observation

Though we may not have all the facts about a photograph, we can learn a lot by recording the details we can observe and by drawing careful inferences from them. Since it is easier to show than describe how this is done, we'll examine how one person used observation and inference to describe the photo on page 115. As you read the description, notice these features:

1. The facts appear first, followed by the inferences that can reasonably be drawn from them.
2. More than one inference can be drawn from each set of facts.
3. The factual information groups together the details of one segment or feature of the photograph at a time.
4. The conclusion draws together the facts and the possible inferences into a plausible explanation of the message, purpose, and meaning of the photograph.

Facts

In the center of this black-and-white photo is a triangular composition in contrasting values of black, grays, and whites that encompasses oval, diagonal, and curved shapes. Behind this center and traversing the top half of the photo is a rectangular shape with a smooth dark wood-like texture. On the lower right side of the photo are the edges of a complex shape: curved, rectangular, and diagonal.

Inferences

1. These central shapes could be identified as representing a young girl and an older man. The rear rectangular shape would seem to be a wall. The complex shape on the right could be a side view of a piano.
2. This is a room with a girl and a man next to a piano.

Facts

In the top center left foreground is a dark-valued two-part mass with the texture and sheen of dark shiny hair. The rear mass hangs in folds ending abruptly on a white- and gray-striped surface; the front mass is domelike and curved, ending on a contrasting white oval.

Inferences

1. This is thick black hair cut shoulder length with thick bangs that cover the brow and ear.

Facts

On the edge of the profile-appearing surface are descending small horizontal and diagonal lines. To their left is a rounded smooth surface.

Inferences

1. These lines represent eyes, a nose, and mouth. The cheek has the smoothness found in a child.

Facts

No eyelid crease line appears in this profile view.

Inferences

1. The shape of the eye together with the dark hair suggest that the girl may be of Asian descent.

Facts

Beneath the dark shapes and profile shape appear a series of alternating broad white and grey stripes. The folds and ripples on its surface suggest a cotton-textured covering of upper arms and chest.

Inferences

1. She is wearing an oversized striped T-shirt.

Facts

Adjacent to this foreground figure are other shapes, colors, and values that configure as another individual's head, chest, arm, and hand. The lightest value on top of the head shape has the texture of thin hair. Beneath this area a paler value suggests facial skin. Short darker horizontal lines on this surface suggest eyes, nose, mouth, and a double chin. Light-valued hairy lines extend over the eyes.

Inferences

1. He is an older Caucasian male, perhaps in his late 60s.

Facts

Beneath the head shape, strong vertical slanting lines suggest a front partial view of a gray-valued business suit. In contrast, within the V opening shape appear the white of a dress shirt and a dark-valued tie with a diagonal striped design.

Inferences

1. He is a professional who prefers formal business attire.

Facts

Another central element of this photo are two curved shapes in a medium-dark value with highlights that enclose a series of white horizontal lines with raised black rectangular areas above the lines. Above this area are upright planes with the texture of dark wood.

Inferences

1. This is a piano; the man is a piano teacher; the girl is a student.
2. This is a piano lesson for which they are seated.
3. He may be retired and teaching as a volunteer.

Facts

Adjacent to the chest area of the man are folds of gray followed by a complex white shape resembling a hand with fingers hanging down. Two of these finger shapes appear longer.

Inferences

1. The piano teacher is resting his left forearm on the piano with his hand over the keys.
2. Two of his fingers point toward the keys as though poised to give her playing support, energy, and direction.

Facts

In the foreground of the photograph, appearing from beneath what seem to be the sleeves of the girl's T-shirt, are two narrow parallel diagonal shapes extending upwards toward the piano.

Inferences

These are her arms and hands.

Facts

The textures of each of these diagonal shapes are different. The top shape is smooth with the light value of skin. The foreground shape has multiple values, sheens, and textures such as those found in plastic, cloth, and wood. No hand is apparent. In what could be the right elbow area two white folds appear that resemble the folds one sees in a jersey knit. A plastic smooth casing shape covers what would be the forearm and wrist areas. Looped over this casing runs a cable line that disappears into a bobbin shape inside a small dark rectangular side slot of a larger knob shape. Another long slot appears on the knob's top surface with a protruding spear shape at the top. The spear is half white, half grey with a black point pointing toward the girl. In what seems to be a plastic casing are also white circles and a white vertical area.

Inferences

1. She is wearing a prosthetic device, both plastic and wooden, that serves as an arm and hand. Underneath the device is a jersey cloth that shows through the holes in the plastic. Beneath the cloth may be a wooden arm.
2. The girl has lost her right hand and arm beneath her elbow.
3. Her left arm and hand are intact.
4. She is reaching toward the piano keyboard.
5. The spear shape is a pencil; she can use its eraser's end to hit the piano keys by sending a signal through the cable.

Facts

The small dark oval areas that represent the eyes of both individuals appear to be gazing down at the piano. The lips and fold shape visible in the profile of the girl seem soft. The mouth line of the man is dark as though open.

Inferences

1. They are both concentrating on how she hits the keys.
2. The girl is relaxed and could be smiling. The teacher's mouth is open as though ready to speak.
3. They both seem comfortably engrossed with the lesson.

Facts

> There is no sheen in what must be the wooden frame of the piano; its texture also has random ragged-edged spots. The area behind both individuals consists of dark panel shapes with a few silver horizontal lines such as one finds in wood molding. On the lower far left of the photo, blonde horizontal shapes of varying thicknesses together with one blonde vertical wide line suggest a table and chair. No shapes that would suggest the presence of other people appear in the background.

Inferences

1. They are alone in a schoolroom that has a table and student chairs.
2. She is playing on an old and scratched upright classroom piano.
3. They are having an after-school lesson in a classroom.

Conclusion

> This photo presents three separate contrasting entities—the girl, the man, and the piano—that keep our attention moving around its revolving circle. The scene is a simple one: that of a piano lesson. What cannot be seen or heard is the music they have made, the limitations overcome. Without pity or sentimentality, the photo presents their intelligent collaboration.

Core Discovery Writing Application

▪ Using Facts and Inferences to Describe a Photograph

1. This is a mental exercise that uses writing. Choose a photograph in this book not already described by the author. For your notes, make yourself a page with columns like this:

Facts of the Photograph	Inferences I Make about This Fact
My description of a detail: a form, texture, shade, relationship, or configuration that I see.	What I imagine this detail represents or what I interpret it to mean.

2. Survey the photograph in a systematic way, beginning with what is central, then moving to relationships of the parts and the background.

3. Write out your list using the columns in step 1 to match each statement of fact with an inference. (Actually, in your thinking, the inference will probably come to mind first. If so, write it down, then restudy the photo to discover and describe the evidence upon which this inference was based.)

4. Write a conclusion that draws your list of facts and inferences together into an explanation of the photograph. (See the example on page 119.) This concluding summary should not introduce new information or provide a story that your evidence cannot support.

5. Now write your description in the form illustrated for you in the preceding exercise on pages 114–119. Remember to end with a summary.

6. The length should be at least two typed pages.

Scoring Using Facts and Inferences to Describe a Photograph

1. Obvious details not ignored. *10 points*
2. Statements of fact described rather than just named or interpreted. *20 points*
3. Systematic organization of data: systematic sectioning of photo—small groupings of related facts, shown with inferences clearly drawn from each grouping. *20 points*
4. Some imaginative use of inferences beyond the obvious. *10 points*
5. Conclusion brings given facts and inferences together in a logical interpretation (not introducing new facts or a fantasy). *20 points*
6. No distracting errors of spelling, punctuation, sentence structure. *10 points*
7. Minimum length of two typed pages. *10 points*

Generalizations Are Inferences

A good scientist, like a good writer, knows how much evidence is needed to support a generalization.

Samuel Scudder, whose encounter with a fish was described in Chapter 1, stated that "Agassiz's training in the method of observing facts and their orderly arrangement was ever accompanied by the urgent exhortation not to be content with them. 'Facts are stupid things,' he would say, 'until brought into connection with some general law.'" We can apply this statement to our concerns about thinking and writing. It is not enough to collect and state facts and inferences alone; we need to look for patterns in them and see how we can make generalizations to describe their organizing principles or "laws."

> "Do you perhaps mean," I asked, "that the fish has symmetrical sides with paired organs?"
> His thoroughly pleased "Of course! Of course!" repaid the wakeful hours of the previous night.

In science, laws are **generalizations** that are based on observations and that deal with recurrence, order, and relationships. Generalizations, in turn, relate individual members of a class or category to a whole. To arrive at laws or generalizations, we must look for information, then look for patterns or configurations, analyze them, and finally draw conclusions about the relationships, recurrences, and order of the gathered data. These were the complex mental actions you followed when drawing conclusions in the last exercise.

It takes experience to know when you have gathered enough information to make accurate generalizations. Beginners, like Scudder, may decide they have seen everything after ten minutes or, at the other extreme, refrain from drawing conclusions for too long. A good scientist, like a good writer, recognizes how much evidence is needed to support reliable generalizations.

When you first listed only facts about a photograph, you may have experienced the sense of the "stupidity" of facts that Agassiz referred to. Perhaps you had a sense of not knowing where to stop or how to separate the relevant details from the irrelevant. However, this first stage of simple-minded observing and collecting is important.

In the second stage of writing and of thinking, we begin to separate, compare, categorize, and organize our information. In the photograph description our intuition may first put everything together. Eventually, we are able to formulate all this into a generalization that is a summary statement. In paragraph writing, this statement becomes our **topic sentence.** This (usually first) sentence states in a general way the main idea to be proven or explained. What then follows is the evidence—the facts and inferences that support the main idea. Therefore what we do is present our topic sentence, which is actually our conclusion, *first* in our writing, although we arrived at it *last* in our thinking. This is exactly what you did in the exercise where you first wrote down your facts and inferences in columns and then drew a conclusion at the end that summarized all your information.

The topic sentence serves both as a statement of commitment and as a guide, aiding us in sorting out what support is needed and relevant. A topic sentence functions like a magnet in this respect. It also *tests* our facts and our inferences about them. We may even discover that the evidence we have selected does not support our topic sentence very well at all. In such cases, we stop and begin again.

The willingness to loop back and forth between the evidence and the generalization takes persistence fueled by a resolve to arrive at truth as best we can. Such a process must be familiar to you from your own writing experience, although you may never have looked at what you were doing in this conscious way before. The following exercise is designed to have you write with this conscious awareness in mind.

Composition Writing Application

▓ Writing a Paragraph from Facts, Inferences, and Generalizations

Choose a photograph from this chapter that you have not described before. Working alone, observe your photograph or cartoon for a while, noticing what is plainly visible.

Make notes by listing your facts and seeing what inferences you can draw from them. Putting this information together, draw a conclusion about the whole. What message, what statement about life do you think is being conveyed here? Write this conclusion at the top of your page. Use this sentence as a topic sentence for a paragraph to follow that makes a general statement or conclusion about your evidence.

Doonesbury

G. B. TRUDEAU

Doonesbury © 1985, G. B. Trudeau. Reprinted by permission of Universal Press Syndicate.

1. What is the professor trying to teach his students?
2. What inferences does he expect them to make?
3. What inferences do they make?
4. What clues led you to your own conclusions about this cartoon?
5. How would you describe the professor's teaching style?

Core Discovery Writing Application

■ *Analyzing the Use of Facts and Inferences in a Newspaper Article*

TABLE 4.4 Analyzing Facts and Inferences

Data Claimed to Be Factual in This Sentence	Inferences Expressed in This Sentence	Pertinent Missing Information	My Own Inference about This Sentence
	"Tougher Grading Better for Students"		Wow! I didn't know that. This must be true since it is based on research.
	"America's high school students may not be getting smarter, but their teachers are getting more generous—at least when it comes to grading."	Who arrived at this conclusion? Was that the unanimous opinion of the teachers surveyed? Or is it the opinion of one or more researchers?	This statement is a rather broad unqualified generalization. Surely there must be a significant number of exceptions.
A national survey released this month showed that a record 28 percent of incoming college freshmen had A averages, up from only 12.5 percent in 1969.		Both private and public college freshmen? And do students take the same high school courses now with the same content and standards offered in 1969?	Maybe teachers don't grade as hard as they used to because students complain more about their grades. Maybe students receive better instruction and training in how to improve their study habits now than in 1969.

1. Work with the article beginning on page 125 called "Tougher Grading Better for Students" or with another article assigned to you by the instructor. Read the article carefully. Then make a chart with four columns, as shown in Table 4.4. After you read each sentence, choose the column that seems appropriate for entering quotes or comments. The examples in Table 4.4 should help you get started. Proceed as in this example, working sentence by sentence, analyzing each one.

2. To save time, you can make a photocopy of the article and cut and paste some sentences into the appropriate columns. When working with quotations, note that although the public statement may be a fact, its content could be an inference. In such cases, put the quote in the first column, and in the second column, note that it expresses an inference.

3. Line for line, as you proceed through the article, notice if you find any information missing. Consider what you or an ordinary reader would need to have in order to understand and believe its claims. Is enough information given about the sources of facts so that they could be verified? Are there enough facts, enough inferences, sufficient explanations? As you read, notice the times you feel puzzled, curious, confused, or suspicious. Then consider if these reactions could be due to pertinent missing information.

4. In the last column, record your thinking about each recorded fact and/or inference. Write down your conclusions, questions, comments, and reactions.

5. When you have finished going through the whole article systematically, prepare your chart in final form by typing and/or by cutting and pasting.

6. On a final sheet of paper, sum up what you learned through your analysis in one paragraph. Did you conclude that the article offers reliable information? Did your final impressions differ from your first?

● R E A D I N G ●

Tougher Grading Better for Students

America's high school students may not be getting much smarter, but their teachers are getting more generous—at least when it comes to grading.

A national survey released this month showed that a record 28 percent of incoming college freshmen had A averages, up from only 12.5 percent in

1969. During much of that period, ironically, student scores on standardized tests actually declined.

Higher grades and lower test scores may be related, according to new research by economists Julian Betts and Stefan Boedeker at the University of California, San Diego. They find a strong relationship between school grading standards and student achievement: The tougher a school grades, the harder its students work and the more they learn.

Their finding is enormously significant. "For thirty years, social scientists have been trying to decide why some schools are good and some are bad," said Betts. "They looked at class size, teacher education and per pupil spending, none of which seem to matter much. So I decided to look at standards set in the schools."

5   If Betts and Boedeker are right, spending more money on schools may help a lot less than simply changing the incentives facing students. If they are allowed to slack off and still earn good grades, most will take it easy. But holding them to higher standards costs nothing and can motivate them to achieve more.

Betts and Boedeker studied the math and science performance of roughly 6,000 middle- and high-school students nationwide over five years, starting in 1987. Students were tested each year to measure how much they were learning. The researchers also had information on grading standards, amount of homework assigned and other factors.

The two scholars found large differences in grading standards between schools and a strong relationship between those standards and how much students learned each year. Over five years, otherwise similar students at tough schools scored about 6 points more than students at easy schools on standardized tests with 100 as the top score. A 6-point difference is huge, Betts said.

Stronger students seem to benefit the most from tougher standards, suggesting that other policies must also be sought to "help the weaker students match the gains in achievement of their (better) prepared counterparts."

One solution to uneven grading standards would be to hold standardized state or national graduation exams to test high school achievement and thus give students more incentive to take their studies seriously. Such exams are routine in Europe and Japan, where graduating students are much further advanced than their American counterparts.

10   Bishop tested this theory by comparing the math performance of 13-year-olds (measured by an international test administered in 1991) in Canadian provinces that have standardized graduation exams and in those that don't.

His findings were striking. In Canadian provinces with testing, students learned about two-thirds of a grade level more than those in provinces without.

"One of the most cost-effective methods of improving achievement in American schools would be to create curriculum-based exams for each state," Bishop said.

Reprinted with permission. ©1995 *San Francisco Chronicle*.

● ● ●

Scoring for Analyzing Facts and Inferences in a Newspaper Article

1. Correct identification of all facts and inferences appearing in the article. *30 points*

2. Does not confuse own inferences with those made in article. *10 points*

3. Shows an understanding that although a quotation may be presented as fact, its content may express an inference. *10 points*

4. Shows understanding that estimates, predictions, and opinions are inferences. *10 points*

5. Missing information column shows thoughtful reflection on *pertinent* missing data. *10 points*

6. Own inferences are drawn systematically, item for item, and show careful reflection on the data. *10 points*

7. Format is systematic, methodical, and easy to read. *10 points*

8. Final conclusion assesses how the information is presented in the article. *10 points*

Building Arguments
Inferences

No reasonable man can for one moment believe that such a beautiful country [America] was intended by its Author [God] to be forever in the possession and occupancy of serpents, wild fowls, wild beasts and savages who derive little benefit from it. (Caleb Atwater, 1850)

Exercise

1. The previous is a claim based on an inference. Put the claim into your own words. Explain how its reasoning is an inference.

2. What conclusion is implied?

3. What evidence is offered in support of the claim?

4. Explain how the claim justifies the author's values.

5. Make a claim that is based on an inference.

Chapter Summary

1. The word *infer* means (a) to derive by reasoning, (b) to conclude, (c) to guess. When we infer, we use imagination or reasoning to provide explanations for situations in which all the facts are either not available or not yet determined.

2. Responsible report writing or descriptive writing lets the facts speak for themselves as much as possible. This often means taking the time to find the right words to describe the obvious and abandoning inferences drawn too hastily that cannot be supported.

3. Writing that offers specific detailed support for its conclusions makes interesting writing. When we perceive and think clearly, we interest both ourselves and others.

4. Reasonable inferences can be used in descriptive writing to tie facts together. Care must be taken to distinguish facts from inferences, nevertheless.

5. In solving problems, inferences can be used as a strategy in planning and choosing alternatives. When we think well, we assess all facts, derive as many inferences as we can, and devise strategies for confirming or obtaining more information.

6. Detectives and consultants of all kinds are valued for their ability to examine facts and make the best inferences from them.

7. Inferences tend to build on inferences in chains of association. Unless each inference is tested for its support of evidence, a series of inferences can mislead us into flights of imagination, away from reliable knowledge.

8. Facts and inferences are linked together through generalizations. Facts have little significance in themselves until generalizations or laws can be derived from them. Generalizing too soon, before we have gathered a sufficient number of facts, is hazardous. This does not mean that we should not generalize at all; it simply means that we should learn how to draw generalizations that can be supported.

9. The topic sentence of a paragraph is a generalization that summarizes the main idea to be demonstrated in that paragraph. When we think, we usually arrive at this generalization last, after we have examined all our facts and inferences; nevertheless, we state it first, at the beginning of the paragraph. The topic sentence is a kind of conclusion, which is repeated again in another form at the end of the paragraph.

10. By the time you have finished this chapter, you should understand more about the thinking operations involved in constructing a paragraph or engaging in descriptive writing. You will understand how observation helps determine facts, imagination, and reasoning to link the facts with explanations, and how a generalization ties all this information together into a meaningful whole.

Chapter Quiz

Write two inferences to explain each of the following events:

1. You see a little girl pushing an elderly woman down Main Street in a large baby carriage.
2. Your best friend leaves you a note saying she has joined the Marines.
3. You have received no mail for the past two weeks.
4. A recent study found that men between 50 and 79 years old married to women one to 24 years younger tended to live longer, with a mortality rate 13 percent below the norm.
5. The same study found that men married to older women died sooner; their death rate was 20 percent higher than the norm.

Rate each of the following statements as *true* or *false*. Explain your choice in each case or give an example to defend your choice.

_____ 6. To state that "annual beef consumption in the United States is 96.8 pounds per capita in 1998, as compared to 11 pounds in China" is to make a generalization without facts.

_____ 7. To state the obvious is to state the sensory details of what is actually seen, as opposed to what is *thought* or interpreted about what is seen.

_____ 8. Good thinking does not continue to build inferences on top of inferences but stops whenever possible to check these inferences against the original facts or to find new ones.

_____ 9. One should always avoid making inferences in every kind of writing.

_____ 10. To state that the United States has the highest per capita use of motor vehicles in the world is to make a generalization without offering the supporting facts.

● R E A D I N G S ●

Friends

Tim O'Brien

This short story is taken from The Things They Carried. *Tim O'Brien was born in Minnesota and was a foot soldier in Vietnam in 1969. Reading this story aloud is the best way to appreciate its bare style but ability to convey powerful feelings. In your second reading, consider how the author uses the interplay of facts and inferences to tell his story.*

Dave Jensen and Lee Strunk did not become instant buddies, but they did learn to trust each other. Over the next month they often teamed up on ambushes. They covered each other on patrol, shared a foxhole, took turns pulling guard at night. In late August they made a pact that if one of them should ever get totally fucked up—a wheelchair wound—the other guy would automatically find a way to end it. As far as I could tell they were serious. They drew it up on paper, signing their names and asking a couple of guys to act as witnesses. And then in October Lee Strunk stepped on a rigged mortar round. It took off his right leg at the knee. He managed a funny little half step, like a hop, then he tilted sideways and dropped. "Oh, damn," he said. For a while he kept on saying it, "Damn oh damn," as if he'd stubbed a toe. Then he panicked. He tried to get up and run, but there was nothing left to run on. He fell hard. The stump of his right leg was twitching. There were slivers of bone, and the blood came in quick spurts like water from a pump. He seemed bewildered. He reached down as if to massage his missing leg, then he passed out, and Rat Kiley put on a tourniquet and administered morphine and ran plasma into him.

There was nothing much anybody could do except wait for the dustoff. After we'd secured an LZ, Dave Jensen went over and kneeled at Strunk's side. The stump had stopped twitching now. For a time there was some question as to whether Strunk was still alive, but then he opened his eyes and looked up at Dave Jensen. "Oh, Jesus," he said, and moaned, and tried to slide away and said, "Jesus, man, don't kill me."

"Relax," Jensen said.

Lee Strunk seemed groggy and confused. He lay still for a second and then motioned toward his leg. "Really, it's not so bad. Not terrible. Hey, *really*—they can sew it back on—*really*."

"Right, I'll bet they can."

"You think?"

"Sure I do."

Strunk frowned at the sky. He passed out again, then woke up and said, "Don't kill me."

5

10

"I won't," Jensen said.

"I'm *serious*."

"Sure."

"But you got to promise. Swear it to me—swear you won't kill me."

Jensen nodded and said, "I swear," and then a little later we carried Strunk to the dustoff chopper. Jensen reached out and touched the good leg. "Go on now," he said. Later we heard that Strunk died somewhere over Chu Lai, which seemed to relieve Dave Jensen of an enormous weight.

● ● ●

Study/Discussion/Writing Questions

1. What inferences do Strunk and Jensen make about how they would react if they were seriously wounded? What inferences do they make about how they should best take care of one another?

2. What stages of reaction does Strunk go through after stepping on the rigged mortar round?

3. How does Jensen react as his friend?

4. How did their experience with the facts and realism of injury transform them both?

5. What inferences do you make as to why Jensen seemed relieved at the end?

He Fixes Radios by Thinking!

Richard P. Feynman

Richard P. Feynman (1918–1988) won the Nobel Prize in 1965 for his work in quantum electrodynamics. During World War II he was one of the Manhattan Project team that developed the atomic bomb. This excerpt is taken from his memoirs, Surely You're Joking, Mr. Feynman! *All his life Feynman took delight in solving problems. Notice, as you read, how, even as a child of 12, he could make careful observations and draw careful inferences from them.*

One day I got a telephone call: "Mister, are you Richard Feynman?"

"Yes."

"This is a hotel. We have a radio that doesn't work, and would like it repaired. We understand you might be able to do something about it."

"But I'm only a little boy," I said. "I don't know how—"

5

"Yes, we know that, but we'd like you to come over anyway."

It was a hotel that my aunt was running, but I didn't know that. I went over there with—they still tell the story—a big screwdriver in my back pocket. Well, I was small, so *any* screwdriver looked big in my back pocket.

I went up to the radio and tried to fix it. I didn't know anything about it, but there was also a handyman at the hotel, and either he noticed, or I noticed, a loose knob on the rheostat—to turn up the volume—so that it wasn't turning the shaft. He went off and filed something, and I fixed it up so it worked.

The next radio I tried to fix didn't work at all. That was easy; it wasn't plugged in right. As the repair jobs got more and more complicated, I got better and better, and more elaborate. I bought myself a milliammeter in New York and converted it into a voltmeter that had different scales on it by using the right lengths (which I calculated) of very fine copper wire. It wasn't very accurate, but it was good enough to tell whether things were in the right ballpark at different connections in those radio sets.

The main reason people hired me was the Depression. They didn't have any money to fix their radios, and they'd hear about this kid who would do it for less. So I'd climb on roofs to fix antennas, and all kinds of stuff. I got a series of lessons of ever increasing difficulty. Ultimately I got some job like converting a DC set into an AC set, and it was very hard to keep the hum from going through the system, and I didn't build it quite right. I shouldn't have bitten that one off, but I didn't know.

10   One job was really sensational. I was working at the time for a printer, and a man who knew that printer knew I was trying to get jobs fixing radios, so he sent a fellow around to the print shop to pick me up. The guy is obviously poor—his car is a complete wreck—and we go to his house which is in a cheap part of town. On the way, I say, "What's the trouble with the radio?"

He says, "When I turn it on it makes a noise, and after a while the noise stops and everything's all right, but I don't like the noise at the beginning."

I think to myself: "What the hell! If he hasn't got any money, you'd think he could stand a little noise for a while."

And all the time, on the way to his house, he's saying things like, "Do you know anything about radios? How do you know about radios—you're just a little boy!"

He's putting me down the whole way, and I'm thinking, "So what's the matter with him? So it makes a little noise."

15   But when we got there I went over to the radio and turned it on. Little noise? *My God!* No wonder the poor guy couldn't stand it. The thing began to roar and wobble—WUH BUH BUH BUH BUH—A *tremendous* amount of noise. Then it quieted down and played correctly. So I started to think: "How can that happen?"

I start walking back and forth, thinking, and I realize that one way it can happen is that the tubes are heating up in the wrong order—that is, the amplifier's all hot, the tubes are ready to go, and there's nothing feeding in, or there's some back circuit feeding in, or something wrong in the beginning part—the RF part—and therefore it's making a lot of noise, picking up something. And when the RF circuit's finally going, and the grid voltages are adjusted, everything's all right.

So the guy says, "What are you doing? You come to fix the radio, but you're only walking back and forth!"

I say, "I'm thinking!" Then I said to myself, "All right, take the tubes out, and reverse the order completely in the set." (Many radio sets in those days used the same tubes in different places—212's. I think they were, or 212-A's.) So I changed the tubes around, stepped to the front of the radio, turned the thing on, and it's as quiet as a lamb; it waits until it heats up, and then plays perfectly—no noise.

When a person has been negative to you, and then you do something like that, they're usually a hundred percent the other way, kind of to compensate. He got me other jobs, and kept telling everybody what a tremendous genius I was, saying, "He fixes radios by *thinking!*" The whole idea of thinking, to fix a radio—a little boy stops and thinks, and figures out how to do it—he never thought that was possible.

• • •

Study/Writing/Discussion Questions

1. Explain how Feynman fixes the radios in the hotel through observing, drawing inferences, and testing to see if his inferences are correct.

2. What inference or explanation does he offer as to why people would hire a child to fix their radios?

3. In the final anecdote, what inference does Feynman draw about his customer upon first meeting him?

4. What inference or conclusion does the customer draw about Feynman?

5. What inference or evaluation does Feynman draw upon first hearing the customer's complaint about the radio?

6. What sensory experience makes Feynman decide he was wrong?

7. Describe how Feynman reasons about the problem after he asks himself the question: "How can that happen?"

8. What inference does the customer draw when he sees Feynman walking back and forth?

9. Why is the man surprised to learn what the boy is thinking?

10. What skills does Feynman have that the customer lacks?
11. How does Feynman test his theory (hypothesis) as to the cause of the problem?
12. What conclusion does Feynman draw as to why the customer changes so much in his attitude towards him?
13. What does Feynman teach the customer?

The Mistake of the Sand Fleas

Paul Krafel

My wife, Alysia, and I camped on the seashore for a week. Each time I walked to and from the ocean, I crossed the strand line of rotting seaweed that marked the high tide. There, each time, I saw countless sand fleas hopping randomly about. I figured that they must spend their lives hopping about, because that was all I ever saw them doing.

After several days of noticing their seemingly mindless behavior, I decided to stop long enough to see what one of these hoppers looked like. I sat down in their hopping midst and waited for one to land close enough and long enough for me to observe it. Within a minute, all the hopping ceased. The sand fleas began going in and out of burrows and digging new ones. Two sand fleas joined together. "Mating," I thought, but then I noticed that they were joined mouth to mouth. The longer I watched, the more behaviors I saw.

I eventually stood up; the sand fleas all began hopping about again. Then I understood! Whenever a large, potential predator like me approaches, the fleas defend themselves by all hopping. The confusing appearance of this random hopping distracts the predator from focusing on one victim long enough to catch it. Everybody hopping protects everybody.

The reason I had seen the sand fleas always hopping whenever I approached them was because I was approaching them. I had mistakenly assumed that the only behavior I ever saw was the only behavior the sand fleas ever had.

● ● ●

Study/Writing/Discussion Questions

1. In this excerpt, what is the first inference made by Krafel to explain why the sand fleas hop about so much? What happens to cause him to begin to doubt that inference?

2. Describe how he arrives at a new insight that explains all the seeming contradictions of the fleas' behavior.

3. Is this explanation an inference?

4. Was his first inference a wrong assumption?

5. Often what gives people expertise is their reputation for making good inferences. How would this be the case for one of the following: a physician, salesperson, car mechanic, cook, antique appraiser?

Objectives Review of Part I

When you have finished Part I, you will understand:

1. The following concepts on an experiential basis: observing, labeling, describing, interpreting, facts, inferences, sensing, perceiving, thinking
2. That it is possible to maintain awareness of one's own thinking–feeling–perceiving process
3. How clear thinking depends on "staying awake" to what is

And you will have had practice in developing these skills:

1. Suspending thinking in order to freshly sense and gather data
2. Describing the obvious evidence without substituting labels and interpretations
3. Recognizing when you and others are formulating facts and when you are formulating inferences
4. Recognizing how facts and inferences can become confused with one another

PART II

Problems of Critical Thinking

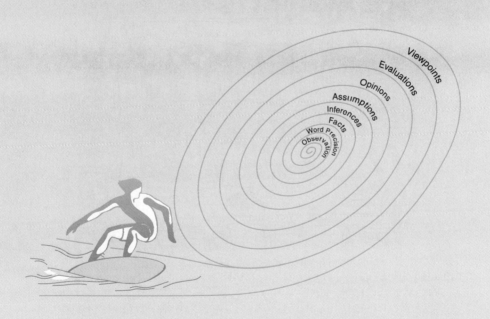

CHAPTER 5

Assumptions:
What's Taken for Granted?

"...so we began asking ourselves, does it really make sense to pay you fifty million when there are C.E.O.'s in Korea and Mexico who would do the same job for twenty-five."

The discovery of an assumption can be amusing, if not shocking. In this chapter, we take a fresh look at that familiar term, *assumption,* and see how it operates in our thinking. We will study types of assumptions, building on what we have already learned about aware observing and inferences. In short, we will continue to build the skills of critical thinking.

DISCOVERY EXERCISES

The following three exercises can be done with a partner or alone, depending on your instructor's directions.

■ Defining Assumption

Using at least two dictionaries, write your own definition of *assumption*.

■ Finding Assumptions in Cartoons

Study previous cartoons and state in words what assumptions brought humor to these situations.

> The word **assume** comes from the Latin *assumere*—to take up. When we assume, we take up or accept something. In reasoning, we assume when we take something for granted or accept an idea without sufficient proof of its truth or certainty.

■ Finding Assumptions in Stories

As you read the stories told in each of the following paragraphs, think how each depends on one or more assumptions. In preparation for class discussion, write your answers to the questions that follow each paragraph.

1. You are a guard at Alcatraz. One day a prisoner is found to be missing. When you inspect his cell you find a hole dug through the concrete under his bed. All that is next to the hole is a bent metal spoon. What assumptions of the guards did the prisoner exploit in order to escape?

2. While visiting Sweden you go with a friend to a grocery store. You are surprised to notice that although the cashier takes the money, the customers bag their own groceries. You take two plastic bags off a hook nearby and begin to fill them. Your friend tells you that you need to pay the cashier for the bags. What assumptions did you make?

3. You have a dinner guest from a foreign country who belches loudly all through the meal. You find him disgusting and want to get rid of him. But he insists that he be allowed to return your hospitality. So you go to his house for dinner. There everyone but you belches loudly all through the meal. Before you leave, your host says, "I am sorry you did not like my dinner, but you didn't have to be so rude about it." What was the assumption of the foreign guest?

4. A woman once proposed marriage to George Bernard Shaw, a witty and erudite English dramatist. "Imagine a child," she said, "with my body and your brains." "Yes," he said, "but what if the child has my body and your brains?" What was his assumption?

5. In his struggles to receive backing for the voyage of his ships to the Far East by sailing west, Christopher Columbus once spent some hours trying to persuade a nobleman to lend his support. The nobleman maintained that he was trying to do the impossible, like making an egg stand on end. Then the nobleman called for an egg and handed it to Columbus, who was sitting across from him at a table. Taking up the challenge, Columbus tried wobbling the egg on one end and then the other, while the nobleman laughed in derision. Then, picking up the egg, Columbus gently smashed its end on the table, allowing it to stand firmly in position, while its contents oozed out. What assumption about the problem did the nobleman make that Columbus did not?

6. On a remote Wyoming highway, a European tourist drives his rental car into a small gas station. An attendant comes out, opens the hood of his car, props up the supporting rod, and looks inside at the engine. Suddenly, without warning, he smashes down the hood, causing the rod to rip through the metal hood. Startled, the tourist puts his head out the window and screams: "What did you do to my car?"

   "Get the hell out of here!" yells the attendant. Frightened, the driver turns on the ignition and pulls out of the station, muttering to himself: "Now I know why they call it 'the Wild West.'" What were the tourist's assumptions?

7. In Oakland, California, a gang of teens—some as young as 13—were arrested in connection with sixty burglaries. All the teens were Asian Americans and the homes they robbed were all in Asian American neighborhoods. Two girls from the gang would knock at the doors. If someone came to the door, they would ask for someone who did not live there, then leave. If no one answered, the girls would signal to two boys, who would go around to the back of the house and break in. The police said, "They acted with impunity because they didn't look out of place in the neighborhood. . . . At times they would wave at neighbors, who would wave back." What assumptions are evident here?

Understanding Assumptions

Assumptions can be forgotten inferences.

Our study of inferences in Chapter 4 leads us naturally into assumptions. We use assumptions in our reasoning, like inferences, to help us bridge what we know with what we don't know. Usually when we infer, we are aware of our reasoning. We infer actively and consciously when we make plans, such as deciding what to pack when we go on a trip. We get into trouble when we make wrong assumptions, however, meaning that we draw some conclusions too hastily, lack some crucial information, or mistake some uncertainties for certainties. For example, it is easy to spot the tourists who visit San Francisco in the cool and foggy summer months. They are the people shivering on the streets dressed in light summer clothing. They only packed for warm weather because most places in North America are warm in July and California has a sunny weather reputation. They would not remember what they took for granted until faced with the fact of the cold damp fog typical of the northern coast's summer season. Thus, many San Francisco shops thrive on catering to tourists' needs for warm clothing because every year new tourists arrive having made the same wrong assumption.

Yet critical thinkers can learn from wrong assumptions by mulling them over. Exactly when and why did I think that? What else might I have considered? Not all assumptions can be prevented, of course, but taking some time out for reflection might prevent their reoccurrence:

- When did I assume my roommate would always pay his half of the rent?
- Why didn't I read the small print in my apartment lease?
- When I bought that car, why did I think I could do without air-conditioning?

Our ability to survive as a species depends on our ability to learn from wrong assumptions. We live on a collective foundation of hard-learned lessons. Each child has to be taught that humans can drown in water, that some mushrooms are poisonous, that we have to protect ourselves from too much heat or cold. Collectively, one reason that we watch the news each day is to learn about new wrong assumptions. Consider these examples:

- In 2005 an Italian journalist, who had been kidnapped and held for months by Iraqi insurgents, was freed by a group of Italian intelligence agents. However, while they were rushing to the Baghdad airport, U.S. soldiers fired on their car. The journalist and two of the agents were wounded; one agent was killed when he threw himself over the journalist.
- A demolition crew in Florida bashed in the roof of a house before learning not only that they had the wrong address but that a family was inside at the time having dinner.
- A woman allowed a longtime friendly neighbor to water her plants while she was on vacation. A year later the woman discovered she was

the victim of identity theft. Her friendly neighbor had gone into her personal files and stolen the necessary private information.

- A Catholic university agreed to accept a donation of several million dollars from an anonymous donor who was vouched for by several board members. Because the money was promised within a year, the university went ahead to contract for some new buildings. A year later the university discovered it was caught in a complex scam with no donation and a large debt.

- In late 2004 the public learned that their favorite star athletes routinely used steroids and other banned substances.

Discussion Break or Writing Questions

1. Which of these examples challenged your assumptions about justice? Which challenged your assumptions about trust?
2. Which situations might have been prevented in some way?
3. Write or describe to a classmate about a time you came to distrust something previously trusted. How was an assumption involved here?
4. Did you learn anything from making this wrong assumption?

Types of Assumptions

Assumptions can be conscious or unconscious, warranted or unwarranted.

The examples of assumptions discussed so far in this chapter have been **unconscious assumptions.** They were assumptions only recognized as such after circumstances revealed their errors. The shooting accident in Baghdad, the demolition crew in Florida, the women with the "friendly" neighbor, and the Catholic university all involved wrong assumptions not fully recognized until injury was done.

Yet assumptions need not always be unconsciously made; they can also be intentionally conceived in the form of **working assumptions;** these are theories designed to serve trial ideas or strategies that might further research. These assumptions are conscious in that it is clear from the outset that these ideas may not be true and may not succeed.

> **Working assumptions** are theories assumed to be true for the purposes of decision making or more research and testing.

The use of a working assumption is illustrated in the story told in the last chapter, *He Fixes Radios by Thinking!* Feynman first develops a theory (also called an hypothesis) to explain why the radio makes so much noise. The theory becomes a working assumption when he theorizes that all he needs to do is get the RF circuit going and the grid voltages adjusted. Secondly, he conceives another working assumption about how best to test this theory. "All right, take the tubes out, and reverse the order completely in the set." As things turned out, the strategy proved that his theory was right because the noise ceased when he reversed the tubes' order. If this test hadn't provided the proof of a radio without noise, then he might have imagined another testing strategy or even another theory to serve as working assumptions.

Working assumptions, however, need not be so complex; we all use them every day.

- You agree to meet your date in front of the local movie theater at 6:00. You arrive but she is not there. You wait until 6:15. You call her on her cell phone. She does not answer. You quickly decide to assume she is on her way. You decide to buy both tickets, save some seats in the theater, and return to wait outside.

Working assumptions help us plan our lives.

- You wonder whether you should pursue a career as a basketball star or a basketball coach. You decide to proceed on the assumption that you will become a basketball star. Then if you don't have what it takes, or get injured, you can always fall back on being a basketball coach. You have an intentional strategy.

Here is another example of a conscious assumption.

- In the year 2000, your parents made an investment decision. They decided to invest in Florida real estate, assuming that property values would continue to increase. Because their assumption was conscious, they realized that some risk was involved: they could have made a wrong assumption. By the year 2008, when prices dropped because of the mortgage crisis, they discovered that their working assumption had been wrong.

The same factors operate in any area of life where people take action based on calculated risks. In mathematics, conscious assumptions are essential. For example, 2 + 2 = 4 is not a fact but a conclusion or theorem based on axioms that are assumed to be fundamental. An **axiom** is defined as a statement assumed as a basis for the development of a subject. Usually, axioms are very acceptable assumptions—not outlandish ones—that can be applied to the real world. Sometimes, as in this case, they are said to be self-evident, but still they are assumptions. We will return in the chapter on Inductive Reasoning (Chapter 11) to the topic of creating working assumptions, or **hypotheses.**

Warranted and unwarranted assumptions have some parallels to conscious and unconscious assumptions. A warranted assumption is based on some knowledge of pertinent standards, codes, customs, or agreements. These agreements make it possible for a group of people to take certain things for granted, as we all must do, in order to proceed efficiently through life together. If a family invites you over to their house for dinner, you can assume that you will not pay for the meal. On the other hand, if you go to a restaurant, it would be unwarranted to expect a free meal. However, if your friends owned a restaurant and invited you over there for dinner, you might not be sure what to expect.

Because many situations can be equally uncertain, we need to stop sometimes to clarify expectations. In public life we form agreements, sometimes in the form of laws or regulations, to help us know what we can assume. Thus if you buy a carton of milk in a grocery store dated for use within one week, your assumption is warranted that it will not be sour when you open it. If you do find the milk to be sour, you can return it to the store for a refund. The same can be said of assumptions that the city buses will arrive and leave on schedule, that the post office will be open on weekdays but not holidays, and that gas and electricity will be available at the flick of a switch. When such events do not occur, citizens can and do complain to those responsible for their maintenance. Thus, warranted assumptions enable societies to proceed through many activities in a routine manner. Nevertheless, it is possible to be unfamiliar with some standard, code, or agreement. If you expect milk to remain fresh in your refrigerator for a month, that would be an unwarranted assumption. If you expect city buses to arrive every half-hour after midnight, that would be unwarranted; and if you go to the post office expecting to mail a package on Christmas day, that assumption would be unwarranted.

Above all, our common safety depends upon warranted assumptions, such as that our pharmacies will not give us bogus medications, that the police will not rob us, that laws will be enforced, and that our own government will not harm us. Training in critical thinking can help us avoid making as many unconscious assumptions as well as unwarranted ones.

Discussion Break Question

1. Write down or explain to your neighbor the difference between a conscious and an unconscious assumption and between a warranted and an unwarranted assumption. Give your own examples of each.

Identifying Hidden Assumptions in Reasoning

Hidden assumptions exert a powerful effect on our reasoning; however, identifying them is not always easy.

- If your friend is Japanese, she must be moody.
- He is a good candidate for mayor; he looks sincere.
- If you love her, you'll give her diamonds.

All of these statements contain hidden assumptions. The first hangs on a stereotype, assumed to be true, about the moodiness of all Japanese people. The second depends on two questionable assumptions: (1) that the appearance of sincerity is actual sincerity; (2) that sincerity is the best qualification for holding office. Finally, the third example is an advertising slogan designed to persuade consumers to accept many assumptions.

If we accept any of these statements, then, we have also agreed to swallow their hidden assumptions. When we think critically, we do not accept and believe statements that hinge upon unspoken, unproven ideas.

Learning how to identify hidden assumptions is a complex skill comparable to catching fish by spotting their shadows underwater. The bait that brings the fish to the surface is the question "What would someone have to believe in order to come to this conclusion?" When we bring forth the words that make hidden ideas explicit, we bring the fish ashore so that its logic and truth can be tested.

All three opening examples depend on hidden stereotypical assumptions. **Stereotypes** are **hasty generalizations** about life that are assumed to be true and are placed in a mental file for further use. To return to two of the opening examples—the sincere mayor and the gift of diamonds— each also represents ideas based on stereotypical assumptions.

He is a good candidate for mayor; he looks sincere.

The claim assumes that people who appear sincere are honest people. Yet a person could also be sincerely deluded or sincerely malevolent. Moreover, many other more substantial qualifications are needed to hold public office.

If you love her, you'll give her diamonds.

For more than a century, the diamond industry has succeeded in persuading millions to believe (1) that crystalline carbons are rare and deserve their high price and (2) that they are the perfect symbol of a pledge of love. The advertising slogan asks you to assume that (1) a gift of diamonds gives a woman proof of her worth and (2) men who don't give women diamonds don't love them. Thus the consumer might be left feeling guilty for not conforming to the expectations cultivated by such propaganda.

Discussion Break Questions

Identify and express the hidden assumptions underlying each of the following statements or situations. The first one is provided as an example.

1. What's a nice girl like you doing in a place like this?

    Hidden underlying assumptions: (1) I am a nice girl. (2) This is a bad place. (3) You can offer me protection. (4) I should trust you. (5) I would fall for a pick-up line as old as this one.

2. I couldn't visit a Buddhist temple because they worship idols there.

3. How can that marriage counselor help people if he himself is divorced?

4. You go into a pharmacy and see a young woman standing behind the counter. You ask her if you can speak to the pharmacist. She tells you she is the pharmacist.

5. I can't understand why I haven't met my soul mate this year. My astrologer said I would.

6. Remark made to a woman in her 60s: What do you do with your time? Do you have grandchildren?

7. In a television program about earthquake preparedness, an expert demonstrated his gas-driven generator. "In the event of a major disaster," he said, "this generator would run our children's television set so that they would have something to do."

Hidden Assumptions in Arguments

Good arguments are not based on assumptions.

The purpose of an **argument** is to be persuasive. A good argument consists of **claims** supported by reasoning, by facts, examples, and evidence.

Facts take the form of statistics, testimony, records, and verified information.

A **good argument** sets forth its claims and reasoning clearly and openly; it examines its own assumptions.

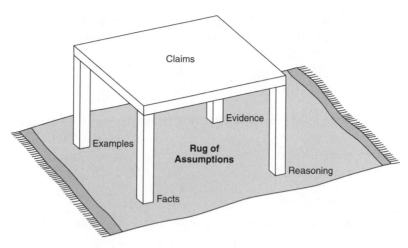

FIGURE 5.1 The Rug Test

Arguments, as the term is used in this text, are structures of reasoning designed to be persuasive. A good argument has a structure of claims supported through reasoning, facts, examples, and evidence. Moreover, all of these elements are made clear and explicit. A poor argument may lack any of these factors. A clever debater can topple the structure of any argument that rests on a rug of hidden assumptions (see Figure 5.1). When critical thinkers compose an argument, they put it to the rug test; they don't wait for their opponents to do it for them.

DISCOVERY EXERCISE

■ *Articulating Hidden Assumptions Underlying Arguments*

Write down the hidden assumptions you find in the following quotations, to share in a later class discussion. Answers are given for the first two by way of example.

1. I am sorry that I totaled your car, but it was just an accident, and accidents do happen.

   Hidden assumptions

   a. An accident is an incident for which no person is responsible.
   b. If I can get you to agree it was only an accident, you will also have to agree that I need not feel guilty or responsible.

2. In 2008 there was a debate about erecting a suicide barrier on the Golden Gate Bridge. Over 1,300 people have jumped off the bridge to their deaths since it was built in 1937. The cost for the barrier was estimated to be $40 million. Arguments pro and con went as follows:

   Pro Our daughter, while in a mood of depression, killed herself by jumping off the bridge last year. If a barrier had stopped her, she might have gone for help.

   Hidden assumptions

   a. She would not have found another way to commit suicide.
   b. She would have benefitted from help.
   c. The public has a responsibility to prevent suicides.

   Con It's a waste of money that would better be spent on suicide patrols. Also, barriers would ruin the design of its beautiful Art Deco architecture.

   Hidden assumptions

   a. Suicide patrols would be effective and inexpensive.
   b. Preserving the architectural beauty of the bridge is of primary importance.
   c. Equally important is to economize in the use of public funds.

3. A senator, concerned about the high mortality rate of children shot by other children, introduced legislation that would require manufacturers to install childproof locks on all handguns.

4. I can't lose weight because I can't stay on a diet.

5. I can't keep your dog for you while you are away overnight; I have a cat.

6. We can't get married; you do not have a job.

7. You can save on food costs if you eat out less, shop smarter, grow your own vegetables, clip coupons, and stock up on cheap canned meat.

8. The U.S. social security system is broken. It won't be there to protect future generations now forced by law to pay into the system. It would be far better for everyone to invest in the stock market so that they can retain control of their money and obtain even greater returns with which to fund their retirement.

Value or Belief Assumptions

Value assumptions are the core beliefs we take for granted. Although we may not be aware of their presence and influence, they greatly affect our reasoning.

Value assumptions are the core beliefs we never or rarely question, the beliefs we assume everyone shares. When first adopted, they may not have been examined at all, especially if they were absorbed through family or culture. Sometimes a visit to another culture can bring them into conscious awareness and reconsideration. An example from the life of the author Jean Liedloff will serve as an illustration.

Liedloff spent two-and-a-half years living with a Stone Age tribe, the Yequana Indians of the rain forests of Brazil. One thing that puzzled her was that the tribe did not have a word for *work*, nor did members distinguish work from other ways of spending time. She observed the women thoroughly enjoying the task of going down to a stream for water several times a day, even though they had to descend a steep bank with gourds on their heads and babies on their backs. Gradually the author came to realize that the idea that work is hard and leisure is fun is only a Western value assumption. She had to consider that this idea was not necessarily a truth about life, but a cultural attitude. This insight led her to reexamine other Western beliefs, such as the idea that progress is good and that a child belongs to its parents.

Other examples of cultural value assumptions emerged in a PBS "reality" series called *Frontier House* that depicted the lives of three families who had agreed to go back in time to 1883 Montana homesteading life for six months. They had to fell trees to build their own homes and furniture, raise their own food, brave a blizzard to care for livestock, wash their

Used with permission of Kirk Anderson.

clothing in a creek, and barter for food and supplies. Many lost weight from hunger and there were fights over food hoarding. Yet in spite of all their hardships, video interviews made after their return to their modern lives revealed a sense of less vitality, less kinship with other family members, and more boredom and emptiness. Their common value assumption had been that modern city life, with all its comforts, possessions, and conveniences, offered the best possible life. Many were surprised to realize that they had found more satisfaction in a life requiring a lot of physical work together with communal activities directed toward common survival.

Thus our lives are shaped and guided by our value assumptions—sometimes well, sometimes poorly. The cartoon labeled "The 7 Virtues of Consumer Culture" depicts some values commonly accepted in our time. Their effect can be startling when we recognize that these values are what our great-grandparents called the seven deadly sins. It awakens us to the possibility that, without awareness, we have transformed what once were sins into virtues. Moreover, the implication is that past traditional virtues (such as thrift, sobriety, generosity, and modesty) are now sins in a consumer culture. Thus, value assumptions differ not only from culture to culture but even reverse themselves over time within a society. Bringing these value assumptions to conscious awareness allows us to choose whether we want to continue to live by them.

Discussion Break Questions

1. What do you think about these two examples of value assumptions as they relate to work and the conveniences of modern life?
2. Do you agree with what this cartoon says about the seven virtues of consumer culture? Why or why not?

Assumption Layers in Arguments

Arguments can contain hidden assumptions that rest on hidden beliefs or value assumptions.

An argument with multiple layers of hidden assumptions could be visualized in the shape of a pyramid buried in sand. As in Figure 5.2, only the tip of the pyramid may be visible in the form of one expressed claim. Beneath the sand lie layers of assumptions resting on a base of one or more value assumptions. Once we know how to identify assumptions, we can sift through the layers in order to expose them.

Hidden value assumptions can sometimes be easier to detect in historical examples than in contemporary ones because they represent beliefs that have already been re-examined or even discarded in many societies. Here are two examples.

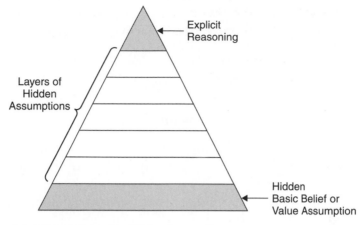

FIGURE 5.2 Pyramid of Value Assumptions

In the United States, women were finally given the right to vote in 1920. Many arguments were raised against allowing them to vote during the 143 years that led up to this achievement. Here was one of those arguments:

> If women had the right to vote, they would hide extra ballots in their voluminous sleeves and slip them into the ballot box all at once.

Assumptions

1. Women, unlike men, are devious and untrustworthy.
2. Women can't understand the importance of honest elections.
3. It won't be possible to stop women from stuffing the ballot box.
4. Women will always wear long wide sleeves.

Possible underlying value assumption

Men are right to dominate women.

Here is a second example. During the Industrial Revolution in nineteenth-century England, debates began to take up the issue of child labor. At that time children from ages 4 to 16 were working from 12 to 16 hours a day in dangerous and heavily polluted factories and mines. Many died or became crippled. Here is one argument raised in favor of child labor:

> Hard work builds character and self-discipline in these children and will help make them valuable members of society.

Assumptions

1. Poor children do not have character and self-discipline.
2. "Hard" work does not have a continuum from tolerable to deadly.

3. Children are the same as adults.

4. Working children will survive to become "valuable members of society."

Possible underlying value assumption

Employers know what is best for their workers.

Discussion Break or Writing Questions

1. Do you agree or disagree with the assumptions and value assumptions given for these arguments? Are there any that you would add or remove?

2. If you wanted to refute these arguments, how would knowledge of their assumptions help you?

3. Choose one of these issues of controversy. Briefly detail what beliefs or value assumptions might shape the reasoning on each side of this issue. Which side speaks to your own values?

   a. The use of torture to extract intelligence information is justifiable.

   b. The use of torture is never justifiable.

   a. Large banks and financial firms should not be allowed to fail.

   b. Large banks and financial firms should be allowed to fail.

   a. Health care insurance should be the right of every citizen.

   b. Health care insurance should be a private matter.

Assumptions, Incongruities, and Thinking

First we have to be alert enough to recognize incongruities; then we need to do the thinking needed to explain them.

Incongruity is something that does not meet our expectations about what is correct, appropriate, logical, or standard. The word comes from the Latin *incongruent,* meaning "not in agreement."

When we see two little girls dressed up in their Sunday best to have their picture taken, we expect to see happy smiling faces as well. But what we see in the photo on the next page instead challenges our stereotypical assumption. This photo may even make us feel uncomfortable. Yet, if instead of turning away, we become curious, we might then come to discover some interesting things about this incongruity. When we can allow ourselves to endure the discomfort of having our assumptions challenged, we learn and grow.

Photo by Arthur Rothstein. Courtesy Library of Congress.

Terms Used by Piaget to Describe Cognitive Development

Equilibrium is the stable inner feeling of balance and well-being we have when the schemas—or mental constructs—of our experiences and beliefs enable us to understand our environments and function well within them.

Assimilation is the process we use when we can explain new events satisfactorily through our existing schemas, thus maintaining equilibrium.

Disequilibrium is the confusion and discomfort we feel when a new experience cannot be adequately explained by our existing schemas.

Accommodation is the process whereby we modify our old schemas in such a way as to improve our understanding and functioning, thus restoring equilibrium.

This topic brings us back to Chapter 1 and the ideas of psychologist Jean Piaget about learning. Piaget says that when we have experiences that we cannot easily assimilate, we then are provoked to think.

We think when we reorder old mental categories. This process is what Piaget calls *accommodation*. It is provoked by an inner sense of disequilibrium. We experience disequilibrium when our assumptions are challenged by momentous experiences, such as witnessing a birth or a death, or more mundanely, discovering we have a flat tire. When our assumptions are challenged, we feel actual physical discomfort; but when we can reorganize our mental categories to accommodate a new experience, our equilibrium is restored. Thus, a feeling of equilibrium is a reward for successful thinking. While describing many of the photographs in this book so far, you may have felt especially uncomfortable. This is because all of them, whether you realized it or not, are based on *incongruities*. In studying the photographs, you have had the choice of either avoiding the disequilibrium they aroused or staying with the task long enough to reach a satisfactory explanation for their incongruities—and thus finding a way to restore your equilibrium.

To return to the picture of the little girls, you might imagine some explanations for their frowns. You could infer (1) they were given dolls they didn't like; (2) they did not want to pose for the picture; (3) the picture was taken when they were off guard; or (4) the photographer only wanted to make a statement of ironic contrasts. If this last explanation seems the most promising, you might wonder if perhaps the photographer was purposely playing with some incongruities. Perhaps the whole composition was intentional: to contrast Hollywood play dolls against two girls dressed up as dolls; to contrast a false concept of little girls with real little girls; to contrast false faces with real faces reflecting the stresses of life.

Sometimes we have to hang in there through a period of doubt and confusion before we can reach an explanation that reconciles all our facts, or until we can bring our information into a satisfying pattern of order. And although we may never be able to confirm the final truth of our explanation, at least we have the satisfaction of having reconciled all the available information. Piaget says that persistence in this process of moving from disequilibrium to equilibrium develops our thinking skills.

Thinking comes about in life through provocation: when we meet situations that do not fit a familiar pattern, that do not fall into familiar stereotypes, that do not meet expectations. In such cases, we have the personal choice to deny or ignore—or to think, to learn, and to grow. When we were toddlers, if we touched a hot stove, the experience of being burned was an unpleasant encounter with reality. And yet, even then, if we had not stopped to analyze even in a simple way what caused the pain, we would have had to suffer the same pain over and over again. Even if we decided to always depend on someone else to think for us and protect us, we would eventually find such a solution to be impractical. We survive best when we can think for ourselves. And the more we think, the more willing, open, and able we are to accept life's challenges of our assumptions.

Discussion Break Questions

1. Give an example of some incongruity that you have experienced that challenged you to recognize one of your assumptions.
2. Can you describe the disequilibrium you felt when you could not resolve this incongruity?

Building Arguments
Assumptions: Building an Argument

Some of our chiefs make the claim that the land belongs to us. It is not what the Great Spirit told me. He told me that the lands belong to Him, that no people owns the land; that I was not to forget to tell this to the white people when I met them in council. (Kannekuk, Kickapoo prophet, 1827)

Exercise

1. What claim is being refuted here?
2. What assumption lies in the claim?
3. What counterclaim is being made?
4. State a claim that you feel contains an assumption. State why you believe it is an assumption. Formulate your own counterclaim.

3. How did you restore your equilibrium?
4. Have you experienced disequilibrium at times while studying this textbook? How was your equilibrium restored?

Chapter Summary

1. An assumption is something we take for granted, something we accept prematurely as being true, something we do not check out carefully. Often, we do not recognize that we have made an assumption until it causes a problem for us.

2. Assumptions can be conscious or unconscious, warranted or unwarranted. Unconscious and unwarranted assumptions can lead to faulty reasoning, whereas conscious and warranted assumptions can be useful tools for problem solving. We need to recognize the difference.

3. Hidden assumptions are unconscious assumptions that greatly influence a line of reasoning. One form of hidden assumptions is stereotypes, where we try to fit new experiences into old or prejudiced categories. Another type is value assumptions, or basic unexamined beliefs that unconsciously influence our thinking.

4. Arguments are the use of reasoning to defend an idea or to persuade someone else to believe in the idea. Good arguments do not rest upon unexamined assumptions.

5. We perceive incongruities when we observe situations that do not meet our expectations or assumptions. This can cause a feeling of disequilibrium. We restore our equilibrium when we reach a new understanding through the process of reexamining our assumptions. This is a familiar and continuous process that results in growth and learning.

6. Someone who brings a fresh perspective to a problem that has stumped others is often able to find a solution because he or she does not buy the assumptions that restrain others. As a conscious tool, we can look for assumptions when we are confronted with a problem to solve.

Chapter Quiz

Rate each of the following statements as *true* or *false*. Justify your answer with an example or explanation.

_____   1. When we articulate hidden assumptions, we simply read what we find in print before us.

_____   2. A good argument invariably contains a few hidden assumptions.

_____   3. A value assumption is a belief assumed to be true that is shared by everyone.

_____   4. "Can you believe it? She is twenty-three years old and not even thinking of getting married." This statement, made by a Puerto Rican mother, contains no value assumption.

_____   5. Assumptions are often recognized only in retrospect because of the problems they cause.

_____   6. In mathematics, conscious assumptions are called *axioms*.

_____   7. A conscious assumption can be used as a strategy to lead us to new information. If a child does not come home from school at the usual time, we might first decide to call the homes of the child's friends; if that turns up no information, we might call the police.

_____   8. Stereotypes contain no assumptions.

_____   9. To be uncomfortable is to be in disequilibrium. Thinking through a problem restores the comfort of our mental equilibrium.

_____ 10. Incongruities can provoke us into thinking in order to resolve their conflict with our assumptions and expectations.

Composition Writing Application

■ Expository Essay: Solving a Problem by Uncovering Assumptions

Think of a major problem from your own life (or someone else's) that was solved by the discovery of one or more hidden assumptions. If you prefer to use historical examples from the lives of explorers, artists, or scientists, do some research on the kinds of problems they succeeded in solving. (Besides using ordinary encyclopedias, you might also look for some special science encyclopedias in the library.) Write in sketch form your basic findings, searching for the following elements to develop and emphasize:

1. What particular problem concerned your subject?
2. What assumptions were embedded in the problem?
3. How were these assumptions discovered?
4. What restraints did these assumptions impose?
5. What, if any, wrong assumptions were made?

Prepare a working outline for an essay of about three typewritten pages. Then begin your essay with a thesis statement that explains what you concluded from your research and analysis.

The **thesis statement**, also called the *thesis,* has some similarity to the topic sentence in that it states a generalization. However, as it is introduced, it may be stated through several sentences instead of one, as it proposes an idea that will be developed, explained, and illustrated over many paragraphs and pages. By definition, the thesis is the idea that the essay intends to prove. Again, in the process of thinking, the thesis, like the topic sentence, may only be mentally formulated after some time has been spent studying the subject. However, when the essay is written in an academic style, the thesis is stated in the first paragraph. A thesis is also called the *controlling idea* because everything written in the essay is based on the dictates of its objective. We can visualize the thesis as a frame, like a picture frame; everything that will appear in that picture—the essay—is contained in and limited by the thesis (see Figure 5.3).

The act of stating the thesis helps us organize our thoughts around one main purpose; it can also serve as a magnet to help us decide what information is relevant for support. Every statement and every fact appearing in the essay should either support or develop the thesis.

Let's look at an example of a thesis. Suppose you decided to write an expository essay to explain a problem you solved at work through the discovery of a hidden assumption. Your thesis might be introduced in this manner:

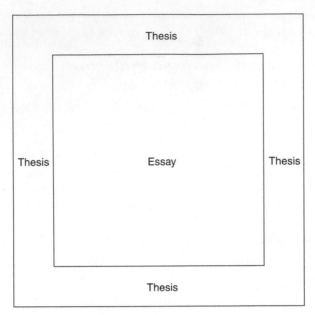

FIGURE 5.3 Thesis as a Frame

(1) All of us have heard fables about villages that suffered long and hard from a particular problem, like a famine or a wayward dragon. (2) Then one day a stranger appeared and solved the problem simply, quickly, and miraculously. (3) In such stories, what seemed to be a miracle to the villagers was only a matter of a newcomer's bringing a fresh perspective, unbiased by any past assumptions. (4) My own life had a parallel situation several years ago when I went to work for the municipal utilities district. (5) And although I did not arrive on a horse or in a suit of armor, I did bring a fresh perspective that solved an "insoluble problem."

These five sentences comprise the thesis statement. The first two introduce the topic and invite reader interest. The third states a principle and a limitation of focus. The fourth makes the transition to a personal incident that will illustrate this principle. And the fifth sentence states the actual thesis that the narrative will develop, support, and illustrate.

Here is a summary of the parameters for this assignment:

1. *Topic:* How one creative individual challenged the restraints of some mistaken assumptions in solving a problem.
2. *Objective:* To describe and explain, through a narrative, a personal or historical achievement from the perspective of how inherent assumptions were worked through.

3. *Form:* Essay using personal or researched information for illustration and exposition to support the thesis statement.
4. *Length:* At least three typed pages.

Submit your working outline with your paper if your instructor requests that you do so. To follow up in class, read your essays to one another in pairs or small groups. Check over one another's work to see whether the parameters were followed. Critique each essay with the following questions.

Scoring for Expository Essay on Assumptions

1. Does the writer state the thesis clearly and develop it through narrative and exposition? *40 points*
2. Does the essay really stay with the topic of illustrating how an individual solved one major problem through working with some mistaken assumptions? *25 points*
3. Is the length at least three typed pages? *10 points*
4. Is the thesis supported with personal or researched information? *15 points*
5. Is the work free of distracting errors in punctuation, spelling, and sentence structure? *10 points*

● STUDENT WRITING EXAMPLE

A MISPLACED ASSUMPTION

Terry Ruscoe

All of us have heard fables about villages that suffered long and hard from a particular problem, like a famine or a wayward dragon. Then one day a stranger appeared and solved the problem simply, quickly, and miraculously. In such stories, what seemed to be a miracle to the villagers was only a matter of a newcomer's bringing a fresh perspective, unbiased by any past assumptions. My own life had a parallel situation several years ago when I went to work for the municipal utilities district. And although I did not arrive on a horse or in a suit of armor, I did bring a fresh perspective that solved an "insoluble problem."

My work as a storekeeper was to receive and distribute merchandise, such as plumbing supplies, to our work crews. Here was the problem: after our trucks rolled out of the yard to make deliveries, we would often get calls asking for a modification in the order. But, we had no way of getting in touch with the trucks once they left. This could mean even more frustration for the frantic caller who needed just one more of those special pipeline fittings to complete the job and get traffic moving again.

"Radios, that's what we need," said the foreman as he burst into the office. He had just been chewed out by the supervisor of maintenance for a work delay of two hours that was due to some missing material. "The only problem is the budget. How can we afford $800 right away to put a radio in each of the trucks?" Carl, the receiving clerk, who was instructing me on the proper manner of keeping stock records, looked up and quipped, "Yeah, not only is that too much money, but say the driver is out of his truck unloading . . . he may not even hear the thing."

Later that day at lunch, several of us were in the break room. We began tossing the problem around. One of the guys came up with a good idea, suggesting that we augment the radios with an attachment to automatically sound the horn of the truck when it was called. But this would be even more expensive and still be useless if the driver was out of range or was out in a pool vehicle.

5   Another problem that arose was the lack of firsthand communication; every message would have to be channeled through the base station operator unless we bought our own base station transmitter, which would cost even more money. And then there was the question of privacy: what if we wanted the driver to stop on the way back to pick up some doughnuts? We didn't need the whole district to know about it. "It's the same old problem," moaned one driver. "Face it, we're just going to have to pop for the whole deal, base station and all, and be done with it. Consider it a long-term investment into our sanity."

I had been listening, just listening, for about twenty minutes when I realized that what we had here were two misplaced assumptions: the first was that we had to reach the truck; and the second was that we had only one way of communicating. It's the driver we need to reach, I reasoned. And what else was there besides radios? Telephones? He couldn't carry a phone around with him, but . . . what about a beeper? That way, when he got our message, he could go to any nearby phone and call us. (Remember that this was back in the times when cell phones were not yet invented and only doctors carried beepers.) "Okay," I said, "why not supply each driver with a remote-controlled beeper, so that when he gets our message he can go directly to a phone and call us. As they say, 'phoning is the next best thing to being there.'" And guess what? It worked. If we wanted to contact a driver we simply beeped him. It was far less expensive, and we were able to rent the beepers immediately. Above all, the troops could now get what they wanted without any of those old-fashioned glazed-or-chocolate mix-ups.

Used with permission of Terry Ruscoe.

● R E A D I N G S ●

Lateral and Vertical Thinking
Edward de Bono

Edward de Bono has been a professor at Cambridge, Oxford, and Harvard universities. He has written many innovative books about thinking, maintaining it is a learnable and teachable skill. He was the first to develop the term lateral thinking, *which is particularly useful for creative problem solving. Lateral thinking allows a person to overcome binding assumptions and see a problem in an entirely different way, thus allowing novel solutions. In the illustrative story presented here, Edward de Bono explains the differences between lateral and vertical thinking.*

Many years ago when a person who owed money could be thrown into jail, a merchant in London had the misfortune to owe a huge sum to a money-lender. The money-lender, who was old and ugly, fancied the merchant's beautiful teenage daughter. He proposed a bargain. He said he would cancel the merchant's debt if he could have the girl instead.

Both the merchant and his daughter were horrified at the proposal. So the cunning money-lender proposed that they let Providence decide the matter. He told them that he would put a black pebble and a white pebble into an empty money-bag and then the girl would have to pick out one of the pebbles. If she chose the black pebble she would become his wife and her father's debt would be canceled. If she chose the white pebble she would stay with her father and the debt would be canceled. But if she refused to pick out a pebble her father would be thrown into jail and she would starve.

Reluctantly the merchant agreed. They were standing on a pebble-strewn path in the merchant's garden as they talked and the money-lender stooped down to pick up the two pebbles. As he picked up the pebbles the girl, sharp-eyed with fright, noticed that he picked up two black pebbles and put them into the money-bag. He then asked the girl to pick out the pebble that was to decide her fate and that of her father.

Imagine that you are standing on that path in the merchant's garden. What would you have done if you had been the unfortunate girl? If you had to advise her what would you have advised her to do?

5   What type of thinking would you use to solve the problem? You may believe that careful logical analysis must solve the problem if there is a solution. This type of thinking is straight-forward vertical thinking. The other type of thinking is lateral thinking.

Vertical thinkers are not usually of much help to a girl in this situation. The way they analyze it, there are three possibilities:

1. The girl should refuse to take a pebble.

2. The girl should show that there are two black pebbles in the bag and expose the money-lender as a cheat.
3. The girl should take a black pebble and sacrifice herself in order to save her father from prison.

None of these suggestions is very helpful, for if the girl does not take a pebble her father goes to prison, and if she does take a pebble, then she has to marry the money-lender.

The story shows the difference between vertical thinking and lateral thinking. Vertical thinkers are concerned with the fact that the girl has to take a pebble. Lateral thinkers become concerned with the pebble that is left behind. Vertical thinkers take the most reasonable view of a situation and then proceed logically and carefully to work it out. Lateral thinkers tend to explore all the different ways of looking at something, rather than accepting the most promising and proceeding from that.

The girl in the pebble story put her hand into the money-bag and drew out a pebble. Without looking at it she fumbled and let it fall to the path where it was immediately lost among all the others.

"Oh, how clumsy of me," she said, "but never mind—if you look into the bag you will be able to tell which pebble I took by the colour of the one that is left."

10   Since the remaining pebble is of course black, it must be assumed that she has taken the white pebble, since the money-lender dare not admit his dishonesty. In this way, by using lateral thinking, the girl changes what seems an impossible situation into an extremely advantageous one. The girl is actually better off than if the money-lender had been honest and had put one black and one white pebble into the bag, for then she would have had only an even chance of being saved. As it is, she is sure of remaining with her father and at the same time having his debt canceled.

Vertical thinking has always been the only respectable type of thinking. In its ultimate form as logic it is the recommended ideal towards which all minds are urged to strive, no matter how far short they fall. Computers are perhaps the best example. The problem is defined by the programmer, who also indicates the path along which the problem is to be explored. The computer then proceeds with its incomparable logic and efficiency to work out the problem. The smooth progression of vertical thinking from one solid step to another solid step is quite different from lateral thinking.

If you were to take a set of toy blocks and build them upwards, each block resting firmly and squarely on the block below it, you would have an illustration of vertical thinking. With lateral thinking the blocks are scattered around. They may be connected to each other loosely or not at all. But the pattern that may eventually emerge can be as useful as the vertical structure.

• • •

Study/Writing/Discussion Questions

1. What role do assumptions play in vertical thinking?

2. How does lateral thinking work with assumptions?

3. "Vertical thinkers take the most reasonable view of a situation and then proceed logically and carefully to work it out. Lateral thinkers tend to explore all the different ways of looking at something, rather than accepting the most promising and proceeding from that." Look again at the story of Columbus and the egg cited in the Discovery Exercises at the beginning of this chapter. Was Columbus a vertical or lateral thinker?

4. Is the author saying that vertical thinking is wrong? Explain why or why not.

5. Edward de Bono once gave this example of lateral thinking: "A granny complains that she can't continue with her knitting because Suzy the three-year-old keeps playing with her wool. A vertical solution would be to put Suzy in a play pen. A lateral solution would be to put the granny there." Explain the role of assumptions in this solution.

6. In the state-operated health care program offered in China, village physicians are paid not for their services to the sick but for the number of their assigned patients who stay well. How does this represent a lateral thinking solution?

7. A persistent problem in the United States is illegal drug use. One unsuccessful solution has been the "war on drugs." Do you think this was a vertical or lateral solution? If you feel it is vertical, suggest some lateral solutions. If you claim it is lateral, then describe some vertical solutions.

8. According to *Time* magazine (August 26, 2002), new ecologically sound products include inflatable sofas and chairs, the Flamp, a lamp that leeches light from other sources without using electricity, and the Eco-Flush Toilet with high, medium, and low settings. What assumptions had to be questioned in order to create each of these products?

An Unexpected Experience

David Wood

This reading appeared in The Sun Magazine *(December 2007) in the section called* Readers-Write. *The theme for readers' submissions in this edition was* Getting Ready.

My cellmate stayed on his bunk and out of my way as I packed two laundry bags with everything I wanted to take. I went through my prison footlocker, tossing out unimportant papers and useless slivers of soap. I had already given away my good sneakers and my old watch to inmates who needed them.

I was getting out after sixteen years, and though I tried to act calm, I could not keep my hands from shaking. The free world had changed: I knew because I'd watched it on television. I'd listened on the radio as the second airplane had hit the tower in New York City. But knowing about the changes and living with them were two different things. I didn't know how to drive, find a job, or do my taxes.

When a prisoner leaves, sometimes his buddies will throw him under the shower and smear lotion and baby powder all over him as a way of saying goodbye. I'd asked my friends not to do that—I was too old for such games—but now I wished they had. It would have been a sign that they cared.

The next morning, when the doors opened after count, I went by each cell to say goodbye. When I stopped by Jack's cell, his towel was over his door because he was on the toilet. He stuck his hand out to shake mine and wished me luck. (He told me later in a letter that he'd been crying and hadn't wanted me to see him.)

5   The corrections officer summoned me to go to the administration building, where I would wait several hours for my release papers. Donnie, who had been my cellmate for a while, helped me carry my laundry bags, heavy with books and papers. We stopped outside the administration building, and I gave him a hug. As bad as I wanted to be out, I would miss him. I would miss a lot of the men I was leaving behind. My hands trembled. Returning to the free world was scarier than my first day in prison. Who would have figured?

Used with permission of David Wood.

● ● ●

Study/Writing/Discussion Questions

1. Explain how this story centers upon the discovery of an assumption.
2. Can you describe a parallel experience in your own life where your reactions did not meet your expectations?

In the Supermarket
John Bul Dau

This excerpt is taken from the latter part of his book God Grew Tired of Us. *Here John describes his first visit to an American grocery store where he is taken by some members of a church that sponsored his visit to the United States.*

. . . We walked through a door that opened on its own as we approached. The interior of the building stretched away in three directions in front of us, all of the space crammed with food. I had never seen so much to eat in my life. Jacob, Andrew, and I must have stood with our mouths open, while Susan and Penny got two shopping carts and tried to herd us to the right side of the store, toward the displays of vegetables.

Susan asked if I wanted some lettuce. I did not know what that was, but it looked as if she were pointing at a bag of leaves, the kind I fed to farm animals in Duk Payuel. I saw something labeled "cucumber" and asked Susan about it. She said it was a good vegetable; it could be sliced and put in salads. It looked like what I fed the goats. I recognized bananas, though. We had those in Africa.

Susan and Penny took us to every counter in the store and asked the workers if we could have samples. The butcher cut a tiny slice of pink flesh.

"What is this?" I asked.

"It is ham."

"What is ham?"

"It's meat. It comes from a pig."

Meat is not meat unless it comes from a cow, I thought. Clams, lobsters, shrimp—do people eat such things? Yes? I didn't want to criticize, but they did not look like anything good to eat. Lobsters and shrimp looked like big bugs. Someone asked if I liked fish. I said no. That wasn't true; I do eat fish. But I didn't want to eat anything that came from the counter next to the giant insects. Not far away I saw lots of chicken roasting on skewers. I wanted to eat those chickens.

One of the grocery store workers handed out doughnuts. I took one but didn't want to eat it in the store. Dinka culture dictated that I go back to the apartment, go inside, and eat. You don't eat in front of other people, not even to peel an orange. Mealtime is separate. And small, sweet foods are inappropriate for grown men, who should eat beef and milk. Popcorn, cookies, sweets—those are for small children. If a baby cries while waiting for dinner, it is okay to drop a kernel of corn near the fire, grab it as it pops, and give it to the child. But it is an insult to offer a trifle such as popcorn or candy to a man . . .

I had my biggest shock when we passed the aisle beneath the sign that said "dog food" and "cat food." My family had dogs in Duk Payuel. We gave them a little food from our dinner. If I wanted to feed the dog, I put a scoop of boiled maize on the floor and continued eating. My dog knew to wait until I had finished and left the room before advancing to eat what I had given him. And later, during the civil war in Sudan, my countrymen starved every day, and tens of thousands went hungry in the dark days in refugee camps, while in America dogs had special meals prepared just for them. Forty-pound bags of dog food took up an entire aisle of the store. An entire industry had sprung up around the need to feed the family pet . . .

Used with permission of *National Geographic*.

● ● ●

Study/Writing/Discussion Questions

1. List the discoveries John Bul Dau makes about American foods and food habits from the perspective of someone raised in the Sudan.
2. Would you say that Dau is contrasting American and African cultural assumptions about food?
3. Why does he keep his reactions to himself instead of sharing them with the two American women who took him to the store?
4. What did you learn from Dau's story about your own cultural assumptions about food?

Advanced Optional Writing Assignment

Write an autobiographical essay of about four typed pages in which you show how you discovered some of your value assumptions through conflicts with another person, your own culture, a visited culture, or a newly adopted culture. Explain what the conflicts were and explain how they resulted from different value assumptions that you may or may not have been aware of at the time. Show how you were able to resolve or not resolve these differences.

Begin the essay with a thesis that involves some statement about value assumptions. Work from an outline that will appear on the first page of this assignment. Construct a draft outline or cluster to help you set up the symmetries for your comparison (how alike) and contrast (how different). You might decide to use a story to describe the conflict, contrasting your value assumptions in conclusion. Or you might want to state the value assumptions first, then compare and contrast people on the basis of each assumption, and end with a summary conclusion.

CHAPTER 6

Opinions:
What's Believed?

Used with permission of Randy Glasbergen.

**"Things always get better after they get worse.
So it's good to make things worse as quickly as possible."**

This chapter explores that familiar word *opinion* and examines how it affects our ability to think critically. Opinions may be wise or foolish, rational or irrational, prejudiced or fair. We form opinions from our own experiences or adopt them from others, then store them in our memory files. Sometimes we mistake them for facts. In this chapter we take an irreverent look at opinions, their characteristics, and their problems.

DISCOVERY EXERCISES

The three discovery exercises that follow can be done either alone or with a partner in preparation for class discussion of this chapter.

■ Comparing a Sample of Opinions

Study the following statements of opinion:

1. My psychiatrist said I need a vacation, not medication.
2. "Why not go to war for oil? We need oil." (Ann Coulter)
3. "Most Americans who are considered 'poor' today have routine access to a quality of housing, food, health care, consumer products, entertainment, communications, and transportation that even the Vanderbilts, the Carnegies, the Rockefellers, and the nineteenth-century European princes, with all their wealth, could not have afforded." (Stephen Moore and Julian Simon, *It's Getting Better All the Time*, Washington, DC: Cato Institute, 2000)
4. "All this . . . persuades us that the word 'person' as used in the Fourteenth Amendment does not include the unborn. . . . We need not resolve the difficult question of when life begins. When those trained in the respective disciplines of medicine, philosophy, and theology are unable to arrive at any consensus, the judiciary, at this point in the development of man's knowledge, is not in a position to speculate as to the answer." (U.S. Supreme Court, *Roe v. Wade*, 1973)

In writing or class discussion, answer these questions about the statements:

1. What do these opinions have in common?
2. How are they different?
3. Do they all have equal weight and value?

■ Why Do We Get Confused by the Word Opinion?

Find at least three different meanings in a dictionary for the word *opinion*. (Be sure to look at the word's etymology.) Write down each definition and compose a sentence that clearly expresses each meaning. Do you find that some of these meanings of *opinion* seem to contradict one another? Explain exactly how.

After you have finished, compare your different meanings to those given here:

1. A judgment that, though open to dispute, seems probable to the *speaker*.
   "No one can say if our weather has changed permanently for the worse or not, but it's my *opinion* that it has."

2. A belief held with confidence but not substantiated by proof.
   "There'll always be an England."

3. A claim or statement about what is considered to be true, supported by reasoning.
   "Americans are overworked. Their average work hours have continued to increase over the past thirty years. It is now not only commonplace in families for both parents to work, but the working poor hold three and four jobs just to make ends meet."

4. A judgment formed by an expert.
   "As your doctor of long standing, it is my opinion that you should not have surgery at this time."

5. Prevailing sentiment.
   "Public opinion supports more environmental protection."

6. A formal judgment drawn after a legal hearing.
   "It is the opinion of the court that the defendant is guilty."

■ An Exercise in Evaluating Opinions

Rate the following opinions as:

A. An opinion I would accept and act on.
B. Worthy of consideration.
C. I'd want another opinion.
D. Forget it!

_____ 1. Your doctor says you need surgery immediately.

_____ 2. A psychiatrist testifies in court that the defendant is not guilty by reason of insanity.

_____ 3. The weather forecaster says it will rain tomorrow.

_____ 4. Your attorney says you should sue your neighbor for damages.

_____ 5. You want to rent an apartment but the neighbor next door says the landlord is a weirdo.

_____ 6. Your best friend tells you your fiancée is tacky.

_____ 7. Your English instructor says you don't know how to think and should see a psychiatrist.

_____　8. Your astrologer tells you not to go on any long trips in May.

_____　9. The judge says you are guilty of driving under the influence of alcohol.

_____　10. An engineer says you can prevent your basement from flooding by blasting holes for drainage in your foundation.

_____　11. Your utility energy advisor says you can conserve energy by having your floors insulated.

_____　12. A Pentagon general advises bombing Mexico.

Types of Opinions

> Opinions take many forms: judgments, advice, generalizations, personal preferences, and general public sentiment.

Let's review what you may have discovered so far by categorizing opinions into types. First, there are the *judgments:* this is *good,* this is *bad;* this is *right,* this is *wrong;* this *should be,* this *should not be.* Look at the following two examples and provide a third example of your own.

1. Men and women should not share college dorms.
2. That car you bought was a lemon.
3.

A second type of opinion involves giving advice: *You should do this; you should not do this.* Examples of such opinions appear as follows:

1. I wouldn't advertise for a roommate if I were you.
2. You need a new car.
3.

As you must have concluded from the earlier rating exercise, whether one chooses to accept advice is an individual matter.

A third category of opinions includes simple *generalizations,* typically preceded by the word *all, no,* or *some.* In this case, the opinion is stated as a generalization in order to suggest that it represents a general truth.

1. Children in the United States are pressured to grow up too fast.
2. Nothing comes without a price.
3.

Here again, support for the opinion may be offered or not. Those who take more responsibility for their opinions do offer reasons and evidence. A critical thinker draws generalizations from evidence and, in turn, examines the generalizations provided by others for their basis in evidence.

A fourth category of opinion involves *personal taste* or *personal preferences: I like this; I don't like this.* Personal preferences need not be rational; they also do not necessarily need to be explained or justified.

1. I can't explain why, but I love the *Survivor* television series.
2. The only shoes I will wear are Caterpillar boots.
3.

A final category of opinion, close to personal taste, is *public sentiment.* Often obtained from polls, public sentiment is a gauge of prevailing public impressions on current issues. Like personal preferences, public sentiment need not be rational or even knowledgeable. Top-of-the-head impressions are as welcome to pollsters as studied opinions. Here are some examples:

1. The president is doing a good job.
2. We have a strong economy.
3.

Distinguishing Between Responsible and Irresponsible Opinions

Not all opinions deserve careful consideration.

You are probably wondering at this point how we can manage to communicate about opinions when we use the same word to convey so many different meanings:

1. An expert's judgment
2. An unsubstantiated belief
3. An argument that is well supported
4. A final legal judgment
5. Personal preferences
6. Public sentiment

When we study critical thinking, we take these differences into account and recognize that we have to evaluate each type differently. A popular truism, which would seem to contradict this idea, states "Everyone is entitled to an opinion." Some might believe that this expression means that all opinions are relative truths and should therefore not be judged. Others believe that "Everyone is entitled to an opinion" only means that every person has a right to free speech. Critical thinkers might be willing to give most opinions a full hearing, but they need not feel compelled to offer blanket tolerance. Moreover, a critical thinker would expect any opinion to measure up to the standards of a good argument if the opinion's intent is to persuade.

Let's give an ordinary example that illustrates the need to evaluate opinions. Suppose you want to decide how to vote on a safe drinking water bond issue. After reading a number of pro and con arguments in the Voter Information Pamphlet, you wonder whose opinion you should respect the most. Would it be that of the League of Women Voters? Of your assembly representative? Of the Save-Us-from-More-Taxes Association? Of your Uncle George? Actually, from all these four choices, your Uncle George might turn out to be the most knowledgeable source you could find. To determine the value of his contribution, you would need to know how well and recently he had studied the subject, how much inside knowledge he had, and what sources he had consulted. You would also want to know whether his viewpoint was independent of vested interests and how sound his reasoning appeared. These questions represent the same standards that we use for a serious evaluation of any opinion offered to influence us.

On the other hand, opinions that are only expressions of personal taste or belief do not require justification or evaluation. If you prefer yogurt to ice cream, jazz to pop music, you do not really need to explain why. The same may be said of personal beliefs. You do not have to defend a statement that you believe in God. However, if you wanted to persuade someone to agree with you, then you would want to use the standards of an argument—that is to say, you would offer the support of reasons. In evaluating opinions, therefore, the first step is to distinguish between opinions that require responsible support and those that do not.

To sum up, critical thinkers have standards for judging which opinions are worthy of their time and consideration and which are not. Thus, when we read a newspaper editorial, we expect it to meet the standards of an argument. When we go to a physician, attorney, or financial advisor, we assume they have the training and experience to offer sound opinions. We can assume they know what facts are available and which are missing, what the variables are, and how much risk is involved in judging and predicting the odds. However, as critical thinkers, we do not assume that all the authorities we consult are always right; in the last analysis, we make our own decisions on the basis of our own judgments about others' opinions.

Looking at Public Opinion Polls

We can have informed or uninformed opinions about polls.

DISCOVERY EXERCISE

■ *Poll on Polls*

Read the following questions. (1) Write out your answers. (2) Form small groups in which to share your answers. (3) Check those items that you need to know more about. (4) Discuss what a critical thinker needs to know about polls.

1. Have you ever been interviewed by a pollster?
2. If so, was it a marketing poll or a public survey?
3. Are you interested in hearing about polls in the news?
4. Have you ever been surprised by a poll result?
5. Do you think polls offer leaders useful feedback about public views?
6. Do government leaders seem to be influenced by public polls?
7. Can polls be designed to influence opinion?
8. What information might help you assess the validity of poll results?
   - Name and reputation of poll-taker
   - Person or organization that sponsored the poll
   - The wording of the polling question
   - The number of people interviewed
   - If they were volunteers or chosen
   - When and how was the poll taken
   - If the margin of error was given
9. Name some polling organizations that you have heard about.

In the past 50 years, just as the United States has grown in population, complexity, and diversity, public opinion polls have grown in their numbers and importance. Often they are taken to serve as "a voice of the people."

For a democracy, the huge advantage of public opinion polls is that they offer relatively fast feedback on specific issues. Yet poll reliance has some significant drawbacks. (1) Both scientific polls as well as pseudo polls exist, and the difference may not always be clear to the public. (2) Polls don't allow for questions to be raised. (3) Polls don't allow for prior study. (4) Depending on the wording of the interview question, poll results can greatly differ. (5) Poll results can be ignored or distorted by media.

In sum, polls can't carry the legal safeguards of a public vote in an election. Unlike elections, poll results depend upon the motives and reputation of the pollster, how the question was phrased, how the sample was chosen, and how the poll was interpreted. Although election results must be made known, the release of poll results is left to the discretion of unknown individuals. The reliability and authenticity of the polls depend upon the reputation of the organization for neutrality and for upholding scientific standards. Moreover, polls must have sponsors, whose identities—and true motives—may not be known. There are, for instance, public relations firms that specialize in using polling as one of many "perception management" tactics. Such pseudo polls are designed to enable their clients to manipulate the public.

Given all these hazards, what can a critical thinker do? Aside from taking out the time to learn about polling organizations, polling methods, and standards, there are a few critical questions you can ask whenever reading or hearing poll results in the news. These questions will help you decide whether to accept polling results or whether to put your judgment on hold until you can get more information.

1. Does this report tell me who conducted this poll and when?
2. Does this organization have a reputation for producing neutral scientific polls?
3. Does this report tell me who paid for the poll?
4. Does it tell me if this was a scientific poll where a random representative sample was chosen or was it an informal poll based on volunteers?
5. Does it say how many people were interviewed and how?
6. Does it tell me the polling questions so that I can examine their wording?
7. Does it offer the margin of error?

Opinions as Claims in Arguments

Opinions function as primary claims in arguments that are supported by facts, other claims, and reasoning. In an essay, the thesis is a statement of opinion.

Arguments begin with opinions. Having an opinion that we want to express and defend motivates us to build an argument. Yet a mere statement of opinion alone is not an argument.

Americans are overworked.

To serve as an argument, this statement needs support. *An opinion only becomes an argument when it provides supporting reasons that might persuade others to agree with this opinion.*

> Unemployment in Americans is growing while the employed are overworked. (*opinion that is a conclusion or principal claim*) Employers are hiring fewer workers because they can use their existing workforce for more hours. (*supporting claim or reason*) In the Detroit area the average workweek is 47.5 hours; Saturn workers have a regular 50-hour week, and in some plants, workers are doing 60 hours a week. The United Auto Workers (UAW) estimates that 59,000 automobile jobs would be created if the plants were on a 40-hour week. (*supporting claims offering verifiable statistics*) (Juliet Schor, *A Sustainable Economy for the Twenty-First Century*, 1995)

Thus, an argument consists of an opinion supported by reasons. To explain an argument we return again to the metaphor of a table: the tabletop holds the opinion or principal claim; its legs are supporting claims, also known as reasons (Figure 6.1). More simply, an argument is a conclusion supported by reasons.

The principal claim in an essay is called a **thesis:**

> Unemployment in America is growing while the employed are overworked.

In the language of argument, this thesis is also called a **conclusion.** It is not a conclusion in the sense that it is a final summary but in the sense that it is the conclusion of a line of reasoning:

> Employers are hiring fewer workers because they can use their existing workforce for more hours.

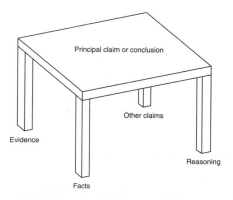

Principal claim or conclusion

Other claims

Evidence

Reasoning

Facts

FIGURE 6.1 Argument Structure

The argument's credibility is greatly increased by the support of additional claims offering verifiable statistics about the working hours of autoworkers. This is known as **evidence**—data offered to prove or disprove something. Evidence includes facts, statistics, testimony, personal experience, witnesses, and records. In short, evidence involves information can be independently examined for its authenticity, accuracy, and reliability.

In the Composition Writing Application that follows, you are asked to write an essay in which you make a short argument in support of an opinion, express an opinion, or analyze three opinions. Such an exercise can remind you how opinions function as primary claims in an argument and how the support of evidence, other claims, and reasoning gives these opinions credibility and persuasiveness.

The word *evidence* comes from the Latin *evidens*, meaning something obvious. When we offer evidence, we seek to make the truth of something obvious. We offer proof in the form of statistics, testimony, personal experience, witnesses, records, and physical objects.

Composition Writing Application

■ *First Option: A Short Argument Supporting an Opinion*

Write a one- to two-page essay stating and defending an opinion you believe in. Follow these steps:

1. *What:* State the opinion or principal claim in one sentence.
2. *Support:*
   a. Give three or more reasons why you believe this opinion to be true.
   b. Also provide evidence in the form of facts, statistics, or specific examples to support your claim.
3. *Persuasion:* Explain why you believe others should accept this opinion.
4. *Conclusion:* Bring your ideas together in a summary or a generalization.

▨ Second Option: A Short Expository Essay About an Opinion

Write a short essay describing an opinion of your own. Follow these steps:

1. *What:* State an opinion.

2. *Source:* Was this opinion based on your own experience or something you heard or read? Be specific about the circumstances in which you formulated it.

3. *Reasons:* Why is it a good opinion or a poor one? What tests of life and time has it survived? Have any experiences suggested that you need to alter this opinion?

The length of your essay should be two to three typed pages. It should take the form of an essay with a thesis. The first paragraph should cover step 1. The second or next two paragraphs should cover step 2. The main part of your essay (two to three paragraphs) should offer the support of reasons described in step 3. The final paragraph should sum up the whole.

▨ Third Option: A Short Essay Analyzing Three Opinions

Study your local newspaper's editorial pages to find some editorials and letters to the editor that interest you. Select three to analyze and photo-copy them. For each, paste your photocopy at the top of a page and then analyze the piece of writing by answering these questions:

1. Is the opinion a judgment, advice, an expression of taste or senti-ment, a belief, or a generalization? Support your answer in each case, providing an example and explaining it fully in these terms.

2. Is this opinion just a personal expression of taste or sentiment, or is it offered in an attempt to influence others? Explain fully.

3. Does the person giving this opinion show any special expertise regarding the subject or have any special qualifications? Explain what information you have and what is lacking.

4. Is the opinion backed up by evidence and sound reasoning? Show why or why not.

5. Does this opinion appear to be based on an objective study of the facts, or does it seem to be motivated by vested interests or a profit motive? Explain your judgment.

6. Would you call this a responsible opinion? Why or why not?

■ *Peer Review*

To follow up in class, form groups of two or more and read your papers aloud. Check one another's work to determine whether all the parameters given were observed. Evaluate the assignment according to the scoring box given below.

> ### *Scoring Sheet for Any One of the Three Opinion Essay Options*
>
> 1. The opinion or opinions are clearly stated. *10 points*
> 2. The support offered is adequate and relevant (or, in the case of option three, clearly stated and analyzed). *30 points*
> 3. Each parameter is followed and/or each question considered. *30 points*
> 4. The essay is clearly organized around a purpose to describe, state and defend, or analyze, depending on the option chosen. *20 points*
> 5. There are no distracting errors of punctuation, spelling, or sentence structure. *10 points*

Chapter Summary

1. Although the word *opinion* is a common one, it is just as commonly misunderstood, because the same word covers so many varieties of thoughts, ranging from expert judgments to expressions of sentiment or personal taste.

2. Opinions can be well substantiated or not. They can be based either on reasons or solely on whim, feelings, emotions, or prejudice.

3. Critical thinking requires that we recognize the difference between responsible and irresponsible opinion and that we distinguish statements based on evidence from statements based solely on feelings.

4. People enjoy expressing and reading opinions.

5. Expert opinion is based on an understanding of evidence and risks in a situation and is important and highly valued.

6. Public opinion polls can be used to *determine* public sentiment on social and political issues as well as to *manipulate* public sentiment.

7. Opinions should not be confused with facts.

Building Arguments
Opinions

Indians ought not to buy whiskey. It is hot in his heart for a little while, then it is gone; the Indian is cold, his head is sore, and he does not remember what he did when the poison was in him. Whiskey is hot poison for the Winnebagoes. My head is like the snow with age, I have seen the ruin that it has brought upon our nation, and I advise them to buy no more whiskey. (Decori, Winnebago chief, 1828)

Exercise

1. What is the principal claim made here?
2. What reasons are given to support it?

8. Arguments consist of supported opinions; the intent of an argument is to persuade.
9. In an essay, a statement of opinion can be the thesis or its principal claim.

Chapter Quiz

Rate each of the following statements as *true* or *false*. Justify each answer.

_____ 1. Expert opinion calculates the risk involved in bridging the gap between the known and the unknown for a particular situation.

_____ 2. Giving advice is not a way of offering an opinion.

_____ 3. The results of public opinion polls are equivalent to votes in elections.

_____ 4. Opinions in the form of judgments state what is right and wrong, bad and good.

_____ 5. Some opinions are based on generalizations, such as stereotypes, as in the statement "All Chinese look alike."

_____ 6. Responsible opinions are based on a careful examination of the evidence.

_____ 7. Opinions are the same as facts.

_____ 8. Gossip is opinion sharing without any requirement for substantiation.

_____ 9. Everyone is entitled to his or her own opinion because all opinions carry equal value.

_____ 10. Prevailing sentiment refers to popular opinion that changes with the times.

● R E A D I N G S ●

Children Deserve Veterinary Care Too

Barbara Ehrenreich

Barbara Ehrenreich is a columnist and essayist as well as the author of over 20 books. This essay was taken from her blog entry for July 26, 2007. Ask yourself as you read, what exactly is this author's opinion about health care?

This year, Americans will spend about $9.8 billion on health care for their pets, up from $7.2 billion five years ago. According to the *New York Times*, New York's leading pet hospitals offer CT scans, MRI's, dialysis units, and even a rehab clinic featuring an underwater treadmill, perhaps for the amphibians in one's household. A professor who consults to pet health facilities on communication issues justified these huge investments in pet health to me by pointing out that pets are, after all, "part of the family."

Well, there's another category that might reasonably be considered "part of the family." True, they are not the ideal companions for the busy young professional: It can take two to three years to housebreak them; their standards of personal hygiene are lamentably low, at least compared to cats; and large numbers of them cannot learn to "sit" without the aid of Ritalin.

I'm talking about children, of course, and while I can understand why many people would not want one of these hairless and often incontinent bipeds in their homes, it is important to point out that they can provide considerable gratification. There's a three-year-old in my life, for example, who gives me many hours a week of playful distraction from the pressures of work. No matter how stressed I am, she can brighten my mood with her quavering renditions of the ABC song or "Twinkle, Twinkle, Little Star."

She has health insurance, as it turns out, and generally high quality care. But you can never be too sure. So I went to the website of VPI Pet Insurance, one of the nation's largest animal companion health insurers, to see what kind of a policy I could get for her. In the application form, I listed her as a three-year-old mixed breed dog—a description made somewhat plausible by the fact that her first words, spoken at the remarkable age of 10 months, were "ruf ruf" and "doggie outside." When I completed the form and clicked to get a quote I was amazed to see that I get her a "premium" policy for a mere $33 a month.

5   But, you may be wondering, could a veterinarian handle common children's ills? On the hopeful side, let me cite the case, reported in June by Bob Herbert of the *New York Times*, of Diamonte Driver, a 12-year-old boy who died recently from an abscessed tooth because he had no insurance and his mother could not afford $80 to have the tooth pulled. Could a vet have handled this problem? Yes, absolutely.

Or there's the case of 14-year-old Devante Johnson, also reported by Herbert, who died when his health insurance ran out in the middle of treatment for kidney cancer. I don't know exactly what kind of treatment he was getting, but I suspect that the $1.25 million linear accelerator for radiation therapy available at one of New York's leading pet hospitals might have helped. The *Times* article also mentions a mixed breed named Bullwinkle who consumed $7000 worth of chemotherapy before passing on to his reward. Surely Devante could have benefited from the same kind of high quality pet care, delivered at a local upscale animal hospital.

It may seem callous to focus on children when so many pets go uninsured and without access to CT-scans or underwater treadmills. But in many ways, children stack up well compared to common pets. They can shed real tears, like Vietnamese pot-bellied pigs. They can talk as well as many of the larger birds, or at least mimic human speech. And if you invest enough time in their care and feeding, they will jump all over you when you arrive at the door, yipping and covering your face with drool.

The Senate Finance Committee has approved a bill that would expand state health insurance cover for children (S-CHIP) to include 3.2 million kids who are not now covered (but leaving about 6 million still uncovered.) Bush has promised to veto this bill, on the grounds that government should not be involved in health coverage. If Bush does veto the bill, the fallback demand should be: *Open up pet health insurance to all American children now!* Though even as I say this, I worry that the president will counter by proposing to extend euthanasia services to children who happen to fall ill.

● ● ●

Study/Writing/Discussion Questions

1. Outline the reasoning Ehrenreich uses to support her proposal.
2. Using at least two dictionaries, write down your own definitions of the words *irony* and *satire*.

3. At what point in this essay did you realize that Ehrenreich might not really be advocating veterinary insurance for children but have some other objective in mind? What would that objective be?

4. Would you say that she was writing satire?

5. Jonathan Swift was the most famous satirist to write in the English language. His essay, "A Modest Proposal," written in 1729, can be found online. Can you see any similarities between his style, values, and objectives and those of Barbara Ehrenreich?

Facing Up to Failure

William Ecenbarger

William Ecenbarger is a Pulitzer award–winning journalist, international correspondent, and travel writer. This essay first appeared in the Los Angeles Times *in 2005.*

It was a numbingly familiar Super Bowl postgame show: seemingly endless coverage of the victorious New England Patriots afire with testosterone-fueled, fist-in-the-air, back-thumping jubilation and a fleeting, almost subliminal shot of an Eagles player, slumped under a yoke of grief, biting his lips to fight back the tears. The TV director must have thought better of it, for he quickly switched back to the Patriots and their 300-watt, gargoyle smiles. We saw no more of the losers.

But how fascinating it would have been to stay with them—any fool can win, it's losing that's the challenge. Moreover, there's a lot to be said for failure. It is so much more interesting than success. Success goes to the head, but losing goes to the heart.

After all, who among us has never lost—in a job, in a relationship, on the tennis court? Losing is part of the price of life. It is the human condition, all of us born to sorrow. Born losers.

It begins early. Little League, science fairs, spelling bees. Later there are pink slips, unrequited love and, finally, death. Losing is a necessary part of competing. For every winner, there is at least one, and usually many more, losers. Losing is one of life's constant companions, ever unwelcome, ever there. The Rolling Stones had it right—you can't always get what you want.

5   Nevertheless, losing is a taboo in our society. The ultimate put-down is "loser," and failure is the ultimate f-word. Hundreds of books have been written on how to win; there are scarcely any on how to lose.

We forget that losers changed the world. Columbus missed his target by thousands of miles. Thomas Edison had most of his inventing triumphs before the age of 40, and in his later years he rolled up an ever-increasing number of failures. Mozart died impoverished and was buried in the pauper's section of the cemetery. Most of the first edition of "Walden" was remaindered into Thoreau's personal library. Churchill distracted himself from defeat with painting, writing, gardening, and breeding butterflies.

Winner worship is embedded early. Children returning from games are asked whether they won or lost, when they should be asked whether they had fun, or asked nothing at all. Parents often play games with their children and allow them to win, ill-preparing them for the game of life. Some educators feel that flunking a class is so detrimental to self-esteem that they move children along to the next grade and to bigger failures to come.

Nowhere is winner worship and loser-loathing more evident than in sports (Vince Lombardi, Leo Durocher and Billy Martin all had bad things to say about losers) or in that other great arena: politics. Few losers suffer more acutely than defeated candidates. Jimmy Carter was stunned by his landslide 1980 loss to Ronald Reagan, and for about five years he all but vanished from the national political scene. He took no part in the 1984 presidential campaign—even though his former vice president, Walter Mondale, was running against Reagan. Several years after he too was swamped by Reagan, Mondale was asked how long it took to recover. "I'll let you know when the grieving ends," Mondale said.

We could pay a terrible price for our loser-loathing. We are a country founded by people who faced down death to start anew, but we could be reduced to wimphood. What better way to avoid losing than to never enter the fray? Americans still revere the image of the lone cowboy, riding off into the sunset in search of his destiny. But how many of us are timid couch potatoes, spectators at the game of life, content to see the spotlight on the winning team, to forget about the other side of every zero-sum transaction?

10   Americans need to confront their losers and their losses. Something as universal as failure deserves our attention. It has its positive side. For one thing, you're among friends. Winning isn't always worth its weight in blue ribbons, and losing can be positive and ennobling if it compels us to examine why we lost. After all, it is the way we learn and the way we live.

Used with permission of William Ecenbarger.

•   •   •

Study/Writing/Discussion Questions

1. Does one sentence in this essay best sum up the author's thesis or main point? If not, how would you put his main idea into your own words?

2. Make an outline of this essay that shows how each paragraph of the essay supports, explains, or defends the thesis.

3. How does this essay concern itself with the connotation of the word *losing?*

4. After reading the essay, did you begin to think of winning and losing in a new way? Explain why or why not.

Advanced Optional Writing Assignment

Consult some newspapers or online sources for current public opinion polls. Select one for analysis or two for analysis and comparison using the questions given in this chapter for rating polls. Did you conclude it was a scientific poll or a pseudo poll? Or did you have a scientific poll to compare with a pseudo poll? State your conclusion as a thesis and then support your argument with your findings. Attach your copy or copies of the poll to your paper.

CHAPTER 7

Evaluations:
What's Judged?

Used with permission of David Cohen.

JUNE 24th + 25th
SAT. + SUN.
3-FAMILY
USELESS CRAP
SALE

©2000 DAVID COHEN

This is a chapter about one variety of opinion called **evaluations.** They can be baldly honest, as in this cartoon, or hidden and manipulative. Their basis can be explicit or vague criteria, clear or vague feelings. Their effects are powerful. When we mistake them for facts or are influenced by them unawares, we get into trouble. This chapter teaches how to both recognize and detach from evaluations.

DISCOVERY EXERCISES

Both Discovery Exercises can be studied either alone or with a partner in preparation for class discussion.

■ *Defining* Evaluate

First, study the etymology of the word *evaluate*. What do its prefix and root mean? Then, write out definitions of the following words:

1. Judge
2. Appraise
3. Estimate
4. Value
5. Evaluate

Based on your work, answer these questions either in writing or in class:

1. What does *evaluate* mean?
2. Is an evaluation an inference?
3. Is an evaluation an opinion?
4. Can an evaluation be based on an assumption?

■ *Recognizing Evaluative Words*

Circle the words in the following passages that express evaluations that pass judgments on the worth of something. Note whether any evidence or reasons are given to support the evaluations.

A reminder before you begin: These Discovery Exercises are not tests in which you are expected to know all the answers; they are meant only to help you acknowledge what you already know and to inspire you to learn more.

1. "Cyclo-cross has got an old-school feel to it, a wacky, super-fun, rad, community feel." (Rachael Lloyd, *San Francisco Chronicle*, November 28, 2004)
2. "It is possible that McCain, because of his boiling moralism and bottomless reservoir of certitudes, is not suited for the presidency." (George Will, *Washington Post*, September 23, 2008).
3. "Florida's system for restoring civil rights to ex-felons is unjust, capricious and unsustainable. It should be scrapped." (Debbie Cenziper and Jason Grotto, *The Miami Herald,* June 12, 2005)

4. *SIGNS.* "The number 1 Movie in America Again. . . and Again! One of the best movies of the year, engrossing, terrifying, and intelligent. A Very Scary Movie. Spooky. Suspenseful. A Wonderful Movie! A Dazzling White Knuckler! Two Thumbs Up! Thrilling, Frightening!" (Advertisement)

5. "*Quintuplets*, a moronic dull-fest that is, in turns, physically painful to watch and jaw-droppingly, stupendously stupid." (Tim Goodman, sitcom review, *San Francisco Chronicle*, June 16, 2004)

On Evaluations

Our values shape our ideals, decisions, and judgments.

> **Evaluate** comes from the Latin *ex* = from, and *valere* = to be strong, to be of value. To evaluate, then, is (1) to determine or fix the value or worth of something or (2) to examine and judge, appraise, estimate.

SIPRESS

Something really bad has happened. Details at eleven.

It takes some hard thinking to evaluate, appraise, and estimate value. We make comparisons and measure them against ideals, yet our standards may be conscious or unconscious. When we do "comparison shopping," we evaluate. We decide what car to buy, what apartment to rent, what school to attend. Using criteria that depend upon our needs, values, and priorities, we decide what candidates to vote for, what beliefs to hold, what friends to spend time with, what movies to attend, what books to read. In addition, our lives are affected by the evaluations of others: the teacher who assigns grades, the boss who hires or fires us, the friends who give or withhold their loyalty. Thus, given the effects of evaluations on our lives, it can be worthwhile to take time to learn how to make the evaluating process more skilled and conscious.

Premature Evaluations

> Our minds tend to evaluate situations before we have had the time to look them over.

If a stranger were to grab your arms and throw you down to the sidewalk, you would immediately think that this person was a thug. But suppose this person was protecting you from being hit by a swerving car? All of a sudden the label "thug" would disappear as you looked up into the face of a new friend. Your first evaluation was understandable, but it turned out to be premature and unfair. Here is another example:

> ALEX: "I knew before I spoke to him that he was too young for the job."
> COREY: "How do you know he is too young for the job?"
> ALEX: "Well, he has acne, for one thing . . . Okay, okay, I'll give him an interview."

Sometimes an evaluator may not be that willing to concede the possibility of prejudice.

> JULIA: "I just can't go out with someone who looks like a *nerd*."
> JANE: "What do you mean by a nerd?"
> JULIA: "You know—a *NERD!*"

Here Julia keeps repeating her evaluation as though it were a fact. A nerd is a nerd is a nerd. She commits the *fallacy of circular reasoning*. (We will learn more about this fallacy in Chapter 10.) It is more common than uncommon for evaluations to be passed off as facts: "He's a genius." "She's a screwball." "He's a scumbag."

Discussion Break Questions

Premature evaluations are snap judgments made before the situation has been adequately studied. Look at the statements below. What questions would you ask the evaluator in each case?

1. Your boyfriend doesn't have a job? He must be a loser.
2. She drives a dirty old clunker. We'd better not take her in as a housemate.
3. Those who share music files are thieves.

Evaluations Are Not Facts

> Critical thinkers try to be fair in their use of evaluations. They don't mistake evaluative words for facts.

JEANIE: Brad Pitt has really gone downhill. That's just a fact!

Suzy: Why do you say that?

JEANIE: Did you see the role he played in *Burn After Reading*? That pompadour haircut with the peroxide streak? And that stupid look on his face!

Suzy: So an actor is going downhill when he plays the role of a loser?

JEANIE: Well, you are right. I only meant that his playing this role shattered my fantasies about him. That is the fact.

In this example Jeanie is showing how our minds tend to work: the evaluation pops up first strong and clear, while the basis for the evaluation may take a little effort to uncover.

Yet this human tendency to evaluate first and think afterwards has a survival function. If we see a car headed toward us in the same lane, the only apt thought is danger! Without having to think, we can swerve to avoid an accident. Yet afterwards, other evaluations might come to mind, such as calling the other driver an idiot. Yet although name-calling can let off the steam of anger, it can also lead to more trouble and confusion.

Thus our innate tendency to rush to judgment might save our lives in some situations but endanger us in others.

Suppose you go to a lot of effort to persuade your brother to enroll in college; he finally agrees to take one English course. Five weeks into the semester, he drops his English class. He tells you he can't stand the instructor. When you question him, he says the instructor is a phony: he wears tweed jackets and horn-rimmed glasses. But as you question him further, he confesses his disappointment with his progress in class. If he had received the help he needed to feel successful, perhaps he would not have cared how the instructor dressed.

To think critically, we need to be aware of how feelings influence evaluations and result in judgments that may not be fair. It is for this reason that most countries have developed courts of law for those who cannot settle their own disagreements. Fair judgments, or evaluations, are achieved by set procedures that require emotions to be controlled and judgments suspended until all testimony has been heard and all evidence considered. Finally, it must be said that although our human tendency to rush to judgment can make it very difficult for us to be fair, nevertheless we still must continuously evaluate our experiences in order to survive.

Discussion Break Questions

1. Share some examples of situations in which you changed your initial evaluation from positive to negative or vice versa. Explain how this occurred.

2. Explain, in your own words, why it is so difficult for us to make fair evaluations.

3. Share some examples of evaluations that you or others made that turned out to be "spot on."

Expectations Influence Evaluations

Expectations influence our perceptions as well as our evaluations.

Psychologist John Enright tells the following story that illustrates the influence of expectations on our perceptions as well as our evaluations.

This morning I had a longing for some orange juice. I knew there must be some in the freezer since my roommate went shopping yesterday. I took an orange-labeled can out of the freezer and made myself a glass; as I did so, I noticed that it was a little darker than usual, but I concluded that it was just a different variety of orange or a different mix of rind and juice. Then when I tasted it, it was just awful. I spit it out in the sink and really made a mess of things, but I was sure that it was spoiled, and I didn't want to make myself sick. Then I decided that I might as well take it back to the grocer's and get our money back. I fished the can out of the garbage and looked at the label. To my surprise it said "Tangerine Juice." I couldn't believe it. I tasted some of the juice left in the glass and . . . *it was good tangerine juice!*

Discussion Break Questions

1. Neither the liquid nor the taste buds of the person changed. How can you explain what happened?
2. What information was missing in the first evaluation?
3. Describe an instance in which expectations influenced your perceptions and evaluations.

Recognizing Evaluations in Word Connotations

Word connotations can be manipulative evaluations.

Evaluations are opinions that can be openly or covertly expressed. Compare these two statements:

- I believe electric cars are impractical because they can't be driven on the freeway at high speeds and they can only be driven a limited number of miles before needing a recharge.
- Electric cars are kiddy-cars for environmental Puritans.

The first example is an up-front evaluation that clearly expresses a personal opinion. It allows us to agree or disagree. The second example is a covert opinion because it evaluates through a choice of words with negative connotations: "kiddy-cars" and "environmental Puritans." It does not invite us to agree or disagree because it implies that these words represent facts.

Word connotations were introduced in Chapter 2. At that time we were studying how to select words with connotations appropriate for what we wanted to communicate. In this chapter we are focusing on the ways in which word connotations carry evaluations that influence our feelings, and thus the formation of our opinions. Sometimes these connotations are so subtle as to influence us unawares. Let's look now at some simple word choices that carry positive or negative word connotations.

Discussion Break Questions

1. Show how the connotations of the following words differ by writing a plus, minus, or zero beside each word that carries a positive, negative, or neutral connotation. Then answer the questions that follow, either in writing or with your neighbor in class.

Girl	Chick	Hot babe	Bitch	Slut
Guy	Dude	Stud	Boy	Hottie

Alcoholic	Alchy	Wino	Dipso
Unintelligent	Airhead	Bubblehead	Stupid

2. Can anyone sum up another's identity through one evaluative word?

3. If you call me an "airhead," does that sum up my identity or does it only represent your evaluation?

DISCOVERY EXERCISE

■ *Recognizing Evaluative Words' Persuasive Powers*

Underline the words in the following passages that contain connotations that could influence feelings, and thus opinion as well.

1. Editor: Your editorial "Added Peril at the Border" criticizes the Minuteman Project for organizing to help our government stop the massive influx of illegal aliens into our country from Mexico. You are wrong in characterizing the Minutemen as vigilantes and extremists. They are just good citizens trying to help our government protect its borders. (Adapted from a letter to the San Francisco Chronicle, April 6, 2005)

2. Green is the new red. When Communism failed, the Left turned to environmentalism which is anti-American and anti-capitalist.

3. "The Karl-Rovian, Swift-Boatian school of smear politics relies on this lag time to discombobulate any real political debate and try to slip their candidates into office on nonsense. Sadly, we're seeing another such effort this year by John McCain and his hatchetmen." (Jim Hightower, "Fight the Smears," September 19, 2008, http://www.jimhightower.com)

4. "Sarah Palin clearly knows nothing and offers only rubbery expressions and glib repetitions, for all the world like a rasping myna bird, of a stream of memorized talking points . . ." (Juan Cole, *"The Non-Debate,"* October 3, 2008, http://www.juancole.com)

Skilled Use of Evaluations

An expert is a person with a reputation for making skilled evaluations.

So far in this chapter we have looked mainly at examples of premature or manipulative evaluations; however, that does not mean that evaluations are wrong. On the contrary, skilled evaluations are highly important and often prized achievements. Experts in any profession, such as law or medicine, are highly paid for their evaluation skills. We visit a physician to get a diagnosis, recommended treatments, and estimates of the time needed for recovery. We go to an attorney to find out whether or not there might be a chance of winning a case. We read editorials in newspapers because we respect editors' evaluations of public issues. We read film, book, art, and music reviews to learn from the reviewers' expertise.

The following reading is an excerpt from a review written by a skilled evaluator, the journalist Vicki Haddock. In this article she offers (1) a movie review, (2) an evaluation of the public response to an Oscar-winning film, and (3) an evaluation of the sport of boxing.

• R E A D I N G •

Million Dollar Brutality

Boxing's violence is unrelenting and, in movies, unremarkable.

Vicki Haddock

What a curious comment on humanity it is that the Oscar-winning best picture *Million Dollar Baby* has ignited fierce debate outside the ring, but not about the subject at its core: professional boxing.

Among inherently treacherous sports, boxing is unique—the only one in which a contestant achieves the pinnacle of success by pummeling an opponent into a state of unconsciousness. It encourages actions that would warrant assault charges if they occurred on the street.

In the multimillion dollar sport of boxing, the violence is unvarnished. There is no ball, no net, no goal lines. Just fists. One database lists 1,200 fighters killed in matches worldwide, and many pro boxers who do survive must cope with some degree of brain damage.

Boxer Mike Tyson has been quoted describing his technique: "I try to catch my opponent on the tip of his nose because I try to punch the bone into his brain."

5   The very premise of boxing is barbaric to the American Medical Association and its counterparts in dozens of other countries. They have clamored, in vain, for a ban on pro and amateur boxing.

The celluloid verdict about the sport by *Million Dollar Baby* director Clint Eastwood is an enigma. Some moviegoers see his film as an unmistakable condemnation of the business: It ultimately renders a spunky prize fighter a helpless quadriplegic. Yet the film also imbues boxing with nobility. Along with figurative sweat and spattering blood, the audience is hit with a string of rationalizations: "Boxing is about respect—getting it for yourself and taking it away from the other guy." Also "The magic of boxing is fighting beyond endurance, through cracked ribs and detached retinas. The magic of risking everything for a dream that no one sees but you."

More significantly, *Million Dollar Baby* seems to absolve the fighter's trainer/manager of blame. The God-like narrator Morgan Freeman reassures us, basso profundo, that the fighter was disabled doing what she *loved* to do.

© *San Francisco Chronicle*. Reprinted by permission.

● ● ●

Study/Writing/Discussion Questions

1. What evaluations does the author offer in her title and subtitle?
2. How does the author open this essay by finding irony in two situations?
3. What three facts does she offer to support her evaluation of boxing as a brutal and violent sport?
4. What contradictory evaluations does she describe in the last two paragraphs of this review?

Propaganda and Hidden Evaluations

The best defense against propaganda is to stay conscious.

Propaganda

Propaganda comes from the Latin *propagare*, meaning to propagate, or breed. The word now has two meanings: (1) to publicize or promote something and (2) to publicize or promote something in a dishonest and manipulative way to further the propagator's hidden aims. Propaganda in this sense uses techniques calculated to arouse such emotions as prejudice, fear, and hatred through the use of evaluative language, slogans, symbols, music, suggestive images, the hypnotic repetition of false ideas, the spreading of false rumors, the omission and distortion of vital information, and the invention of misinformation.

The word **propaganda** means the manipulation of public opinion for the benefit of the propagator. One thing is certain about propaganda: it shows no respect for truth and rational argument. Instead, psychologically sophisticated maneuvers are used to affect the unconscious mind and sway emotions toward a predetermined purpose.

The influence of propaganda is not as distant as an airplane dropping pamphlets on the enemy, but as close as your television set or the checkout stand in your neighborhood supermarket. While you are waiting your turn in line, bored and tired, even the magazine rack's accounts of lurid gossip and familiar celebrities can have their appeal. Consider these magazine headlines:

Thugs Mourn the Death of Their Dictator

Senator X Grovels for Votes

The First Lady, Our Comforter in Times of War

In each case, evaluations offer to do our thinking for us. Advertisers also prefer to persuade us into accepting their own evaluations of their products. One useful technique is just to keep repeating the desired evaluative words. "Reach for aspirin for relief, aspirin for relief, for relief. Reach for aspirin for relief whenever you have those awful headaches, those awful headaches. Aspirin for relief." This technique has the additional advantage of not requiring evidence. It is only necessary to get the message imprinted in the readers' or viewers' brains within the few seconds required to turn a page or glance at a TV commercial.

"Tiggerrific! What a gem! A fun, heart warming story for the whole family. A gem of a movie! The Tigger Movie. What a gem!"

In order to be most effective, propaganda should not be easily recognizable. Early attempts at propaganda, as seen in old World War II movies, seem ludicrous to us now. Today propaganda can entice our attention with the latest styles in entertainment. It holds our eyes and touches our feelings with colorful, stirring, even frightening images. It provides us with well-dressed experts or authority figures who tell us what we should know, who comfort us with reassurances that they are taking the best care of our interests. Today's propaganda is created by highly sophisticated public relations firms. Celebrities and public figures hire them to shape their images, tell them how to dress, write their speeches, prepare them for talking to the press, plant articles about them in the newspapers, arrange for talk show appearances. At present, public relations firms are hired routinely by organizations wishing to influence the larger American public. They include not only large corporations, but also the Catholic Church, the Pentagon, and foreign governments such as those of Kuwait and Saudi Arabia. At present, PR advisors are even hired to plan and carry out publicity campaigns for U.S. presidents that will influence public perceptions, gain consent, and thus advance the policies of their administrations.

Modern public relations firms have a sophisticated knowledge of human psychology. They play on our dreams and desires, our secret unconscious wishes, and even our fatigue and lethargy. The television viewer who lies down on his sofa to "relax" at the end of a hard day is especially prone to manipulation. According to the book *The Plug-In Drug* (by Marie Winn, Bantam, 1978), television itself induces an immediate trance state in viewers, regardless of the content shown. Perhaps you have become aware of this phenomenon yourself when you found you had to make an extreme effort to get up out of your chair and turn the television off. The next day you might not even wake up to the realization that you had been hypnotized to reach for that bottle of aspirin on the grocery shelf or cast a vote for that sincere-looking politician. Thinking critically requires that we simply

Building Arguments
Evaluations

Yet, while there were whites who preferred to live like Indians, there were few, if any, Indians who regarded a completely civilized form of living as superior to their own way of life. This is true even of Indian children who were educated in the schools of the white colonists and who were later permitted to return to their own people. With the opportunity of choosing between the two ways of life, they rarely cast their lot with civilization.

The reason for this decision was because the Indian was convinced that the white man's style of life, with its lack of freedom; innumerable laws and taxes; extremes of wealth and poverty; snobbish class divisions; hypocritical customs; private ownership of land; pent-up communities; uncomfortable clothing; many diseases; slavery to money and other false standards, could not possibly bring as much real happiness as their own ways of doing. The great mass of white people and the great mass of Indians realized that their two ways of life were directly opposed. Each race looked upon the other as inferior; neither felt inclined to adopt the ways of the other; and that is why the Indians and the whites could not get along together. (Alexander Henry, American trader, 1764)

Exercise

1. What is the principal claim made in the first paragraph?
2. What behavior is cited to support this claim?
3. What characteristics of the white man did the Indians find objectionable?
4. What do these evaluations tell us about the values of the Indians?

wake up. If you want to retain the power of making your own choices, you need to learn to recognize propaganda strategies. In short, you have to continuously reclaim the right to think for yourself.

Short Discussion Break Questions

1. What images do you remember most from commercial advertisements?
2. What words, or advertisement jingles, stay in your mind?
3. What advertised products do you buy? Do you think you were hypnotized?

Chapter Summary

1. Evaluations make judgments about worth on the basis of standards that may be conscious or unconscious.
2. Evaluations can help us react quickly to situations in which our survival is at stake. But this same tendency to evaluate first instead of last may be problematic when we don't reexamine our evidence to make sure our evaluation is warranted.
3. Evaluations are not facts. Factual reports keep the distinction between facts and evaluations clear.
4. Premature evaluations are hasty evaluations that contain unexamined or faulty support.
5. Feelings and expectations affect both our perceptions and our evaluations.
6. All of us need to learn how to make fair and sound evaluations because they affect our lives constantly. Experts are those who have a reputation for offering skilled and reliable evaluations.
7. Connotative words convey evaluations that can be used to sway our opinions. When we think critically, we recognize how these connotations affect our feelings so that we can choose or not choose to accept the opinions they contain.
8. Evaluations are used in advertising and journalism to persuade us, sometimes hypnotically, to make positive associations with products and purchase them.
9. Critical thinking requires that we stay alert to manipulative advertising techniques that are most effective when we can be enticed to enter into a trance state.

10. Propaganda uses many sophisticated manipulative techniques of persuasion. One of these is the use of hidden evaluations. A critical thinker knows how to recognize and detach from the influence of propaganda.

Chapter Quiz

Rate the following statements as *true* or *false*. Give an example to substantiate your answer in each case.

T   1. Evaluations are not facts but judgments based on conscious or unconscious standards.

T   2. Premature evaluations can result from hasty observing and thinking.

T   3. Opinion can be influenced unawares by the use of highly connotative words.

F   4. Evaluations should never be used in writing reviews, such as of films and books.

T   5. Repeating evaluations, as is done in advertising, can serve as a hypnotic technique.

T   6. A critical thinker notices when evaluations are substituted for facts, information, and evidence.

T   7. Prior expectations influence perceptions and our evaluation of these perceptions.

T   8. Our first reactions, before we have had time to examine the evidence, are always the most reliable.

T   9. To evaluate wisely, we need to observe and think carefully while also being clear about our standards.

T   10. Many advertisements want us to let them do the evaluating for us.

Composition Writing Application

■ First Option: Observing and Analyzing Evaluations in Advertisements

Select two printed advertisements of the same product or type of product and make a list of all the evaluative words used. Also consider the images that accompany these words and how the two interact to persuade you to buy this product. Photocopy the ads to hand in with your paper, or attach the originals. Write at least a one-page analysis of each advertisement; then compare the ads to one another in a final page. Write a summary at the end that states your thesis.

In your one-page analysis of each ad, go over every major evaluative word you have listed and thoroughly discuss both its literal and connotative (associative) meanings. Notice what appeals these words carry to make you want to buy the product. Do the words make a pattern of evaluation that conveys a subliminal message? Is one key or primary evaluation repeated a lot, reinforced by secondary or lesser evaluations?

In your conclusion, rate each ad for its trickery or honesty and effectiveness.

In review, the parameters are:

1. *Topic:* Comparison of the use of evaluative language and imagery in two advertisements of the same or related products. The original ads, or photocopies of them, should be attached.
2. *Method:* Descriptive analysis using explosion, comparison, and evaluation.
3. *Length:* Three typed pages.
4. The summary at the end states your conclusion as a thesis.

■ Second Option: Writing a Critical Review

Write a review that evaluates a film, music album, or concert. Be conscious of your standards for evaluation. Try working with just three criteria that you discuss at the beginning, such as exciting, instructive, and entertaining. Be sure to define each one. Describe the strengths of the work as well as weaknesses.

Make this into a short essay of about three pages. Let your thesis be your recommendation for (or against) buying or going to see this work. In review, the parameters are:

1. *Topic:* A review of a film, music album, or concert.
2. *Method:* A summary and evaluation of an event or product on the basis of three criteria. The thesis states your recommendation as a reviewer.
3. *Length:* Three typed pages.

Scoring for Evaluative Words in Advertising or a Critical Review

1. Directions followed for choice of comparison of two advertisements or the writing of a review. *25 points*
2. Method directions followed for descriptive analysis, or a summary and evaluation in the review on the basis of three explicit criteria. *30 points*
3. Length of three typed pages. *20 points*
4. Summary states thesis. *15 points*
5. No distracting errors of spelling, punctuation, or sentence structure. *10 points*

• R E A D I N G S •

Rachel Carson and *Silent Spring*

Al Gore

Al Gore has had many careers, including Vice President of the United States from 1993–2001. He is also well known for his writings on critical thinking, The Assault on Reason *(2008), and for his critiques of environmental issues, including such books as* Earth in Balance *(1992) and the book and film* An Inconvenient Truth *(2006). This reading is an excerpt taken from his Introduction to* Courage for the Earth *edited by Peter Matthiessen (2007).*

In 1962, when *Silent Spring* was first published, "environment" was not even an entry in the vocabulary of public policy. In a few cities, especially Los Angeles, smog had become a cause of concern, albeit more because of its appearance than because of its threat to public health. Conservation—the precursor of environmentalism—had been mentioned during the 1960 Democratic and Republican conventions, but only in passing and almost entirely in the context of national parks and natural resources. And except for a few scattered entries in largely inaccessible scientific journals, there was virtually no public dialogue about the growing, invisible dangers of DDT and other pesticides and chemicals. *Silent Spring* came as a cry in the wilderness, a deeply felt, thoroughly researched, and brilliantly written argument that changed the course of history. Without this book, the environmental movement might have been long delayed or never have developed at all.

Not surprisingly, both the book and its author, who had once worked as a marine biologist for the Fish and Wildlife Service, met with considerable resistance from those who were profiting from pollution. Major chemical companies tried to suppress *Silent Spring*, and when excerpts appeared in *The New Yorker*, a chorus of voices immediately accused Carson of being hysterical and extremist—charges still heard today whenever anyone questions those whose financial well-being depends on maintaining the environmental status quo. (Having been labeled "Ozone Man" during the 1992 presidential campaign, a name that was probably not intended as a compliment but that I wore as a badge of honor, I am aware that raising these issues invariably inspires a fierce—and sometimes foolish—reaction.) By the time the book became widely available, the forces arrayed against its author were formidable.

The attack on Rachel Carson has been compared to the bitter assault on Charles Darwin when he published *The Origin of Species*. Moreover, because Carson was a woman, much of the criticism directed at her played on stereotypes of her sex. Calling her "hysterical" fit the bill exactly. *Time* magazine added the charge that she had used "emotion-fanning words." She was dismissed by others as "a priestess of nature." Her credibility as a scientist was attacked as well: opponents financed the production of propaganda that supposedly refuted her work. It was all part of an intense, well-financed negative campaign, not against a political candidate but against a book and its author.

Carson brought two decisive strengths to this battle: a scrupulous respect for the truth and a remarkable degree of personal courage. She had checked and rechecked every paragraph in *Silent Spring*, and the passing years have revealed that her warnings were, if anything, understated. And her courage, which matched her vision, went far beyond her willingness to disturb an entrenched and profitable industry. While writing *Silent Spring*, she endured a radical mastectomy and then radiation treatment. Two years after the book's publication, she died, of breast cancer. Ironically, new research points strongly to a link between this disease and exposure to toxic chemicals. So in a sense, Carson was literally writing for her life.

5   She was also writing against the grain of an orthodoxy rooted in the earliest days of the scientific revolution: that man (and of course this meant the male of our species) was properly the center and the master of all things, and that scientific history was primarily the story of his dominion—ultimately, it was hoped, to a nearly absolute state. When a woman dared to challenge this orthodoxy, one of its prominent defenders, Robert White Stevens, replied in terms that now sound not only arrogant but as quaint as the flat-earth theory: "The crux, the fulcrum over which the argument chiefly rests, is that Miss Carson maintains that the balance of nature is a major force in the survival of man, whereas the modern chemist, the modern biologist and scientist, believes that man is steadily controlling nature."

The very absurdity of that world view from today's perspective indicates how revolutionary Rachel Carson was. Assaults from corporate interests were to be expected, but even the American Medical Association weighed in on the chemical companies' side. The man who discovered the insecticidal properties of DDT had, after all, been awarded the Nobel Prize.

But *Silent Spring* could not be stifled. Solutions to the problems it raised weren't immediate, but the book itself achieved enormous popularity and broad public support. In addition to presenting a convincing case, Carson had won both financial independence and public credibility with two previous bestsellers, *The Sea Around Us* and *The Edge of the Sea*. Also, *Silent Spring* was published in the early years of a decade that was anything but silent, a decade when Americans were perhaps far readier than they had been to hear and heed the book's message. In a sense, the woman and the moment came together.

Eventually, both the government and the public became involved—not just those who read the book, but those who read the news or watched television. As sales of *Silent Spring* passed the half-million mark, *CBS Reports* scheduled an hour-long program about it, and the network went ahead with the broadcast even when two major corporate sponsors withdrew their support. President Kennedy discussed the book at a press conference and appointed a special panel to examine its conclusions. When the panel reported its findings, its paper was an indictment of corporate and bureaucratic indifference and a validation of Carson's warnings about the potential hazards of pesticides. Soon thereafter, Congress began holding hearings and the first grassroots environmental organizations were formed.

Silent Spring planted the seeds of a new activism that has grown into one of the great popular forces of all time. When Rachel Carson died, in the spring of 1964, it was becoming clear that her voice would never be silenced. She had awakened not only our nation but the world. The publication of *Silent Spring* can properly be seen as the beginning of the modern environmental movement.

Used with permission of Al Gore and The Wylie Agency, Inc.

• • •

Study/Writing/Discussion Questions

1. In his opening paragraph, how does Al Gore rate Rachel Carson's achievement?

2. What hardships did she have to overcome in order to get her book written and published?

3. In the fifth paragraph, what basic orthodox belief did she bring into question? Why does this idea seem quaint to us now?

4. What groups opposed her and why?

5. What turned the tide in support for her?

6. Explain how, for you, Rachel Carson was or was not a model of a critical thinker.

How Films Feed the Mind

Bill Swanson

Before his untimely death in 2007, Bill Swanson was a textbook author and instructor of humanities, writing, and film at South Puget Sound Community College in Olympia, Washington. This reading is an excerpt taken from an essay titled "How Films Feed the Mind or When I'm Hungry, I Don't Want to Eat Candy." Notice as you read how he evaluates what he calls "Comfort Zone films." What are his criticisms of these films? What are his standards?

. . . If you think of a film as a purely imaginary experience, as a dream created by all the people listed in the credits, then the movie viewer is someone who pays money to inhabit someone else's dream in order to make sense out of it. When we watch a movie, we dream someone else's dream just for a little while. We accept the illusion that we are looking at the real world. We forget, as soon as the lights go down, that we are sitting in a theatre looking at lights and shadows projected on a screen. The real world—the actual world we live in—resides outside the theatre. Audiences experience the *reel* world of fabricated illusions dancing around on a screen acccompanied by dialogue and music. Films thus become an interior, psychological experience. They resemble the real world, but they are only analogies for the real world that condense time and experience into a two-hour story. During this time anyting can happen. It could be anything, from *Beauty and the Beast* to *A Beautiful Mind*. Whatever it is, we just accept it as real and participate in it by identifying with the characters and the actions they take.

Filmmakers have various motives for making films because filmmaking is both an art form and a business. Certain films like *Star Wars* or *Titanic* are blockbusters because they create an easily accessible world with fantasies that appeal to almost any audience. They make it easy to get involved with the story because they simplify human experience into familiar categories of good and evil, and love and death. Films that make it easy for audiences to participate are more immediately entertaining than films that ask audiences to stretch a bit and experience something new and unfamiliar. Every person has a Comfort Zone within which are contained their unquestioned assumptions about the world, their basic beliefs, their familiar ways of thinking about what is natural or normal or right. Films that reinforce the borders of the Comfort Zone are entertaining. They are "feel good" movies because they make viewers feel more comfortable about themselves and what they believe. Filmmakers who make Comfort Zone films are often rewarded by vast profits.

For examples of Comfort Zone films, here is a list of the "Top Ten Grossing Films World Wide" as rated by the Internet Movie Database for the years between 1993 and 2004:

1. *Titanic* 1997
2. *Lord of the Rings: The Return of the King* 2003
3. *Harry Potter and the Sorcerer's Stone* 2001
4. *Star Wars: Episode 1: The Phantom Menace* 1999
5. *The Lord of the Rings: The Two Towers* 2002
6. *Jurassic Park* 1993
7. *Shrek 2* 2004
8. *Harry Potter and the Chamber of Secrets* 2002
9. *Finding Nemo* 2003
10. *The Lord of the Rings: The Fellowship of the Ring* 2001

Source: imdb.com

What do these films have in common? The Comfort Zone movies are essentially children's movies in which human beings behave like cartoon characters. This doesn't apply to *Finding Nemo* or *Shrek* because they *are* cartoons. Adventure stories with melodramatic villains, elaborate quest journeys and plenty of action, they are spectacles that thrill the eyes and the imagination with threats to the main characters that are always external beings—dinosaurs, dragons, space aliens—or forces of nature—icebergs, predatory animals. The main characters are usually good and innocent. Their motives are transparent and child-like (though real children are never this simple). The special effects represent the latest in action film technology. The happy, triumphal endings provide both emotional closure and plot points that allow for continuation, that is, sequels. They are very expensive and successful serials. The earliest of these films, *Star Wars*, was made in 1977, but most are more recent. These films have benefited from young people who like to see a favorite film several times and from older people who want to return to their Comfort Zone when they see a film. Usually called "escapist" entertainment, they represent an escape from the actual conflicts, frustrations and disappointments of everyday life.

In these films the good guys and the bad guys are clearly defined and the good guys win—or at least their values are shown to be true and valid. Values like love, friendship, loyalty, and honesty are shown to be the greatest sources of human fulfillment. Messages like this easily gain universal approval. These values **are** the greatest sources of human fulfillment, but these films do not adequately represent the psychological struggle involved in making conflicting values a functional part of everyday life. It is not a mistake for films to champion these values, but it is a mistake to put them in the pure realm of fantasy, to remove them from the complexity of lived psychological experience. By creating such stark contrast between good and evil these films eliminate mixed motives, difficult choices, and moral ambiguity. The characters rarely have to choose between conflicting ethical values. Designed for maximum international distribution, simple mythic stories communicate to people everywhere because the conflicts are external and don't require conflicted, personal dialogue or particular cultural knowledge.

5   Though these films have dialogue, they might be described as pre-verbal. When I saw *Titanic* (number one on the list), I was struck by how much it resembled a silent film; I would have enjoyed it more if it was a silent film! The dialogue was so predictable and wooden most audiences could have imagined better lines if they'd been allowed to. *Titanic* uses a plot idea very popular in the silent era: the damsel in distress. In 1914, only two years after the real Titanic went down, Pearl White starred in a twenty-part serial called *The Perils of Pauline* in which a fair-haired girl must escape from her rich guardian in order to run off with her true love and in the process falls from an air-balloon, escapes a burning house and is nearly run over by a train, among other life-threatening events. Eighty-three years later James Cameron was able to recycle this movie fantasy, add computer graphics, and bring in close to two billion dollars. An old-fashioned tear-jerker, it succeeded so well because it adds so little to a formula for sentimental adventure that is based upon putting virtuous young girls in danger and pinning all their hopes on the redeeming power of love. This was a melodramatic cliché in 1914! Yet the film had unprecedented success because it was aimed directly at the center of the Comfort Zone, and it hit its target. The performances of Kate Winslet and Leonardo DiCaprio carried the whole thing off because audiences liked them and believed in their innocence. They were the very image of Young Love. Cooler heads, mostly film critics, snickered and sniffed their noses at the whole thing, but it made little difference.

Think of the differences between *Titanic* and *Memento*. Christopher Nolan's film literally reverses our expectations by having the story move backward in time. Also, he mixes black and white with color footage, and gives the story a narrator who can't retain short term memories. *Memento* asks audiences to identify with a character who is not a conventional hero, not even a conventional *film noir* hero. A difficult film, it gets better and better with multiple viewings as various bits of information begin to cohere in the mind. Its tightly constructed story raises questions about the nature of memory, the relation of memory to a sense of self, the necessity of memory in order to have conscience. It is not simple entertainment in which we sit back amused by special effects and daring actions. Films like *Memento* are more engaging than entertainment because they require us to put clues together, to perceive subtle details, and come up with our own coherent understanding of the film. Though few people will experience the unusual brain injury depicted in *Memento*, all of us struggle to remember things, and eventually realize that the things we remember define who we are. When we lose our memories, we lose a big part of our identity.

Used with permission of Lynda Swanson.

● ● ●

Study/Writing/Discussion Questions

1. Respond to Swanson's comment that "The Comfort Zone movies are essentially children's movies in which human beings behave like cartoon characters." If you have seen any of these ten films yourself, how did you react to this evaluation?

2. What does Swanson say, in the same paragraph, about the general characteristics of these films?

3. What values does he say are shown to be the greatest sources of human fulfillment? What does he say is wrong about their treatment?

4. What reasons does he give for his classification of *Titanic* as "an old-fashioned tear-jerker"?

5. What does he find to commend, by comparison, in a film such as *Memento?*

Advanced Optional Writing Assignment

Write an essay with a thesis that demonstrates the power of images in transmitting evaluations to the public. Base your essay on one or two photo ops of political figures or celebrities. Illustrating your essay with magazine cut-outs or Internet print-outs, discuss what qualities their images and activities seem to convey. Do the male politicians seem fatherly, powerful, decisive, and trustworthy? If you choose a celebrity, what about their dress, appearance, and possessions might invite your admiration or envy?

CHAPTER 8

Viewpoints:
What's the Filter?

Used with permission of John Heine.

When one's own viewpoint is mistaken for reality, there are no other viewpoints. In this cartoon, we see how such narrow awareness affects our lives on this planet. We might also wonder if the animals have the wiser perspective.

The ability to detach from one's own point of view and assume another's is an important skill; it enables us to communicate better with others and gain new perspectives. However, if we forget that all information must flow through the filters of human biases, we confuse information with reality. A person trained in critical thinking always looks for the source of any piece of information and evaluates that information within the context of its viewpoint and inherent bias. The purpose of this chapter is to demonstrate the benefits of such attitudes and skills.

DISCOVERY EXERCISES

■ *Understanding the Term* Viewpoint

Using at least two dictionaries, formulate your own definitions of the following words:

1. Viewpoint
2. Point of view
3. Attitude
4. Bias
5. Perspective
6. Frame of reference
7. Opinion

■ *Discussion or Writing Questions*

1. Explain how viewpoints can be both collective and individual.
2. Explain why the term *viewpoint* is far more than a synonym for the word *opinion.*

■ *What Types of Viewpoints Are There?*

This is an exercise that will involve the whole class working in small groups. Each group will use brainstorming to construct one cluster or mind map illustrating a viewpoint. The mind maps may be drawn on sections of the blackboard or be drawn with crayons or felt-tip pens on large sheets of paper. Each group will begin by choosing one of the categories in the following list. Each mind map will record all the different viewpoints the group can imagine would fit under the chosen category.

Type of Viewpoint	Examples to Get You Started
Socioeconomic	Homeless, working class
Political	Red states, blue states
National	Chinese, Korean
Ethnic	Native American, Armenian
U.S. high school youth	Skaters, thugs

Type of Viewpoint	Examples to Get You Started
Religious	Islam, Catholicism
Financial world	Stock market, banking
Education	Students, administration
Occupation	Plumber, journalist
Citizenship	Immigrant, voter
Pastimes	Bikers, shopping mall visitors
Consumer groups	Internet users, Harley-Davidson owners

■ Study Questions

1. What did you learn from this exercise?
2. Take any one subgroup within a viewpoint (such as bikers) and describe how its members identify themselves through clothing, symbols, possessions, language, or shared opinions.

Viewpoints in Literature

When we study the elements of literature—such as plot, theme, and character—a crucial element is the point of view that tells the story. In literature an author can choose a third person to tell the story with omniscient or limited understanding. Other choices of viewpoint include a first-person narrative told by one character or the multiple points of view shared by several characters. In each case, the author must decide how much information and sensitivity this viewpoint will allow and how this perspective will shape the story and affect the reader. The science fiction novel *Flowers for Algernon,* by Daniel Keyes, is a first-person narrative told through the diary of a young man whose range of awareness expands and then contracts. By reading the diary entries, we learn that he is the subject of a scientific experiment that gradually raises his I.Q. from 70 to 185. He goes through a career change—from being a baker's assistant to becoming a linguistic scientist; he also enters into more complex social interactions. In time, however, his intelligence allows him to discover that the scientific experiment of which he is the subject will fail. The diary then reveals a gradual return to retardation. Thus, the plot hangs on distinct changes in his consciousness reflected through his writing. Here are three entries from this diary.

Progris riport 1 martch 3

My name is Charlie Gordon I werk in Donners bakery where Mr. Donner gives me 11 dollars a week and bred or cake if I want. I am 32 yeres old and next munth is my brithday . . . (p. 1)

Progress report 13

Am I a genius? I don't think so. Not yet anyway. I'm exceptional—a democratic term used to avoid the damning labels of gifted and deprived (which used to mean bright and retarded) and as soon as exceptional begins to mean anything to anyone they'll change it. Exceptional refers to both ends of the spectrum, so all my life I've been exceptional. (p. 106)

Nov. 21

I don't know why Im dumb agen or what I did rong. Mabye its because I din't try hard enuf or just some body put the evel eye on me. Anyway I bet Im the frist dumb persen in the wrold who found out some thing inportent for sience. I did something but I don't remembir what. (p. 216)

(Quotes taken from *Flowers for Algernon* by Daniel Keyes (New York: Bantam, 1975). © by Daniel Keyes.)

Discussion Break Question

1. Most of you will probably have read this story in middle school or have seen it on film. What did this story teach you about the way in which lives are shaped by awareness and intelligence?

2. Describe some other films and stories that enabled you to enter into unfamiliar viewpoints and thus learn more about yourself and other human beings as a result.

On Unconscious Viewpoints

Viewpoints, like assumptions, opinions, and evaluations, may or may not be consciously recognized.

In earlier chapters of this text, distinctions were drawn between the conscious and the unconscious uses of assumptions, opinions, and evaluations. To understand assumptions, we have to know that an assumption can be unconscious. To appreciate well-supported opinions, we need to distinguish them from superficial sentiment or fixed opinions that defy reexamination. To make sound evaluations, we need to guard against premature judgments. In this chapter, as we work with viewpoints, the issue of conscious and unconscious use appears again.

Both conscious and unconscious viewpoints are illustrated in the excerpts from *Flowers for Algernon*. In the first entry, Charlie only identifies himself through his work, his salary, and his age. One might say that he is not even aware that he has a viewpoint, nor at that time would he have been able to grasp the concept of viewpoint. By the time of the second diary entry, he has long since learned that he has a personal viewpoint, that other viewpoints exist beyond his own, and that he can enter into them or step out of them. Nevertheless, learning how "to step into others' shoes" does not require a genius I.Q.

The psychologist Jean Piaget, who studied learning stages in children, theorized that before the age of seven most young children lack the ability to see the world through any viewpoint other than their own. The ability to move beyond this cognitive limitation varies from one individual to another, depending on a number of educational, cultural, and emotional factors. As we grow out of egocentrism, we also develop the ability to be *exterior* to our own viewpoint—to see and recognize it from the outside, objectively. We learn how to see the world through the eyes of others. Such a capacity enables us to respect life more and to separate who we are as human beings from how we sometimes think and behave. We learn the meaning of the word *compassion* and move from the unconsciousness of egocentrism to the consciousness of objectivity.

Other less conscious viewpoints that share this feature of self-identification include ethnocentrism and religiocentrism. *Ethnocentrism,* in its milder forms, is an attitude that judges other people by one's own cultural practices, values, and standards, as though these were the only reasonable norms. The relativity of ethnocentrism becomes clearer to us when we go to live in another country and find that we can adapt to new cultural mores, such as eating with our hands, that we might have judged as backwards before. However, ethnocentrism also has tragic consequences, as in the case of Yugoslavia's "ethnic cleansing." The United States, in turn, shows its ethnocentricity when it justifies morally questionable actions as being "in America's best interests." Thus, ethnocentricity is always easier to see in other nations, especially if they are considered enemies.

Religiocentrism is a word used to describe an attitude that assumes one's own religion is the only religion, or the only religion with the right beliefs. Of course, usually this assumption is based on unfamiliarity with other religions. Here are two examples of religiocentric reasoning:

1. All any couple needs to have a happy marriage is to be good Christians.
2. Women who don't keep their hair covered don't deserve to marry or be married.

Now notice how the religiocentrism disappears when the same idea is recognized as representing a viewpoint.

1. Christians believe that happiness in married life is inevitable when a couple lives by Christian values.
2. According to Islam, women should dress in a modest manner so as not to arouse men's interest.

Discussion Questions

Rate the following statements as either (1) ethnocentric, (2) religiocentric, (3) both, or (4) neither. Defend your answer.

1. U.S. settlers brought the blessings of Western civilization to a nation of pagans and savages.

2. In the thirteenth century at the time of the Crusades, Pope Innocent IV proclaimed it necessary to send missionaries to infidel lands; he also let it be known that if the infidels did not allow his missionaries to preach, armies would follow.

3. "What we have to fight for is the freedom and independence of the fatherland, so that our people may be enabled to fulfill the mission assigned to it by the Creator." (Adolf Hitler)

4. "We live in times of tremendous change, but the United Kingdom is still, thankfully, a predominantly white, Christian country." (Ann Winterton, British member of Parliament, 2005)

5. "Take up the White Man's burden—Send forth the best ye breed— Go bind your sons to exile To serve your captives' need; To wait in heavy harness, On fluttered folk and wild—Your new-caught, sullen peoples, Half-devil and half-child." (Rudyard Kipling, "Recessional" written in support of U.S. invasion of Philippines, 1899)

6. "The Jewish Question is as old as the history of Jewry itself. From the days of antiquity to the present, the peoples have always risen up to defend themselves against Jewish parasitism. The defense was often bloody. Greater Germany is the first country in the world to find a legal way to separate from the alien Jewish people." (Max Eichler, *The Jewish Problem*, 1939)

7. "The Japanese dislike Koreans. Korean people's characters are utterly different from Japanese people's. Koreans often break promises without hesitation . . . and they often tell lies, but they don't have a sense of sin at all. We Japanese should not trust Korean people. They do any dirty thing in order to accomplish their own goal. It is very dangerous to trust Korean people." (Nishimura Shingo, member, Japanese Diet, YouTube, September 14, 2006)

8. Islam is a very evil and wicked religion. . . . the God of Islam is not the same God. He's not the Son of God of the Christian or Judeo-Christian faith. It's a different God, and I believe it is a very evil and wicked religion.

Used with permission of David Sipress.

Discussion Questions

1. Cite some ideas that represent ethnocentric or religiocentric thinking.

2. Those who believe it is important to strongly advocate the truth of nationalist or religious beliefs might argue that at least they are not *relativists*. Compare several dictionary definitions of *relativism* and share your views on this subject.

3. What do the terms *androcentric, anthropocentric, Eurocentric,* and *biocentric* mean? Would you call these unconscious viewpoints?

DISCOVERY EXERCISE

■ *Recognizing Political and Social Points of View*

Read the following passages and notice how they express very different viewpoints based on different concerns, values, and priorities. See if you can assign each a political or social label, such as "radical left," "right conservative," or "feminist," on the basis of the language used and the ideas expressed.

1. I say without any pride that I did my job as a soldier [in Iraq]. I commanded an infantry squad in combat, and we never failed to accomplish our mission. But those who call me a coward are also right. I was a coward, not for leaving the war, but for having been a part of it in the first place. (Camilo Mejia, *Stop the Next War Now,* 2004)

2. "But also, all of the news, whether it's social security, bankruptcy laws, the economy, the wars—they're never looked at through a gender lens, and they all impact women differently than they do men. Welfare reform—all of that. And we're the majority of humanity . . ." (Jane Fonda, interview with Marianne Schnall, October 28, 2006)

3. "Conservatives are independent, rugged individuals who believe the 'American Dream' is achieved through hard work, sacrifice and an unrelenting commitment to excellence. . . . We detest able-bodied bloodsuckers who live off the sweat equity of others by refusing to be equal to those who try harder . . ." (Ted Nugent, Opinion page, February 10, 2008. *WacoTrib.com*)

4. "Usually it's the bandits robbing the banks. But now it's getting harder to tell the bankers from the bandits. Where have they stashed the loot—that 350 billion dollars of our money that the Bush Administration lavished on them to jump-start our economy?" (Bill Moyers, *Bill Moyers Journal*, January 23, 2009. *www.pbs.org/moyers/journal*)

5. "We affirm that God-given dominion is a sacred responsibility to steward the earth and not a license to abuse the creation of which we are a part . . . Because clean air, pure water, and adequate resources are crucial to public health and civic order, government has an obligation to protect its citizens from the effects of environmental degradation." ("For the Health of a Nation: An Evangelical Call to Civic Reponsibility," 2005, p. 11. *www.nae.net/images/civic_responsibility2pdf*)

Discuss these questions in writing or in class:

1. Which quotes were the most difficult for you to identify?

2. What were the clues that helped you decide how to label the viewpoint?

Recognizing Viewpoints: Left and Right

Even though their meanings keep shifting, the terms *liberal* and *conservative, left* and *right,* are still used as yardsticks to describe political viewpoints.

Today's students often find it both frustrating and confusing to apply the labels *left* and *right* to the shifting world patterns of political ideas. These are polar ideas about how governments should best govern in

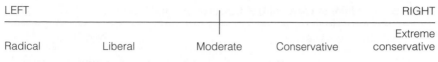

FIGURE 8.1 The Left-to-Right Political Spectrum

order to assure the survival and prosperity of their nations; they are based on different clusters of political, social, economic, and religious values.

During the first half of the twentieth century, the left-to-right political spectrum as displayed in Figure 8.1 seemed easy enough to understand: all one had to do was draw a scale with radicals placed on each end and moderates in the middle. Anarchism and communism found their position at the far left end, fascism on the far right.

In the past 50 years, the scale of the U.S. spectrum has contracted to reflect a two-party system based on the old liberalism and conservatism. During the years of the Bush administration (2000–2008), the spectrum of power remained predominantly to the right.

The problem with the left–right paradigm is that it is not only constantly changing but that it also leaves out more political perspectives than it includes. More recently multi-axis models have been developed that divide viewpoints around such polarities as community or individualism, equality or privilege, free trade or fair trade, the exclusion or inclusion of religion in political affairs, foreign interventionism or isolationism, domination of the U.S. as the world's sole superpower or peaceful international cooperation.

Table 8.1 offers some traditional observations about the liberal and conservative values. However, in order to fully understand the viewpoints currently shaping American politics, both time and study are needed to examine definitions of such words as *liberal, conservative, neoconservative, the religious right, progressivism, populism, libertarian,* and *green.* A good place to begin is with an online encyclopedia such as Wikipedia. Such a source will list each group's characteristic issues of concern as well as provide lists of their publications, think tanks, and chief commentators. In addition, the next Discovery Exercise is designed to enable you to arrive at your own conclusions about their characteristic beliefs, concerns, and rhetoric.

Today our so-called "mainstream" city newspapers and corporate network radio and television stations fall far short of fully reflecting this country's diverse range of opinion. Nevertheless, this vacuum has become filled by the Internet's offering of an ever growing range of viewpoints. Libraries also offer access to viewpoints both online and in print that are underrepresented in the mainstream media. Most of these publications clearly identify their social, religious, or political

TABLE 8.1 Traditional Values of U.S. Conservatives and Liberals

U.S. Conservatives	U.S. Liberals
1. Chief concern is preserving and generating wealth, assets, and resources, both personal and national. Belief in personal initiative and responsibility. Dedication to free market capitalism.	1. Chief concern is government protection of the public from the inequities and excesses of the capitalist economic system.
2. Concern about safety, law, and order—personal, national, and international. Belief in strong police and military force and strong punishment of offenders.	2. Concern for law, order, and safety, but equally concerned about ensuring justice and respect for civil rights. Tendency to believe more in prisoner rehabilitation than punishment.
3. Concern about personal freedom: least taxation of wealth, least government regulation. Right and left Republicans divided on how much government regulation they want of personal life.	3. Concern about social responsibility. Support for regulations and funding to assure community needs are fairly met.
4. Preference for traditional social conformity. Opposition to abortion and gay marriage.	4. Greater tolerance of nonconformity and alternative lifestyles, ethnic diversity, and other religious orientations.
5. Support for a high military budget and military solutions to problems.	5. Support for a strong military defense but more critical of military interventions.
6. Support for pro-business legislation, less gun control, school vouchers, tax reductions for those with higher incomes, elimination of capital gains taxes, expansion of military spending, government deregulation, privatization of government programs.	6. Support for legislation such as minimum wage increases, stricter gun control, equitable taxation, universal health care, federal subsidies to public schools and farmers, labor protection, public financing of elections.
7. Wary of federal spending and administration of programs dealing with welfare and health care. May or may not oppose Social Security, affirmative action, student loans, public housing, public education, environmental protections.	7. Opposed to tax loopholes and subsidies for corporations, low fines for environmental pollution, federal deregulation of banks, huge corporate mergers, media monopolies.
8. Committed to furthering the interests of corporations.	8. Committed to furthering the interests of corporations but more wary of how they can harm the public good.
9. Prominent in the Republican Party.	9. Prominent in the Democratic Party.

affiliations. Browsing through such small newspapers and magazines can help you reach your own understanding of what values, ideas, and rhetoric characterize right-wing opinion, left-wing opinion, green opinion, and so on.

In the next discovery and writing assignments you will have an opportunity to carry out this kind of exploration, while finding provocative and stimulating reading as well.

DISCOVERY EXERCISE

■ Learning to Recognize Political Viewpoints

This is an inductive exercise designed to enable you to arrive at your own conclusions about the differences between left and right viewpoints. Go to your library and sample a few—or all—of the magazines and newspapers from each column. Most of these publications can also be sampled online. Note how their beliefs, issues of concern, and rhetoric differ. Report your findings to the class.

Left Progressive

Mother Jones
In These Times
The Progressive
The Nation
The New Republic

Left Centrist

The New Yorker
Harpers
The Atlantic
The Washington Post
New York Times

Left Christian

Sojourner Magazine
Christian Science Monitor

Neoconservative

American Enterprise
Weekly Standard

FrontPage.com
NewsMax.com
Insight on the News
Policy Review
Commentary

Conservative

National Review
American Spectator
Wall Street Journal
Washington Times
New York Sun

Christian Conservative

World Magazine

Mass Media Corporate

Time
Fortune

Composition Writing Application

■ A Survey of Some Alternative Viewpoints

This assignment is designed to introduce you to some viewpoints rarely heard on corporate-owned TV stations, newspapers, and radio stations. Most of these magazines or websites clearly identify their viewpoints and affiliations. Some offer information, some advocate ideas, some focus on media criticism. A few appear as publications available in your local library or bookstore; all can be found online.

First skim through the following list of magazines, then read the assignment directions that follow.

Adbusters

The Advocate

Aljazeera.com

Arab American News

Asia Times

The Beat Within

Bioneers

Chicano.org

Common Dreams News Center

Earth Island Journal

Feminist Weekly News

Foundation for Individual Rights
in Education

Guerrilla News Network

Independent Media Center

Indian Country Today

The Korea Times

Mexican Labor News & Analysis

MoveOn.org

New American Media

Public Citizen (consumer news from
Ralph Nader)

The Onion

Teen Voices Magazine

Tikkun

Utne Reader

WatchingAmerica.com

■ Assignment Directions

Choose four publications from the list and write down your notes about each in the following order:

1. *Name, date, and form* of publication (print or online).
2. *Cover or home page.* Describe the magazine cover or website home page, concluding with a statement about the mood or impact that it might have on the reader.
3. *Purpose.* Does this magazine openly state its mission or purpose? If so, what is it?

4. *Table of contents or headlines.* Study the feature topics of this magazine and summarize them. How would you describe the magazine's overall slant, values, and interests?

5. *Advertising.* If there are any advertisements, note what products are featured. If this is a print magazine, generalize about the types of advertisers, their products, and their presentation. Note also the ratio of articles to advertisements. Describe a typical advertisement.

6. *Audience.* What might you infer, on the basis of the topics chosen and language used, about (a) the political and/or ethnic group to whom this publication seems directed and (b) the readers' level of education, social class, and income.

7. *Content.* Does this publication offer perspectives rarely found in mainstream publications, national TV networks, and radio stations? Explain why or why not.

8. *Other.* Write down anything remarkable that you learned from studying this magazine.

Select *two* of these magazines to write up for an oral or written report. If the instructor agrees, you can write up your notes in outline form based

---

Scoring for Survey of Some Alternative Viewpoints

1. Choice of two publications whose unfamiliarity poses some challenge. *10 points*

2. Description of cover or home page conveys its calculated effort to attract readers through mood, choice of images, symbols, words, and topics. *20 points*

3. Table of contents or headlines are not just listed; discussion shows thoughtful attention to the details that give evidence of the publication's interests, slant on life, values, and ideology. *20 points*

4. Advertisements: Specific examples show the types of advertisers, the types of products, and how they are presented. Speculation may be offered about what the ads, or lack of ads, suggest about the values of the magazine and its readers. *20 points*

5. Audience: Thoughtful conclusions are drawn about the social, ethnic, income, and educational characteristics of readers. *10 points*

6. Content: Thoughtful conclusions are offered about the uniqueness of this perspective. *10 points*

7. No distracting errors of spelling, punctuation, sentence use, word use. *10 points*

on your answers to these eight questions. The report should be at least four typed pages. Attach to your report photocopies of the cover and table of contents of each magazine or attach printouts of some pages from each website. Be sure to review the criteria given in the scoring box before you turn in your final draft to the instructor.

Hidden Viewpoints: The Use of News Framing

News framing describes the way an editor uses layout design, placement, and headlines to sensationalize, downplay, exaggerate, or convey importance.

When we begin to understand that information is filtered through human viewpoints, we begin to ask more questions about "the daily news." We begin to wonder *who* decides *what* is news? Are they truth seekers dedicated to public service? The book *How To Watch TV News,* by Neil Postman and Steve Powers, says "no" in answer to this last question, casting doubt even on the assumption that the intention of the news media is to keep you informed. The media's purpose, these authors maintain, is to keep you entertained and sell you products:

> You may think that a TV news show is a public service and a public util- ity. But more than that, it is an enormously successful business enter- prise. The whole package is put together in the way that any theatrical producer would proceed, that is, by giving priority to show business values. (p. 161)

The authors then go on to say that acquiring media literacy means taking the time to inquire about the viewpoint, or the economic and political interests, of those who run TV stations:

> Keep in mind that other professionals—doctors, dentists, and lawyers, for example—commonly display their diplomas on their office walls to assure their clients that someone judged them to be competent. . . . But diplomas tell more than station "owners" and news directors and jour- nalists tell. Wouldn't it be useful to know who these people are? Where they come from? What their angle is? And, especially, where they stand in relation to you? (p. 163)

Learning the identity of the owners of any given TV network (as well as mag- azines or newspapers) remains a challenge in this decade of constant and overlapping media mergers. It can require ongoing research to learn what combinations of business conglomerates (including banks, insurance com- panies, industries, publishers, and individuals) control which newspapers or television stations or which of these media groups are merging with still other media groups.

The Discovery Assignment that follows is designed to introduce you to the technique of *news framing analysis.*[*] A news frame is basically the layout, placement, and prominence given to any story in a publication. The editor, representing the policies and values of the publishers, owners, and advertisers, chooses the frame for any given story. The editor must decide what stories go on the front page, which will have pictures, which will be short, which long, which sensationalized, which minimized. Although journalists may write the stories, editors decide on the wording of the headlines. A comparison of two newspapers from the same day will show how the same stories are given different prominence and treatment.

When we conduct frame analysis, we remove our attention from story content and bring our awareness to the influence of newspaper layout, story prominence, and headline language. Such analysis helps us recognize which information a given viewpoint will tend to emphasize, minimize, or omit. We then understand how all of these more subtle elements have a calculated effect on the reader. Frame analysis habits teach us to detach from the influence of the frame and gain a more objective perspective on the hidden viewpoint it expresses.

DISCOVERY ASSIGNMENT

▓ *Observing How a Newspaper Frames Its Information*

1. Each student should bring a copy of that day's newspaper to class for this exercise, which will involve either small-group or general class discussion. Newspapers might include *USA Today,* the *Wall Street Journal,* the *New York Times,* a local city newspaper, or an online newspaper.

2. Study the front page of each newspaper. What subject was chosen for the main headline? How is the headline worded? What are the subjects of stories accompanied by pictures? Which stories are given less prominence? What are the differences in depth of treatment?

3. Now study the inside pages. Which news stories are given less prominence in each? Which stories do not appear in some papers? How do the editorials differ? How do the advertisements differ?

4. Choose one news item that appears in all the newspapers to compare how it is treated in each one. Consider the following items:

   a. How much prominence is given to this story?

   b. Does the headline use words that suggest evaluations?

[*]The author is indebted to Ralph H. Johnson and William Dorman for their lectures on how to teach frame analysis.

c. Does the story have balance, giving more than one point of view?

d. Are opinions and judgments mixed in with the facts?

e. Does the headline accurately reflect the article's data and conclusions?

5. What can you infer about the different values of each newspaper from the way in which each frames its information?

Building Arguments
Viewpoints

Much has been said of what you term Civilization among the Indians. Many proposals have been made to us to adopt your laws, your religion, your manners, and your customs. We do not see the propriety of such a reformation. We should be better pleased with beholding the good effects of these doctrines in your own practices than with hearing you talk about them, or of reading your newspapers on such subjects. You say, "Why do not the Indians till the ground and live as we do?" May we not ask with equal propriety, "Why do not the white people hunt and live as we do?" (Old Tassel of the Cherokee tribe, 1777)

Exercise

1. What argument is Old Tassel refuting?

2. Given what you know about U.S. history from 1777 to the present, was Old Tassel's viewpoint heard or understood by the white men?

3. How can you explain that Old Tassel could describe and compare the two opposing viewpoints while the white men only saw their own?

Chapter Summary

1. Critical thinking means learning to recognize viewpoints and how they shape the content of any message.

2. Viewpoints—like assumptions, opinions, and evaluations—can be either conscious or unconscious.

3. We communicate best when we are aware of our own viewpoint and can understand and respect the viewpoints of others as well.

4. Writers shape their stories through their choice of a point of view; their choices include third-person, first-person, and multiple points of view. These viewpoints may be omniscient or humanly limited.

5. Unconscious viewpoints include the egocentric, ethnocentric, and religiocentric.

6. Left, right, and centrist perspectives exist within both the Republican and Democratic parties.

7. The Internet provides a vehicle for the expression of a wide range of viewpoints not well represented in the U.S. corporate media. Such viewpoints include third political parties, feminists, gays and lesbians, ethnic minorities, labor, environmentalists, religious groups, and immigrants.

8. Periodicals can express viewpoints through images, words, and in the framing given to information. Framing decisions made by an editor can exercise a hidden influence over the reader.

Chapter Quiz

Rate each of the following statements as *true* or *false*. Rewrite any false statements to make them true.

_____ 1. Viewpoints can be either consciously or unconsciously assumed.

_____ 2. To be exterior to one's own viewpoint is to see it objectively as just one viewpoint among many.

_____ 3. Egocentrism means being absorbed in one's personal viewpoint without being able to put oneself in other people's shoes.

_____ 4. Religiocentrism means believing one's country is morally superior to any other.

_____ 5. Nations tend to become more ethnocentric in wartime.

_____ 6. Authors only tell their stories from one viewpoint.

_____ 7. Conservatives are prominent in the Republican party.

_____ 8. Liberals are best known for their opposition to programs such as social welfare.

_____ 9. A newspaper editor implies the relative importance of a news story by the framing given to the story.

_____ 10. We communicate best when we ignore the viewpoints of others.

• R E A D I N G S •

I Got This Part . . .

Margaret Cho

Margaret Cho was born into a Korean family in San Francisco in 1968. At the age of 16 she launched her career as a stand-up comic. This excerpt is taken from her book I Have Chosen to Stay and Fight.

I don't need any more people calling me up, saying, "I have this script that you're gonna love. There's this part for an ASIAN WOMAN—it's really not the lead, but it's such a great part. Call me." The first thing that I do when I get a call like that is to press 3 for "Delete," because there's no way this part is gonna be anything good.

I have never had any desire to play a maid, a liquor store owner kicking a black person out of my store, a rude and harried waitress, a worldly-wise acupuncturist, an early-rising, loose black cotton pants–wearing elderly woman practicing tai chi in the park, a manicurist, a prostitute, a student in an English as a Second Language course, a purveyor of exotic mushrooms and ginseng, an exchange student, a newscaster covering gang warfare in Chinatown, a woman drowning my newborn baby in a bowl, a daughter crying with my mom over our constant battle between East and West yet finally coming together over a particularly intense game of mah-jongg, a queen sitting on her throne in the Forbidden City being served a bowl of turtle soup by a eunuch, a peasant carrying a yoke on my shoulders like a yak trudging up Gold Mountain delivering precious water to my village, a young girl being raped and killed by GIs in the Killing Fields, a woman balancing a basket of any kind on my head, being the second wife and committing suicide to avenge the first wife by coming back as a ghost and scaring the shit out of everyone, or, alternately, committing suicide because my white lover did not come back to Japan after the war, or having him come back for me and fooling him successfully for years and years into thinking I am a woman when really I'm a dude, as if my race castrates me so much that this deception is completely feasible, or a girl, barely out of grammar school, playing violin for the president in a long, black velvet dress, or a mother, out of nowhere, screaming and then sullenly freezing out my children in an effort to terrorize them into getting better grades in school, especially in math and science, through emotional blackmail and coercion, or a teenager, figure-skating in the Olympics and winning the Gold but never getting a major endorsement contract because even though I fucking won that goddamn medal for America I will never be considered the hero that I truly am because, no matter what anybody says, this is still a racist country, or a woman giving birth to the Dalai Lama, or holding my breath for over three minutes while diving for pearls, or arguing with Elaine from *Seinfeld* about her dry cleaning, or saying, "Welcome to Japan, Mr. Bond," or being a hired assassin and flinging a ninja star, or sword-fighting up a tree, or writing my Geisha memoirs . . .

• • •

Study/Writing/Discussion Questions

1. Why does Margaret Cho reject all of these Asian woman parts? What is it about them that offends her?
2. What is she saying about the way in which Asian women are portrayed in the media?
3. What is she saying about her own identity?

The N Word

Jabari Asim

Jabari Asim writes a column of politics, popular art, and social issues for the Washington Post. He is also a playwright, fiction writer, and literary critic. This excerpt is taken from the epilogue from his 2007 book, The N Word.

> We African Americans are perceived as acceptable in a token amount, toxic beyond it. This is a devastating commentary on the majority's perception of our nature.
>
> —Arthur Ashe, 1992

"Our country shall be peopled," Patrick Henry observed, "shall it be with Europeans or with Africans?" As we noted in the first chapter, Henry spoke for many of his peers when he expressed concern that blacks would someday outnumber them. They needn't have worried: a few years into the twenty-first century, African Americans make up a little more than twelve percent of the U.S. population. However, our outsize public image—or our image in the minds of whites—often leads whites to overestimate our numbers. In national polls, some whites estimate that blacks make up as much as fifty percent of the populace.

This exaggerated perception doubtless also derives in part from African Americans' disproportionate influence on many aspects of popular culture, ranging from movies, television, and popular music to the wide world of sports. Bolstered also by the unprecedented explosion in technology that makes popular culture more ubiquitous and accessible than ever, black athletes and entertainers are aggressively pursuing roles that would have been unthinkable even a mere thirty years ago. Whereas, for example, black sports stars and celebrities were routinely shut out of lucrative endorsement deals in the past, Michael Jordan and Tiger Woods are the dominant product pitchmen of recent years.

In the world of big-screen entertainment, the lascivious, dimwitted Gus of *The Birth of a Nation* has given way to black characters played by genuine black actors, accepted and even embraced in heroic roles such as savior of the world (Will Smith in *Independence Day*) and ruler over all Creation (Morgan Freeman in *Bruce Almighty*).

The new mass media, while helping to perpetuate damaging images of African Americans, have often been used to counter the most virulent stereotypes. While Willie Horton and O. J. Simpson were exploited to sustain the old negative images in the 1980s and '90s, respectively, during that same period blacks in very disparate fields emerged to set forth new images of profound impact. In addition to celebrity endorsers and box office champions, Oprah Winfrey and Jesse Jackson were just two of the prominent blacks who made masterful use of television exposure. Winfrey parlayed her talk show popularity into profitable forays in movie and theater productions and magazine publishing, resulting in her being nicknamed "the queen of all media." While Jackson's media moment was considerably briefer, it remains historically significant. His speech at the 1988 Democratic convention elevated his own image as a statesman of stature and skill and helped pave the way for future political aspirants on both sides of the political divide, including Condoleezza Rice, Colin Powell, and Barack Obama. Obama's own turn in the spotlight at the 2004 Democratic convention promoted a new image of wise, committed black leadership capable of organizing and speaking on behalf of all Americans.

5   During the civil rights era, black visionaries had taken similar advantage of the advent of the mass media to promote the image of nonviolent, spiritually inclined seekers of justice maintaining their dignity and courage in the face of violence and madness. The televised pictures of peaceful, patient African Americans in their Sunday best, forthrightly arrayed against violent, ragtag, and raging mobs of whites, changed hearts and minds and brought about a permanent, *significant* transformation of American culture.

Civil rights activists claimed the moral high ground, a meaningful stance in a nation that has always fancied itself as morally astute, despite a bloody and hypocritical history that suggests a far less noble existence. The public profile of the civil rights vanguard was not adopted by succeeding generations of African Americans, who kept alive the notion of creative rebellion but dressed it up in dramatically different clothing. Somewhere along the line, the romantic rebel in the Bigger Thomas–Stokely Carmichael–Sweet Sweetback tradition became a "gangsta," a self-absorbed sellout who peddles everything from cognac to sneakers to vitamin water while pushing tall tales of sex, drugs, and destruction. While it is true that Jordan, Woods, and other post-civil rights celebrities have carefully nurtured clean-cut personae reminiscent of the marchers of yesteryear, they have done so at the risk of losing credibility in the eyes of their African-American peers. The apparent abandonment of the high ground, exacerbated by the 24–7 display of choreographed black dysfunction through cable television, cell phone, ring tone, iPod, and Web site, elevates a misbegotten philosophy of "street-cred" nihilism while obscuring African Americans who do their utmost to uphold the finest traditions of our past. The forces of uplift and excellence continue their steady tread, but beneath the shadow of a commoditized "gangsta" culture that both titillates mainstream audiences and keeps alive the very images of black depravity that white supremacy feeds on . . .

●　●　●

Study/Writing/Discussion Questions

1. What is the main point that Jabari Asim makes in his first paragraph?
2. How does the next paragraph account for this misperception?
3. In the following paragraphs, what does he say about the way in which the media has enhanced both negative and positive stereotypes of African Americans?
4. How would you describe the author's viewpoint?

Awakening from the Nightmare of Zoos

Derrick Jensen

Derrick Jensen is an environmental activist, author, and philosopher. The book from which this excerpt is taken received the 2008 Eric Hofer Award, an award that honors "free-thinking writers and independent books of exceptional merit." The full title of this 2007 book is Thought to Exist in the Wild: Awaken from the Nightmare of Zoos.

I'm at a zoo. Everywhere I see consoles atop small stands. Each console has a cartoonish design aimed at children, and each has a speaker with a button. When I push the button, I hear a voice begin the singsong: "All the animals in the zoo are eagerly awaiting you." The song ends by reminding the children to be sure to "get in on the fun."

I look at the concrete walls, the glassed-in spaces, the moats, the electrified fences. I see the expressions on the animals' faces, so different from the expressions of the wild animals I've seen. The central conceit of the zoo, and in fact the central conceit of this whole culture, is that all of these "others" have been placed here for us, that they do not have any existence independent of us, that the fish in the oceans are waiting there for us to catch them, that the trees in the forests stand ready for us to cut them down, that the animals in the zoo are there for us to be entertained by them.

It may be flattering to believe that everything is here to serve you, but in the real world, where real creatures exist and real creatures suffer, it's narcissistic and dangerous to pretend nobody matters but you.

Sometimes I fantasize about imprisoning zoo advocates and zookeepers to give them a taste of their own medicine. I would confine them for a month and then ask if they were still eager to make jokes about the pacing monkey they call "Jogging Man." I would ask them if they felt grief, sorrow, resentment, and homesickness, and if they still believe that animals do not need freedom. I wouldn't listen to their answers, though, because I would not care to hear about their experiences. In fact, I wouldn't believe that these zookeeper animals—for humans are animals, too—could meaningfully experience the world, which means it would be a projection on my part to believe they had anything to tell me. Indeed, it would be a projection on my part to believe these animals might wish a certain condition to continue or change.

5   I would leave the human animals there, in their cages, and I would ask them these questions again in a year. During that time they would never be allowed to speak to another human, but they would be given cardboard boxes and paper bags to play with. I think that after twelve months of confinement they would tell me they agreed that animals need freedom. But I would not listen to them. I would not believe they could speak. I think that in time they would no longer tell me anything at all; they would silently walk around their cages—their "habitats"—taking seven steps forward, dipping their heads, turning to the left, and back again.

It is often said that one of the primary positive functions of zoos is education. The ending to the standard zoo book uses elevated language to state that because the earth has become a battlefield with the animals losing the war, zoos really are the last hope for beleaguered wildlife. Only through unleashing the full potential of zoos for education will people ever learn to care enough about wildlife not to destroy the planet. As author Vicki Croke puts it, the challenge for zoos is "to allow living, breathing animals to inspire wonder and awe of the natural world; to teach us that animal's place in the cosmos and to illuminate the tangled and fragile web of life that sustains it; to open the door to conservation for the millions of people who want to help save this planet and the incredible creatures it contains."

Have you watched people at zoos? I see no awe and wonder on their faces. Instead I hear children laughing at the animals—not the sweet sound of innocent laughter, but the derisive kind you hear in the schoolyard: the laughter at someone else's misfortunes. I see parents and children giggling at the fat orangutan, making scary faces at the snake, ignoring the pacing bear. They shriek at the silly monkeys who pick their noses and stare straight through the glass at them. The children laugh and pound on the window.

Even if we accept at face value the claims for the educational potential of zoos, study after study has shown that zoos fail miserably at this task. A tally of observation periods at the London Zoo found that spectators stood in front of the monkey enclosure for an average of forty-six seconds. These forty-six seconds included time spent reading—or, rather, skimming—the information posted about the animals. Not surprisingly, studies show low retention rates: even while patrons are in the zoo, standing directly in front of the animals in question, they consistently fail even rudimentary nomenclature questions: they still call gibbons and orangutans "monkeys"; vultures "buzzards"; cassowaries "peacocks"; otters "beavers"; and so on.

The traditional method for capturing many social creatures, including elephants, gorillas, and chimpanzees, was—and, in some cases, is—to kill the mothers. Most of us never hear about this; much better to believe that zoos rescue animals from the wild. To hear the truth about how animals are captured would impinge on the fantasy that the eager ocelots and elephants are "waiting" to meet us. Zookeepers know this. They have always known it. William Hornaday, director of the Bronx Zoo, wrote in 1902 to Carl Hagenbeck, considered by many to be the father of the modern zoological gardens and a trader in animals on an almost inconceivable scale: "I have been greatly interested in the fact that your letter gives me regarding the capture of the rhinoceroses; but we must keep very still about forty large Indian rhinoceroses being killed in capturing the four young ones. If that should get into the newspapers, either here or in London, there would be things published in condemnation of the whole business of capturing wild animals for exhibition."

10   If you are a mother, what would you do if someone tried to take your child? When you were a child, how would you have felt if someone shot your mother so they could put you on display? What would you feel as you poked at her, hit her, wanted her to wake up so together you could make your escape, but she did not awaken? What would you feel if they put you in a cage?

These are not rhetorical questions. What would you do? What would you feel?

One of the things I dislike most about Western culture is the unexamined belief that humans are superior to and fundamentally separate from "the animals"; that animals are animals, and that humans are not animals; that an impermeable wall stands between.

In this construct, humans are intelligent. Animals—by which is meant all animals except humans—are not, or if they do have any sort of intelligence, it is dim, rudimentary, just sufficient to allow them to meaninglessly navigate their meaningless physical surroundings.

Whereas human behavior is based on conscious, rational choices, our culture suggests animal behavior is fully driven by instinct. Animals do not plan, do not think. They are essentially machines made of DNA, guts, and fur, feathers, or scales.

15   Humans feel a wide range of emotions. Animals reportedly do not. They do not grieve the loss of a mother, of freedom, of a world. They do not feel sorrow. They do not feel joy. They do not feel homesickness. They do not feel humiliated.

This culture thinks that human life is sacred (at least, some human life is sacred, but the lives of the poor, the nonwhite, the indigenous, as well as the lives of any who oppose the wishes of those in power, are only a little sacred, or sometimes not sacred at all), but animal life is not sacred. In fact, the entire animate world is not sacred.

Humans are supposedly the sole bearers of meaning, the sole definers of value, the only creatures capable of moral behavior. Animals' lives have no inherent value—indeed, no value at all, except insofar as value is assigned to them by humans. This value is almost always strictly utilitarian. Most often it is monetary, and usually it is based not on their lives but on the price of their carcasses. And, of course, animals are incapable of moral behavior.

Finally, this culture constantly stresses that all that is human is good: humans have humanity and are humane; the civilized are civil. Human traits are to be loved. Animal traits are to be hated—or, rather, hated traits are projected onto animals. Bad humans are "animals," "brutes," and "beasts." My thesaurus lists as synonyms for *animal: inferior, mindless, unthinking, intemperate, sensualist.*

We are discouraged from anthropomorphizing animals—that is, we shouldn't attribute human characteristics to them. This means that we must do everything within our power to blind ourselves to animals' intelligence, their awareness, their feelings, their joys, their suffering, their desires. It means we must ignore their selfhood, their individuality, and their value entirely independent of our own uses for them . . .

● ● ●

Study/Writing/Discussion Questions

1. What does the word *anthropocentric* mean? How does that concept apply to this essay?
2. Why does the author fantasize about imprisoning zoo advocates and zookeepers in cages?
3. How does the author refute the argument that the positive function of zoos is that they are educational?
4. What does he say about how the animals are captured?
5. What mistaken ideas does he claim that Western culture has about animals?
6. After reading this essay, how do you feel about zoos?

Objectives Review of Part II

When you have finished Part II, you will understand:

1. The concepts and complexities of assumptions, opinions, evaluations, and viewpoints
2. How these concepts are mental experiences
3. How they are problematical when confused with facts
4. How a viewpoint frames information
5. The meaning of conscious and unconscious viewpoints

And you will have practice in developing these skills:

1. Recognizing the mental formation of assumptions, opinions, evaluations, and viewpoints
2. Assessing assumptions, opinions, evaluations, and viewpoints for strengths and limitations
3. Identifying underlying assumptions and value assumptions in discourse
4. Separating opinions and evaluations from facts
5. Recognizing hidden opinions within evaluative words
6. Identifying social and political viewpoint characteristics
7. Analyzing the news frame

PART III

Forms and Standards of Critical Thinking

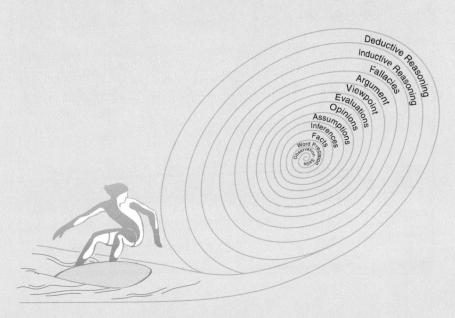

CHAPTER 9

Argument:

What's a Good Argument?

In each previous chapter you have been learning something more about argument fundamentals. Now is the time to integrate what you have learned into a focused study of argument structure and standards. When you finish studying this chapter, you will not only know more about how to construct, support, and analyze arguments but also feel ready to prepare for the argument research assignments described in Appendix One.

DISCOVERY EXERCISE

■ *Reading and Judging Arguments*

Read the six points of view offered here on a controversial issue. Then answer the questions that follow, in writing and/or class discussion.

1. Illegal immigration has a clear economic logic: It provides U.S. businesses with the types of workers they want, when they want them, and where they want them. If policy reform succeeds in making U.S. illegal immigrants more like legal immigrants, in terms of their skills, timing of arrival, and occupational mobility, it is likely to lower rather than raise national welfare. (Gordon H. Hanson, Professor of Economics, University of California San Diego. *The Economic Logic of Illegal Immigration*, Council on Foreign Relations No. 26, April 2007)

2. Illegal immigration into the United States is a highly profitable proposition for both employers and the U.S. government, and it also benefits Mexico, which is the largest source country of undocumented immigrants into the United States. The U.S. and Mexican government actively entice illegal immigrants to enter this country and to work illegally for profit-hungry U.S. employers. Poverty-stricken immigrants, who are often desperate to house and feed their families, respond to the financial enticements, and then are blamed by U.S. citizenry for illegally being in the United States. (Deborah White, journalist, "Illegal Immigration Explained—Profits & Poverty, Social Security & Starvation." *About.com: US Liberal Politics*. No date provided.)

3. "I have to tell you that we are facing a situation, where if we don't control immigration, legal and illegal, we will eventually reach the point where . . . we are no longer a nation at all. That is the honest to God eventual outcome of this kind of massive immigration combined with the cult of multiculturalism that permeates our society. . . ." (Tom Tancredo, Republican congressman from Colorado, *Right Wing News* interview with John Hawkins. No date.)

4. "While illegal immigrants burden the social infrastructure— schools, hospitals and housing—they also revitalize many neighborhoods as they open new businesses and buy additional goods and services. . . . At the very bottom of the wage scale, illegal immigrants probably take a few jobs away from uneducated and marginalized American laborers. But the effect is minimal, according to researchers. The most comprehensive analysis has found that

illegal immigration depresses wages no more than 50 to 60 cents an hour—hardly a figure that makes or breaks a budget." (Cynthia Tucker, columnist, "Immigrant Bashing Goes Its Sorry Way," *Atlanta Journal Constitution*, February 10, 2008)

5. "Hispanics see firsthand every day the drain illegal immigration has on institutions such as school systems, law enforcement, the criminal justice system, health care, and jobs, and as a factor in the depression of wages. Our taxpayer-funded institutions are reeling from this migration into the United States, particularly those that are primarily supposed to be serving the low-income people of this country." (Waldo Benavidez, "Speakout: Illegal immigration hurting Hispanics," *Rocky Mountain News*, October 2, 2006)

Study Questions

1. Is there one common question addressed by all these arguments?
2. How would you label each viewpoint here?
3. State the basic pro or con position taken by each one.
4. Take one viewpoint for analysis. What reasons are given in support of its position?
5. Which arguments do you find to be the most persuasive and why?

Critical Reading of Arguments

What an argument first needs is an objective reading or hearing.
Afterwards criticism can begin with five questions.

As you will remember from the short discussion in the second chapter about critical reading, accurate comprehension must precede any criticism of the material. In reading arguments, maintaining openness is not always easy, especially when the arguments express values that differ from your own. It can require a lot of restraint to slow down those inner objections in order to make sure that you really understand what is being said. You may have found it a struggle to give a fair hearing to some of the viewpoints expressed in the opening Discovery Exercise. Yet critical analysis cannot be fair unless it is based on a careful and accurate reading of the material.

In this chapter you will be guided by some questions that will help you fairly assess the arguments you read. By using these questions, you will be able to make rapid evaluations of newspaper editorials, letters to editors, voter information pamphlets, and any other form of persuasive writing. The skills of critical analysis will also enable you to write more effective arguments yourself, whether in the form of simple letters of complaint or in the longer argumentative essay assignments that appear in Appendix One of this book.

What follows are five guiding questions to help you quickly analyze any argument. After completing this analysis, you will know whether to accept the argument, reject it, or simply suspend judgment for the time being.

1. What viewpoint is the source of this argument?
2. What is the issue of controversy?
3. Is it an argument? Or is it a report?
4. How is the argument structured in terms of reasons and conclusion?
5. What are the argument's strengths and weaknesses?

What Viewpoint Is the Source of This Argument?

Arguments represent the bias, interests, and objectives of a viewpoint.

This chapter's opening Discovery Exercise gave you an opportunity to apply what you learned in the previous chapter about the way viewpoint shapes content. You might have begun by first skimming through each argument, reading the names, titles, and affiliations of each speaker, then rereading the argument in light of this information. From such clues, you might have been able to make inferences about the speaker's values, motives, and beliefs. You would have begun by asking the first question of critical reading: *What viewpoint does this argument express?*

What Is the Issue of Controversy?

To assess an argument, we first must determine the issue.

Argument: offers reasons to support a conclusion with the intent to persuade
Topic: a subject of interest
Issue: a controversial topic that arouses debate
Debate question: a neutrally formulated question that provides a focus for pro and con positions on the issue

Arguments are based on issues or controversial topics that generate pro and con arguments. A few examples of topics that have stirred up controversy include the financial bailout of Wall Street, the war in Iraq, nuclear energy and weapons, and genetically modified foods.

One topic can generate hundreds of issues. Moreover, surrounding each issue can be many debate questions. The opening Discovery Exercise began with pro and con arguments on the topic of illegal immigration. You might have decided that the common issue was whether illegal immigration benefited the United States. Other issues raised by illegal immigration could include proposed solutions such as amnesty for illegal residents, mass raids and deportations, increasing border officers, completing a border wall, and the use of foreign guest programs.

Debate questions provide a clear common focus for pro and con positions on selected issues. In the opening Discovery Exercise, the arguments might be paired or clustered according to such debate questions as follow:

- Is illegal immigration of economic benefit to the United States?
- Does illegal immigration harm the United States?
- Do the social costs of illegal immigration outweigh its economic benefits?

As is customary in debates, the question addressed by both sides, pro and con, is expressed in neutral language free of biased wording. The questions begin with open-ended words such as *Does, Can,* or *Should.* Thus, a debate question, like a good polling question, does not favor one side or the other.

Debate questions can also be more specific than the three mentioned previously; they can address more specific problems:

- Do illegal immigrants take the jobs that Americans don't want?
- Does illegal immigration lower the wages and job opportunities of unskilled American workers?
- Should illegal immigrants receive drivers' licenses?
- Should the children of illegal immigrants born in the United States become American citizens?

Debate questions generally appear in the headings above pro and con arguments on newspaper editorial pages or in magazines such as the *Congressional Digest.* However, more often the debate questions are not made explicit, requiring that they be supplied from our own thinking. Indeed, this was what you had to do in the opening Discovery Exercise.

Class Discussion

Read each of the following condensed pro and con arguments. For each one, first state the issue and then formulate one debate question that addresses their common issue.

1. **Pro** Ex-convicts should not be denied the right to vote. Denying felons the vote assumes that they can never repay their debt to society.

   Con Felons would have to have bad judgment; otherwise they never would have committed crimes. Therefore, why should we allow people with bad judgment the right to vote?

2. **Pro** DRE or direct recording electronic voting machines are efficient, secure, and easy to use; they eliminate the need for paper ballots; and they provide instant tabulation of the results. Their touch screens or buttons make it easier for the disabled to vote.

   Con DRE voting machines are untrustworthy: they can be hacked or tampered with; and they do not provide voters with a paper trail for verification. They subvert the democratic process.

3. **Pro** The production of ethanol for fuel has many advantages. It reduces the toxic air pollutants caused by gasoline. It can be produced locally, it produces a harvest within six months, and it reduces our reliance on imported oil.

   Con The production of ethanol requires nearly as much energy as it ends up supplying as fuel. The crops made into ethanol use up vast tracts of land needed for growing food in a planet where more people are now starving.

Is It an Argument or a Report?

Arguments and reports are each structured differently and have different objectives. We cannot analyze one according to the standards of the other.

Although arguments and reports have very different objectives and forms (see Table 9.1), they can be mistaken for one another if their differences are not fully understood. Moreover, to add to the confusion, arguments can sometimes be disguised as reports while actually offering a biased perspective. (More will be explained about this hybrid later.)

The main purpose of a **report** is to offer information; this can be done by offering facts and findings or relating and explaining events. Its objective is not to advocate an opinion. If the situation is controversial,

TABLE 9.1 Arguments and Reports: Making the Distinction

Report	Argument
Purpose: To inform in a manner that wins trust in its reliability.	*Purpose:* To persuade others to agree with an idea.
Structure:	*Structure:*
1. Data presented and explained.	1. Assertion of an opinion, thesis, or conclusion that has a clearly committed bias.
2. Offers hypotheses for interpreting the data. Tries to avoid bias.	
3. Offers support to confirm data's accuracy and veracity, such as corroborating evidence, independent studies, examples, expert testimony, records, surveys, polls, investigations, statistics, analogies.	2. Reasons given to support this conclusion are offered just as they are in a report. However, material that supports the conclusion is emphasized, whereas material that does not may be omitted or downplayed.
4. Summary of findings in manner that leaves final assessment up to the reader.	3. Summary seeks agreement for own conclusion.

the reporter should present arguments from all sides, but not favor one argument or another. Likewise in writing scientific reports, the author might make recommendations, but not advocate.

Arguments, on the other hand, do advocate opinions; information may be used to explain an idea, to justify it, or to persuade others to accept that idea. Arguments are not supposed to be neutral but express a position.

Let's review these differences by means of some condensed examples on this question: Should concealed guns be allowed on college campuses?

Argument

Pro Students should be allowed to carry concealed guns on any college campus. This right would protect them from more mass shooting episodes. They would not even have to fire the guns; just knowing that others were armed would deter any maniac from going on a shooting spree.

Con If students were allowed to carry concealed guns, life on college campuses would turn into the Wild West. Fear, distrust, and mayhem would prevail. Moreover, since mass shooters are usually suicidal, they would hardly be deterred. The idea of legislating to allow all students to arm themselves is a misguided solution.

Report

In 2008, fifteen states were considering legislation to allow people (students, faculty, and staff) to carry concealed guns on college campuses. Proponents of such legislation claim that no one would go on a shooting spree if they knew that their victims would be armed and could return fire. They say that in past incidents, the police have not been able to arrive in time to prevent massacres. If students were armed, they might be able to hold off a shooter until the police arrive. Opponents of such legislation claim that arming the campus would not deter shooters, who are suicidal anyway, and would only create a climate of fear and possibly more shooting incidents. A third view claims that this debate only distracts us from the core problem: the failure of U.S. gun control laws. They point to countries such as Australia, Britain, France, China, and Sweden that maintain low homicide rates through strict gun control laws. Meanwhile, licensed individuals can now carry concealed handguns at state universities in Utah, Colorado State University, and Blue Ridge College in West Virginia.

A report can tell a story, it can present findings, interview supporters and detractors, summarize arguments, and offer theories. Nevertheless, a report in the pure sense of the word leaves the final conclusions up to the reader.

Another difficulty we face in separating arguments from reports is that arguments may sometimes have the appearance of reports. This practice is particularly prevalent in many of the so-called news magazines, which offer news reports that are actually opinion pieces because of their slanted language, selection of information, and emphasis. Here is an example of an argument that could be mistaken for a report.

> "During the week of April 21–25, 2008, thousands of college students throughout the United States, organized under the banner of Students for Concealed Carry on Campus (SCCC), will attend classes wearing empty holsters, in protest of state laws and school policies that stack the odds in favor of dangerous criminals and armed killers by disarming law abiding citizens licensed to carry concealed handguns virtually everywhere else." (*Concealed Campus.com*)

Discussion Break Question

Working in small groups, or with a partner, explain how the first report differs from the pro and con arguments on this issue. Then discuss how the first report differs from the second one.

Class Discussion

Identify the following as either reports or arguments:

1. Don't buy water in plastic bottles. For one thing, you don't know whether you are paying for city tap water. Secondly, the plastic can leach cancer-causing chemicals into the water, and thirdly, our landfills are already choking with the billions of plastic bottles.

2. "Nuclear power, apart from nuclear war, is the greatest threat to life on this planet. In fact, 95% of the total nuclear waste in the United States has been generated by nuclear power plants. Nuclear waste will last for 500,000 years, and there is no safe means to prevent these radioactive elements from entering and concentrating in the food chain." (Helen Caldicott, 2004)

3. U.S. railroads, after being in decline for decades, are now part of a booming business. They are being rediscovered as the answer to congested highways and rising fuel prices. Moreover, they are being marketed as eco-friendly and low in fuel consumption.

4. Stonehenge has remained a mystery for centuries. This circular monument of stones, built around 4,500 years ago in southwest England, was thought to be mainly a temple to the sun and an astrological calendar. In 2008 archeological research came up with a new theory: that it served primarily as a royal burial ground. But will this be the final explanation?

How Is the Argument Structured in Terms of Reasons and Conclusions?

A quick method for analyzing an argument is to disassemble its structure, first identifying its conclusion and then separating that statement from the reasons offered to support it.

Conclusion: A clear statement of what an argument intends to prove. This statement serves as the argument's thesis, final opinion, or judgment. It clearly shows the author's position on an issue.

Reason: Statements offered to explain, justify, or support the conclusion of an argument. Reasons can take the form of statements of facts, statistics, evidence, or reasoning. Any number of reasons can be offered to support one conclusion.

In the chapters that follow, you will be learning more about standards and forms for inductive and deductive reasoning. You will learn that with induction, arguments are structured in this manner:

- Data
- Data
- Data
- Data

Conclusion

In deduction we use the syllogism:

- Major Premise
- Minor Premise

Conclusion

Arguments use both inductive and deductive reasoning. Simplified models such as these reveal their structure. We will learn more about how these models help us understand the rules of reasoning in the next chapter. For now we only want to focus on the two essential aspects of an argument: (1) what point is being made and (2) how this point is supported. If we can identify these two elements quickly in an argument, we can size up its structure. Thus, when reading the chapter's opening arguments on outsourcing, you may have sensed that some of them were better reasoned than others, but you may not have been really sure how to explain why or why not. Seeing arguments in terms of their structure can help us begin to do that. It also helps us write better arguments.

The next few pages offer a rapid method for recognizing these two elements in arguments; this method explains arguments as structures consisting of *reasons* and *conclusions*. Both inductive and deductive arguments consist of both conclusions and reasons. As you will discover in the following chapters, the term *reasons* can be used to include both the premises of deduction and the factual evidence of induction, and the term *conclusion* includes inductive hypotheses as well as deductive conclusions. In both cases, separating conclusions from their reasons is not always easy. Yet we have to make this separation in order to determine what conclusion we are being asked to accept, and whether or not sufficient and adequate reasons are given in its support. This portion of the chapter will offer exercises for practice in identifying and analyzing arguments in terms of their reasons and conclusions.

Identifying the Conclusion of an Argument

The key to understanding any written argument is to first search for its conclusion. Although the word *conclusion* is generally understood as a final summary statement in an argument, the conclusion functions more like the thesis of a composition, which sometimes appears first. In the formal reasoning of induction and deduction, a conclusion is the *last step* in a reasoning process:

Inductive

Yesterday I was happy singing.

Last week I was happy singing.

Every time in my life I sing, I feel happy.

Conclusion: Singing makes me happy.

Deductive

Singing makes me happy.

I am singing.

Conclusion: I am happy.

In an argument, a conclusion is the bottom line of a decision, while the reasons are the evidence and thoughts that support this decision. Yet the problem remains that although we know our own conclusions, it is not always that easy to find them in the written arguments of others, especially because statements of reasons can look like very much like conclusions.

Consider this argument on illegal immigration. Here the conclusion is clearly separate from the reasons although each reason could serve as a conclusion in a different context.

Illegal immigration is good for America. (conclusion) It provides U.S. businesses with eager low-wage workers. (reason) Employers do not have to provide them with benefits. (reason) Their low wages and lack of benefits are offset through social services provided by U.S. taxpayers. (reason) Finally, all U.S. consumers enjoy the lower prices for goods and services allowed by their low cost labor. (reason)

Sometimes it is not that easy to separate the conclusion from the reasons. Consider this example:

Illegal immigrants from Mexico living in the U.S. are poor although usually not as poor as they were in Mexico. They are blamed for burdening U.S. social services and for taking jobs away from legal residents. They have no rights when arrested and incarcerated. All these stresss factors leave illegal immigrants more susceptible to exploitation.

Here you would have to decide where the conclusion lies. What statement encompasses all the rest of the sentences? Is it the first or the last?

One method for recognizing conclusions is to look for the so-called inference indicator words that precede conclusions. Here are examples of the ways in which these words signal the conclusions of arguments:

1. *The truth of the matter is* that illegal immigration is not good for the United States.
2. *In my opinion*, illegal immigration is good for the United States.
3. *It all goes to show that* illegal immigration is not good for the United States.
4. *Therefore* illegal immigration is good for the United States.

Identifying Reasons

Reasons are statements offered to explain, justify, or support conclusions.

1. I am not in favor of completing the border wall between the United States and Mexico. (conclusion) First of all, it is costing billions of dollars. (reason) Second, it is damaging the environment in many locations. (reason) Third, determined refugees will find their way over or around it. (reason)

2. I am in favor of completing the border wall between the United States and Mexico. (conclusion) Good fences make good neighbors. (reason) A secure wall could save the lives of immigrants who would otherwise die in the desert on its other side. (reason) Its success would force Mexico to do more to help its poor and unemployed, and thus stem its flood of mass emigration. (reason)

As is the case with conclusions, reasons are easier to identify when we supply them ourselves than when we read or hear them in someone else's argument. Yet, we need to identify the reasons in an argument we hear or read in order to decide if they provide adequate and sufficient support for the conclusion. In both arguments given in the previous example, if only one reason had been offered, the support would have been insufficient. Both reasons together make for stronger arguments, although both will need more expansion and development to be convincing, as would occur in a longer, complete argument.

The task of analysis then begins by flushing out the reasons, which means looking for the conclusion first. In a short argument, once we identify the conclusion the reasons are simply what remain.

Another technique for identifying reasons is to look for the so-called inference indicator words that often introduce reasons. In the first example given previously, you may have noticed the use of the words *first, second*, and *third*, which signaled that you were being given reasons in support of the conclusion stated in the first sentence. Other reason indicator words include *because, for one thing, in view of the fact that, for the reason that, is supported by, also*, and *for example*.

1. I am in favor of amnesty for illegal immigrants *because* it is not good to have a country full of second-class citizens.
2. I am opposed to the idea of amnesty. *For one thing*, it gives a signal that it is OK to break this country's laws.
3. I favor amnesty *in view of the fact* that we could never track down and deport all the illegals living in this country.

Conclusion indicator words include *therefore, so, in fact, the truth of the matter is, in short, it follows that, shows that, indicates that, suggests that, proves that, we may deduce that, points to the conclusion that, in my opinion*, and *the most obvious explanation is*.

Reason indicator words include *because, first . . . second, since, for, for one thing, in view of the fact that, for the reason that, is supported by, for example, also*.

EXERCISE

■ *Identifying Reasons and Conclusions*

In the following statements, underline the conclusions and number the reasons. Notice that some of these may be arguments and some may be reports since both have reasons and conclusions.

1. I opened these fresh blueberries as soon as I got home from your store and found they were moldy on the bottom. You owe me a refund.
2. People used to say that they were working their way through college. Nowadays either you need scholarships, family help, a loan, or all three. No longer can you pay all your college expenses by working as you go.
3. He said he didn't want to interrupt his studies to cook dinner and wash the dishes. I said we couldn't afford a restaurant. I ended up cooking the dinner.

4. You can save on gas in a lot of ways. Ride your bike to school and work. Live in a neighborhood where you can walk to buy food and use a collapsible cart to push the groceries home.

5. It is possible to get your garbage down to one full can a month. Almost everything can go into compost or recycling bins. Do your part to reduce landfill waste.

6. You can get super rich by buying commercial real estate! Commercial properties are easier to own, produce greater cash flow, and are more profitable than owning rentals.

7. Some people don't like dogs but I do. Their affection is constant, as is their loyalty, and their needs are simple.

8. "Experts say the depletion of groundwater threatens the food security and economic stability of India, China, the United States, Mexico, Spain, and North Africa. In China, the agricultural use of groundwater has skyrocketed, causing water tables to drop in many places by a rate of 5 feet a year." (Daniel Pepper, *San Francisco Chronicle*, May 9, 2008, p. A-1)

More on Distinguishing Reasons from Conclusions

Conclusions at the Beginning

Conclusions often appear at the beginning of arguments, functioning like thesis statements or topic sentences. You would have first noticed this in the two chapter opening arguments on page 235.

> Illegal immigration has a clear economic logic.

> Illegal immigration into the United States is a highly profitable proposition for both employers and the U.S. government, and it also benefits Mexico . . .

Conclusions Implied

Sometimes the conclusion is not stated explicitly but only implied. Examine opening quotes 4 and 5 on pages 235–236. In each of these cases we find hints of the conclusion in the titles of the articles from which the excerpts were taken:

> *Immigrant Bashing Goes Its Sorry Way*
> *Illegal immigration hurting Hispanics*

Sometimes title clues may not be present. Consider this example:

> The U.S. government continues to build a border wall costing millions of dollars and untold environmental damage. In the meantime, hundreds of immigrants continue to cross the border daily from Tijuana hidden in automobiles waived through by bribed border guards. Even if the immigrants are caught at the border, their only penalty is to be sent back to Tijuana, free to try again.

Here the implied conclusion could be formulated as follows:

> An expensive new border wall cannot keep out illegal immigrants as long as our highway border crossings are not secure and as long as those who are caught can continue to return.

Conclusions in the Middle

Sometimes a conclusion appears in the middle of a series of statements. Consider this example:

> The U.S. needs a continuous influx of young workers to feed revenue into the Social Security system. Now as the lifespan of our population has increased, we have an unfavorable ratio of workers to retirees. Amnesty for the 20 million illegal immigrants in this country could save our Social Security system. (conclusion) Since the majority of illegal immigrants are young workers or parents of future workers, their participation could turn things around.

In summary, when we want to analyze arguments the first step is to identify the conclusion. Obviously, we need to determine clearly *exactly what the author is claiming to prove* before becoming involved in a reaction of agreement or disagreement. By identifying the conclusion, we know the author's exact position. We may agree or disagree with this position—but first we must know what it is. If we should mistake one of the reasons for the conclusion, we may find ourselves going off on a wrong track in our analysis and rebuttal. But once we have identified the conclusion, we can easily determine the reasons and isolate them for examination and evaluation.

The final advantage of learning how to identify conclusions and reasons is that it saves us the time of wrestling with poor arguments. When we have the skill to quickly survey and assess an argument's structure, then we can decide whether or not this argument is worth our serious consideration. Moreover, when we are writing our own arguments, we will know how to build them on a clear and aware foundation and thus demonstrate a visible structure of conscious thought.

EXERCISES

■ More Practice in Identifying Reasons and Conclusions

Analyze the following arguments by underlining the conclusions, or by supplying the conclusion in writing if it is only implied. Note that sometimes a conclusion may be part of a sentence, or the conclusion may be offered alone without any reasons attached.

1. Frequent snacks of high-energy food are not harmful to backpackers. Indeed, hikers are found to have more energy and less weariness if they snack every hour.

2. Broadcast television is not appropriate in the courtroom. The relentless pressure of the media threatens the balance between the First Amendment's press freedom and the Sixth Amendment's fair trial rights.

3. Whereas birth is a cause for celebration, death has become a dreaded and unspeakable issue to be avoided by every means possible in our modern society. Perhaps it is that death reminds us of our human vulnerability in spite of all our technological advances. (Elisabeth Kübler-Ross)

4. Do not stop thinking of life as an adventure. You have no security unless you live bravely, excitingly, imaginatively; unless you choose a challenge rather than competence. (Eleanor Roosevelt)

5. There's nothing like the taste of fresh, hot brownies. Bake your own the easy way with Brownlee's Brownie Mix! (advertisement)

6. No doctor should have the right to allow a patient to die. No doctor is God.

7. Videos are a good way to entertain children. You can control what they watch, and there are many worthwhile films to choose from.

8. Since the 1920s, sperm counts have declined among American men. The underlying causes are uncertain, but the factors of stress and toxic chemicals are being considered.

9. If only 1 percent of the car owners in America did not use their cars for one day a week, they would save 42 million gallons of gas a year and keep 840 million pounds of CO_2 out of the atmosphere.

10. Because of their greater use of prescription drugs, women turn up in hospital emergency rooms with drug problems more frequently than men. (FDA consumer report)

▪ More Practice with Longer Arguments

Analyze the arguments that opened this chapter by underlining the conclusions and numbering the reasons given. Then do the same for each of the following arguments:

1. People think non-violence is really weak and non-militant. These are misconceptions that people have because they don't understand what non-violence means. Non-violence takes more guts, if I can put it bluntly, than violence. . . . We are convinced that non-violence is more powerful than violence. We are convinced that non-violence supports you if you have a just and moral cause. If you use violence, you have to sell part of yourself for that violence. Then you are no longer a master of your own struggle. (Cesar E. Chavez)

2. An enigma presents itself which in all ages has agitated inquiring minds. How can it be that mathematics, being after all a product of human thought which is independent of experience, is so admirably appropriate to the objects of reality? Is human reason, then, without experience, merely by taking thought, able to fathom the properties of real things? In my opinion, the answer to this question is briefly, this: as far as the propositions of mathematics refer to reality, they are not certain; and as far as they are certain, they do not refer to reality. (Albert Einstein)

3. Many economists believe that water is a natural resource like any other and should be subject to the laws of supply and demand—and market pricing. Since the turn of the century, U.S. water use has risen at least six fold. . . . Nowhere is demand greater than in the West—whose population has soared nearly 70 percent in 25 years. Scarce water has been misdirected because of a hodgepodge of regulations and federal subsidies—which have created a lot of waste. If farmers were encouraged by market pricing to use just 5 percent less water, the demands of urban users could be met for the next 25 years. ("Making Water Plentiful," *Investor's Business Daily*, February 17, 1997)

4. A growing movement of people believe that the imperatives of economic globalization—unlimited growth, a seamless global consumer market, corporate rule, deregulation, privatization, and free trade—are the driving forces behind the destruction of our water systems. These must be challenged and rejected if the world's water is to be saved. Water as a fundamental right is guaranteed in the Universal Declaration on Human Rights. ("Water as Commodity—The Wrong Prescription" by Maude Barlow, quoted in *Institute for Food and Development Policy Backgrounder*, Summer 2001)

Core Discovery Writing Application

■ Writing a Short Persuasive Argument: A Letter of Complaint

This assignment is about claiming your own power. It is a practical opportunity to stand up for something you believe in, to defend yourself or others against some injustice, and to initiate or restore communication with someone. This assignment will take the simple form of writing an effective argument in a short letter of complaint. In this letter, you will only need to describe what you consider to be an injustice and then communicate clearly what you want.

■ The Steps

1. Address the letter to a specific individual: to a friend, a parent, an elected official, a landlady, or a newspaper editor. In short, address it to someone who has some power to do something about the situation that concerns you. It may take some research to determine who this person is, but that is a key part of the assignment.

2. As you outline your letter, use neutral, descriptive, and nonblaming language to explain

   a. What the situation is

   b. What is unfair about it

   c. What you want from the other person now

   Your final paragraph should serve to keep the two of you connected by asking for reactions, a call, an appointment, or an agreement within a time frame that you suggest. (For instance, you might conclude by saying "I would like very much to hear what you have to say in response, and I would welcome hearing from you by phone or letter. If I have not heard from you within a week, then I will call you.")

3. Use reasoning and evidence to support your case. Make your conclusions straightforward and simple. Be clear about what you want but also remain courteous and respectful.

4. The length of your letter should be one to two pages typed; use a business letter format.

■ Writing Preparation

In choosing your topic, select a situation that feels genuinely unjust and unfinished to you, one that you have not been able to handle in a way that you would like. The more emotion you feel on the subject, the greater the challenge will be to formulate an effective, well-reasoned argument. When we feel very angry, sad, or apathetic, it is difficult to think clearly or make ourselves heard. Yet, writing and revising to work through your emotions can summon the clarity and power needed to present your case effectively. If at the beginning you feel overwhelmed by feelings, write them out or hit some pillows until you blow off steam. When you feel more collected, you can compose your argument. After you have finished your first draft, reread it, asking yourself whether your purpose was to make the other party feel ashamed, guilty, or wrong. Blaming the other person may make you feel better temporarily, but will not help you get what you really want. If you try to make people feel guilty, they will resist hearing what you have to say and not want to cooperate. Instead use neutral descriptive language; report what happened with objectivity. Be quite specific about how you see the problem and what you want the other person to do for you. Remain respectful both of yourself and of the person you are addressing. Do not make demands or give ultimatums, but make requests that the other party can meet.

Scoring for Letter of Complaint

1. Letter is addressed to a specific person who has the power to do something about the situation. *10 points*

2. Organization is simple and clear, describes the situation and the complaint, and is requesting a specific action. *10 points*

3. Request made that is clear and possible to fulfill. *10 points*

4. Conclusion is clear; sufficient and adequate reasons are given. *10 points*

5. Topic chosen involves challenge of self-control. (Not a routine letter returning a defective product.) *20 points*

6. Language does not blame, make guilty, or cause defensiveness. *10 points*

7. A final connecting statement is made, requesting, but not demanding, a response within a stated period of time. *10 points*

8. No distracting errors of punctuation, sentence structure, spelling. *20 points*

■ Peer Review

To follow up on this exercise in class, exchange your letter or essay with a partner and do the following:

1. Underline the conclusion and circle the reasons.

2. Answer these questions on a sheet to attach to your partner's work:

   a. Which reasons clearly support, justify, or explain the conclusion? Which do not?

b. Are more reasons needed? Explain.

3. If any portion is not clear to you, circle it and ask your partner to explain it to you.

When you receive your work back, consider the comments. If you cannot agree with the critique, seek another partner and go through the same process verbally. If you find the criticisms helpful, revise your work accordingly.

What Are the Strengths and Weaknesses of This Argument?

To make a list of standards for judging the strengths and weaknesses of an argument would mean reviewing most of the material covered in the past several chapters of this text. These six questions summarize such standards:

1. Are the reasons adequate to support the conclusion?
2. Are there any hidden assumptions in this argument?
3. Are any central words ambiguous or slanted to incite prejudice?
4. Are there fallacies in the reasoning? (You will learn how to use this question in the next chapters.)
5. Is any important information omitted?
6. Is any information false, contradictory, or irreconcilable?

All but the final three questions have already been discussed in this text. Fallacies will be explained in the next chapters. What follows now is an explanation of the last two questions.

Is Any Important Information Missing?

In any communication, crucial information can be purposely or inadvertently omitted. A critical thinker pays attention to what is relevant but missing.

When studying arguments or reports, it is just as important to consider what is missing as what is present. Since missing information does not come with a label or announcement, we have to make use of our capacities to read or listen carefully, notice gaps, and ask questions. When crucial information is omitted, standards for clarity, completeness, and fairness cannot be met.

If you are writing a research paper and have read up on your subject, then it can be easier to spot significant omissions. Yet, even if you are relatively unfamiliar with a topic, you can still detect essential missing elements, such as a missing date or identified author. A routine checklist of the basics to look for would include the following:

- Missing definitions
- Missing supportive details
- Missing reasons or conclusions
- Missing facts and citations
- Missing frame identifiers such as dates and sources

Some of these elements have already been discussed in this text. The importance of definitions was emphasized in Chapter 2, where you learned how undefined central words cause confusion in an argument. In Chapter 3 you learned that facts need verification. In later chapters you learned how inferences, opinions, and evaluations might be substituted for facts. Finally, in this chapter, you have been learning about the need both for conclusions and supporting reasons.

Investigative journalism may be described as the pursuit of missing information. Beginning with mysteries and armed by curiosity, journalists can spend months gathering information, conducting interviews, and gathering and confirming facts before writing up their notes for publication.

In analyzing an individual piece, a researcher also has to consider whether crucial omissions might be purposeful or inadvertent. Purposeful omissions can range from acts of censorship to simple editing decisions about how best to accommodate the space available. Newspaper articles, for instance, will not provide the amount of supporting evidence or citations required in scientific papers or academic studies. Inadvertent omissions, on the other hand, might be due to factors such as ignorance, carelessness, or insufficient research. Although we may not be able to determine whether crucial omissions were intentional, we nevertheless need to consider these omissions when assessing the relative reliability of an argument or a report.

Following Up on Missing Information

Arguments are meant to be persuasive. Yet sometimes this purpose can collide with ethical considerations such as truthfulness and fairness. Here is an illustrative story that begins in the form of a brief advertisement: *Spacious* *sunny apartment available! Great rent: $750. Secure building. Close to freeway connections. One block from buses and subway. Call 946-7708.*

Since you are looking for a low-rent apartment near public transportation, you make the call. However, when you are given the street address, you pause since you realize that the apartment building is located in an intercity area once known for its high crime rate. You call the police department; they tell you that although cars continue to be vandalized or stolen on that street, there haven't been any muggings there for the past year. This information leaves you wary, but drawn by the prospect of low rent, you decide to see the place for yourself. When you arrive, you note that the building is secured by a buzzer let-in system that seems to provide a fair amount of safety.

The landlord leads you up the stairs to the apartment; it is on the fifth floor and there is no elevator. When you enter the apartment, you discover that although the apartment could be called spacious because of the large rooms and high ceilings, it seems more dark than sunny. As the landlord turns on the lights, he tells you that the sun will be streaming from the kitchen into the living room in the late afternoons at sunset. Since the kitchen faces west, you wonder why the sun only arrives that late.

You open the kitchen curtains and find that the windows look out directly onto a freeway overpass that blocks the path of the sun. It is only at that time that you feel the shaking of the floorboards from the constant roar of freeway traffic.

You tell the landlord that you are thinking of buying a car and ask him if it would be safe parked out on the street. After a short pause, he says, "Well, you would keep it locked, wouldn't you?"

At that point you excuse yourself, saying that you have decided not to take the place.

Class Discussion

1. Make a list of the things that the storyteller found to be significant omissions about the apartment.

2. At what point in this story does the storyteller decide that the landlord is untrustworthy?

3. Was the landlord wrong to put the best spin in his ad, stating only the apartment's best features? How might the landlord have justified his omissions?

4. Working in small groups or pairs, share a parallel situation from your own life or someone else's. How was it discovered that some important information was being withheld? Were you or the other person adversely affected?

Is Any Information False, Contradictory, or Irreconcilable?

Although we may not be able to prove falsehoods, we can pay attention to such warning signs as discrepancies, contradictions, incongruities, and inconsistencies.

Discrepancy: Something diverges from what we expect: an inconsistency, as between facts and claims. *(American Heritage Dictionary)*

Incongruity: Something that does not meet our expectations about what is correct, appropriate, logical, or standard. The word comes from the Latin *incongruent*, meaning *not in agreement*.

Consistency: Something that is consistent has constancy and therefore dependability. The term comes from the Latin *consistens*, meaning *to stand firmly*. Something that is **inconsistent** lacks constancy or logical coherence, and may contain contradictions.

Contradiction: To make claims that cannot both be true or both be false at the same time; to do or say something, then deny it was done or said; to say one thing but do the opposite.

Irreconcilable: Conflicting ideas, beliefs, or information that cannot be fully explained or resolved.

A final topic for this chapter concerns ways of approaching information suspected to be false. As critical readers, we cannot conduct court hearings to prove lies, but our knowledge of critical thinking standards can help us assess information reliability. An early signal that something may be wrong is the appearance of **discrepancies, inconsistencies,** or **contradictions.** Read the definitions of these and related terms given in the box. Then consider the following situations.

1. "Termites? No problem. [Online] $64.99 buys a 20-ounce bottle of XXXX. That's enough for anyone with a credit card and a shipping address to make 24 gallons of anti-termite spray. Never mind that the manufacturer, XX Corporation, authorizes only licensed exterminators who have undergone a special training program to handle the pesticide, according to the product's website. (Julian Olsen, "World Wide Web of Pesticides Can Endanger Consumers," The Center for Public Integrity, September 12, 2008)

2. Energy saved is energy found. At *Big Oil*, we recognize the world's needs for all the energy we can develop. With technology and with respect, *Big Oil* finds the oil lying deep beneath the ocean. We believe that conservation is the cheapest, most reliable form of new energy.

3. [Scott] McClellan, [White House Press Secretary from 2003–2006] told Keith Olbermann in an interview on June 9, 2008 regarding the Iraq War planning: *"I don't think there was a conspiracy theory there, some conspiracy to deliberately mislead. I don't want to imply a sinister intent. There might have been some individuals that knew more than others and tried to push things forward in a certain way, and that's something I can't speak to. I don't think that you had a bunch of people sitting around a room, planning and plotting in a sinister way. That's the point I make in the book. At the same time, whether or not it was sinister or not, it was very troubling that we went to war on this basis."* (Wikipedia, Scott McClellan, *http://en.wikipedia.org/wiki/Scott McClellan*)

4. Mom: "I can't understand how you could have put 10,000 miles on that car I gave you two months ago when you say you have only used it to drive between the dorm and your classes or into town for errands. Has your boyfriend been using your car?"

   Daughter: "If I had known you were afraid I would wear the car out by driving it, I would have been more careful."

5. Today a prestigious peer-review journal of occupational and environmental medicine published the results of the largest study ever conducted on the effects of toxic PCB chemicals. The study, financed by XX Incorporated, found no significant increase in cancer deaths among plant workers. XX Incorporated faces potential liabilities of hundreds of millions of dollars for cleaning up waters contaminated by PCBs. For many years it vigorously opposed federal government requirements to dredge the sediments in waters contaminated by PCBs. It has frequently cited scientific studies that it says show no link between exposure to PCBs and cancer. The study did not address other health risks associated with PCBs such as neurological dysfunction, liver damage, skin irritation, and reproductive problems.

Class Discussion

Divide into four groups that will each consider one of the preceding examples. Then answer the following questions.

1. What exactly is the discrepancy here? Are there any contradictions? If so, what are they?

2. What critical thinking standards are not being met here?

As we all know, contradictions need not always signal a faulty cover-up; they can also stem from careless thinking. For our purposes as critical thinkers, however, it may not be necessary to determine whether carelessness or lying was involved. We need only refer to the standard that says that any argument that contains contradictions is unsound.

> A **sound argument** (or one that is both true and correctly reasoned) does not contain contradictions.

Contradictions appear not only in arguments but also in other situations, such as those that involve contradictions between

- Words and action
- Evidence and denials
- Different testimonies
- Different facts
- Claims and consequences
- What we are told and what we know to be true

The challenge of contradictions is that they don't appear with labels; their detection only results from alert perception and thinking.

Aside from the presence of contradictions, there are many other warning signs of possible dishonesty. We might encounter them in situations ranging from live encounters at home or work to events reported on the nightly news. Here are some signs that call for closer attention:

1. Person who, when confronted with a contradiction, either flatly denies it or engages in diversionary tactics such as name-calling, red herrings, and straw man arguments.
2. Person who makes a false statement and, when confronted with evidence that it is false, only continues to make the false statement.
3. Person who offers "facts" without citing sources, thus making it difficult to corroborate their veracity.
4. Person who uses "double-talk," choosing words that can mislead or deceive.

Class Discussion

Break into small groups. Share your knowledge of personal or public examples that illustrate any of these warning signs. In which cases was there a confirmation that some form of deceit had occurred?

Chapter Summary

1. The critical reading of arguments is an active endeavor that requires involvement, interaction with questions, and evaluation.

2. The questions asked in the critical reading of arguments are:
   a. What viewpoint is the source of this argument?
   b. What is the issue of controversy?
   c. Is it an argument or a report?
   d. How is the argument structured in terms of reasons and conclusions?
   e. What are the argument's strengths and weaknesses?

3. The analysis of arguments in terms of their reasons and conclusions applies to both inductive and deductive arguments. Reasons include data, evidence, and premises, while conclusions include those deductively drawn as well as hypotheses.

4. The conclusion of an argument is the last step in a reasoning process. However, it may be stated at any time during an argument or not at all.

5. Reasons support conclusions. They may be generalizations that could function as conclusions in another context. Once the argument's main conclusion is uncovered, the reasons offered in support becomes clear.

6. Arguments state and defend a claim in an attempt to persuade. Arguments disguised as reports slant the facts and language toward a bias.

7. Reports that only relate events or state facts cannot be analyzed as though they were arguments.

8. An issue is a topic of controversy upon which positions may be taken. Surrounding each issue are many debate questions.

9. The following questions can serve as guidelines for analyzing the strengths and weaknesses of arguments:
   a. Are the reasons adequate to support the conclusion?
   b. Are there any hidden assumptions?
   c. Are any central words ambiguous or slanted so as to incite prejudice?
   d. Are there fallacies of reasoning?
   e. Is any important information missing?
   f. Is any information false or contradictory?

● R E A D I N G S ●

Is Illegal Immigration a Crime?

Here are a pair of pro-and-con arguments on the topic of illegal immigration. The pro argument appears at the website of FAIR (Federation for American Immigration Reform).

This version was last updated in March 2005. The con argument is by David Bacon, a writer and photographer. It appeared in the San Francisco Chronicle *on May 1, 2008. He is the author of* Illegal People—How Globalization Creates Migration and Criminalizes Immigrants.

Illegal Immigration Is a Crime

Federation for Immigration Reform

U.S. Illegal Immigrant Laws

Each year the Border Patrol makes more than a million apprehensions of aliens who flagrantly violate our nation's laws by unlawfully crossing U.S. borders. Such entry is a misdemeanor, but, if repeated, becomes punishable as a felony.

In addition to sneaking into the country (referred to as "entry without inspection—EWI") in violation of the immigration law, others enter with legal documentation and then violate the terms on which they have been admitted. The immigration authorities currently estimate that about two-thirds of all illegal immigrants are EWIs and the remainder is overstayers. Both types of illegal immigrants are deportable under Immigration and Nationality Act Section 237 (a)(1)(B) which says: "*Any alien who is present in the United States in violation of this Act or any other law of the United States is deportable.*"

Illegal Immigration Is Not a Victimless Crime

Apologists for illegal immigration try to paint it as a victimless crime, but the fact is that illegal immigration causes substantial harm to American citizens and legal immigrants, particularly those in the most vulnerable sectors of our population— the poor, minorities, and children.

Illegal immigration causes an enormous drain on public funds. The seminal study of the costs of immigration by the National Academy of Sciences found that the taxes paid by immigrants do not begin to cover the cost of services received by them. The quality of education, health care and other services for Americans are undermined by the needs of endless numbers of poor, unskilled illegal entrants.

5   Additionally, job competition by waves of illegal immigrants desperate for any job unfairly depresses the wages and working conditions offered to American workers, hitting hardest at minority workers and those without high school degrees.

Illegal Immigration and Population Growth

Illegal immigration also contributes to the dramatic population growth overwhelming communities across America—crowding school classrooms, consuming already limited affordable housing, and increasing the strain on precious natural resources like water, energy, and forestland. The immigration authorities estimate that the population of illegal aliens is increasing by an estimated half million people annually.

Illegal Immigration Undermines National Security

While most illegal immigrants may come only to seek work and a better economic opportunity, their presence outside the law furnishes an opportunity for terrorists to blend into the same shadows while they target the American public for their terrorist crimes. Some people advocate giving illegal aliens legal status to bring them out of the shadows, but, if we accommodate illegal immigration by offering legal status, this will be seen abroad as a message that we condone illegal immigration, and we will forever be faced with the problem.

Border Patrol: Necessary But Not Sufficient

The Border Patrol plays a crucial role in combating illegal immigration, but illegal immigration cannot be controlled solely at the border. The overstayers as well as the EWIs who get past the Border Patrol must be identified and removed by the interior immigration inspectors of Immigration and Customs Enforcement (ICE).

What Can Be Done?

There must be a comprehensive effort to end illegal immigration. That requires ensuring that illegal aliens will not be able to obtain employment, public assistance benefits, public education, public housing, or any other taxpayer-funded benefit without detection.

10   The three major components of immigration control—deterrence, apprehension and removal—need to be strengthened by Congress and the Executive Branch if effective control is ever to be reestablished. Controlling illegal immigration requires a balanced approach with a full range of enforcement improvements that go far beyond the border. These include many procedural reforms, beefed up investigation capacity, asylum reform, documents improvements, major improvements in detention and deportation procedures, limitations on judicial review, improved intelligence capacity, greatly improved state/federal cooperation, and added resources.

What About the Costs?

Effective control and management of the laws against illegal immigration require adequate resources. But those costs will be more than offset by savings to states, counties, communities, and school districts across the nation.

Updated 3/05 http://www.fairus.org/site. Used with permission of FAIR Federation for Immigration Reform.

● ● ●

Mayday for Undocumented Workers

David Bacon

In the big immigrant marches that swept the country on May Day in 2006 and 2007, one sign said it all: "We are Workers, not Criminals!" Often it was held in the calloused hands of men and women who looked as though they'd just come from work in a factory, cleaning an office building, or picking grapes.

The sign stated an obvious truth. Millions of people have come to this country to work, not to break its laws. Some have come with visas, and others without them. But they are all contributors to the society they've found here, not people who mean it harm.

Again this May Day, immigrant workers are filling the streets, making the same point. Yet today, the federal government is taking actions that make holding a job a criminal act. Some states and local communities, seeing a green light from the Department of Homeland Security, are passing measures that go even further. These actions need a reality check.

Last summer, Homeland Security Secretary Michael Chertoff proposed a rule requiring employers to fire any workers who couldn't correct a mismatch between the Social Security number they'd provided their employer, and the Social Security database. The regulation assumes that those workers have no valid immigration visa, and therefore no valid Social Security number.

5   With 12 million people living in the United States without legal immigration status, the regulation would lead to massive firings, bringing many industries and businesses to a halt. Citizens and legal visa holders would be swept up as well, since the Social Security database is often inaccurate.

Under Chertoff, the Bureau of Immigration and Customs Enforcement has conducted sweeping workplace raids, arresting and deporting thousands of workers. Many have been charged with an additional crime—identity theft—because they used a Social Security number belonging to someone else to get a job. Yet workers using another number do no harm, and actually deposit money into that holder's account. These immigrants will never collect benefits their contributions paid for.

The Arizona Legislature has passed a law requiring employers to verify the immigration status of every worker through a federal database called E-Verify, which is even more incomplete and full of errors than Social Security. The employers must fire workers whose names get flagged. And Mississippi passed a bill making it a felony for an undocumented worker to hold a job, with jail time of one to 10 years, fines of up to $10,000, and no bail for anyone arrested.

Congress is now debating two bills, the SAVE Act and the New Employee Verification Act, that would require similar use of the E-Verify database.

In 1986, the Immigration Reform and Control Act made it a crime, for the first time in our history, to hire people without papers. Defenders argued that if people could not legally work, they would leave. Life was not so simple, though. Undocumented people are part of the communities they live in. They will not simply go—nor should they. They seek the same goals of equality and opportunity that everyone else in our country believes in.

10   For most, there are no jobs to return to in the countries from which they've come. Rufino Dominguez, an Oaxacan community leader in Fresno, says, "The North American Free Trade Agreement made the price of corn so low that it's not economically possible to plant a crop anymore. We come to the U.S. to work because there's no alternative."

When Congress passed NAFTA, 6 million displaced people came to the United States as a result. If Congress stops passing new free trade agreements, and instead faces the damage NAFTA and other procorporate measures did in Mexico, the poverty and desperation that fuel migration can eventually be reversed.

Trying to push people out of the United States who've come here for survival simply won't work. The price of trying is that the vulnerability of undocumented workers will increase. Unscrupulous employers use that vulnerability to deny overtime, minimum wage, or fire workers when they protest or organize. Increased vulnerability ultimately results in cheaper labor and fewer rights for everyone. Children live in fear that their parents will be picked up in raids.

After deporting more than 1,000 workers at Swift meatpacking plants, Chertoff called for linking "effective interior enforcement and a temporary-worker program."

The government is really after giving cheap labor to large employers. Deportations, firings and guest worker programs all make labor cheaper and union organizing harder. They contribute to a climate of fear and insecurity for everyone. Instead of making work a crime and treating immigrants as criminals, we need equality, security, jobs and rights for everyone.

Used with permission of David Bacon.

●   ●   ●

Study/Writing/Discussion Questions

Working alone or with a partner or group, write an outline that analyzes one of the two preceding arguments.

Begin by stating the debate question addressed by both arguments. Write your statement of the debate question at the top of your outline. Now begin your analysis by making an outline that answers the following questions:

1. What is the viewpoint of the writer? What are this writer's qualifications and affiliations?

2. What is the final conclusion of the argument? Quote or summarize.

3. What reasons does the writer give in support of this final conclusion? Number and summarize each, using quotes as needed.

4. Do you find any key words that are ambiguous (not clearly defined) or words with connotations that convey hidden evaluations, bias, or prejudice? Quote and discuss each.

5. Is any essential information missing in the argument?

6. Discuss any information you find that seems to be false, inconsistent, or irreconcilable.

CHAPTER 10

Fallacies:

What's a Faulty Argument?

SIPRESS

"Your stress is stress-related.

Used with permission of David Sipress.

Of course the doctor's diagnosis is absurd. But would you recognize it as the fallacy of circular reasoning? You will find twenty different types of fallacious reasoning discussed in this book; each has a different name to describe a different reasoning error. Fallacies may be accidental or intentional; many are amusing; all are manipulative; each sidesteps the work of constructing a fair and well-reasoned argument. In order to make learning these twenty fallacies easier, they will be presented in two segments. Three groups of fallacies are presented in this chapter; a fourth group, fallacies of inductive reasoning, will be discussed in Chapter 12. This placement, following a review of the principles of inductive reasoning, should make their fallaciousness more evident and therefore easier to understand. All in all, this division into two parts is intended to make it easier for you to recognize and remember each one.

> **Fallacy** comes from the Latin word *fallacia*, which means deceit or trick. A fallacy is a statement or argument that presents itself as soundly reasoned when it is not.

DISCOVERY EXERCISE

■ *Recognizing Fallacies*

Environmental zealots threaten four industries in California—agriculture, mining, timber, and construction—and the people will no longer tolerate what the zealots are doing to the ability of Californians to make a living. The zealots can shut down the American economy. (Rep. William Dannemeyer, R-Calif.)

1. Do you tend to agree with this opinion or not?
2. What exactly is right or wrong about the argument?
3. If you are familiar with some fallacies, do any of the following apply: poisoning the well, slippery slope, bandwagon, slanted language, appeal to fear, hasty generalization, use of ambiguous words?

The Fallacies

Since the times of the Greeks, fallacies of reasoning have been given names and categorized for study and identification. When we learn the names and characteristics of these fallacies, we gain the following advantages:

- We learn more about the rules for good reasoning.
- We avoid using them ourselves.
- We are not influenced by arguments that contain them.

The effectiveness of fallacies rests in their pseudo-reasoning, their use of hidden appeals to our emotions, and their ability to distract our attention from their weaknesses. On the surface their argument may appear plausible, but a closer study reveals confusion or intentional manipulation. Fallacies fan the smoke of fear, pity, or prejudice; they distract from the issue, play with language, and assume what they should prove. In this chapter, you will learn how to avoid using—or being influenced by—the following fallacies that manipulate through language, emotions, and distraction.

Manipulation Through Language

1. **Word ambiguity:** Seeks to gain an advantage in an argument by using vague or undefined words.

2. **Misleading euphemisms:** Hides meaning by creating words that make a less acceptable idea seem positive or unrecognizable.

3. **Prejudicial language:** Attempts to persuade through the use of loaded words that convey a bias.

Manipulation Through Emotions

4. **Appeal to fear:** Seeks to persuade by arousing fear.

5. **Appeal to pity:** Seeks to persuade by arousing pity.

6. **Appeal to false authority:** Seeks to persuade by citing a fake or inappropriate authority or by appealing to the authority of vague entities, tradition, and popular wisdom or to popular momentum known as bandwagon.

7. **Appeal to prejudice:**
   a. **Personal attack:** Attacks a person's character on matters irrelevant to the issue.
   b. **Poisoning the well:** Seeking to prejudice others against a person, group, or idea so that their arguments will not be heard on their own merits.

Manipulation Through Distraction

8. **Red herring:** Instead of proving a claim, diverts attention into other issues.

9. **Pointing to another wrong:** Distracts attention from a wrongdoing by claiming that similar actions went unnoticed and unpunished.

10. **Straw man:** Misrepresents or caricatures an opponent's position, then refutes the false replica created; also attacks a minor point in an argument, then claims this maneuver invalidates the whole argument.

11. **Circular reasoning:** Assumes what it is supposed to prove by merely repeating the conclusion—sometimes in different words—without providing any supporting reasons. The assumption—or pretense—is that the conclusion is self-evident and needs no support.

Fallacies That Manipulate Through Language

Fallacies that use deceptive language include the fallacies of word ambiguity, misleading euphemisms, and prejudicial language.

Fallacious arguments can be based on an inept use of words or a purposeful selection of words that are vague, ambiguous, and prejudicial in connotation. When the selection is intentional, such words can ward off questioning and hide the weaker aspects of an argument. Three fallacies that attempt persuasion through deceptive word use are called the fallacies of word ambiguity, misleading euphemisms, and prejudicial language.

Word Ambiguity

The **fallacy of word ambiguity** occurs in an argument when a key word with several meanings is left undefined; as a result, the reader must assume what meaning was intended.

A good argument makes careful and conscious word choices. It wants to persuade, and to make its language as clear as possible. A faulty argument tries to gain an unfair advantage by using words that might confuse others and lead them to agree with a claim they don't fully understand. The fallacy of ambiguity uses vague or ambiguous words for this purpose: "We should treat *drug* use as a private right that harms no one but the user." Here, what is meant by *drug* is undefined. The reader trained in critical thinking will stop and wonder what substances the author would include under the term *drugs*. If such a question cannot be answered, then the argument is not worth further study.

Let's consider some other examples. Two expressions frequently seen in print or heard in the media are "the American dream" and "the American way of life." Have you ever wondered if everyone agrees on what these two ideas mean? Here is your chance to find out.

Class Discussion

Choose one or both of these expressions to work with. Write down your answer to the first question given below. Next, break into small groups in order to share your definition or definitions; then discuss the remaining questions.

1. Explain what one or both of these expressions mean to you.

2. Do you all agree on one meaning for each one?

3. In 1992, at the Earth Summit—a UN conference concerned with protecting the global environment—George H.W. Bush said: "The American way of life is non-negotiable." How would you paraphrase what he meant?

4. A number of U.S. mortgage companies have named their companies "The American Dream." What would such a title suggest to you?

5. In your discussion, did you discover anything new about these familiar expressions?

Class Discussion

Here are some examples of statements that contain ambiguous words. Underline the words or expressions that are ambiguous. Write down or explain to a classmate what purpose such ambiguity might serve in each case.

- Disregard what they say; they are a special interest group.
- Society is to blame for crime, not criminals.
- You should be willing to do anything for love.

Weasel words are words that appear to say one thing when in fact they are saying nothing at all. (Weasels are predators who steal into the nests of other animals, make small holes in their eggs, suck out the insides, and leave the hollow eggs standing.)

Ambiguous words can be not only words with more than one meaning, but also words that say nothing at all. Advertisers frequently use weasel words in order to lure buyers into projecting their own desires onto advertising claims. The advantage of this approach for advertisers is that they can later deny responsibility for the buyer's interpretations. Such ambiguities may take the form of hollow words such as *helps*, as in "Helps prevent cavities," or *as much as*, as in "Saves as much as 1 gallon of gas." A few other familiar weasel words appear in the following ads:

- Save on digital TV sets from a leading maker! SALE! SALE! $200! Made to sell for $495! (Here the word *sale* only tells you the store has something to sell. Perhaps it was overpriced in the first place.)

- Women's coats—$54. A $75 value. (The word *value* is relative. Perhaps the store bought the coats especially for the sale and set the previous value arbitrarily.)
- These blouses have the *feel* of silk. (That an item has the *feel* of silk does not mean it is silk.)
- Come see our sheepskin-look seat covers. (Remember, they are not saying that the items *are* sheepskin.)

Class Discussion

Identify the ambiguous words in the following sentences by underlining the words and stating how they function for persuasion.

1. All ingredients in this ice cream are natural and nutritious.
2. These pies have that old-fashioned country taste.
3. Ace aspirin provides relief up to eight hours.
4. This detergent leaves drinking glasses virtually spotless.
5. No other chocolate bar like it.
6. You can be sure if it is a Zippo motorcycle.

Misleading Euphemisms

> **Euphemism** comes from the Greek word meaning "good voice," or to use words of good omen. Euphemisms are inoffensive words used to maintain a level of social formality. All of us know what is meant when we hear *remains* for corpse or *bathroom* for toilet. **Misleading euphemisms,** on the other hand, are deliberately created for the purposes of evasion and manipulation.

Ordinary euphemisms allow us to avoid taboo subjects and maintain polite social interactions. Misleading euphemisms manipulate and deceive; they are the staples of commercial and political propaganda. They can make the bad seem good and the good seem bad.

Misleading euphemisms perform the tasks of promoting and lying (also known by the euphemism of "public relations"). They sanitize and camouflage actions, things, or events that could appear unacceptable in light of professed values. They intentionally distort truth and meaning. In George Orwell's novel *1984,* misleading euphemisms are grimly parodied in his creation of a state built on the slogans "War Is Peace," "Freedom Is

Slavery," and "Ignorance Is Strength." Here the government ministries include the Ministry of Truth (which produces lies and propaganda), the Ministry of Love (which practices imprisonment, brainwashing, and torture), and the Ministry of Peace (which concerns itself with war).

The term *double-talk* is also used to describe misleading euphemisms, as when politicians speak of "disinformation" to describe lies planted in media releases. Public relations employees, both inside and outside the U.S. government, specialize in creating euphemisms. In the U.S. military, lists of official euphemisms are distributed to military officers for their use in relating to the public. Sometimes euphemisms serve as code words to sanitize military actions that might raise uncomfortable questions and offend our professed national values. Here are some examples of misleading euphemisms:

Misleading Euphemism	Conventional Term
Incursion	Military attack
Transfer tubes	Vinyl shrouds for dead soldiers
Take out, take down	Kill, assassinate
Kick butt	Blow up, maim, and kill
Defensive action	War
Asymmetric warfare	War against an enemy without an army
Aerial ordinance	Bombs and missiles
Sanction	Punish
Conventional weapons	Non nuclear weapons
Enhanced interrogation	Torture
Draw down	Military retreat
Detainee	Prisoner of war
Insurgent	Resistance fighter

Class Discussion/Writing Assignment

Following are some controversial terms coined in the last decade. To some they represent valuable new concepts; to others they are intentionally misleading euphemisms. Divide into groups, with each group selecting a few of these words; if you decide that one is misleading, explain why.

Climate change
Clear Skies Act
Healthy Forests initiative
No Child Left Behind Act

Ownership society
Extraordinary rendition
Coalition of the Willing
Extremist environmentalists
Iraq time horizon

Prejudicial Language

The **fallacy of prejudicial language** is an attempt to persuade through the choice of slanted or loaded words that convey a bias. The implication in such a tactic is that the words chosen only describe what is real and true.

In earlier chapters, we studied how word connotations convey positive or negative feelings. Let us now consider how highly connotative words might be chosen to function as hidden persuaders. Study the following three headlines:

- Earth Day Birdcage Liner. What better occasion to honor the shameless press coverage of environmental wackies and wackos. (*American Spectator,* April 22, 2005)
- Earth Day: Sleepwalking Into an Apocalypse. (Institute for Public Policy, April 20, 2005)
- Let's Stop the "Free Trade" Nutballs. (Jim Hightower, Alternet, April 20, 2005)

Discussion Break Questions

1. Underline the words in these headlines that carry strong connotations.
2. What slant do they lend to this information?
3. What associations do you have with these words?
4. Compare the following translations of these headlines. Do they convey the same message?
    - Earth Day Worthless News. Valuable only for viewing press favoritism.
    - Earth Day: Are we moving unaware into world destruction?
    - Let's oppose those who talk of "free trade" but mean no government protections.

5. Read the following quotations and circle the words that seem prejudicial:

   a. "Cultic America: A Tower of Babel"

   b. "Liberals love the UN because it reminds them of the form of government they support in the United States: bloated, ineffectual, anti-capitalist, and anti-American." (Mark W. Smith, *The Official Handbook of the Vast Right-Wing Conspiracy,* 2004, p. 79)

   c. "The latest draconian maneuver [in housing initiatives] comes from the mind of . . . a tantrum-prone manchild who is infamous for his fits of legislation. . . . He has had an especially bad year in pushing through special interest, pro-tenant laws. But give him credit—he's not sensible enough to know when to quit." (Ken Garcia, columnist, *San Francisco Chronicle,* November 15, 2004)

Some of the words you circled in the previous exercise may contain evaluations that you agree with, but they do require acceptance of a bias. In these quoted excerpts, no supporting reasons are provided (although, to be fair, some reasons appear in the full arguments from which they are excerpted). Within these quotations, persuasion is attempted chiefly through evaluative word choices. The task for the critical reader is to separate word choice from word meaning and thus detach from the emotional power of word connotations. Having said all this, however, one has to allow that journalists will often use highly connotative words in order to grab their readers' attention. In this age of hype and hucksterism, when ideas need to be shouted in order to be heard, even writers who know how to construct sound arguments in neutral language may feel they have to turn the volume up to be heard.

Class Discussion

Which of these arguments rely primarily on slanted words in order to be persuasive?

1. The latest mortgage bailout boondoggle has cleared another congressional hurdle.

2. Spud fans tell us that Spud Cigarettes has proved itself in the real smoking "tough spots" . . . where smoking is hardest and heaviest . . . because Spud's moist-cool, clean taste never fails. That's why so many are switching to Spud as a constant smoke. Have you discovered how Spud's mouth-happiness increases tobacco enjoyment? (Advertisement in *The Literary Digest,* May 6, 1933)

3. "The story of the credit rating agencies is a story of colossal failure," said Henry Waxman, chairman of the House Oversight and Government Reform Committee. "Millions of investors rely on them for independent, objective assessments. The rating agencies broke this bond of trust, and federal regulators ignored the warning signs and did nothing to protect the public. The result is that our entire financial system is now at risk." (Andrew Taylor, "Credit raters admit they succumbed to pressure," Associated Press, October 23, 2008)

4. The GOP campaign, in short, is a brew of red-baiting and free-market zealotry, a concoction with a poisonous purpose: resurrecting the everyone-for-themselves pathologies that perpetuate the status quo.

Fallacies That Manipulate Emotions

Some fallacies manipulate by seeking intentionally to arouse such emotions as fear, anxiety and pity, insecurity, hatred, and prejudice. Once influenced by such emotions, the lack of a sound argument can be overlooked. Fallacies that manipulate emotions seek to persuade by exploiting our weaknesses instead of inviting conscious consideration and consent. They can be insidiously effective in attracting interest and clouding rational study of an issue. All of this does not mean that any argument that arouses emotion is fallacious. Usually we are not motivated to formulate arguments unless aroused by feelings. To be sane on many topics is to feel clear anger, indignation, or grief. However, a fallacious argument avoids or omits sound reasoning and depends primarily on arousing reactions that overwhelm clear rational thinking. What follows are the fallacies of Emotional Appeals to Fear and Pity, Appeal to False Authority, and Appeals to Prejudice.

Emotional Appeals to Fear and Pity

Appeals to fear are the staples of commercial advertising. The following examples may serve as familiar reminders:

1. "What your best friends won't tell you . . ."

2. (Picture of a frantic traveler who has lost her traveler's checks.) "Next time be safe with our fast call-in service."

3. (Picture of man in hospital bed in a state of shock after seeing his bill.) "Did you think one insurance coverage plan was enough?"

4. (Picture of burglars breaking into a house.) "Are you still postponing that alarm system?"

Class Discussion

The use of an appeal to anger has not been considered fallacious in the tradition of argumentation; apparently such an appeal is assumed to be legitimate because anger usually arouses people from complacency. Listed here are some appeals to fear, pity, and anger. Read the arguments and decide which you think are appropriate calls for fear, anger, or pity, and which are appeals based on exaggerations. Again, your judgments may depend on your personal values. Defend your answers.

1. Berkeley, California has become a police state as police presence has increased from 12 cops to 40 to 60 on any given weekend night. Cops are everywhere, on foot, bicycle, motorcycle, undercover, and in both marked and unmarked cars. The police mobile substation, a menacing blue bus with smoked windows, cruises the area for added effect. Sinister jump squads, followed by a paddy wagon, keep tensions high by making quick arrests. (*Copwatch Report,* Fall 1992)

2. Loretta Fortuna wants out. Sickened by odors wafting from the red toxic pools near her home, angered by the political battleground she's had to maneuver, grief-stricken by two miscarriages within a year and perpetually worried for the health of her two small sons, she finally had enough. Fortuna has spent the past year waging a campaign on behalf of her family and neighbors to get a leaking waste dump near her home cleaned up. But now she has decided to move elsewhere, a disheartened casualty of a frustrating battle. The Gloucester Environmental Management Services landfill . . . is one site among 1,175 toxic nightmares nationwide waiting to be cleaned up. (Robert J. Mentzinger, *Public Citizen,* May/June 1990)

3. Get out of here! The building is going to collapse!

4. "We are God in Here . . ." That's what the guards in an Argentine prison taunted Grace Guena with as they applied electrical shocks to her body while she lay handcuffed to the springs of a metal bed. Her cries were echoed by the screams of other victims and the laughter of their torturers. (Appeal letter from Amnesty International USA)

5. In 2008 Congress was voting by overwhelming majorities to pass an enormous, wasteful, ridiculous farm bill that provides massive subsidies to wealthy people who grow wheat, corn, soybeans, rice and cotton as well as thoroughbred horses. (Gail Collins, June 19, 2008)

6. The consequences of the Democratic health care plans will be ruinous, tax increases, job losses, less money in your pocket to spend the way you want to spend it. (Political advertisement, 1994)

Appeal to False Authority

> **Appeal to false authority** is an argument whose chief or only support is a false, questionable, or vague authority. The argument is not upheld by sound reasons but instead by alleged endorsements of celebrities without pertinent credentials, vague general entities, and bandwagon claims of popular appeal.

The appeal to false authority has many variations, beginning with an appeal to a popular public figure:

- *Buzz Bonanza,* star of stage and screen, prefers Tasty Toothpaste.
- *The President of the United States* says that brushing your teeth once a week is enough.

Here Buzz Bonanza is clearly not a toothpaste expert. Yet, for those who adore him, such a discrepancy might be overlooked. Advertising psychology research has shown that if a consumer can be manipulated into equating a positive figure with a product, then the consumer will assume that owning the product will also mean owning the positive attributes of the figure. Thus, we have so many product testimonials by film stars, athletes, and even former politicians. Admittedly, this ploy is both entertaining and highly effective.

An appeal to a false authority can also refer to authorities in the form of vague entities:

- *Some people say* we don't need to brush our teeth.
- *Doctors say* you should brush your teeth every day with Florident.
- *Experts agree* you should use an electric toothbrush.
- *Inside sources* at the White House say the President doesn't like to brush his teeth.

An argument can also place false authority in tradition, popular wisdom, and the bandwagon. Here are some examples of the appeal to the authority of tradition:

- You can't be an American male unless you like beer and football.
- You have to go to law school. Every oldest child in this family for the past four generations has gone to law school.

False authority can also be claimed to reside in popular wisdom, or the infallible knowing of the masses:

- If you have any doubts about the status of American health care, just compare it with that in the other industrialized nations! *Ask anyone you know* from a foreign country where they would most like to be treated if they had a medical emergency. Ask them which country is the envy of the world when it comes to health care. (Rush Limbaugh)

- It is not fair to blame the U.S. government for not signing the international treaty to destroy all existing land mines. *Ask anyone in the world* about the U.S. record on human rights and about all it has done to alleviate human suffering.

Another variety of false authority is called the *bandwagon fallacy.* If a herd is headed in one direction, that must be the right direction. The bandwagon fallacy promises the exhilaration of joining in a march of irrepressible instinctive wisdom. It offers all the comfort of joining the crowd and coming over to the winning side. Here are some examples of bandwagon appeals:

- Don't vote for Proposition 9. The polls show it will lose 5 to 1.
- Everyone else does it; why can't I?
- Last year over 10 million people switched to Buckaroo Trucks!
- Buddy Springs! America's Beer!
- Join the Pepsi Generation!

In all these appeals to false authority, you will notice the conclusions are unsupported by reasons. What appears instead is the pressure to trust bogus authorities or to trust the wisdom of conformity. Whereas a good argument lays all its claims and proof on the table, an appeal to false authority suggests that one should not trust one's own reasoning but depend on some vague others who know better. However—and this is most important to remember—the existence of the fallacy of false authority *does not mean that a good argument should avoid using and quoting authorities.* On the contrary, authorities with relevant expertise provide excellent support for reasons and are used routinely to lend them more credibility.

> The first comprehensive study of the geographic skills of America's youngsters shows they are "getting the message that they are part of a larger world," Education Secretary Richard Riley said yesterday. "We're not at the head of the class yet, but it's a good start," said National Geographic Society President Gilbert Grosvenor in releasing the results of National Assessment of Educational Progress tests. Nearly three-quarters of the 19,000 students tested in the first national study of geographic knowledge showed at least a basic understanding of the subject, the Education Department reported. (Associated Press, October 18, 1999)

In this example you will notice that each claim is attributed to an authority. If you, as the reader, are in doubt about the qualifications of Richard Riley and Gilbert Grosvenor to offer opinions, at least you have been given enough clues for further research. However, when you decide to use authorities to support your own argument, admittedly it is not always easy to determine their suitability and reliability. So-called experts may have credentials, but you must also research their track records; furthermore, you might want to know whether other authorities agree or disagree with them. In summary, authority citation can offer impressive support for an argument, but assessing the qualifications and appropriate expertise of the authority requires experience and research.

> An **authority** is someone who has expertise in a particular subject. Authority expertise depends on the person's credentials, accomplishments, reputation for competence and reliability, and peer recognition. *A confirming quotation from an appropriate, reputable, and unbiased authority can provide excellent support for claims made in an argument.*

Class Discussion

Explain how the following statements are different kinds of appeals to authority. Which are fallacious? Which are legitimate?

1. My doctor says that I should take a nap every afternoon.
2. A ten-year study by leading scientists has found that Tuff toothpaste prevents decay in four out of five cases.
3. Buzz Bonanza, star of stage and screen, drives a Macho Motorcycle.
4. I read it in the newspapers.
5. Interviewer: "Do you feel national parks should be privatized?" Woman: "My husband says they should."
6. "Women have babies and men provide the support. If you don't like the way we're made you've got to take it up with God." (Phyllis Schlafly)
7. For over a quarter of a century our teachers have been committed to the idea that the best way to teach students is to withhold criticisms and build self-esteem. But both Alfred Binet, the father of intelligence testing, and Sigmund Freud, the father of psychoanalysis, described the development of self-criticism, which we learn from the criticisms of others, as the essence of intelligence.
8. "One out of every five Americans experience a mental disorder in any given year, and half of all Americans have such disorders at some time

in their lives but most of them never seek treatment, the surgeon general of the United States says in a comprehensive new report." (Robert Pear, *New York Times*, December 13, 1999)

Appeal to Prejudice: Personal Attack and Poisoning the Well

Prejudice is a complex feeling: a mixture of envy, fear, and resentment. A person who feels prejudice cannot maintain the openness necessary for clear reasoning. Arguments that seek to incite prejudice avoid the hard work of constructing a sound argument; the hope is that once the prejudice virus is transmitted, those infected will not even notice the argument's weaknesses. There are two basic fallacious appeals to prejudice. The first makes a direct attack. The second "poisons the well" or contaminates a whole environment so that it will be distrusted and avoided.

■ Personal Attack

This fallacious argument is familiar when political campaigns turn negative and opponents begin to trash one another. The fallacy of personal attack occurs when arguments are not considered on their own merits, but their authors are attacked instead. They can include frontal attacks, such as abusive name-calling, or rear attacks, such as innuendo. Such arguments are fallacious because they incite prejudice and divert attention from the lack of a sound argument.

- "Richard Clark is a politically motivated historical revisionist. His attacks on our administration are scurrilous." (Condoleezza Rice *CNN.com*, May 6, 2004)
- He's another rich Republican pinhead birdbrain.
- "He's a scoundrel! Look at his face! The guy's sick! A typical schizoid! Any psychiatrist will tell you the guy's a wacko!" (Russian presidential TV debate, February 20, 2008)
- Senator Brown: Senator Green has opposed farm subsidy bills in the past. Why, then, should we believe him now when he says he is committed to more farm subsidies?

    Senator Green: My opponent, being the politician that he is, is just obfuscating in order to win your votes.

In this last example, Senator Green does not respond to the issue of his record on farm subsidy support; instead, he discredits his opponent by labeling him as a politician trying to win votes. He misses the irony that he is a politician himself.

It must be emphasized, however, that the fallacy of personal attack does not mean one should never confront a person's actions. There are often times when a person's character and motives are the issue. If Senator Green could prove that Senator Brown accepted bribes from agribusiness, such information would raise pertinent questions about Senator Brown's character and motives.

Class Discussion

Which of the following are personal attacks used to divert attention from the issue? Which raise pertinent issues?

1. This former press secretary, who just published a scurrilous book about the government administration, misrepresents himself as a former insider. In fact, he was invariably out of the loop; now he seeks to profit from sensationalizing his imaginings.

2. It doesn't matter what my wife says about why she needs a new car. She is just a spoiled kid who always wants her way.

3. "There are plenty of friendly places for the [financial services] industry to make its wishes known on Capitol Hill . . . According to the Center for Responsive Politics, the top two recipients of money from the finance, insurance and real estate industries combined is the Democratic presidential nominee, Sen. Barack Obama ($27.8 million). He's trailed only by his Republican rival, Sen. John McCain ($25.2 million)." (Brian Wingfield, "The Street Version of Financial Reform," Forbes.com, October 21, 2008)

4. Judge: Did you or did you not hit your neighbor's car while backing out of your garage on May 25?

> The **fallacy of personal attack** (also known as *ad hominem*) does not respond to an argument but instead tries to discredit the person who made the argument. Such attacks could consist of abusive name-calling, suggestive remarks, or irrelevant claims.
>
> The **poisoning the well fallacy** uses contamination rather than direct attack. It incites prejudice against persons or groups so that whatever they might do or say will be distrusted.

■ *Poisoning the Well*

This fallacy is another variety of personal attack. When any amount of poison is poured into a well, all its water becomes contaminated, so that no one dares drink from the well. Thus, when a person, idea, or cause is discredited at the outset, people could be made to feel aversion, rather than neutrality and openness. This fallacy has four variations. The first variety of poisoning the well uses a string of words with negative connotations:

- Of all the screwball, asinine, muddle-headed letters I have ever seen from this newspaper's readers, the one from Detroit advocating the legalization of drugs takes the cake.

- Every criminal, every gambler, every thug, every libertine, every girl ruiner, every home wrecker, every wife beater, every dope peddler, every crooked politician is fighting the Ku Klux Klan. Think it over. What side are you on?

- Anticipating the deluge of enraged, frustrated letters from your core (read ultra-liberal, closed-minded) constituency, following an extremely well-crafted well-delivered acceptance speech by the president, I will provide some rational balance to the irrational liberal tirade. (Letter to the editor, *San Francisco Chronicle,* November 4, 2004)

- Next year, thousands of you will enter the bowels of academia. The track to a productive career is fraught with exposure to faculties decidedly left-leaning. (*Pittsburgh Tribune Review,* November 2, 2004)

- Whatever a right-wing Fox News pundit may have to say, believe the opposite.

Poisoning the well can also take subtler forms when it uses innuendo:

- This president, who has never worn a uniform, announced today that he would send our troops overseas.

- Senator Smith, known as the "waste-fill senator" because of the tons of propaganda he mails from his office, made a speech in favor of increasing immigration quotas before Congress today.

The second example is a fallacious argument because even if Senator Smith deserves a bad reputation for his mailings, he might be able to make a well-informed, persuasive speech on immigration quotas. If it could be shown that he bought extravagant amounts of paper from paper mill lobbyists who exploited immigrant labor, such information might make this criticism relevant. But as this argument stands, his "waste-fill" reputation is beside the point. It only serves to incite prejudice against what he might have to say.

Poisoning the well can be directed not only against individuals but also against ideas or collective groups:

- The news media has been sounding the alarm lately, loudly decrying the terrorists, tax-evaders, and assorted huddled masses poised to over-run us. These racist and alarmist stories are in sync with the message from Washington. (Kelly Gettinger, *Progressive,* August 1993)

Poisoning the well can serve to discredit and thus ward off any argument a person or group might be prepared to offer:

- You are a man. I don't want to hear what you have to say. You can't understand what women feel.
- Bought politicians and PR firms will be trying to persuade you that handing our national parks over to private corporations is good for all of us. Don't let yourself be conned.

Class Discussion

Which of the following are examples of poisoning the well?

1. Those who object to irradiated foods are picky purists whose ideas run counter to common sense.
2. *Three to Tango.* Here is a sex soufflé that falls flat. . . . This is the kind of movie that TV stars do when they're on hiatus and trying to squeeze one in. (Peter Travers, *Rolling Stone,* November 1999)
3. Today's teenage girls are aware of the outside world, and it makes them fearful. They are a generation that knows more but does less. (Jancee Dunn, *Rolling Stone,* November 1999)
4. "Many companies charge drivers more than twice as much as other companies for identical insurance coverage . . ." That's the word from the California Department of Insurance following a new State survey on automobile insurance rates. (Ad from 20th Century Insurance)

Fallacies That Manipulate Through Distraction

Fallacies based on distraction include red herring, pointing to another wrong, straw man, and circular reasoning.

Fallacies that use the ploy of distraction can be classified in many ways, but what they all have in common is a lack of support for their arguments. All use different tricks to divert attention away from their arguments' weaknesses. Some, like red herring and pointing to another wrong, distract attention from the issue at hand to a different issue. The straw man fallacy falsely represents the opponent's position, pretends this depiction is accurate, and then destroys its own misrepresentation. Circular reasoning distracts through the illusion of support. Each of these fallacies can be difficult to identify because they can really succeed in distracting us.

Red Herring

> The **fallacy of red herring** does not offer reasons to support its conclusion but diverts attention to other issues that are irrelevant. The term *red herring* comes from a ruse used by prison escapees who would smear themselves with herring in order to throw the dogs off their scent.

The red herring fallacy diverts our attention from the question at hand and throws us off track into irrelevancies. Four red herring tactics can be identified.

This first example shows a typical red herring sidetracking maneuver:

- Marijuana smoking is not all that harmful. I would feel safer in a car with a driver who had smoked weed than one under the influence of liquor any day.

Here, the claim that needs to be defended is "marijuana is not all that harmful." However, instead of offering support for this claim, the writer diverts our attention into comparing the safety of drivers under the influence of marijuana versus alcohol. Thus, we become completely sidetracked as we discuss their relative effects on reflexes and perception. Meanwhile, the original claim that marijuana was not all that harmful is either forgotten or incorrectly assumed proven.

A red herring can be the most difficult of all fallacious arguments to detect because it can actually prove a claim; however, the claim proven will not be the claim that was originally presented.

- Guns are not America's major problem, or even high on the list of our problems. Cars, cancer, accidents in the kitchen all kill far more people than guns do. It is not *guns* that we should be frightened of but the effects of poverty, lack of education, a judicial system that sends criminals and psychopaths back out into the streets. Guns are not a solution, but they are not the problem, either!

In this case, it could easily be shown that guns do not cause the majority of American fatalities. Also it would not be difficult to support the claim that the problems of gun violence are tied into a complex social system. But the argument never supports the claim that "guns are not America's major problem or even high on the list of our problems."

Another red herring tactic is to make one claim and pretend to support it with another claim, without ever supporting either claim.

- I cannot understand why the environmentalists feel it is harmful to cut down the redwood forests. This work provides a good living to loggers and their families.

Here, no reasons are given as to why it is not harmful to cut down the redwoods. Nor is the meaning of the word *harmful* clarified. Instead, the writer diverts our attention to other issues by introducing another ambiguous phrase "good living to the loggers." He could then lead us into debating whether the loggers have a right to maintain their livelihood, diverting attention from the profits and responsibilities of the lumber companies. We might not even notice the writer's assumption that nothing is harmful as long as it provides an income for someone.

Finally, there is the more familiar bumper-sticker example of a fallacious red herring argument:

- Guns don't kill people. People do.

In this case, the argument does not prove the claim that guns do not kill people. Nor does it prove an implied claim that guns in themselves are not harmful. Instead it distracts attention into arguing about the nature of people. In addition, this slogan also serves as a false dilemma argument, since the issue is not a matter of either people or guns, but of both necessarily operating together to kill other people.

Class Discussion

Study the following examples of red herring arguments. For each one, determine (a) the issue and (b) the diversion.

1. TV can't be harmful to children, because it occupies their attention for hours and keeps them off the streets. (S. Morris Engel, *With Good Reason,* St. Martin's Press, 1982)

2. Congressman: Did you use steroids?
   Baseball player: I am not here to talk of my past; I am only here to make a positive influence.
   Congressman: What do you mean by a positive influence?
   Baseball player: I am here to let all young athletes know that they should never resort to using steroids.

3. Christie Whitman, EPA chief in 2001, was accused in a senate hearing of having been "dead wrong" in assuring the public that it was safe to breathe the Manhattan air in the weeks after 9/11. This was her reply: "There are indeed people to blame. They are the terrorists who attacked the United States, not the men and women at all levels of government who worked heroically to

protect and defend this country." (Devlin Barrett, "Whitman on Hot Seat over 9/11 Aftermath," Associated Press, June 26, 2007)

4. Neighbor A: I am sorry, but I need to ask you to turn down your television. I can hear it from every room in my apartment.
Neighbor B: Well, you have good reason to be sorry. You are always waking me up by taking showers at midnight.

5. Policeman: It is against the law to smoke in a car with children present.
Driver: Well, I only smoke when I have my window open. I exhale and hold the cigarette outside.

Pointing to Another Wrong

> The **fallacy of pointing to another wrong** is also called *two wrongs make a right*. It distracts attention from a wrong-doing by claiming that similar actions went unnoticed or unpunished.

This fallacy is also called *two wrongs make a right* because it assumes that two wrongs cancel one another out. This weak defense can go unnoticed because it diverts attention into other issues, such as discussing whether or not the other instances are relevant or related. Pointing to another wrong can also divert attention from the issue by making attacks that would lure another to focus on self-defense. Consider these examples of pointing to another wrong, and discuss, either with a class partner or in writing, how each argument lacks reasonable support.

1. On hearing that China now exceeds the United States as the world's top carbon polluter, a Chinese diplomat said: "Given that the United States has been a major polluter for so long, it has no right to ask the Chinese to cut down on their emissions."

2. Motorist to police officer: "Why are you giving me a ticket for going the wrong way on a one-way street? Didn't you see that red sedan I was following doing the same thing?"

3. So what if I don't separate the cans and newspapers out from the garbage for recycling. I don't have that much time. Neither do most other people.

4. The politically correct people will tell you that Columbus brought oppression, slavery, and genocide to the peaceful Indians. But Indians committed as many atrocities against the white people as well as against one another.

5. Why do you complain about cruelty to animals in scientific experiments? Look at the way animals are cruel to one another. Have you ever seen the way lions bite into the necks of zebras, rip open their insides, then eat their hearts and entrails?

Straw Man

> The **straw man fallacy** makes a false replica of an opposing argument, then destroys it. It uses caricature, ridicule, and oversimplification by way of refutation. It can also attack and disprove an insignificant point in an argument, then claim that the whole argument has been demolished as a result.

This fallacy appears in three variations. In the first, it misrepresents and distorts the argument opposed.

- Those who are in favor of national health care want to give us army-style medicine. If the government starts running health care for us, we'll find ourselves waiting all day in barracks full of sick people, while the doctors are shuffling through piles of red tape in their offices and leaving for home by the time our turn arrives.

- When you support picketing, you are supporting a conspiracy to commit extortion through disruption of business, intimidation, and slander. I have no sympathy for strikers who always have the option of going to work for someone else if they don't like the compensation or conditions offered by their employer. I feel they have no right to force the employer to change employment policy to suit them. Why does hiring people to do a specific job, for specific pay, force the employer to practically adopt the employee, catering to him or her from the cradle to the grave? It must be stopped and the extortionists jailed for long terms.

- I am bewildered by those who support the "three strikes and you're out" law. This tough position denies all possibility for change in people. With it, we turn our backs on these people, saying they can never get better. Thus, we buy into a cycle of hate and fear in a total rejection of love and compassion, locking ourselves up in our houses of fear just like we lock up the prisoners in our prisons.

Second, the straw man fallacy can attack one trivial aspect of an idea, cause, or person and then pretend that this one aspect represents what is most essential about the whole.

- I can't respect Hindus because they wear those red spots painted on their foreheads.
- He can't stand the Germans; you know, all those "oompah pah" bands, the beer drinking, and all those thigh-slapping guys dancing in their leather shorts.

Third, a straw man argument may seek to discredit an idea on the basis of objections that are beside the point.

- Doctor: "You need to get more exercise. Why don't you walk to work?"
  Patient: "I can't walk to work—I work at home!"
- Father: "Why don't you wear your helmet when you ride your motorcycle? It's both unsafe and illegal to go without it."
  Son: "Dad, I can't do that. It's not cool."
- Boss: "What we need to get this business off the ground is for all the employees to meet together on a regular basis."
  Manager: "But we don't have a meeting room large enough for all of us!"

Circular Reasoning

> The **fallacy of circular reasoning** is the assertion or repeated assertion of a conclusion without reasons being given to support it. It may imply that the conclusion is self-evident or rephrase the conclusion to sound like a reason.

The fallacy of circular reasoning creates an illusion of support by simply asserting its conclusion as though it were a reason, or by reasserting the same claim in different words. In translation, this argument says that "*A* is true because *A* is true."

- Kerosene is combustible; therefore it burns.

This fallacy also has another name: *begging the question,* which means to assume what one is supposed to prove, or to beg for acceptance rather than earning it through a sound argument. However, it may be easier to remember this fallacy by the term *circular reasoning* because that is just what it does: it goes in circles. Let's look at some examples:

- Taxing inheritances is justified because people should pay a tax on money they have been given by their families.

Here, the first half of the sentence is repeated in different words in the second half, as though the second half were a supporting conclusion.

- Running is good for your health. If you want to be healthy, you should run.

Circular reasoning can deceive by offering inference indicator words like *therefore* that suggest an inference is being drawn from the first claim. In actuality, however, no valid inference follows. Instead of having a conclusion and a reason, we have two conclusions.

- Adultery and fornication are wrong. Therefore, it follows that contraception is wrong.

Here, the gap between the first claim and the second is huge. If we agree that adultery and fornication are wrong, why is contraception also wrong? To make a good argument, we have to provide links of explanation to show that one claim follows logically from another.

Class Discussion

See if you can find the circular reasoning in these examples:

1. Movie stars are intelligent. If they weren't intelligent, they wouldn't be movie stars.
2. Concealed weapons should be discretionary. After all, people should have the right to conceal their guns if they wish.
3. To curse is immoral because it is wrong.
4. Elect Donna Brown supervisor—she is a mother and realtor.
5. Isn't it obvious that when we have the best-funded defense in the world, we will have the best defense in the world?
6. Interviewer at 1994 Miss USA Beauty Pagent: "Miss Alabama, if you could live forever, would you and why?"
   Miss Alabama: "I would not live forever because we should not live forever, because if we were supposed to live forever, then we would live forever, but we cannot live forever, which is why I would not live forever."

Chapter Summary

1. Word ambiguity uses undefined and vague words in an argument, seeking to gain an advantage by using words that could be interpreted in more than one way.
2. Misleading euphemisms are words that hide meaning by wrapping a less acceptable idea in positive or neutral connotations. The use of euphemisms is fallacious in an argument when the goal is to be evasive, to mislead, or to disarm awareness and objections.

3. Prejudicial language persuades through the use of loaded words that convey a bias while pretending to convey objective information.

4. Appeals to fear and pity seek to persuade by affecting emotions rather than through sound rational support for an argument.

5. Appeal to false authority seeks to influence others by citing phony or inappropriate authorities. This false authority may be a person, a tradition, or conventional wisdom. However, the appeal to an authentic and appropriate authority is not a fallacy; it can provide excellent support for claims.

6. Appeal to bandwagon is another example of the appeal to authority. In this case, the authority is the exhilarating momentum of the herd instinct.

7. Personal attack refutes another argument by attacking the opponent rather than addressing the argument itself. This fallacy can take the form of using abusive language or name-calling.

8. Poisoning the well seeks to prejudice others against a person, group, or idea and prevent their positions from being heard. This technique seeks to remove the neutrality necessary for listening and to implant prejudice instead.

9. The red herring is a ploy of distraction. It makes a claim, then instead of following through with support, it minimizes the issue or diverts attention into irrelevant issues.

10. The straw man is an argument that misrepresents, oversimplifies, or caricatures an opponent's position; it creates a false replica, then destroys the replica. The straw man also invalidates by attacking a minor point as though the whole argument depended upon it.

11. Pointing to another wrong is also called *two wrongs make a right*. It says, "Don't look at me; he did it too!"

12. Circular reasoning is the assertion or repeated assertion of a conclusion as though the conclusion were a reason. It can also pretend that no supporting reasons are needed. Circular reasoning assumes what it is supposed to prove.

Chapter Quiz

Identify the following arguments either as *NF* for *not fallacious* or as one of the types of fallacious arguments indicated for each section. In some cases, you may find that more than one fallacy applies; choose the one you consider the most appropriate. Be prepared to defend your answers.

■ Part I

In this section, look for arguments that are *misapplied euphemisms, band-wagon,* or *appeal to fear.*

_____ 1. It was announced today that our troops, who have been shelled for some weeks now in Lebanon, have made a *strategic transfer* to their ships offshore of that country.

_____ 2. In China, Europe, and Brazil, efforts are being made to control the population growth that adds one billion people to the planet every decade.

_____ 3. Africa, the birthplace of humankind, provides a disturbing clue to our future. As I fly across areas that were forests just years ago and see them becoming desert, I worry. Too many people crowd this continent, so poor they strip the land for food and wood for fuel. The subject of my life's work and our closest living relatives, the chimpanzees and gorillas are slaughtered for food or captured for the live-animal trade. Pollution of air, land, and water abounds. (Jane Goodall, National Geographic Society)

_____ 4. Five million people have already seen this movie. Shouldn't you?

_____ 5. Why do I think the president's program is sound? It is sound because the polls show that the vast majority supports it.

_____ 6. By a margin of two to one, shoppers prefer Brand X to any of the leading competitors. Reason enough to buy Brand X.

_____ 7. What if your bank fails and takes your life savings? Buy diamonds—the safe investment.

_____ 8. There is *virtually no tar* in these cigarettes.

_____ 9. It has been estimated that illegal aliens are costing taxpayers in excess of $5 billion a year. Should our senior citizens be denied full health care benefits, should our children suffer overcrowded classrooms in order to subsidize the costs of illegal aliens?

_____ 10. There are plenty of people out there on the streets waiting to get your job. If you go on strike, you may find yourself out there with them.

_____ 11. The *natural* way to relieve muscular pain is through our vitamin ointment. It *relieves* pain from burns, stiff neck, backache, swelling, and so forth.

■ Part II

In the following arguments, look for *straw man, poisoning the well, appeal to pity,* and *appeal to false authority.*

_____ 12. The majority of American educators, in a recent survey, agreed that longer school days, more homework, and longer school years would only penalize children and not necessarily result in better learning.

_____ 13. The President of the United States says that the problem of illiteracy can be solved only by longer school days, more homework, and longer school years.

_____ 14. No use listening to those repressive environmentalists and economic zero-growthers who don't have anything under their thick skulls. They oppose any sane domestic policies that allow timber companies to do their jobs.

_____ 15. Elijah Jones was the tenth victim of police brutality this year. Arrested for murdering his two children in a fit of insanity due to the pressures of poverty, he had hoped, on release from a mental institution, to make a new life for himself. But Sunday he was shot down mercilessly by the pigs when he ran from a police officer after robbing a liquor store.

_____ 16. Cigarettes are not addictive. I know this to be true because the chairman of the R. J. Reynolds Tobacco Company testified before Congress that tobacco is not an addictive substance.

■ Part III

In this section look for arguments that use _pointing to another wrong, red herring, prejudicial language,_ and _circular reasoning._

_____ 17. Using hidden notes on a test is not unethical; our professors wouldn't be where they are today if they hadn't done the same thing.

_____ 18. Maybe I do cheat on income tax, but so does everyone else.

_____ 19. When you support picketing, you support a conspiracy to commit extortion through disruption of business.

_____ 20. Some people would have us eliminate the use of all pesticides on fruits and vegetables. But both fruits and vegetables are essential for health and excellent sources of vitamins and minerals.

_____ 21. Why do you object to people smoking? What are you doing about the problems of smog pollution? Exhaust fumes are far more likely to give people lung cancer.

_____ 22. Capital punishment is justified for murder and rape because people should be put to death for violent and hateful acts.

_____ 23. The reason I believe in a large tax cut is because it's what I believe.

_____ 24. Why do you always expect me to carry out the garbage? I don't expect you to drive me to work every day.

_____ 25. The U.S. government has no right to accuse us Chinese of human rights violations when the United States has the highest crime rate in the world.

_____ 26. A spokesman for a chemical industrial firm, when charged and fined for disposing of toxic wastes in the lakes of Illinois, protested, "Thousands of other industries are doing the same thing."

CHAPTER 11

Inductive Reasoning:

How Do I Reason from Evidence?

Great Moments in Science

1962: Bell Labs scientists discover that gravity does not function inside a ketchup bottle.

Inductive reasoning is a method used to discover new information or to supply missing information. When we use inductive reasoning, we observe, test, and check things out in some systematic fashion. Although it is an open-ended method of learning and discovering, it is not hit or miss, or trial and error, but has its own rules for arriving at the most reliable answers. This chapter serves as an introduction to the forms, methods, and rules of inductive reasoning.

DISCOVERY EXERCISES

■ Defining Key Terms

Using at least two dictionaries, write down definitions of the following terms:

1. Induction
2. Reasoning
3. Empirical
4. Scientific method
5. Inductive reasoning

■ Answering a Survey on Test Performance

Write your answers to the following questions in preparation for discussion. Use a mindmap or cluster if you wish. Pay attention to the way in which you must reason in order to reply.

1. Think of a time when you made a high score on a challenging test. What steps did you take to prepare yourself mentally, physically, and in actual study?
2. Think of a time when you did poorly on a challenging test. How did you prepare? What did you fail to do?
3. What conclusions can you draw on the basis of this comparison?

Now discuss the following questions in class:

1. Explain how you were reasoning in order to answer these questions. Was this inductive reasoning?
2. How was this reasoning similar to, or different from, the way you worked mentally as you worked in the first exercises describing a fruit, vegetable, or tool?

Looking at Inductive Reasoning

Induction comes from the Latin *inducere*, to lead in. In logic, induction is to reason to a conclusion about all members of a class on the basis of an examination of a few members of a class. Induction reasons from the particular to the general.

Your study of this text began with descriptive exercises that required you to use the inductive thinking process. Now is the time to step back and consider the forms and rules of inductive reasoning.

In this last discovery exercise, as well as in the descriptive work you did at the beginning of this book, you used inductive reasoning. You observed, gathered data, then drew inferences about patterns, configurations, and meanings. You recorded your findings and reported them. This method of researching from personal observation is basic to the **empirical** or **scientific method.** It was the approach, you will remember, used by Samuel Scudder. In this chapter, we are going to look more abstractly at the nature and structure of inductive reasoning. You will also review the rules and standards used to guide scientific research that has been developed over many centuries.

Induction reasons from evidence about *some* members of a class in order to draw a conclusion about *all* members of that class. We use inductive reasoning to help us out in situations where an examination of all the data would be an impossible or impractical task. Samplings

"Hence, there is a direct relationship between how the ball bounces and the way the cookie crumbles."

and extrapolation enable us to estimate how many voters nationwide favor a particular candidate, how many needles there are in a haystack, or how many stars there are in the universe. This chapter discusses a number of the methods that have traditionally been used to learn about the whole from a study of its parts. They include sensory observation, enumeration, analogical reasoning, pattern recognition, causal reasoning, and statistical reasoning.

Reasoning from Sensory Observation

> Major scientific discoveries have resulted from accidents that just happened to be given close attention by someone who was both a curious skilled observer and an inductive thinker.

> **Sensory observation** is the awareness of self and of the world through the basic senses of sight, touch, taste, smell, and hearing. Ancillary senses include a sense of time, weight, energy, pressure, motion, balance, direction, sexuality, feelings, emotions, pain, strength, weakness, solidity, lightness, darkness, color, fluidity, heat, cold, pitch, tonality, and vibration.

The ability to observe and infer will always remain the primary skills of a scientist. (Indeed, such skills have always been indispensable for human survival.) Even a scientist who uses instruments such as a computer, microscope, or X-ray machine still depends primarily on personal skills of reasoning from sensory information. Moreover, some of the most dramatic discoveries in the history of science resulted from simple observing of the right thing at the right time. The book *Serendipity: Accidental Discoveries in Science* by Roysten M. Roberts tells many stories of accidental discoveries that led to such inventions as quinine, electric batteries, synthetic dyes, rayon, nylon, and antibiotics. Here is a summary of one of these stories:

> In 1903 the French chemist, Edouard Benedictus, dropped a glass flask one day on a hard floor and broke it. However, to the astonishment of the chemist, the flask did not shatter, but still retained most of its original shape. When he examined the flask he found that it contained a film coating inside, a residue remaining from a solution of collodion that the flask had contained. He made a note of this unusual phenomenon, but thought no more of it until several weeks later when he read stories in the newspapers about people in automobile accidents who were badly hurt by flying windshield glass. It was then he remembered

his experience with the glass flask, and just as quickly, he imagined that a special coating might be applied to a glass windshield to keep it from shattering. Not long thereafter, he succeeded in producing the world's first sheet of safety glass.

Class Discussion Question

Parallel stories of lucky scientific discoveries lie behind the inventions of penicillin, X-rays, Teflon, dynamite, and Post-Its. Describe how one of these discoveries, or any other you are familiar with, depended on both sensory observation and inductive reasoning.

Reasoning from Enumeration

Induction can involve a simple counting of parts in order to draw conclusions about wholes.

> **Enumerate** means (1) to count off or name one by one or (2) to determine a number from counting.

Induction uses enumeration in a range from simple counting to gathering statistics. The rules for good induction are concerned with how to draw the most likely and probable conclusions about wholes on the basis of a controlled sampling of parts.

This can of Chock Nuts contains exactly 485 peanuts.

This second can of Chock Nuts contains exactly 485 peanuts.

This third can of Chock Nuts contains exactly 485 peanuts.

(Therefore) all cans of Chock Nuts must contain exactly 485 peanuts.

You will notice that the conclusion drawn here uses the word "must," suggesting that its conclusion is a guess. It is a probability estimate, a projection, or an **extrapolation.** If you open a fourth can and find 500 peanuts, then you will know that the conclusion was incorrect because the sampling was insufficient. Therefore, you would have to revise your experiment to count more samples until a reliable average could be obtained.

Conclusions drawn from samplings can never be totally certain; at best they reflect probabilities. Yet probability estimates help out considerably in situations where all the facts cannot be known. If you have an old car that begins to have one or two major repair problems every six months, you can extrapolate a trend that may well continue until all parts are replaced. On the basis of this extrapolation, you may decide to buy a new car. However, you might wonder if that old clunker would have been the exception that held up forever.

Analogical Reasoning

Inductive reasoning also draws conclusions from making comparisons in the form of analogies.

> **Analogy** means (1) to find a correspondence of similarity between things that seem different or (2) an inference that if two things are alike in some respects, they will be alike in other respects.

Inductive reasoning can also be based on analogies, which are a form of comparisons. All of us learn from making comparisons. Even a one-year-old can get the idea that if adults can stand upright and walk, then so can he or she. Analogies are used in the teaching of all subjects in order to make the unfamiliar more understandable by comparison to the familiar. In the study of macroeconomics, a principle, such as how a government can control an economy, can be explained by comparison to the way a person can control the water level in a bathtub by judicious use of the faucet and the plug.

Analogical reasoning also serves as a mainstay of legal argumentation in countries such as Canada, England, and the United States, where the decisions depend on precedents; the rule of precedents means that similar cases must be decided in a similar manner. Thus, when an attorney argues a case, comparisons are made between the case in question and the past rulings and decisions.

Finally, in the sciences, analogical reasoning has resulted in many discoveries and inventions. Here are two famous examples:

- Ben Franklin proved by a simple experiment that materials of different colors absorb heat differently. He put squares of cloth of different colors on some banks of snow and left them in the sun. In a few hours he noticed that a black piece had sunk into the snow, the deepest, lighter-colored pieces less, and a white piece not at all. From this Franklin reasoned that dark colors absorb the sun's heat more readily than the paler ones, which reflect part of the sun's radiation. By analogous reasoning, he decided that people who live in tropical climates should wear white clothing.

- The invention of Velcro was based on a study of cockleburs. In the 1950s George de Mestral began to wonder why cockleburs would stick to his jacket when he went out for nature walks. When he put one under a microscope, he discovered that each seed bur was covered with hooks that were caught in the loops of his cloth jacket. Next he began to wonder if this pattern of hooks and loops could be put to some practical use. By analogous reasoning he came up with the concept of an alternative kind of fastener, which was eventually realized through manufacturing research.

Discovering Patterns

Inductive reasoning looks for patterns, notes their characteristics, and draws conclusions about their nature and significance.

> **Pattern** is a design or form that is perceived. A pattern can involve shapes, images, ideas, words, signs, entities, sounds, or smells that suggest some recognizable configuration or rhythm.

In the inductive process, sensory observation is used to note details and forms, to compare similarities and differences, and thus to recognize designs. This was the case in the discovery of Velcro, when a microscope revealed the pattern between seed bur hooks and fabric loops. Gradually such a discernment of pattern leads to inferences about their correspondences, trends, and tendencies as well as to explanations or conclusions about their nature and meaning. All the accumulated evidence might be called the *parts* and the generalizations the *whole*. In medicine, the name given to the whole is called the *diagnosis*.

A child is brought to the doctor with the following symptoms: fever, cough, and eye inflammation. The doctor examines the patient and finds small red spots with white centers on the insides of her cheeks. The doctor begins to recognize a pattern of symptoms that could lead to a diagnosis of common measles. He knows that if a rash appears first on her neck and then on the rest of her body within three to five days, and if there is a diminution of the fever, then he can be sure of this diagnosis. However, the onset of other symptoms or the worsening of the patient's condition could suggest other possibilities.

Thus, the process of examining a patient and arriving at a correct diagnosis (and with that a correct treatment) requires not only considerable knowledge but also skills in discerning patterns and forming dependable hypotheses about them.

Reasoning from and About Causes

We use inductive reasoning to determine the probable causes of events.

> **Cause** comes from the Latin *causa*, meaning reason or purpose. Cause means that which produces an effect, or result, or a consequence; something that is responsible for an event; or a source of influence.

Induction is one form of reasoning that seeks to explain why certain things have occurred or might occur. Because our forebears wondered what caused our days to be divided between light and darkness, we gradually moved from the explanations of myths to the scientific explanations of astronomy and physics.

All humans show curiosity about causation because such knowledge makes life more predictable and thus more controllable. Many theories have been advanced to explain the 2001 anthrax attacks in the United States following 9/11. By 2008 there were still no conclusive explanations for the cause, motives, and identities of the perpetrators. Although Bruce Ivins, a U.S. military anthrax researcher, was named a primary suspect in that year, his suicide before his trial left the public with many unanswered questions.

Discussion/Writing Break Questions

1. Describe a time in your life when you needed to discover the cause of some event. (It could be something simple like a physical symptom or mechanical breakdown.)
2. List the causes that you first considered possible.
3. What steps did you take to discover the actual cause?
4. How did you know you had found the right answer?

Class Discussion

Inductive reasoning, whether using sensory observation, enumeration, analogies, pattern recognition, or guesses about causation, has its own rules or standards for producing the most reliable or probable conclusions. Study the following examples that use inductive reasoning and explain why each one is well or poorly reasoned.

1. The leaves on our maple tree turn red in October.

   Some years it is cold in October, and some years it is warm through October. No matter what the temperature, our tree always turns in October.

   _____

   October makes the leaves of maple trees turn red.

2. I always get a cold after I go swimming.

   I only get a cold when I go swimming.

   _____

   The cause of my colds is swimming.

3. The last ten times I flipped this coin, it came up tails.

   _____

   The next time I flip it, it is certain to be tails.

4. I get nervous when I drink coffee.

   I get nervous when I drink tea.

   I get nervous when I drink cola.

   _____

   All drinks make me nervous.

5. Jules and Jim like the same dogs.
   Jules and Jim like the same foods.

   Jules and Jim must like the same people.

6. My lover promised to come see me at 8:00 P.M.
   I have waited until 4:00 A.M.

   He is not coming.

7. When I stopped smoking, I gained 10 pounds.

   Smoking keeps my weight down.

8. My wife and I know how beneficial fresh garlic can be to health, but we worried about the smell. Then we found a solution. We chop up pieces of garlic and put them inside a banana to share just before going to bed. Afterward I have never noticed any garlic on the breath. Even the next morning, there is no garlic smell.

   We believe we have discovered a cure for garlic breath.

9. I had a wart that was protruding and sore. I decided to try vitamin E. I applied the oil about two or three times a day, and in less than ten days the wart was gone.

   This proves that vitamin E cures warts.

Reasoning with Hypotheses

Science formulates and tests hypotheses in order to explain and predict phenomena.

> **Hypothesis** comes from the Greek word *hupothesis,* meaning a supposition. A hypothesis is the name given to a trial idea, tentative explanation, or working assumption that can be used to further investigation.
>
> The **conclusion of an inductive study** generalizes to produce a universal claim based on empirical findings. This conclusion may or may not confirm the hypotheses tested. Yet such a conclusion remains probable rather than totally certain because further evidence could challenge its findings.

A preliminary conclusion derived from inductive reasoning is called a *hypothesis.* All of the "conclusions" given in the preceding examples were prematurely drawn; their sampling was insufficient to warrant their conclusions. In actuality they expressed untested hypotheses. Yet even if a hypothesis becomes confirmed through extensive testing, it may never be considered certain. The discovery of even one exception, or counterexample, challenges the truth of a hypothesis. Because inductive generalizations have these limitations, special precautions have to be taken in order to reach the most probable hypothesis. Thus, we learn the rules for gathering and examining evidence, for controlling variables, and for creating experiments that can be duplicated and thus tested by others. Moreover we have to be continually willing to modify and refine our hypotheses depending on the feedback we receive.

It takes time and testing to establish the truth of a hypothesis. Obviously Sir Isaac Newton's hypothesis that gravity explains an apple's perpendicular fall to the ground has not been improved upon. The discovery that a vaccination could prevent smallpox also proved to be true, although it took the interweaving of many hypotheses and many tests to establish its reliability. By 1979, vaccination had eradicated the disease worldwide.

The first hypothesis is not always the last; indeed, one hypothesis can lead to another and another, or can serve as an imaginative guide for further research. Here are two examples of the way in which hypotheses can function as working assumptions:

- A patient developed a high fever and complained of pains in the kidney area; the doctor first diagnosed a kidney infection (first hypothesis). However, on a second visit, an examination of the patient's mouth and throat revealed enlarged and swollen tonsils (new evidence), and it seemed more likely at this point that the fever and kidney pains were due to the infected tonsils (new hypothesis).

- In the eighteenth century, Europeans began to experiment with the nature of electricity. The similarity between lightning and electric sparks was observed, and it was conjectured that lightning was simply a big electric spark. Ben Franklin decided to test this hypothesis. Using analogous reasoning, he noticed that lightning and electric sparks were similar in color and in shape, that they traveled at about the same speed, and that both killed animals. Franklin published a proposal suggesting that a "sentry box" be built on a high tower with a man inside on an insulated platform who would draw sparks from passing clouds with a long pointed iron rod (test for a hypothesis). Before Franklin got around to trying out this experiment himself, it was conducted in France, and it was proved that clouds are electrified (confirmation of the hypothesis). Franklin then found a way to verify his hypothesis again, using his well-known kite experiment. He fixed a sharp-pointed wire to the top of a kite, then knotted a large iron key between the kite string and a length of ribbon used for insulation.

When a storm cloud passed by, Franklin saw the fibers of the kite string stand on end and drew a spark from the key with his knuckle (second confirmation of the hypothesis in an experiment conducted under different conditions).

Class Discussion

Following are four examples of inductive reasoning that include hypotheses. Read and underline the hypothetical statements, and discuss whether you find adequate support for these hypotheses. What other hypotheses might better explain some of these situations? Note also whether each example uses analogies, extrapolates and predicts from patterns, speculates about cause and effect, or gathers data and statistics.

1. A study of high school students in ten major U.S. cities showed that four out of every five were not coffee drinkers. It was conjectured that this statistic could be due to TV commercials showing only older people drinking coffee. A new advertising promotional scheme was devised to seek to change this ratio by showing teenagers enjoying coffee at athletic events, during class breaks, and on dates to see if it might change this ratio.

2. I have been wearing a wool knitted cap for the past ten years. People think it is strange, but it has kept me from having sore throats. Before I started wearing the cap, I had sore throats all the time. But since I started wearing it, I have not had any.

3. Japanese government officials and auto industry spokesmen said American drivers might be having trouble with their Japanese-made seat belts because their cars are too dirty. They reported finding animal hair in American cars, pieces of food, and soft drink drippings. In Japan, people do not drink or eat in their cars or even wear shoes. This explanation for the faulty seat belts (whose release button gradually became brittle and would not lock securely) came in response to reports that federal safety officials in the United States were planning to recall and repair defective seat belts in 9 million cars. The Japanese manufacturers said that they had received no complaints in Japan about the 4.79 million vehicles on the road with the same seat belts. (Summarized from an article in the *San Francisco Chronicle*, May 23, 1995)

4. World bicycle production increased to more than 110 million units in 1994. The trend has been rising steadily since 1970. Bikes have been found to be speedier and more efficient than cars in gridlocked U.S. cities for couriers, pizza deliverers, police, and paramedics. Developing countries, where bikes have long been

popular, are also finding new uses for bikes, such as in El Salvador where they are used for trailer towing. The potential for their further growth is great. They hold promise of becoming a valuable, environmentally friendly means of transportation. (Data summarized from *Vital Signs 1995*)

Reasoning Through Statistics and Probability

Induction uses the sciences of statistics and probability to gather, organize, and interpret data and make predictions with these data.

Statistics: The mathematics of the collection, organization, and interpretation of numerical data.

Probability: In statistics, the ratio of the number of actual occurrences of a specific event to the total number of possible occurrences.

Inductive reasoning can work with statistical samplings (a form of enumeration) and make predictions on the basis of an estimate of probabilities. For example, the payoffs for betting on the winners of horse races are determined by inductive reasoning. Suppose you read in the papers that today at Green Meadows racetrack the following horses will run with the odds as listed: Post Flag, 9.90 to 1; Bru Ha Ha, 3.40 to 1; Plane Fast, 6.80 to 1; En-Durance, 5.20 to 1. These odds are based on the Racing Association's estimates of each horse's chance of winning. Bettors who pick winners will be paid an amount equal to the first number in each of these odds for each dollar bet.

The field of mathematics known as statistics is a science that seeks to make accurate predictions about a whole from a sampling of its parts. Probability and statistics have yielded some basic rules for evaluating the reliability of conclusions drawn by inductive reasoning from statistical samplings. For the purposes of our introduction to the subject, there are five basic rules:

1. The *greater the size of the sample* (or number of study subjects), the greater is the probability that that sample is representative of the whole population or group it is supposed to represent.

The results of a survey of the coffee-drinking habits of students in one high school based on questioning only ten students would obviously not be as reliable as the results of a survey of the whole student body. However, samplings are made for the sake of convenience or necessity, and the same information can be extrapolated for a full population when some rules for size, margin of error, and random selection are followed. These rules are taught in the study of statistics. Yet, without knowing all these rules, you can still estimate that a survey of ten students could not speak for a whole high school, or one high school for all U.S. high schools.

2. The *more representative* the sample is of a population, the more likely it is that accurate conclusions will be drawn about the full population from the sample.

In a poll seeking a representative sampling of menopausal women in Illinois, the most representative respondents would probably be Illinois women between the ages of forty and sixty. Less likely to be representative would be women under the age of thirty. Moreover, a survey limited to women in their forties would also not be representative, nor would a survey of women in the city of Chicago only.

3. One *counterexample* can refute a generalization arrived at through inductive reasoning.

If you complain that your friend *always* comes late and is *never* reliable, and then one day your friend arrives early, you have a counterexample that refutes your generalization.

4. If statistical evidence is offered, it should be offered in *sufficient detail* to permit verification. Sources or background material about the researchers should also be cited so others can determine their reputation and independence from vested interests in the study's outcome.

In the following example, consider the vague references to "independent laboratory tests" as well as to the research data used to support the claims:

> FATOFF has been proven to cause weight loss. After years of research and expensive experimentation, an independent laboratory with expertise in biotechnology has finally uncovered a naturally occurring substance that can be taken orally in tablet form. Now it is being made available to millions of overweight men and women who are losing as much as 10 lbs. a month. It has taken over 15 years of research and over 200 medically documented studies to produce FATOFF. But there is only one catch: FATOFF is expensive to produce.

5. When polls are taken, it is important to know not only whether a *reputable organization* or agency (such as Gallup, Roper, or Harris) took the poll but also the *exact formulation* of the question.

Compare the following questions:

a. Do you favor a constitutional amendment that declares, "The English language shall be the official language of the United States"?

b. English is the language of the United States by custom, although not by law. In order to avoid the political upheavals over language that have torn apart Canada, Belgium, Sri Lanka (Ceylon), India, and other nations, would you favor legislation designating English the official language of the United States?

The first question might elicit quite a different response than the second.

When you hear or read about polls, be sure to see if the exact wording of the question is given so that you can analyze it for bias. Also, do not accept without question results from polls identified only vaguely as "a recent poll." If the pollster's name is given, consider whether it was an independent source or a source filtering information to represent its own political or commercial interests. You need to be able to determine whether the source was unbiased and whether the results are verifiable.

Class Discussion

The following examples offer statistical evidence. Rate the statistics given in each as *reliable* or *not reliable* and then state what rule or standard you used in making your judgment.

1. According to the Center for Academic Integrity at Duke University, three quarters of college students confess to cheating at least once. And a *U.S. News* poll found 90 percent of college kids believe cheaters never pay the price. [*U.S. News* poll of 1,000 adults (including an oversample of 200 college students) conducted by Celinda Lake of Lake Snell Perry & Associates and Ed Goeas of the Tarrance Group. Oct. 18–23, 1999. Margin of error: plus or minus 3.5 percent.] (*U.S. News & World Report,* November 22, 1999)

2. I would guess that the average office female makes 509 visits to the lavatory to a male's 230, and spends 10.7 minutes there to a male's 2.5. What management is going to put up with this "primp time" featherbedding at equal pay? (Edgar Berman, guest columnist, *USA Today*)

3. It was May 1971 when Russell Bliss, a waste hauler, sprayed oil at Judy Piatt's stables in Moscow Mills, Mo., to help control the dust. A few days later hundreds of birds nesting in the stable's rafters fell to the ground and died. Soon, more than 20 of her cats went bald and died, as did 62 horses over the next three and a half years. Piatt herself developed headaches, chest pains and diarrhea, and one of her daughters started hemorrhaging. In 1974 the federal Centers for Disease Control in Atlanta identified the culprit as dioxin and traced it to Bliss's oil, which contained wastes from a defunct hexachlorophene plant that had paid him to dispose of it. Bliss, it turned out, had

sprayed the waste-oil mixture on horse arenas, streets, parking lots and farms throughout the state, leaving what state Assistant Attorney General Edward F. Downey called "a trail of sickness and death." (*Newsweek,* March 7, 1983)

Composition Writing Application

■ *Working from Facts to Inferences to Hypotheses*

Follow these steps in this assignment:

1. Skim through books that list facts, such as *The Information Please Almanac, The Book of Lists, The People's Almanac,* and *Statistical Abstracts of the United States.*
2. Find a group of related facts on one subject and write them down.
3. Draw all the inferences you can that would explain what these facts mean. Write them down as a list of potential conclusions.
4. From these, select one conclusion that seems to you to be the most likely hypothesis to explain the facts' meaning.
5. Discuss this hypothesis and list what further facts you would need to determine whether or not it is true.
6. Make this a short essay assignment of at least two pages.
7. Title your paper with a question your hypothesis seeks to answer.
8. Make your thesis the answer to that question.

● STUDENT WRITING EXAMPLE

WHY ARE THERE FEWER INJURIES IN HOCKEY THAN IN OTHER TEAM SPORTS?
Shamma Boyarin

The Facts

Team sport injuries reported in U.S. hospitals in 1980*:

    463,000 injuries related to football
    442,900 injuries related to baseball
    421,000 injuries related to basketball
    94,200 injuries related to soccer
    36,400 injuries related to hockey

*Source: Susan Baker, *The Injury Fact Book* (Lexington, MA: Lexington Books, 1984).

Why Were Fewer Injuries Related to Hockey Reported?
Potential Conclusions or Hypothesis

1. Hockey is a less dangerous sport.
2. People who play hockey are tougher and less likely to go to the hospital with injuries.
3. Hockey is a less popular sport, so fewer people are injured.
4. Hockey is more safety conscious than other sports.

Discussion

On the basis of my knowledge of all five sports, I would say that hockey is the most dangerous. And this factor of danger leads to three practices that make hockey different from the other team sports:

1. Hockey players, even nonprofessionals, are more likely to wear protective gear.
2. The rules of hockey are designed to prevent unnecessary injuries as much as possible. Referees enforce these rules more rigorously than in other sports.
3. Because it is a very tiring game, players are allowed to rest more often. A player with a minor injury can rest more and not aggravate the injury.

Because of these precautions, I do not think that the first two hypotheses are likely. As for the third, hockey may be a less popular sport, and this may contribute to the smaller number of injuries, but I don't think this can account for its dramatic difference from the rest. I do not think that hockey is a less popular sport than soccer, which reported nearly three times as many injuries. Therefore, I select the final hypothesis as the most likely reason for fewer injuries in hockey; namely, hockey's players and officials are more safety conscious.

Supporting Argument for the Thesis

I don't know how many people injured in hockey were in fact wearing protective gear, or how many of the injuries could have been prevented by such gear, so I can't prove that protective gear prevented injuries. I also don't know how many games with injuries were official games following strict rules. After all, a player injured in a neighborhood game can step out whenever he feels like it. Also the word *related* is vague. Does this include bystanders? Is a baseball fan hit in the stands with a baseball included in "baseball related injuries"? During the 1994 football game between Atlanta and San Francisco, two players started fighting. Their teams were penalized, but they continued playing. If it had been a hockey game, both players would have been thrown out of the whole game. Since hockey has such a violent reputation, the referees are more strict with brawling players.

Finally, I can compare hockey to what I have read about injuries in football. Last year, *Sports Illustrated* ran an article on head injuries in professional football. The magazine pointed out that many injuries could be prevented by changing the rules a little as well as by putting an extra shell on players' helmets. They cited one player who said that wearing such a shell did not hinder his performance. However, the NFL has not adopted these suggestions, which seems to indicate my theory is correct: there are fewer injuries in hockey because its players and officials are more safety conscious.

Used with permission of Shamma Boyarin.

Scoring for Working from Facts to Inferences to Hypotheses

1. Minimum of two pages. *10 points*
2. Title includes question your hypothesis seeks to answer. *10 points*
3. Group of related facts listed taken from identified source. *10 points*
4. Imaginative list of (more than three) inferences that could be drawn from these facts. *20 points*
5. Further facts needed to determine reliability of hypotheses listed. *10 points*
6. Adequate support for argument defending hypothesis. *30 points*
7. No distracting errors of spelling, punctuation, sentence structure. *10 points*

Chapter Summary

1. Inductive reasoning is the process of thinking that you used in describing a fruit, vegetable, or tool in Chapter 1 when you began by not knowing the identity of the covered object.
2. The inductive method is also called the empirical or scientific method. It appeared in the reading by Samuel Scudder.
3. Induction reasons from evidence about some members of a class in order to form a conclusion about all members of that class.
4. Induction can be done through sensory observation, enumeration, analogous reasoning, causal reasoning, and pattern recognition.
5. A hypothesis is a trial idea that can be used to further investigation in an inductive study. The conclusion of an inductive study is a generalization that is probable but not certain.

6. Inductive reasoning is used as a method for obtaining information when it would be impossible to examine all the data available. This is done by taking statistical samplings or by making extrapolations.

7. The five basic rules for evaluating the reliability of hypotheses based on statistical samplings are as follows:

   a. The greater the size of the sample, the greater is its probability of being representative of the whole of a population.
   b. A sampling must be representative in order to lead to reliable results.
   c. One counterexample can refute a generalization arrived at through inductive reasoning.
   d. Statistical evidence should be offered in sufficient detail for verification.
   e. When evaluating the results of polls, it is important to examine both the polling agency and the polling question for bias.

Chapter Quiz

Rate the following statements as *true* or *false*. If you decide the statement is false, then revise the statement to make it a true one.

_____   1. Inductive reasoning is also known as the scientific method.

_____   2. You are out swimming in the ocean and you see some fish with prominent sharp teeth swimming around you. You know that some fish with sharp teeth are predatory. You take off without waiting around to see if they might harm you. Your decision is based on analogous reasoning.

_____   3. You could use inductive reasoning to put together a picture puzzle if all the pieces were available, even if there were no box cover to show what the whole picture would look like when it was finished.

_____   4. There is a contest to guess how many gumballs are in a jar. You can use inductive reasoning to figure this out.

_____   5. Inductive reasoning could help you cook a new dish by carefully following instructions from a cookbook.

_____   6. Inductive reasoning can extrapolate reliable predictions from only one or two examples of a phenomenon.

_____   7. Counterexamples can test or refute theories or generalizations.

_____   8. A hypothesis is a theory that can lead to new facts and discoveries, but the hypothesis itself is not a certainty.

_____   9. Statistical evidence is always reliable regardless of the attitudes of the people who research and present the information.

Building Arguments
Induction

The first of May 1779, the troops under General John Sullivan commenced their march but did not arrive at Wyoming until the middle of June. . . . The fourth day it reached a beautiful region, then, almost wholly unknown to the white man. . . . As the weary columns slowly emerged from the dark forest and filed into this open space . . . they seemed suddenly to be transported into an Eden. The tall, ripe grass bent before the wind—cornfield on cornfield, as far as eye could reach waved in the sun—orchards that had been growing for generations, were weighted down under a profusion of fruit—cattle grazed on the banks of a river, and all was luxuriance and beauty. . . . All about were scattered a hundred and twenty-eight houses—not miserable huts huddled together, but large airy buildings, situated in the most pleasant spots, surrounded by fruit trees, and exhibiting a civilization on the part of the Indians never before witnessed.

Soon after sunrise immense columns of smoke began to rise the length and breadth of the valley, and in a short time the whole settlement was wrapped in flame, from limit to limit; and before night those one hundred and twenty-eight houses were a heap of ashes. The grain had been gathered into them, and thus both were destroyed together. The orchards were cut down, the cornfields uprooted, and the cattle butchered and left to rot on the plain. A scene of desolation took the place of the scene of beauty, and the army camped that night in a desert.

The next day, having accomplished the object of their mission, Sullivan commenced a homeward march. . . . The thanks of Congress was presented to Sullivan and his army for the manner in which they had fulfilled their arduous task. (Joel Tyler Headley, *Washington and His Generals,* 1859, an account of the 1779 tragedy in New York State when President George Washington ordered troops to secure the frontier against the Iroquois in case they should be influenced by the English to attack Americans)

Joel Tyler Headley, *Washington and His Generals,* Vol. II, Charles Scribner, 1959.

Discussion Questions

1. Is this a neutral report? Is it an ironic inductive argument?
2. What words suggest where the author's sympathy lies?
3. Does the author draw a conclusion about the significance of this event or does he leave it up to the reader?

• R E A D I N G •

The Beekeeper

Sue Hubbell

Sue Hubbell is an American author who lives in the Missouri Ozarks. In this short chapter, titled "Summer" and taken from her book The Country Year, *Hubbell describes one event that occurred on her beekeeping farm. Notice as you read how her writing has its basis in her observation skills, and how she draws the reader into her keen interest in the ordinary life that surrounds her.*

I keep twenty hives of bees here in my home beeyard, but most of my hives are scattered in outyards across the Ozarks, where I can find the thickest stands of wild blackberries and other good things for bees. I always have a waiting list of farmers who would like the bees on their land, for the clover in their pastures is more abundant when the bees are there to pollinate it.

One of the farmers, a third-generation Ozarker and a dairyman with a lively interest in bees, came over today for a look at what my neighbors call my honey factory. My honey house contains a shiny array of stainless-steel tanks with clear plastic tubing connecting them, a power uncapper for slicing open honeycomb, an extractor for spinning honey out of the comb, and a lot of machinery and equipment that whirs, thumps, hums and looks very special. The dairyman, shrewd in mountain ways, looked it all over carefully and then observed, "Well . . . ll . . . ll, wouldn't say for sure now, but it looks like a still to me."

There have been droughty years and cold wet ones when flowers refused to bloom and I would have been better off with a still back up here on my mountain top, but the weather this past year was perfect from a bee's standpoint, and this August I ran 33,000 pounds of honey through my factory. This was nearly twice the normal crop, and everything was overloaded, starting with me. Neither I nor my equipment is set up to handle this sort of harvest, even with extra help.

I always need to hire someone, a strong young man who is not afraid of being stung, to help me harvest the honey from the hives.

5   The honey I take is the surplus that the bees will not need for the winter; they store it above their hives in wooden boxes called supers. To take it from them, I stand behind each hive with a gasoline-powered machine called a beeblower and blow the bees out of the supers with a jet of air. Meanwhile, the strong young man carries the supers, which weigh about sixty pounds each, and stacks them on pallets in the truck. There may be thirty to fifty supers in every outyard, and we have only about half an hour to get them off the hives, stacked and covered before the bees get really cross about what we are doing. The season to take the honey in this part of the country is summer's end, when the temperature is often above ninety-five degrees. The nature of the work and the temper of the bees require that we wear protective

clothing while doing the job: a full set of coveralls, a zippered bee veil and leather gloves. Even a very strong young man works up a considerable sweat wrapped in a bee suit in hot weather hustling sixty-pound supers—being harassed by angry bees at the same time.

This year my helper has been Ky, my nephew, who wanted to learn something about bees and beekeeping. He is a sweet, gentle, cooperative giant of a young man who, because of a series of physical problems, lacks confidence in his own ability to get on in the world.

As soon as he arrived, I set about to desensitize him to bee stings. The first day, I put a piece of ice on his arm to numb it; then, holding the bee carefully by her head, I placed her abdomen on the numbed spot and let her sting him there. A bee's stinger is barbed and stays in the flesh, pulling loose from her body as she struggles to free herself. Lacking her stinger, the bee will live only a short time. The bulbous poison sac at the top of the stinger continues to pulsate after the bee has left, its muscles pumping the venom and forcing the barbed stinger deeper into the flesh.

I wanted Ky to have only a partial dose of venom that first day, so after a minute I scraped the stinger out with my fingernail and watched his reaction closely. A few people—about one percent of the population—are seriously sensitive to bee venom. Each sting they receive can cause a more severe reaction than the one before, reactions ranging from hives, difficulty in breathing and accelerated heartbeat, to choking, anaphylactic shock and death. Ky had been stung a few times in his life and didn't think he was seriously allergic, but I wanted to make sure.

The spot where the stinger went in grew red and began to swell. This was a normal reaction, and so was the itchiness that Ky felt the next day. That time I let a bee sting him again, repeating the procedure, but leaving the stinger in his arm a full ten minutes, until the venom sac was emptied. Again the spot was red, swollen and itchy, but had disappeared the next day. Thereafter Ky decided that he didn't need the ice cube any more, and began holding the bee himself to administer his own stings. I kept him at one sting a day until he had no redness or swelling from the full sting, and then had him increase to two stings daily. Again the greater amount of venom caused redness and swelling, but soon his body could tolerate them without an allergic reaction. I gradually had him build up to ten full stings a day with no reaction.

10   To encourage Ky, I had told him that what he was doing might help protect him from the arthritis that runs in our family. Beekeepers generally believe that getting stung by bees is a healthy thing, and that bee venom alleviates the symptoms of arthritis. When I first began keeping bees, I supposed this to be just another one of the old wives' tales that make beekeeping such an entertaining occupation, but after my hands were stung the pain in my fingers disappeared and I too became a believer. Ky was polite, amused and skeptical of what I told him, but he welcomed my taking a few companionable stings on my knuckles along with him.

In desensitizing Ky to bee venom, I had simply been interested in building up his tolerance to stings so that he could be an effective helper when we took the honey from the hives, for I knew that he would be stung frequently. But I discovered that there had been a secondary effect on Ky that was more important: he was enormously pleased with himself for having passed through what he evidently regarded as a rite of initiation. He was proud and delighted in telling other people about the whole process. He was now one tough guy.

I hoped he was prepared well enough for our first day of work. I have had enough strong young men work for me to know what would happen the first day: he would be stung royally.

Some beekeepers insist that bees know their keeper—that they won't sting that person, but *will* sting a stranger. This is nonsense, for summertime bees live only six weeks and I often open a particular hive less frequently than that, so I am usually a stranger to my bees; yet I am seldom stung. Others say that bees can sense fear or nervousness. I don't know if this is true or not, but I do know that bees' eyes are constructed in such a way that they can detect discontinuities and movement very well and stationary objects less well. This means that a person near their hives who moves with rapid, jerky motions attracts their attention and will more often be blamed by the bees when their hives are being meddled with than will the person whose motions are calm and easy. It has been my experience that the strong young man I hire for the honey harvest is always stung unmercifully for the first few days while he is new to the process and a bit tense. Then he learns to become easier with the bees and settles down to his job. As he gains confidence and assurance, the bees calm down too, and by the end of the harvest he usually is only stung a few times a day.

I knew that Ky very much wanted to do a good job with me that initial day working in the outyards. I had explained the procedures we would follow in taking the honey from the hives, but of course they were new to him and he was anxious. The bees from the first hive I opened flung themselves on him. Most of the stingers could not penetrate his bee suit, but in the act of stinging a bee leaves a chemical trace that marks the person stung as an enemy, a chemical sign other bees can read easily. This sign was read by the bees in each new hive I opened, and soon Ky's bee suit began to look like a pincushion, bristling with stingers. In addition, the temperature was starting to climb and Ky was sweating. Honey oozing from combs broken between the supers was running down the front of his bee suit when he carried them to the truck. Honey and sweat made the suit cling to him, so that the stingers of angry bees could penetrate the suit and he could feel the prick of each one as it entered his skin. Hundreds of bees were assaulting him and finally drove him out of the bee-yard, chasing him several hundred yards before they gave up the attack. There was little I could do to help him but try to complete the job quickly, so I took the supers off the next few hives myself, carried them to the truck and loaded them. Bravely, Ky returned to finish the last few hives. We tied down the load and drove away. His face was red with exertion when he unzipped his bee veil. He didn't have much to say as we drove to the next yard, but sat beside me gulping down ice water from the thermos bottle.

15   At the second yard the bees didn't bother Ky as we set up the equipment. I hoped that much of the chemical marker the bees had left on him had evaporated, but as soon as I began to open the hives they were after him again. Soon a cloud of angry bees enveloped him, accompanying him to the truck and back. Because of the terrain, the truck had to be parked at an odd angle and Ky had to bend from the hips as he loaded it, stretching the fabric of the bee suit taut across the entire length of his back and rear, allowing the bees to sting through it easily. We couldn't talk over the noise of the beeblower's engine, but I was worried about how he was taking hundreds more stings. I was removing the bees from the supers as quickly as I could, but the yard was a good one and there were a lot of supers there.

In about an hour's time Ky carried and stacked what we later weighed in as a load of 2,500 pounds. The temperature must have been nearly a hundred degrees. After he had stacked the last super, I drove the truck away from the hives and we tied down the load. Ky's long hair was plastered to his face and I couldn't see the expression on it, but I knew he had been pushed to his limits and I was concerned about him. He tried to brush some of the stingers out of the seat of his bee suit before he sat down next to me in the truck in an uncommonly gingerly way. Unzipping his bee veil, he tossed it aside, pushed the hair back from his sweaty face, reached for the thermos bottle, gave me a sunny and triumphant grin and said, "If I ever get arthritis of the ass, I'll know all that stuff you've been telling me is a lot of baloney."

● ● ●

Study/Writing/Discussion Questions

1. Does this story elicit inductive reasoning skills? How so?
2. How does the story center on two trial experiments?
3. How is the first experiment a controlled experiment?
4. What is Hubbell trying to find out?
5. What theories does she mention about why bees sting some people and not others? What theory does she tell about bee stings and arthritis?
6. What trials does Ky go through in proving his ability to do the job?
7. Were you surprised by the story's ending? Why or why not?
8. How was the ending a confirmation of the author's hunch about his suitability for the job?

CHAPTER 12

Inductive Fallacies:

How Can Inductive Reasoning Go Wrong?

Used with permission of Mark Stivers.

©1997 Stivers

Two out of three farmers approve of genetically engineered produce.

You will probably realize that this cartoon is not only satirizing the acceptance of genetically modified foods but also playing with the fallacy of questionable statistic. While studying the material in the first part of this chapter, you learned some standards for inductive reasoning that included a few examples of poor inductive reasoning. In this chapter you will study the chief fallacies of inductive reasoning; in other words, you will learn a great deal more about how inductive reasoning can go wrong. Following is a list of the fallacies covered in this chapter.

1. **Hasty generalization:** A conclusion based on insufficient evidence.
2. **Either-or fallacy:** An argument that oversimplifies a situation, asserting that there are only two choices when actually there are many.
3. **Questionable statistic:** Backing up an argument with statistics that are either unknowable or unsound.
4. **Inconsistencies and contradictions:** Offering evidence that contradicts the conclusion or making claims that contradict one another.
5. **Loaded question:** Using a biased question to obtain a predetermined answer.
6. **False analogy:** Comparing two things that have some similarities but also significant differences that are ignored for the sake of the argument.
7. **False cause:** Claiming a causal connection between events without reasonable evidence to support the claim.
8. **Slippery slope:** An unwarranted claim that permitting one event to occur would lead to an inevitable and uncontrollable chain reaction.

The Hasty Generalization

> **Hasty generalization** is the fallacy of overgeneralizing, of drawing a conclusion about the whole from an insufficient sampling of its parts.

The hasty generalization is the fallacy that occurs most often in inductive reasoning. A hasty generalization is a conclusion reached prematurely without a fair and adequate study of sufficient evidence. Often it expresses stereotypes.

1. All used car salesmen are crooks. One of them sold me a lemon.
2. All old people are cheap. They never give me a fair tip when I park their cars.
3. No car mechanic can be trusted. They are only out to make a buck.
4. I waited half an hour for him to get dressed. Men are really more vain than women.
5. Chinese are tall, thin, and skinny.

In all five cases, the samplings were too small to justify the conclusions drawn from them about all used car salesmen or other groups. Hasty generalizations are familiar to all of us; we tend to make them when we feel angry, or too impatient to deal with complexities.

Hasty generalizations can also result from careless interpretations of the data:

> I read recently in a survey of U.S. medical students that tuition costs, on the average, $30,000 a year. This means that only the wealthy can still make it into the medical profession.

This is a hasty generalization because it does not consider the possibility of receiving scholarships or loans. Instead only one assumption is made to account for cost payment.

How do we avoid hasty generalizations? First, by being very careful in our use of the words *all, every, everyone,* and *no.* A single exception will disqualify any generalization preceded by one of these words, which are called *quantifiers.* Test to see if what you actually mean calls for *qualifiers* such as *in this case, in some cases,* or *it appears* or *seems* or *suggests that.* A careful use of quantifiers and qualifiers can often make the difference between an accurate statement and a fallacious one. Let's see how the following generalization differs significantly from the one given previously.

> Although this survey states that the average cost of medical school tuition is $30,000 a year, it does not state how medical students manage to pay for it. Some could be wealthy, while others might qualify for scholarships or loans. All that can be said is that a student who wants to attend medical school does have to consider the cost.

Class Discussion

Which of the following statements contain hasty generalizations? Underline the generalization and then explain why its use of quantifiers or qualifiers seems careless or based on insufficient sampling.

1. Most poor black people who live in cities are anti-Semitic. That's because their landlords are Jewish.
2. Every woman in the military that I ever met was a lesbian. They are all either lesbians or about to become lesbians.
3. Because Asian students are now becoming the majority ethnic group accepted for math and science studies into West Coast graduate schools, this suggests that Asians may be either genetically gifted in abstract thinking and/or culturally encouraged in it.
4. From 1993 to 1996, network news coverage of homicide increased 721% while the national homicide rate decreased by 20%. . . . TV executives

know that if they spend more time examining stories about violent crimes, more people will tune into their broadcasts. (*The Better World Handbook*, 2001, p. 32)

5. Throughout history people have preferred the slum and the sweat-shop to the even more confining poverty of the farm. She reaches back into history, quoting a North Carolina woman born in 1899. "We didn't like the farming. It was so hot from sunup to sundown. No, that was not for me. Mill work was better." (Quoted from *The Travels of a T-Shirt in the Global Economy* by Pietra Rivoli in a book review by Tom Abate, *San Francisco Chronicle*, April 3, 2005)

6. The lower economic people are not holding up their end of the deal. These people are not parenting. They are buying things for kids—$800 sneakers—for what? And won't spend $200 for *Hooked on Phonics*. (Bill Cosby on *Jim Lehrer News Hour*, July 15, 2004)

The Either-Or Fallacy, or False Dilemma

> The **either-or fallacy** or **false dilemma** is a fallacious argument that over-simplifies a situation, maintaining that there are only two choices when actually other alternatives exist.

An argument that presumes that there are only two ways of looking at a situation—or that only one of two choices can be made—when other alternatives do exist is called the either-or fallacy, or false dilemma. Sometimes these false dilemmas appear in those frustrating questions on personality assessment tests:

1. When you see a friend coming toward you on the sidewalk, do you rush forward to greet the person or do you cross to the other side of the street?

2. Do you act impulsively rather than deliberately?

3. Do you have only a few friends or a large circle of friends?

More often, false dilemmas appear in poll questions: "Are you for or against the war on drugs?" Such questions are convenient for tabulation purposes but do not allow for weighed discriminations that reflect actual opinion. You may be in favor of aggressive federal programs to prevent the import of cocaine, but not marijuana. Or you may prefer that more funding be given to programs of rehabilitation and prevention. When confronted with either-or questions, a thoughtful person is faced with another dilemma: that of refusing both choices or of compromising with an answer that plays into the questioner's assumption and bias. The usual false dilemma argument oversimplifies a complex issue; sometimes it seeks to intimidate:

- Live free or die.
- America. Love it or leave it.
- When you have a headache, all you can do is reach for aspirin.
- Either you are with me or against me.
- The Cougar convertible: you'll either own one or want one.

In each of these cases, the argument is based on a dilemma that over-simplifies the situation to fit assumptions. Sometimes, as in these slogans and commercial appeals, the false dilemma serves as an intentional ploy to negate resistance and force agreement. Here is such an example: "Mothers of young children can either have careers or stay at home. But they can't expect both to have careers and to raise happy children." This argument is based on many assumptions.

1. A father supports the family.
2. A mother (or father) has to leave home to pursue a career.
3. Parents pay attention to their children when at home.
4. Another family member or child-care worker cannot give a young child what it needs.

A false dilemma assumes that there is only one choice, whereas imagination will allow for other options.

Class Discussion

Analyze the false dilemmas just given and offer reasons for your agreement or disagreement with their designations as such.

The Questionable Statistic

> The **questionable statistic** is the fallacy of offering statistics that are unknowable, faulty, or misleading.

Inductive reasoning requires some knowledge of statistics and how statistics can be used or misused as evidence. As you learned earlier, to evaluate whether statistics are used fairly, you need to look for such things as the size of the sample, whether it was representative and random, whether a margin for error was considered, and what the margin was. These are only some of the basics involved in assessing the reliability of statistics. The fallacy of the questionable statistic refers to confusion or deception in the use of statistics, even to the point of citing figures that would be impossible to obtain.

Recall this use of statistics, quoted earlier:

> I would guess that the average office female makes 509 visits to the lavatory to a male's 320, and spends 10.7 minutes there to a male's 2.5. What management is going to put up with this "primp time" featherbedding at equal pay?

In this case, the author is lightly mocking the use of statistics, suggesting that his estimate can be this precise because everyone knows that his claims are true. From there he jumps to a conclusion (in the form of a question) that lacks any evidence to back up his claim about either featherbedding or equal pay.

When statistical claims are false or deliberately misleading, they are not always easy to detect unless we have knowledge of the laws of statistics. A sure warning sign is *unattributed figures,* or figures given without a citation of source, purpose, and methods of calculation.

> Why isn't alcohol illegal? It has the same rate of addiction (10 percent) as cocaine.

In this case, a critical thinker would want to know how *addiction* is being defined, how this figure was derived, who conducted the study, and whether this 10 percent figure was quoted out of context.

Here is another example, also uncited, with a flashing red sign attached:

> Illegal aliens cost American citizens $5 billion a year.

First, the word *cost* is undefined; what expenses does this term cover? Second, "illegal aliens" refers to undocumented immigrants; therefore, how were they counted, on what basis was their cost to the public estimated, and by whom? Whoever made this statement should not have made this claim at all unless she could have supplied this information as well as its source. Otherwise the reader is left wondering if the 5 billion is an *unknowable statistic.*

Here is a clearer example of pure guesswork:

> If we legalize drugs, drugs would become much cheaper, at least one-fifth the cost. Then five times as many people would buy them. Then we would have five times as many addicts, and instead of 100,000

addicted babies born to addicted mothers each year, we would have a million.

The chief weakness of this argument is that it is based on the assumption that if drugs were legal, they would be less expensive. From there, the figure of "at least one-fifth the cost" seems to be drawn out of a hat. Next are repetitions of *five,* concluding with the dreadful statistic of 1 million addicted babies. The argument commits the fallacy of the unknowable statistic, not once but four times, seeking to establish as factual guesswork calculations for a hypothetical situation with too many variables and unknowns.

Sometimes it is more obvious that the statistics quoted could not have been gathered. Consider these examples:

- Two-thirds of all thefts are never detected.
- Two-thirds of all people have thoughts they would never admit to.
- Loss in federal taxes from those who barter instead of paying cash for goods is $1 billion annually.

Class Discussion

What questions would you ask about the statistics used in the following statements?

1. Only 106 of an estimated 895 cases of rape that occurred in New England last year were reported.
2. If it is elitist to say that 30 percent of the American people are dumb in the sense of uninstructed, then I'm an elitist. But it's true. (William F. Buckley, Jr.)
3. It is a known fact that people use only 10 percent of their actual potential.
4. If the *Roe v. Wade* decision remains in force until the beginning of the twenty-first century, our nation will be missing more than 40 million citizens, of whom approximately 8 million would have been men of military age. (From "It's 'Life for a Life,'" quoted in "Notes from the Fringe," *Harper's,* June 1985)
5. Milk consumption is probably the number-one cause of heart disease. America's number-one killer. By the time the average American reaches the age of fifty-two, he or she will have consumed in milk and dairy products the equivalent cholesterol contained in one million slices of bacon. In 1994 the average U.S. citizen consumed 26 ounces of milk and dairy products per day. One 12-ounce glass of whole milk contains 300 calories and 16 grams of fat. Beer is taking a bad rap—protruding

stomachs on overweight people should be called milk bellies, not beer bellies. (Robert Cohen, "Milk: the Deadly Poison," *Earth Island Journal,* Winter 1997–98)

Contradictions and Inconsistencies

> **Contradictions and inconsistencies** is the fallacy of making claims or offering evidence that contradicts the conclusion.

In the Sipress cartoon on page 325, the daughter surprises her mother by pointing out her use of two contradictory claims or premises. The daughter implies that one of the claims must be false. Here's another example of reasoning from contradictory claims.

> All men are equal; it is just that some are more equal than others.

In political life we often hear contradictions made within or between speeches or announcements. If someone wants to please as many people as possible, discrepancies often become the consequence. Here is an example of contradictions within statements:

> Of course I cannot approve of hecklers disrupting my opponent's speeches. However, I would also say that in a democracy, they also have the right to be heard as much as the speaker.

In this case, the politician wanted to defend himself from any implication that he might have benefited from a tactic that prevented his opponent from being heard. He declares his disapproval while also taking the high road of defending the hecklers' right of free speech. He does not consider the rights of the audience to hear the speaker or how a democracy might function without some rules of order.

Here is an example of a contradiction expressed in a television program interview:

> VETERAN: We should not send American troops to Bosnia. No American life is ever worth being shed on foreign soil.
>
> INTERVIEWER: But didn't you fight in World War II when American soldiers died in both Europe and Asia?
>
> VETERAN: Well, that war was fought because one man was trying to control the world. Hitler took over Europe and his allies controlled the East.

Used with permission of David Sipress.

In this case, the veteran is not able to defend his claim that "No American life is ever worth being shed on foreign soil." He makes a generalization that allows for no exceptions. Then when the interviewer confronts him with the way in which his own military career contradicts this generalization, he is unable to revise his generalization accordingly. In other words, he would have to say, "You are right. No American life is ever worth being shed on foreign soil unless it would be to stop someone like Hitler."

Class Discussion

List the contradictions you find in the following examples.

1. I love mankind; it's just that I can't stand people.

2. The Nuclear Regulatory Commission has imposed strict penalties for employees at nuclear plants found to be stoned from illicit drug use on the job; but no penalties were prescribed for workers discovered to be drunk at the nuclear controls. (David Freudberg, KCBS Radio, February 16, 1990)

3. I'd like to order one Big Mac, large fries, twenty chicken nuggets, two apple pies, one chocolate sundae, and a diet Coke, please.

4. Capital punishment is our society's recognition of the sanctity of human life. (Sen. Orrin Hatch, R-Utah)

5. The more killing and homicides you have, the more havoc it prevents. (Richard M. Daley, mayor of Chicago)

The Loaded Question

> The **loaded question** is the fallacy of using a biased question in order to obtain a predetermined result.

Loaded questions occur often in polls, as discussed earlier, in order to create a bias toward a certain answer: "Do you believe pornography should be brought into every home through television?" We are all familiar with the loaded questions "Have you stopped beating your wife?" and "Are you still a heavy drinker?" In such cases, the guilt is assumed and not proven. Any reply to the question traps the respondent into either an admission of guilt or a protest that could be interpreted as a guilty defense. Loaded questions are related to the fallacy of circular reasoning (begging the question), where conclusions are asserted without evidence or premises to support them.

Class Discussion

Which of the following are loaded questions and which are not?

1. Do you feel that a school voucher program should be permitted to dismantle U.S. public schools?
2. Where did you hide the murder weapon?
3. When are you going to stop asking me so many silly questions?
4. Are you going to be good and do what I say?
5. What would you like for dinner tonight?
6. What do you think about the new brain research that says that emotional stability is more important than IQ in determining success in life?
7. Forty-three percent of U.S. grade school children are reading below grade level. Why? Is this because they are not learning phonics?
8. What will you do on the day you discover our number one brand of arthritis medication? (Ad with picture of a woman running along a beach)1
9. Why do Senate Democrats hate America?

The False Analogy

> The **false analogy** is the fallacy of basing an argument on a comparison of two things that may have some similarities, but also significant differences that are ignored for the sake of the argument. (The Greek word *analogos* means "according to ratio.")

As you learned earlier, an analogy is a form of reasoning in which two things are compared. A good analogy often compares some abstract principle that is difficult to understand to a concrete familiar experience in order to make the abstract principle clearer. A good or sound analogy must compare two things or ideas that have major parallels in ratio. If one uses the analogy of a pump to explain the heart, the heart does not have to physically look like a metal pump with a handle, but it should at least function on the same principles. Here is an analogy taken from physics about the nature of subatomic particles: "If you wish to understand subatomic particles, think of them as empty space that is distorted, pinched up, concentrated into point-like ripples of energy." Here the appearance is the essential parallel that permits a visualization of something invisible to us.

In a false analogy essential parallels are missing, either overlooked or willfully disregarded.

> Well, it's too bad that so many Indians had to die as America was settled by the white men. But you can't make an omelet without breaking a few eggs.

How do we decide whether an analogy is a true or a false one? A recommended technique is to first write out the equation that the analogy offers; then under two columns, headed Similarities and Differences, compare the chief characteristics of each:

Claim: There is no convincing evidence to show that cigarette smoking is harmful. Too much of anything is harmful. Too much applesauce is harmful. (cigarette manufacturer)

Equation: Too much cigarette smoking = too much applesauce.

When we see the equation, we sense that something is not right here. For a further check, make a list of the similarities and differences between each. If the differences far outweigh the similarities, you have a false analogy.

Similarities	Differences
1. Ingested into body	1. One ingested through lungs first and is not digestible
	2. One a food, other not a food
	3. One addictive, other not
	4. Both don't affect body and consciousness in same way
	5. No evidence applesauce causes cancer, but evidence that cigarette smoking does

DISCOVERY EXERCISE

■ Evaluating Analogies

Use the procedure just demonstrated to analyze the following analogies.

1. There are no grounds for the claim that the incidence of lung cancer is higher in this county because of the presence of our oil refineries. Cancer can be caused by all kinds of things. People don't stop eating peanut butter because it causes cancer, do they? (Biologist working for an oil refinery)

2. Who is the endangered species? The spotted owl or the loggers of the Northwest?

3. We welcome immigrants because our country needs them the way old soil needs new seeds.

4. Nature is cruel. It is our right to be cruel as well. (Adolf Hitler)

5. Vote for the incumbent. Don't change horses in midstream!

Class Discussion

Rate the following examples as either good analogies or false analogies and tell why.

1. If a ban on same-sex marriages violates their civil rights, then the refusal to issue a driver's license to a blind man violates his civil rights as well. After all, gay couples can not procreate any more than a blind man can safely drive a car in traffic. (Letter to the editor, *San Francisco Chronicle*, March 16, 2005)

2. People and politicians, who really . . . don't know enough about the issue of acid rain have been brainwashed by the media and

environmentalists into believing that we, in Ohio, are the primary cause of the decay. The biggest killers of human life in the U.S. are automobiles, cigarettes and alcohol. Yet none of these products have been banned. Americans, and no Americans more than we in the coal fields, want to see a healthy and safe environment for all generations to come, but we just cannot accept legislation such as this without a scientific basis. (Rep. Douglas Applegate, D-Ohio, speaking against a House bill to require federally mandated emission limitations on the largest sources of sulphur dioxide)

3. If you take a piece of meat and throw it in a pack of hungry dogs, they are going to kill each other over it. If you don't have any opportunities available to you, and something that can make you easy money (selling crack cocaine) comes up, what are you going to do? (Paris, Oakland rap artist)

4. Measuring a country's health by measuring its gross domestic product is rather like measuring a person's health by how much medical care he buys. Thus, a person who just had bypass surgery and cancer radiation treatments would be considered healthy.

5. If children cannot be executed for crimes, why should we execute retarded people with the minds of children?

False Cause

> **False cause** is the fallacy of claiming a causal connection between events without reasonable and sufficient evidence to support the claim.

Inductive reasoning is used to speculate about cause or to determine cause. The criminal justice system uses inductive reasoning to gather evidence to determine guilt or innocence. Faulty reasoning about causality can result in the arrest and conviction of an innocent person or the release of a guilty person. A trial presents evidence to the jury as support for causality in a crime.

False cause is a fallacious argument that insists on a causal connection between events that cannot reasonably be connected. False cause can also be an interpretation that is oversimplistic. Sometimes false cause reasoning can be ludicrous, as shown in the little Sufi teaching stories about a character named Nasrudin. In one of these stories Nasrudin was seen throwing crumbs around his house. When someone asked what he was doing, Nasrudin answered, "I'm keeping the tigers away." The person then objected, "But there aren't any tigers in this part of the world!" And Nasrudin replied, "That's right. That's because it is so effective!" In another story Nasrudin boasts to a friend that he once caused an entire tribe of desert nomads to run. When asked how he did it, he said, "I just ran and they ran after me."

Blaming the wrong target is one kind of false cause. More frequent are those false causes that vastly oversimplify a situation, such as scapegoating. The term *scapegoating* refers to the ancient practice of offering ritual sacrifices for the appeasement of some god or some person or persons. Although we may now think sacrificing maidens on altars to the gods is barbaric, scapegoating rituals still abound in our personal, political, and social lives.

Another version of false cause is known in Latin as *post hoc ergo propter hoc,* meaning "after this, therefore because of this." The post hoc fallacy reasons in a childlike way that because one event happened after another event, the second was caused by the first.

- First my cat ate a mouse, and then she had kittens. The mouse gave her the kittens.

- He committed the murder, but he couldn't help himself because he was under the influence of a sugar high after eating Twinkies.

Sometimes false cause arguments center around debates on the chicken-or-egg questions. The fictional character Nasrudin confuses us with his own confusion as he attributes his running away from the Bedouins as the cause of their running after him. Here are two contrasting chicken-or-egg arguments:

- The violence on the home screen follows the violence in our lives. (Del Reisman, president, Writers Guild of America)

- Violence on TV is definitely a cause of the growing violence in our lives. It presents violence as an appropriate way to solve interpersonal problems, to get what you want out of life, avenge slights and insults and make up for perceived injustices. (Leonard D. Eron, professor of psychology)

Finally, all the examples of causal reasoning discussed here contain a traditional Western assumption that causality is linear, that one effect must result from one cause. More recently, science has begun to use *systems thinking* to study causality in a manner that is ecological, taking the widest perspective of context, of interrelated parts and cycles. Systems thinking is concerned with the way in which the wolf's predator role is actually essential to the health of the deer. Systems thinking reveals the folly of attempting to protect the deer by killing off the wolves, which leads in turn to an overpopulation of the deer, overgrazing, and eventually mass deer starvation. When we engage in systems thinking, we avoid the fallacious reasoning that results from the assumption that causality is always single and linear.

Class Discussion

False or questionable cause is a fallacy that is often found in political arguments. Analyze the following statements. Decide if you agree or disagree that they are examples of the fallacy of false cause and state why.

1. As a white nation, we wish to survive in freedom in our own father-land, and we demand to be governed by our own people. South Africa must retain the fatherland given us by God. (Andries P. Treurnicht, leader, far-right conservative party, South Africa; speech reported in *The Los Angeles Times,* May 28, 1986)

2. The corruption of American youth has been caused by rock and roll music. Its rhythms and lyrics, together with the role models provided by its singers and musicians, have encouraged experimentation with drugs and promiscuity.

3. Forests are disappearing fast from the world. Loss has been caused by logging, mining, the development of energy, farming, pollution. During the 1980's eight percent of the world's tropical forest was lost. Another 10 percent of all the world's forests may be lost by 2050. (*Atlas of the Future,* 1998)

4. Americans buy Japanese cars, cameras, and stereos because they are unpatriotic. An ad campaign appealing to their patriotism could reverse this trend.

5. State-sponsored affirmative action, bilingual education, and multi-culturalism are promoting dangerous levels of ethnic group tensions and conflicts.

The Slippery Slope

> **Slippery slope** is the fallacy of arguing, without sufficient proof, that if one event is allowed to occur, a disastrous and uncontrollable chain reaction will result. The slippery slope appeals to fear and urges agreement on the basis of a situation that contains too many variables and unknowns.

The slippery slope is another fallacy that deals with causation. In this case the claim is made that permitting one event to occur would set off an uncontrollable chain reaction. In politics this is also called the domino theory: if one country falls, so will all the rest like a line of dominoes. This argument was often given as a reason that the United States should stay in Vietnam: if Vietnam fell to the communists, China would take over the rest of Asia.

The same argument was also cited for the U.S. presence in El Salvador: if El Salvador fell to the guerrillas, so would all of Central America and Mexico, thus jeopardizing the whole Western hemisphere. Although these were predictions of a possible scenario, as arguments they were fallacious in that they urged agreement on the basis of logic for a position that contained many variables and unknowns.

Here are three examples of arguments built on the fallacy of the slippery slope:

- If you offer people unemployment insurance, they will become lazy and expect the government to support them for life.
- Sex education in the schools leads to promiscuity, unwanted pregnancies, and cheating in marriages.
- If you teach critical thinking in an Indian university, the young people would go home and question, then disobey their parents. Their families would quarrel and break up. Then they would question their bosses and everyone else. The next thing you know the whole country would fall apart. (comment made by a University of Bombay professor)

Class Discussion

Which of the following arguments are slippery slopes? Explain why.

1. I cannot support the "three strikes and you're out" law. This tough position denies all possibility of change in people. With it, we turn our backs on these people, saying they can never get better. Thus, we buy into a cycle of hate and fear in a total rejection of love and compassion, locking ourselves up in our houses of fear just like we lock up the prisoners in our prisons. (Letter to the editor, *San Francisco Chronicle*, November 30, 1997)

2. A widely acclaimed and disturbing study out of the University of Vermont has shown a "decline in emotional aptitude among children across the board." Rich and poor, East Coast or West Coast, inner city or suburb, children today are more vulnerable than ever to anger, depression, anxiety—a massive emotional malaise. The result is that boys who can't control their emotions later commit violent crime; girls who can't control emotion don't get violent, they get pregnant. (Daniel Goleman, *Emotional Intelligence*, New York: Bantam, 1995)

3. Considering the legal union of same-sex couples would shatter the conventional definition of marriage, change the rules that govern behavior, endorse practices which are completely antithetical to the tenets of all the world's major religions, send conflicting signals

about marriage and sexuality, particularly to the young, and obscure marriage's enormously consequential function—procreation and childrearing. (William Bennett, "Leave Marriage Alone," *Newsweek,* June 3, 1996)

4. We are using about two-thirds of our oil supply right now to burn in cars and airplanes and trucks. But we're producing about 40 percent of what we use in this country. And we're using 25 percent of the entire world's production of oil right now and we only have five percent of the population. So what's going to happen when a country like China, for example, comes on line and begins to rise to the level of consumerism that we have in this country? They purchased about two million cars last year; we put about 17 million on the road. And as that goes up in China we're going to see an incredible increase in world demand for oil. And when demand goes up and supply does not keep pace with it, then the prices go up. And that's what we mean by the end of cheap oil. (Bill Allen, "The End of Cheap Oil," Editorial, *National Geographic,* 2004)

Chapter Summary

1. Hasty generalization is the fallacy of basing a conclusion on insufficient evidence.

2. The either-or fallacy, or false dilemma, is an argument that oversimplifies a situation, asserting that there are only two choices when actually other alternatives exist.

3. The questionable statistic is the statistic that is either unknowable or unsound.

4. Inconsistency in evidence is the fallacy of offering evidence that contradicts the conclusion.

5. The loaded question is the use of a biased question that seeks to obtain a predetermined answer.

6. The false analogy is a comparison of two things that have some similarities but also significant differences that are ignored for the sake of the argument.

7. False cause is the fallacy of claiming a causal connection between events without reasonable evidence to support the claim.

8. The slippery slope is the fallacy of claiming without sufficient proof that permitting one event to occur would lead to a chain reaction that could not be stopped. It ignores the many variables or unknowns in the situation.

Chapter Quiz

Identify the following ten arguments in this section by name, either as *NF* for *not fallacious* or as *slippery slope, false cause, questionable statistic,* or *inconsistencies and contradictions.*

_____ 1. All riders on the buses in a Boston suburb now pay for their rides with special credit cards. All buses are equipped with electronic scanners that record account number, route, time, and date. The American public is being conditioned for the complete Big Brother totalitarian surveillance of the future.

_____ 2. The French and the German objections to importing British beef are purely a matter of their stubborn national pride. There is no reason to fear that this beef would infect any of their citizens with mad cow disease.

_____ 3. Any regulations that dampen corporate profits in the oil and coal industries will backfire because environmental preservation depends heavily on the health of the U.S. economy. The richer the United States is, the more it can help poorer countries with their pollution problems. (Public representative of a coalition of oil and gas producers)

_____ 4. Some people hesitate to have children because of the expense and trouble. The trouble of having children is entirely secondary to the blessing.

_____ 5. Legalizing marijuana would reduce the price by 50 percent.

_____ 6. The reason that I didn't stop for that light was that it was two o'clock in the morning.

_____ 7. If the baseball players start using drugs, then so will the managers, and the next thing you know all the games will be fixed and baseball will no longer be a real American sport.

_____ 8. You should never lie to your partner, although a little white lie never hurts.

_____ 9. A CIA internal investigation found no evidence linking its employees, agents or operatives with the crack cocaine epidemic in the U.S. and no connection between the agency and three men at the center of that drug trade. The findings . . . dispute allegations made by the *San Jose Mercury News* in 1996 of a CIA link to cocaine trafficking in California. The CIA released the first of two volumes of conclusions reached by agency Inspector General Frederick Hitz, who led a 17-member team that reviewed 250,000 pages of documents and conducted 365 interviews. (Associated Press release, January 30, 1998)

_____ 10. All people are equal but some deserve more privilege.

Identify the remaining ten arguments as *nonfallacious, loaded question, false analogy, hasty generalization,* or *either-or fallacy.*

_____ 11. More than any other time in history, mankind faces a crossroads. One path leads to despair and utter hopelessness. The other, to total extinction. Let us pray we have the wisdom to choose correctly. (Woody Allen, "My Speech to the Graduates" *Side Effects,* 1980)

_____ 12. Son, listen, you talk like I do, you even like the same food I do. You're gonna become a musician like me. Don't fight it!

_____ 13. Are you still getting into the movies without paying?

_____ 14. Either you stay in school or you get a job. You can't do both!

_____ 15. One of the major causes for the rapid growth of the European population in the nineteenth century was the improvement of medical knowledge.

_____ 16. When you do laundry, you should separate light clothing from dark clothing and wash each separately, because light articles streak dark ones and the dark items bleed on the light ones.

_____ 17. Is two months' salary too much to spend for something that lasts forever? (ad for diamonds)

_____ 18. I was turned down in two job interviews. I guess I just don't have what it takes.

_____ 19. Are you still fooling around with that guy?

_____ 20. Women, like rugs, need a good beating occasionally.

Advanced Optional Short Research Assignment

■ Detecting Fallacies in an Argument

So far, you have been examining fallacies in examples abstracted from the context in which they appear. The purpose of this assignment is to give you the opportunity to search for fallacies in an argument, to extract them, and to discuss the manner in which they affect the argument as a whole. This is a research assignment, for which you will need to find a short argument. A good source for short arguments that often contain fallacies is letters to editors. Comb newspapers and magazines for your choice, and photocopy it to accompany your analysis. Your parameters will be as follows:

1. *Topic:* Fallacies in an argument.
2. *Approach:* Critical analysis.
3. *Form:* Exposition and argumentation. Identify the fallacies involved and explain whether they affect or do not affect the soundness of the argument.
4. *Length:* Two typed pages, plus a photocopy of the argument.

CHAPTER 13

Deductive Reasoning:

How Do I Reason from Premises?

"I was a good boy, grandpa was a good boy, his father was a good boy. In fact, since the dawn of history, there have only been good boys in this family. That's why you have to be a good boy."

Used with permission of David Sipress.

In this cartoon, the father uses both inductive and deductive reasoning to make his point. Yet his son looks more dismayed than convinced. If the son could defend himself, what logical error would he find in his father's reasoning? The answer to that question comes with the study of deductive reasoning, also known as logic. This chapter will explain the fundamental standards that govern deductive reasoning. It will introduce you to logic's basic vocabulary and explain how deduction and induction interplay in our thinking.

DISCOVERY EXERCISES

▪ What Is Deductive Reasoning?

Using at least two dictionaries, look up the terms *deduction*, *deductive logic*, and *reasoning*. Then write out in your own words a definition of deductive reasoning.

▪ Evaluating Deductive Arguments

Study the following short deductive arguments. Which of these seem to you to be based on good reasoning and which do not? Explain the basis for your decision in each case.

1. Most Americans under age thirty don't believe Social Security will be there for them when they retire. Therefore, most Americans under age thirty favor private accounts.

2. God made men to serve women. Therefore, men should obey their women.

3. People get warts from touching toads. This child has a wart on her finger. This child has touched a toad.

4. The Supreme Court's *Miranda* ruling (giving defendants the right to have a lawyer present during questioning) is wrong and only helps guilty defendants. Suspects who are innocent of a crime should be able to have a lawyer present before police questioning. But the thing is you don't have many suspects who are innocent of a crime. That's contradictory. If a person is innocent of a crime, then he is not a suspect. (Attorney General Edwin Meese, quoted in the *Oakland Tribune*, October 6, 1985)

5. If she had been the last person to leave the house, she would have locked the door. However, the door was unlocked. Therefore, she was not the last person to leave the house.

6. If the temperature goes below freezing, the orange crop will be lost. The temperature went below freezing. The orange crop will be lost.

Now write down your answers to the following questions in preparation for class discussion:

1. Which of the preceding arguments contain statements that are false?
2. In the examples with the false statements, are the inferences nevertheless reasonable?
3. Are there any that may contain true statements but seem illogical in their reasoning?
4. Are there any that contain statements that are true and seem well reasoned?
5. Can you infer any rules for deductive reasoning from what you have learned here?

About Deductive Reasoning

Deduction is taught through the study of formal logic, or the science of good reasoning.

Deduct comes from the Latin *deducere*, to lead away. In deductive reasoning we infer, or lead away, from a general principle in order to apply that principle to a specific instance.

Logic is the science of good reasoning. Both **inductive logic** and **deductive logic** are concerned with the rules for correct reasoning.

We learn *deduction* through the study of formal logic. It is called *formal* because its main concern is with creating *forms* that serve as models to demonstrate both correct and incorrect reasoning. Unlike induction, in which an inference is drawn from an accumulation of evidence, deduction is a process that reasons, in carefully worded statements, about relationships between classes, characteristics, and individuals. You will notice that these statements seem obvious, even childlike, in their simplicity:

All humans are mammals.
Jane is a human.
_____

Jane is a mammal.

All horses are herbivorous.
This animal is a horse.
_____

This animal is herbivorous.

All cats are night animals.

This creature is a cat.

This creature is a night animal.

In these examples, the first statement is about all members of a class; here the classes were humans, horses, and cats. The second statement identifies something or someone as belonging to that class:

- Jane is a human.
- This animal is a horse.
- This creature is a cat.

At this point, the two statements lead to an inference that becomes the conclusion:

- Jane is a mammal.
- This animal is herbivorous.
- This creature is a night animal.

Here you will notice that the conclusion is inevitable. The only inference one could possibly draw from the two statements "All humans are mammals" and "Jane is a human" is that Jane is a mammal. In contrast to the inductive hypothesis, which always remains open, the deductive conclusion is unavoidable. The only objective of deductive reasoning is to draw a correct inference from a group of claims. And that inference is a final conclusion. Nevertheless, deduction often begins with a generalization that has been derived from inductive reasoning. Such is the generalization "All horses are herbivorous." This is a conclusion based on inductive observations repeatedly confirmed.

Deduction also works with generalizations not necessarily derived from inductive reasoning. For instance, it can begin with a belief:

- Horses are not humans.

Indeed, deduction starts with any statement that makes a claim. And a claim, which is an assertion about something, can be worked with logically, regardless of whether the claim is true or not. This is possible because deduction's main concern is not with sorting out evidence and searching for truth; its main concern is studying implications. The focus of deduction is on logic, or the rules of reasoning. Nevertheless, the truth of a statement is important in logic, and the objective of deductive reasoning is to arrive at conclusions that are true.

To summarize, the purpose of deductive logic is to help us reason well with the information we have already acquired. It offers us models, guidelines, and rules for correct reasoning that can lead us to draw reliable conclusions from that information. Thus, *logic,* by definition, is the science of reasoning or the science of inference.

One major barrier to understanding logic is its technical vocabulary. This vocabulary is needed to identify the components of deductive arguments and to convey its rules for correct usage. However, for the student, the task of mastering this terminology can seem formidable at first.

The Basic Vocabulary of Logic

The following are key terms needed to understand the basics of logic: *argument, reasoning, syllogism, premise* (major and minor), *conclusion, validity, soundness.* They will be defined and explained one at a time.

Argument

Arguments appear in both deductive and inductive forms. As we have seen before, deductive arguments involve one or more claims (also called *premises*) that lead to a conclusion:

> All people who flirt are showing interest in someone.
>
> She is flirting with me.
> _____
>
> **She is showing interest in me.**

Inductive arguments also establish claims through reasoning based on experiences, analogies, samples, and general evidence. Compare the following example to the preceding deductive argument:

> This woman seeks me out whenever she sees me having my lunch on the lawn. She comes over and sits next to me. She asks for a sip of my coffee.
>
> She teases me and makes me laugh a lot.
> _____
>
> **She is interested in me.**

Reasoning

Both arguments use reasoning to arrive at a conclusion. *Reasoning* draws conclusions, judgments, or inferences from facts or premises. Deductive arguments start with one or more premises, then reason to consider what conclusions must necessarily follow from them.

If I flirt back, she will encourage me further.

I will flirt back.

She will encourage me further.

Sometimes these premises appear in long chains of reasoning:

If I am nice to her, she'll think I'm flirting.

And if she thinks I'm flirting, she'll come on to me.

And if she comes on to me, I'll have to reject her.

And if I reject her, she'll be hurt.

I don't want her to be hurt.

Therefore, I won't be nice to her.

Argument is a set of claims in the form of reasons offered to support a conclusion.

Reasoning is to draw conclusions, judgments, or inferences from facts or premises.

Syllogism

Logic arranges deductive arguments in standardized forms that make the structure of the argument clearly visible for study and review. These forms are called *syllogisms*. We do not speak in syllogisms, which sound awkward and redundant, but they are useful constructs for testing the reliability of a deduction according to the rules of logic. We have already considered a number of syllogisms, beginning with:

All humans are mammals.

Jane is a human.

Jane is a mammal.

Premises and Conclusion

A syllogism usually contains two premises and a conclusion. The first statement is called the *major premise* and the second is called the *minor premise*.

No flirts are cross and mean. (major premise)

This man is cross and mean. (minor premise)

This man is not a flirt. (conclusion)

In deduction, the reasoning "leads away" from a generalization about a class to identify a specific member belonging to that class—or it can lead to a generalization about another class. In the preceding deductive argument, the major premise states a generalization about the class of flirts: none is cross and mean. The minor premise asserts that a specific individual does not belong to that class: *because* he is cross and mean, he *must* not be a flirt. Between the word *because* and the word *must* lie the inference and the logic. Such reasoning can be checked for reliability by outlining the argument in the strict form of the syllogism.

> **Syllogism** is a standardized form that makes the structure of a deductive argument visible. A syllogism consists of two premises and a conclusion. From the Greek *syllogismos*, a reckoning together.
>
> **Premises** are the claims made in an argument that provide the reasons for believing in the conclusion. In a syllogism, they usually appear as two statements that precede the conclusion. *Premise* comes from the Latin *praemittere*, to set in front.

Validity

The standards used for testing reliability are based on some specific rules that determine an argument's *validity* and *soundness*. Validity has to do with reasoning; and soundness, with both reasoning and truth. A deductive argument is said to be valid when the inference follows correctly from the premises:

All fathers are males.

Jose is a father.
_____

Jose is a male.

Here, because Jose is a member of the class of fathers, and all members of that class are males, it follows logically that Jose must be a male. Moreover, even if we only *assume* these premises are true, it is entirely reasonable to infer that he is a male. We do not have to ponder the matter any further.

On the other hand, invalid reasoning might proceed like this:

All fathers are males.

Jose is a male.
_____

Jose is a father.

In this argument, the first two premises do not imply this conclusion. The conclusion may be true or it may not be true. But we cannot make that determination on the basis of this line of reasoning. Even if we are certain that all fathers are males and that Jose is a male, we still cannot infer from these premises alone that Jose is a father. The conclusion could be false. Therefore, this argument is invalid.

Soundness

Standards for judging arguments refer not only to correct reasoning but also to the truth of the premises. These standards are conveyed by the use of the word *sound*. A deductive argument is sound if the premises are true and the argument is valid. A sound argument is one that uses true premises and correct reasoning to arrive at a conclusion that cannot be false. By this definition, this argument is sound because its premises are true and its reasoning is valid:

> All fathers are males.
>
> Jose is a father.
> _____
>
> **Jose is a male.**

However, the following argument is not sound because, although it contains true premises, the reasoning is invalid, leading to a conclusion that could be false.

> All fathers are males.
>
> Jose is a male.
> _____
>
> **Jose is a father.**

So far, so good. Yet there are some other complexities. An argument can be valid *even though the premises are not true:*

> All men are fathers.
>
> All fathers are married.
> _____
>
> **All men are married.**

In this case, if all men are fathers and all fathers are married, then it would follow that all men are married. Yet common sense tells us that both the premises and the conclusion are false. Here is another such example:

> All fathers are baseball fans.
>
> All baseball fans like beer.
> _____
>
> **All fathers like beer.**

Thus, the logician makes a distinction between the truth or falseness of statements in an argument and the validity of the entire argument. The term *sound* is used to signify that an argument is valid and the premises are true. The rule for determining soundness is that if the premises are both true and the argument is valid, the conclusion cannot be false.

An argument can be valid even though the premises are not true.

The **rule for determining soundness** is that if the premises are both true and the argument is valid, the conclusion cannot be false.

To summarize, deductive arguments can be structured into a unit for the purposes of simplicity, clarity, and analysis according to standards for good reasoning. With this understanding of the basic vocabulary of logic, we can now consider in greater detail the unit of deductive argumentation—the syllogism.

A **valid** argument is one in which the conclusion has been correctly inferred from its premises. *Valid* comes from the Latin *valere*, to be strong.

Deductive logic is concerned with the rules for determining when an argument is valid.

A **sound** argument is one in which *the reasoning is valid and the premises are both true*. The word *sound* comes from an Old English word, *gesund*, which means healthy.

Standardized Forms in Syllogisms

Syllogisms have been discussed as a standardized form that makes the structure of a deductive argument visible. A syllogism presents claims concerning a relationship between the terms (classes or individuals) given in the premises and those in the conclusion. A standardized language, which makes these relationships clearer, has also been developed for phrasing the premises within the syllogism. Here are six examples of the standardized phrase forms used for expressing premises:

1. All _____ are _____.
2. All _____ are not _____.
3. No _____ are _____.

4. Some _____ are _____.

5. Some _____ are not _____.

6. If _____, then _____.

You will notice that in the first five forms, each of the blanks offers space for an adjective or noun phrase; in addition, each is connected by forms of the verb *to be* expressed in the present tense. This simplification allows a reduction of everyday language into verbal equations, thus making the task of argument analysis much easier. Now let's see how natural language has to be translated into this kind of standardized language for use in syllogisms. Compare the following translations:

Natural Language	Standardized Language
Ice cream always tastes sweet.	All ice cream food is sweet food.
Cats never take baths.	No cats are animals that take baths.
Some airlines have lower fares.	Some airlines are lower-fare transport.
If she is over seventy, she must be retired.	If she is a person over seventy, then she is a retired person.

DISCOVERY EXERCISE

■ *Practice in Constructing Syllogisms**

1. Rephrase each of the following sentences, if necessary, into a standard major premise. Then see if you can add a minor premise and a conclusion.

   a. All horses have exactly four legs.

   b. Everybody's got needs.

   c. Many eighteen-year-olds are college students.

   d. Lead is poisonous.

   e. If he's late, he'll be sorry.

2. Fill in the blanks in the following sentences so that all the syllogisms are valid.

   a. All horses are mammals.

   All _____ are animals.
   _____
   All horses are animals.

*For the style and method used in these exercises, I am indebted to Matthew Lipman's *Philosophical Inquiry: An Instructional Manual to Accompany Harry Stottlemeier's Discovery,* 2nd ed. Published by the Institute for the Advancement of Philosophy for Children, Upper Montclair, NJ, 1979.

   b. All horses are living things.

   All living things are things that reproduce.

   All _____ are things that reproduce.

   c. No sheep are creatures that sleep in beds.

   This creature is sleeping in a bed.

   Therefore, this creature is _____.

   d. If today is Tuesday, this must be Belgium.

   This is _____.

   This must be _____.

3. Choose the correct answer in each of the following cases.

   a. All beers are liquids.

   It therefore follows that:

   (1) All liquids are beers.

   (2) No liquids are beers.

   (3) Neither (1) nor (2).

   b. Florida is next to Georgia.

   Georgia is next to South Carolina.

   It therefore follows that:

   (1) Florida is next to South Carolina.

   (2) South Carolina is next to Florida.

   (3) Neither (1) nor (2).

   c. Ruth is shorter than Margaret.

   Margaret is shorter than Rosie.

   It therefore follows that

   (1) Ruth is shorter than Rosie.

   (2) Margaret is shorter than Ruth.

   (3) Ruth is taller than Rosie.

What Syllogisms Do

The logician accomplishes a number of purposes by standardizing the phrasing of arguments in syllogisms. Syllogisms help us

1. Clarify the claims of the premises

2. Discover and expose any hidden premises
3. Find out if one thought follows logically from another

Each of these objectives will be discussed in turn.

What Is Said and Is It True?

> Of course John is cheating on his wife. Doesn't he always come home late?

You will sense that something is wrong with this statement, but where do you begin? Here is where a syllogism helps, because a translation into a syllogism exposes an argument's structure:

> All husbands who always come home late are wife cheaters.
> John is a husband who always comes home late.
> _____
> **John is a wife cheater.**

Here the syllogism reveals a stereotype or hasty generalization in a *hidden major premise*. The words *all* and *always* make the claim in this hidden premise false. We could easily point out exceptions, such as "wife cheaters" who are punctual or loyal mates who work late. But in addition, *wife cheater* is an ambiguous term. What actions constitute wife cheating? The second premise also contains the vague terms *always* and *late*, which could be exaggerations. What does *late* mean? One minute or four hours? Does this mean *late* according to one person's expectations or according to a mutual agreement? Then there is the vague term *always*. If the person accused came home early only once, the generalization would not hold. Thus, although the reasoning may be valid, the argument's use of vague terms and false generalizations makes it unsound.

Now, let's consider another example:

> Our guest is Japanese. We had better cook rice rather than potatoes for dinner.

Here is the syllogism that such reasoning is based upon.

> No Japanese person is a potato eater.
> Our guest is Japanese.
> _____
> **Our guest is not a potato eater.**

The syllogism shows the reasoning is valid, but again the major premise, which had been hidden, is revealed as containing too broad a generalization to be true. For this reason, the conclusion is uncertain. Therefore, the argument is unsound.

Here is another example. You may have seen this claim on billboards:

Milk does a body good.

Because the billboard supplements this claim with attractive happy people, you may well conclude that you should remember to drink more milk. However, a syllogism will reveal some hidden aspects in this claim worth studying. First there is the ambiguity of the word *good*. *Good* has at least two meanings in this context: healthy and tasty. But a syllogism cannot function with words that have double meanings. In poetry, double meanings are effective. But in arguments, double meanings can be manipulative: they encourage assumptions and escape accountability. If the milk cooperative that paid for the ad were sued, its attorney could claim in court that the company was not claiming that its product was healthy, but only tasty. Nevertheless, suppose you assume that *good* means healthy in this case. You would write out the syllogism thus:

People who drink milk are people made healthy.

I am a person who drinks milk.

I am made healthy.

Thus, if you assume that the premises are true, the reasoning is valid. But when you want to know whether the argument is sound, you must ask questions to test the truth of the generalization in the major premise. Are there exceptions that would challenge its universality? What if my brother is allergic to milk? What about nutritionists who say that cow's milk is good only for cows? Again, as this syllogism shows, we have a false generalization, leading to an uncertain conclusion, and therefore the whole is an unsound argument.

Is There a Hidden Premise?

A major advantage of using syllogisms is that they reveal hidden premises—as you found in the major premises of the preceding examples. Consider the following examples, which contain questionable hidden premises. Note how the form of the syllogisms requires that they be exposed.

Senator Jones is a Democrat. Expect him to tax and spend.

All Democrats are taxers and spenders. (hidden premise)
Senator Jones is a Democrat.

Senator Jones is a taxer and spender.

Do I think he's sexy? Well, he drives a truck, doesn't he?

All those who drive trucks are sexy. (hidden premise)
He drives a truck.

He is sexy. (implied conclusion)

In the second example, both the major premise and the conclusion are hidden or implied. This often happens in advertising slogans:

The burgers are bigger at Burger John's!

As a syllogism, this reads as follows:

Bigger burgers are better burgers. (hidden premise)
Burger John's burgers are bigger.

Burger John's burgers are better. (hidden conclusion)

You should buy Burger John's burgers. (additional hidden conclusion)

Is the Reasoning Correct?

Here the logician is concerned with validity, or correct reasoning. The following argument is obviously valid:

She is either married or single.
She is married.

Therefore, she is not single.

The inference expressed in the conclusion automatically follows: she cannot be both married and single at the same time. Therefore if she is married, she cannot be single. The syllogism makes the validity of the reasoning transparent.

Now let's consider a more difficult example, one that appeared in a discovery exercise that opened this chapter.

Suspects who are innocent of a crime should be able to have a lawyer present before police questioning. But the thing is you don't have many suspects who are innocent of a crime . . . If a person is innocent of a crime, then he is not a suspect.

Here is a translation of that statement into a syllogism:

All innocents are not suspects.

You are a suspect.

You are not innocent.

In this case the reasoning is valid if you assume that both of the premises are true. It follows logically that if the categories of innocents and suspects are mutually exclusive, then if you belong in the category of suspects, you cannot belong in the category of innocents. However, the argument is not sound, because the major premise "All innocents are not suspects" is not true even though the minor premise "You are a suspect" might be.

Now let's take this argument a step further.

If you are a suspect, then you are questioned by the police.

You were questioned by the police.

You are a suspect.

Here, even if both the major and the minor premises were true, the conclusion could still be false. Suspects are not the only category of individuals questioned by the police. Police also question witnesses and bystanders. (Moreover, the implication of this line of reasoning is that if you are a suspect, you are guilty. But police do not make judgments about guilt or innocence; this is the function of a judge and jury.) However, simply on the basis of what is stated, the argument is invalid because the conclusion "You are a suspect" is not implied by its premises. Suspects are not necessarily always questioned by the police, and not all people questioned by the police are suspects. The illogic of the reasoning here can be recognized intuitively, but the syllogism exposes the way in which it is illogical.

Logicians have a number of rules for helping them determine whether or not an argument is valid. However, understanding these rules requires knowledge of further technical terms, which will be discussed in the next section of this chapter.

EXERCISE

■ *Reviewing the Vocabulary of Logic*

Work with a classmate to write down the definitions you can remember of the following words: *logic, reasoning, deductive* and *inductive reasoning, premise* (major and minor), *conclusion, argument, syllogism, true statement, valid argument, sound argument, hidden premise, hidden conclusion*. When you have finished, compare your definitions with those in the chapter summary on page 355. If there is a discrepancy, or if any of the definitions are still unclear to you, review the text discussion until you can explain the terms to your partner.

The Interplay of Inductive and Deductive Reasoning

> Whether we are aware of it or not, our thinking moves back and forth
> between inductive and deductive reasoning all the time.

Inductive and deductive thinking are not isolated modes. They interweave in our minds constantly throughout the day as we confront both serious problems, such as environmental degradation, and mundane ones, such as daily transportation. Let's consider the latter for illustration purposes.

Suppose you have an apartment in the Boston suburb of Needham and commute to Boston University downtown. You have a car, but you prefer to commute by the T train. You made this decision by reasoning deductively:

> All public trains are faster than car transport.
> I want faster-than-car transport.
> _____
> **I will take public trains.**

Suppose this reasoning stands you in good stead for some months. However, one morning you arrive at the station to find an unusually large crowd of people waiting there. You wonder what this means. Are there fewer trains today? Has there been an accident? Will everyone be delayed? You form hypotheses through inductive reasoning. You seek to test each hypothesis by searching for more information from those waiting. But all they can tell you is that their expected train has been delayed. Therefore you reason deductively:

> Delayed trains are unpredictable in schedule.
> This train is delayed.
> _____
> **This train is unpredictable in schedule.**

Then you reason inductively again in order to decide whether to wait or go home and get your car. You weigh the unknown factor of when the train will arrive against the time it might take to go home, get your car, and drive through heavy traffic. You decide that although the delayed train *may* make you late, driving your car will *certainly* make you late. And so, on the basis of your estimate of time and probability, you choose to wait in the station. Because you made this decision carefully, you will not get upset if the train is delayed for yet another thirty minutes. Moreover, you can be glad you did not impulsively run home to get your car without thinking the matter through, only to feel your blood pressure go up when you found yourself stuck in traffic with the train passing you by. You made a conscious decision to take the consequences with responsibility.

In college we study deduction and induction separately both for convenience and because of their different structures and standards (see Table 13.1). But whether we are aware of it or not, in our thinking we move back and forth between the two modes all the time. Yet, taking conscious notice of how our thinking moves between deductive and inductive modes has considerable advantages; we then can purposely direct our thinking to the mode that is more appropriate. This awareness also allows us to use the different standards of the two modes to evaluate what we are doing. Thus, we have a greater probability of arriving at better decisions. And even if we are disappointed with the results of our decisions, at least we know that we made a conscious choice that we can learn from.

TABLE 13.1 Comparing Inductive and Deductive Reasoning

Inductive Reasoning	Deductive Reasoning
Specific to general (usually, not always).	General to specific (usually, not always).
Purpose is to reach a conclusion for testing and application.	Purpose is to reach a conclusion that cannot be false.
Discovers new laws.	Applies known laws to specific circumstances.
Thinking guided by theories, observation, research, and investigation.	Thinking makes inferences about the relationship of claims.
Data are collected and analyzed.	
Sudden insights and unexpected discoveries can occur.	
Tests verify measure of truth in terms of reliability, accuracy, applicability, and their ability to be replicated.	Truth of premises is assumed or determined by reasoning.
Even if the premises are true, the conclusion is only probable and could even be false. More data or major changes could call for further testing.	If the premises are true, or assumed to be true, and the reasoning valid, the conclusion cannot be false.

Composition Writing Application

■ *Writing a Deductive Argument*

Write a deductive argument within the following parameters:

1. *Topic:* Application of an aphorism, or wise saying, to life.
2. *Approach:*
   a. Explain the aphorism.
   b. Define its terms.
   c. Illustrate it.
   d. Choose to agree, disagree, or both.
3. *Form:* Exposition and argumentation—explain, justify, and persuade through logic, reasoning, and example.
4. *Length:* Concise two pages.
5. *Subject:* Choose your own aphorism or select one of the following:
   a. The most savage controversies are about those matters as to which there is no evidence either way. (Bertrand Russell)
   b. Man is a social animal who dislikes his fellow men. (Delacroix)
   c. Competition brings out the best in products and the worst in people. (David Sarnoff)
   d. Failure is when you stop trying.
   e. People get the kind of government they deserve.
   f. Prejudice is never easy unless it can pass itself off as reason. (William Hazlitt)
   g. Life was meant to be lived, and curiosity must be kept alive. One must never, for whatever reason, turn his back on life. (Eleanor Roosevelt)

Chapter Summary

1. Deductive reasoning is the process of starting with one or more statements called premises and investigating what conclusions necessarily follow from these premises.
2. Deduction is the subject of formal logic, whose main concern is with creating forms that demonstrate reasoning.
3. Logic has its own technical vocabulary. The following is a summary of the definitions of key terms:

Argument:	A conclusion supported by reasons.
Claim:	A true or false assertion about something.
Conclusion:	The last step in a reasoning process. It is a judgment based on evidence and reasoning, an inference derived from the premises of an argument.
Hidden premise or conclusion:	A premise or conclusion that is not stated but implied in an argument. When the argument is cast in a syllogism, the missing premise or conclusion is expressed.
Hypothesis:	A theory, explanation, or tentative conclusion derived through inductive reasoning based on a limited view of facts or events.
Inductive reasoning:	The process of noting particular facts and drawing a conclusion about them.
Logic:	The science of reasoning; also called the science of inference.
Premises:	Statements, evidence, or assumptions offered to support a position.
Propositions:	Claims, statements, or assertions used in an argument. They can be either premises or conclusions and either true or false statements.
Reasoning:	The act or process of arriving at conclusions, judgments, or inferences from facts or premises.
Sound:	A sound argument is one in which all the premises are true and the reasoning is valid.
Syllogism:	The formalized structure of a deductive argument, usually written, in which the conclusion is supported by two premises.
True:	Corresponding to reality.
Valid:	A valid argument is one in which the reasoning follows correctly from the premises to the conclusion. An argument can be valid without the premises or conclusion being true.

4. The standardized language of syllogisms allows a reduction of everyday language into verbal equations.

5. Syllogisms allow logicians to determine what is being said, to identify hidden premises, and to find out if the argument makes sense.

6. Deductive and inductive reasoning are not isolated pursuits but are mentally interwoven both in major and mundane problem solving.

7. It is possible to infer the rules of valid and invalid reasoning from the study of models.

Building Arguments
Deduction

Great Spirit, my Grandfather, you have said to me when I was still young and could hope, that in difficulty I could send a voice four times, once for each quarter of the earth, and you would hear me.

Today I send a voice for a people in despair.

To the center of the world you have taken me and showed the goodness and the beauty and the strangeness of the greening earth, the only mother, and there the spirit-shapes of things, as they should be, you have shown me, and I have seen. At the center of the sacred hoop you have said that I should make the tree to bloom.

With tears running, O Great Spirit, my Grandfather—with running eyes I must say now that the tree has never bloomed. A pitiful old man, you see me here, and I have fallen away and done nothing. Here at the center of the world, where you took me when I was young and taught me; here, old I stand and the tree is withered, my Grandfather.

Again, and maybe the last time on earth, I recall the great vision you sent me. It may be that some little root of the sacred tree still lives. Nourish it, then, that it may leaf and bloom and fill with singing birds. Hear me, not for myself but for my people; I am old. Hear me, that they may once more go back into the sacred hoop and find the good road and the shielding tree. (Black Elk, shaman of the Oglala Sioux, 1912)

Speeches of the Native Americans offered in this series, together with the quotations from Alexander Henry and Joel Tyler Headley, were taken from Virginia Irving Armstrong, *I Have Spoken* (Swallow Press, 1971). Used with permission of Ohio University Press/Swallow Press.

Exercise

1. Can a prayer or prophecy be a deductive argument?

2. Write out the syllogism behind the reasoning of the first statement (major premise, minor premise, and conclusion). Also write out the syllogism behind the narrator's reasoning about the sacred hoop.

3. Write a deductive argument in which you make a claim about Black Elk's prayer. Support it with premises and draw a conclusion.

Chapter Quiz

Rate the following statements as *true* or *false*. If you decide the statement is false, revise it in the simplest manner to make it read true.

_____ 1. A premise is a reason given to support a conclusion.

_____ 2. Syllogisms are used in logic because logicians like to make their knowledge arcane, or hidden and secret.

_____ 3. Logic is less concerned with truth than with whether one statement follows reasonably from another.

_____ 4. Reasoning occurs only in deduction—not in induction.

_____ 5. A generalization reached through induction can become a premise used in a deductive syllogism.

_____ 6. "All homeowners are taxpayers. He is a property owner. Therefore, he is a taxpayer." This is a valid argument.

_____ 7. "Bloodletting reduces fever. This patient has fever. This patient needs bloodletting." This syllogism shows valid reasoning although both premises may not be true.

_____ 8. "White-skinned people are superior to dark-skinned people. Therefore, it is the manifest destiny of white-skinned people to rule dark-skinned people." No country would ever accept such fallacious reasoning as this.

State whether the reasoning in each of the following syllogisms is correct or incorrect:

_____ 9. If the two parties agree, then there is no strike.

   The two parties agree.
   _____

   Therefore, there is no strike.

_____ 10. If the two parties agree, then there is no strike.

   There is no strike.
   _____

   Therefore, the two parties agree.

_____ 11. If the two parties agree, then there is no strike.

   The two parties do not agree.
   _____

   Therefore, there is a strike.

_____ 12. If the two parties agree, then there is no strike.

   There is a strike.
   _____

   Therefore, the two parties do not agree.

After you have decided, compare your answers to those given here. Explain why these answers are correct.

9. correct 10. incorrect 11. incorrect 12. correct

• R E A D I N G S •

The Declaration of Independence (excerpt)

Thomas Jefferson

Based on a clear line of deductive reasoning, this great historical document written in 1776 is also an enduring work of literature. Jefferson begins by stating some "self-evident truths," or axioms, which set off a revolution and formed the ideological basis for the laws of a new government. This document can be studied as a structure of reasoning in four parts. Following are the first and last parts. Notice as you read how they function as the major premise and conclusion of an argument.

When in the Course of human events, it becomes necessary for one people to dissolve the political bands which have connected them with another, and to assume among the powers of the earth, the separate and equal station to which the Laws of Nature and of Nature's God entitle them, a decent respect to the opinions of mankind requires that they should declare the causes which impel them to the separation.

We hold these truths to be self-evident, that all men are created equal, that they are endowed by their Creator with certain unalienable Rights, that among these are Life, Liberty and the pursuit of Happiness. That to secure these rights, Governments are instituted among Men, deriving their just powers from the consent of the governed. That whenever any Form of Government becomes destructive of these ends it is the Right of the People to alter or to abolish it, and to institute a new Government, laying its foundation on such principles and organizing its powers in such form, as to them shall seem most likely to effect their Safety and Happiness. Prudence, indeed, will dictate that Governments long established should not be changed for light and transient causes; and accordingly all experience has shown, that mankind are more disposed to suffer, while evils are sufferable, than to right themselves by abolishing the forms to which they are accustomed. But when a long train of abuses and usurpations, pursuing invariably the same Object evinces a design to reduce them under absolute Despotism, it is their right, it is their duty, to throw off such Government, and to provide new Guards for their future security. Such has been the patient sufferance of these Colonies; and such is now the necessity which constrains them to alter their former Systems of Government. The history of the present King of Great Britain is a history of repeated injuries and usurpations, all having in direct object the establishment of an absolute Tyranny over these States. To prove this, let Facts be submitted to a candid world . . .

We, therefore, the Representatives of the United States of America, in General Congress, Assembled, appealing to the Supreme Judge of the world for the rectitude of our intentions, do, in the Name, and by Authority of the good People of these Colonies, solemnly publish and declare, That these United Colonies are, and of Right ought to be Free and Independent States; that they are absolved from all Allegiance to the British Crown, and that all political connection between them and the State of Great Britain, is and ought to be totally dissolved; and that as Free and Independent States, they have full Power to levy War, conclude Peace, contract Alliances, establish Commerce, and to do all other Acts and Things which Independent States may of right do. And for the support of this Declaration, with a firm reliance on the protection of divine Providence, we mutually pledge to each other our Lives, our Fortunes and our sacred Honor.

● ● ●

Study/Writing/Discussion Questions

1. In the first sentence it is stated that people are entitled by "the Laws of Nature and of Nature's God" to separate and equal stations. What does this mean? Is there any evidence offered to back this claim?

2. Outline the deductive reasoning offered in the second paragraph. Which truths does Jefferson claim to be self-evident? What is the purpose of governments? From where do they derive their power?

3. How does Jefferson anticipate the argument that this kind of reasoning would allow people to overthrow governments "for light and transient causes"?

4. In the last paragraph, in the name of what authorities does he make the declaration?

5. Compare this document, and the reasoning used therein, with two of its offspring, *The Seneca Falls Declaration* written by Elizabeth Cady Stanton (1848) and the *Universal Declaration of Human Rights* (1948), which was, in large part, authored by Eleanor Roosevelt.

Letter from a Birmingham Jail (excerpt)

Martin Luther King, Jr.

This letter was written by Martin Luther King, Jr., in 1963 after his arrest at a sit-in to protest segregation of eating facilities. His actions resulted in a turning point for the civil rights movement in that, in the same year, the Supreme Court ruled that Birmingham's segregation laws were unconstitutional. Notice how in this short excerpt he draws major premises from statements made by authorities and then reasons from these premises.

I would agree with St. Augustine that "an unjust law is no law at all." . . . How does one determine whether a law is just or unjust? A just law is a man-made code that squares with the moral law or the law of God. An unjust law is a code that is out of harmony with the moral law. To put it in the terms of St. Thomas

Aquinas: an unjust law is a human law that is not rooted in eternal law and natural law. Any law that uplifts human personality is just. Any law that degrades human personality is unjust. All segregation statutes are unjust because segregation distorts the soul and damages the personality. It gives the segregator a false sense of superiority and the segregated a false sense of inferiority. Segregation, to use the terminology of the Jewish philosopher Martin Buber, substitutes an "I–it" relationship for an "I–thou" relationship and ends up relegating persons to the status of things. Hence segregation is not only politically, economically, and sociologically unsound, it is morally wrong and sinful. Paul Tillich has said that sin is separation. Is not segregation an existential expression of man's tragic separation, his awful estrangement, his terrible sinfulness? Thus it is that I can urge men to obey the 1954 decision of the Supreme Court, for it is morally right, and I can urge them to disobey segregation ordinances, for they are morally wrong.

● ● ●

Study/Writing/Discussion Questions

1. State King's argument in the form of a syllogism.
2. Why do you suppose King chose to refer to the authorities of Catholic church philosophers (St. Augustine and St. Thomas Aquinas) as well as a Jewish and a Protestant theologian (Martin Buber and Paul Tillich)?
3. Which terms does he define and why?
4. What conclusions does he draw from his premises?
5. Explain how the sound logic of his reasoning makes his argument so compelling.

Objectives Review of Part III

After you have finished Part III, you will understand:

1. Why arguments are supported claims
2. How reasons differ from conclusions
3. What questions to ask in analyzing arguments
4. Why fallacies make arguments deceptive
5. Definitions and examples of twenty informal fallacies
6. The forms and standards of inductive and deductive thinking
7. The concepts of empirical reasoning, scientific method, hypothesis, probability, and causal reasoning
8. The basic vocabulary of logic
9. The functions of the syllogism
10. The differences between deductive and inductive reasoning
11. How inductive and deductive reasoning interplay in our thinking

And you will have practice in developing these skills:

1. Identifying conclusions and separating them from reasons
2. Identifying reports and separating them from arguments
3. Articulating the question at issue
4. Analyzing arguments
5. Writing a persuasive argument under the pressure of strong feelings
6. Evaluating deductive arguments for validity and soundness
7. Identifying hidden premises
8. Applying different standards to inductive and deductive reasoning
9. Researching and preparing your take-home final

The Research Paper

Research Paper Assignments in This Text

If you have been assigned a research paper due at the end of the semester, you should begin your research by the time you finish Chapter 9 on Arguments. Instructions are provided in this appendix for two research writing assignments. Each assignment will challenge you to integrate all the critical thinking skills you have learned and apply them to writing about a controversial issue of your own choice. You may be asked to do only the first assignment, an outline analysis of two arguments, or you may be required to write a longer argumentative essay.

This section includes instructions for these two assignments together with suggestions for scheduling and researching. To give you a visual model to follow, a portion of one student writing sample also appears in this section. This sample offers an analysis of the two arguments on illegal immigration that appear in the Readings section at the end of Chapter 9.

FIRST OPTION:
Analysis of Two Arguments Pro and Con on a Recent Controversial Issue

This assignment can also serve as a final take-home exam, because its purpose is to allow you to demonstrate all the knowledge and skills you learned while studying this book. Nevertheless, you should begin to prepare for it at least a month before the end of the semester, before you finish reading the text. Indeed, having this assignment as a goal will help you understand the last three chapters even better. The skills that this assignment requires include being able to do the following:

- Isolate a recent controversial issue.
- Research to find two arguments from two different sources, if possible, representing two different viewpoints on one debate question related to that same issue.

- Identify the political or social orientation of a viewpoint.
- Select a complete argument, either in full or extracted from a larger article, in order to analyze its structure, strengths, and weaknesses according to standards learned in this text.
- Compare, evaluate, and summarize both arguments. Then choose the better argument on the basis of critical thinking standards.
- Follow instructions and communicate your findings clearly.

▪ Overall Format

Follow your instructor's directions for presenting your work. You might use a simple folder to contain your take-home final research paper. The folder would contain a title page, a table of contents, four to six pages of analysis, and the photocopied arguments. The whole paper should come to about ten pages. Take pride in giving your work a professional appearance.

▪ Research Preparation

Choose one topic of recent controversy that interests you. Stimulate your thinking by following the daily news, by browsing in the library or on the Internet, and by studying magazines and newspapers representing different points of view. Remember you are looking for a subject of current

---

Instructions for the Argument Analysis Assignment

This assignment is not an essay assignment but an outline analysis of two arguments. Read the instructions given below first. Then skim through the student sample to see how it serves as a visual model of the outline format you will be using. Finally, return to read the remainder of the guidelines offered here.

Outline Form Used in This Assignment

Offer your complete analysis of each argument one by one. Use the outline topic form that appears in the following, and follow through all these steps with each argument. A photocopy of each argument you selected to analyze should appear at the end of each outline.

Part I: Title Page: Write the debate question on the title page followed by your name, the date, your course number, and a short table of contents.

Part II: Headings: At the top of your first page fill in the following information:

1. **The debate question:**
2. **Title:** (of the article or argument, magazine or newspaper)
3. **Date of publication:**
4. **Form:** Argument Pro or Con (This is to test your ability to distinguish an argument from a report.)
5. **Viewpoint:** Label the viewpoint politically or socially.

Part III: Basic Structure of the Argument

6. **Conclusion:** State the argument's conclusion using your own words or short quotes.
7. **Reasons:** List all the reasons given in the argument to support this conclusion. (Do this in your own words or with short quotes.)

Part IV: Critique Questions: Review the argument according to the following items. Discuss each fully and systematically. Remember this is not just an exercise in finding flaws; you may find much in the argument to commend.

8. **Argument structure:** How is the argument structured? Briefly describe and evaluate the way it is put together without getting into too many details. Generalize about its special features and mention how the conclusion and the reasons are presented.
9. **Ambiguous or prejudicial words:** Are any central words in the argument ambiguous or prejudicial?
10. **Fallacies:** Does the argument contain any fallacies? If so, identify each fallacy and discuss each one with specific examples.
11. **Hidden assumptions:** Does the argument make any hidden assumptions? What are they and how do they affect the argument?
12. **Missing information:** Is any important information missing?
13. **Contradictory or false information:** Is any information false, irreconcilable, or contradictory?

Part V: Final Summary Comparing the Two Arguments: On a final page, summarize the two arguments. Which viewpoint do you find the more persuasive and why? Remember you are not being asked to defend your own viewpoint on this issue but only to show why you find one to be the more persuasive argument.

controversy—one that will demand more thinking than a topic that has been around long enough to accumulate a lot of familiar opinions.

Let's suppose, for instance, that you pick up a recent magazine called *Natural Health* and notice an article on irradiated foods. You might be surprised to read that Congress is considering a bill that would no longer require irradiated foods to bear prominent labels. Your curiosity might motivate you to find out more about this whole subject. You might first go onto InfoTrak or the Internet and enter "irradiated foods" in search engines such as Google or Yahoo. Should irradiated foods be a current hot news item, you could also go online to read such newspapers as *The Washington Post, The New York Times,* and *The Los Angeles Times* for articles written on irradiated foods during the past year; you could also use their archives for articles published in years past. After making an initial survey of the topic, you could then begin to print out a collection of the best reports and arguments for your research file. Before long, you should feel reasonably informed on the topic. The test would depend on whether you know the following:

- What are the main issues or unresolved problems related to irradiated foods?
- What are the arguments pro and con on each issue?
- What are the debate questions being addressed?
- What groups, individuals, or organizations are representing each position?

Suppose the issue of the *safety* of irradiated foods is what interests you most. However, you may decide not to work with this issue, because it would involve technical opinions and speculations. You may then decide to search for pro and con arguments on the *labeling* of irradiated foods; however, as it turns out, you can only find one suitable argument. On the other hand, you have found two good pro and con arguments on the issue of the *need* for irradiated foods. At this point, you decide to select this issue for your research paper. Therefore you formulate the debate question that both of your arguments address: "Do we really need irradiated foods?" Debate questions are sometimes stated within arguments; sometimes they appear in their headings above pro and con arguments that appear on editorial pages of newspapers. They are spelled out in publications like *Speeches of the Day* or *The Congressional Digest.* Nevertheless, in most cases, you will need to study your argument selections carefully in order to recognize the debate question they are commonly addressing. Here you may need the assistance of your instructor. Before proceeding, you need confirmation that you have formulated your debate question correctly. (If you want to learn a great deal more about preparing and writing the research paper, refer to the list of handbooks on page 368.)

■ Arguments, Not Reports

A second confirmation that you will need concerns your selection of an argument rather than a report. *No matter how much work you do on this assignment, you will not succeed if you try to work with reports rather than arguments.* Reports sometimes give short quotes of pro and con arguments; however, what you need are two single coherent arguments written each by one person expressing one person's point of view. If you are unsure whether you have an argument or a report, get your instructor's opinion before beginning this assignment.

■ Length and Viewpoints of Arguments Selected

Your argument selections should be short—not more than twelve paragraphs. If you want to excerpt your argument from a longer article, photocopy the whole article and attach it to your final paper with a border around the section you chose to analyze. (However, make sure the section you choose is a complete argument in itself.) Newspaper editorials and letters to the editor can also serve as short arguments. If you are working on a political topic, find two different views, such as liberal and conservative, from two different published sources. If you choose a sociological issue, such as physician-assisted suicide, find two different perspectives such as a physician's view, a minister's view, and/or a relative's view.

Scoring for Analysis of Two Arguments

1. Two different arguments (not reports) from two different authors addressing the same issue and taken from two different publications. *20 points*

2. Follows the format required; photocopies are attached. *10 points*

3. Conclusion and reasons correctly identified; all reasons are listed. *20 points*

4. Accurate and insightful critique that addresses:
   Analysis of argument structure
   Ambiguous and prejudicial words
   Fallacies of reasoning
   Hidden assumptions
   Missing information and/or false information
   Any other pertinent characteristics
   42 points (7 points each)

5. Final summary that compares the two and chooses the better argument. *8 points*

SECOND OPTION:
An Argumentative Research Essay

Here is an opportunity for you to express and defend your own view in depth on one current controversial issue. You can prepare by completing the previous assignment or by taking up a different issue that you have researched independently. This will be a research paper from ten to thirty pages in length, depending on your instructor's specifications.

▪ *Preparation Instructions*

Prepare to write an argumentative essay by following these steps:

1. Write out fully your own viewpoint on the issue that you have researched for several weeks, either for the previous assignment or in consultation with your instructor. Write freely without self-censorship for as many pages as it takes to exhaust what you have to say.

2. Now shape your principal claim into a thesis, taking care to choose your key terms carefully. Use clustering as needed.

3. Leaving wide spaces between each statement, outline your support for this thesis in terms of claims and/or evidence.

4. Consult your research file and notes to see what information you have that might be pertinent to use for illustration and support. Take notes on what further research you may need to complete now and as you go along. Make notes on your outline concerning where you need supporting information or quotations. As you organize the data in your research file, remember that you will be quoting or referring to sources in the MLA style of documentation. Use a reference handbook recommended by your instructor for information about the new 2009 MLA style. You will need to prepare a "Works Cited" list as well as a bibliography. Therefore, as you do your research, be sure to record all the citation data you will need in order to save yourself a frantic search the night before your paper is due. You might also want to consult a handbook for more research suggestions or review the skills of proper summarizing, quoting, and paraphrasing in order not to plagiarize your sources.

5. As you write and revise your outline, note where you need to acquire more evidence or examples and where you already have enough material to write the number of required pages.

6. Keep your outline before you as you write. Tack it up on the wall. Read and reread it to make sure that each part of the essay relates to your thesis. Revise it as needed.

■ *Writing the First Draft*

7. Now start to flesh out the skeleton of your outline. Introduce your subject, stating the issue in your first paragraph. Explain why this issue interests you and why it should be of interest to the reader. You might summarize some of the different positions taken on this issue. Then state your position—your thesis or principal claim. Also provide any definitions necessary to explain how you are using your terms.

8. As you write, seek to be as clear as possible. Guide your readers so that they can know exactly what you are doing at each step as you pursue your argument. Read your work aloud to friends to discover what they need to hear to understand you.

9. In the second paragraph or paragraphs give an argument to defend your principal claim, clearly stating your premises and conclusion as well as your evidence.

10. In the paragraph that follows, state any major objection or objections that others might have to your argument. You can counter these with further arguments or evidence.

11. If you think of further criticisms that might be made of your counterargument, reply to these.

12. As you continue to write your draft, decide at some point whether you can fully support your original thesis or whether you might need to modify it. If this should occur, go back to your outline and revise accordingly.

■ *Final Touches*

13. When you have finished your final draft, find another good listener. Notice where you are not understood or where, in explaining, you find that you need to say more in writing.

14. Rewrite your work as necessary to improve coherency and correct errors.

15. The following handbooks are recommended for guidance in research writing:

   - Slade, Carole & Perrin, Robert. *Form and Style: Research Papers, Reports, Theses*, 13th edition. Cengage Learning, 2008.
   - Kirszner, Laurie G., & Mandell, Stephen R. *The Brief Wadsworth Handbook*, 6th edition. Cengage Learning, 2010.
   - *MLA Handbook for Writers of Research Papers*, 7th edition. Modern Language Association of America, 2009.

Scoring for Argumentative Essay

1. Thesis is clearly stated with all key terms defined. *10 points*
2. Support is adequate and complete in defense of the thesis. *30 points*
3. Paper shows the author is well informed on the issue selected. *20 points*
4. All citations and bibliography are correctly presented in MLA form. *10 points*
5. The argument is persuasive. *10 points*
6. Writer is able to summarize, use quotations, or paraphrase as needed. *10 points*
7. No distracting errors in spelling, mechanics, and sentence structure. *10 points*

Student Model Paper

Analysis of Two Arguments on the Question:
Are Illegal Immigrants Criminals Who Harm America?

Andrea Welch
University of California, Santa Barbara

Table of Contents

Part 1: Pro Argument

Title: "Illegal Immigration Is a Crime" by Federation for American
                 Immigration Reform
Publication: FAIR website, last updated in March of 2005
Form: Argument
Viewpoint: Conservative

Conclusion:
Illegal immigrants are criminals whose presence harms the United States and its people.

Reasons:
1. Illegal immigrants break our nation's laws: illegal entry is a misdemeanor and, if repeated, a felony. Both immigrants and overstayers are deportable under the Immigration and Nationality Act.
2. Illegal immigration is not a victimless crime. Such immigrants harm American citizens by their "enormous" drain on public funds, which is not covered by the taxes they might pay.
3. Their desperation for work depresses wages and working conditions for American citizens and legal workers.

4. They contribute to "dramatic population growth," overcrowding problems in schools and housing, and strain natural resources. Immigration authorities estimate they increase by a half million people annually.
5. They are a threat to national security; their presence outside the law in this country opens the door for terrorists.
6. Current border control efforts are inadequate.
7. We need a comprehensive effort to end illegal immigration, including "ensuring that illegal aliens will not be able to obtain employment, public assistance benefits, public education," and public housing. Congress also needs to strengthen immigration control through "deterrence, apprehension and removal."
8. The costs will "require adequate resources" that will be more than offset by the savings.

Structure

The FAIR argument's introduction uses the word "alien" in the first sentence. This sets the tone for the following paragraphs that seek to prove that illegal immigrants are criminals whose presence damages our country. The authors cite the appropriate laws, and define the two types of illegal immigrants under the law. The remainder of the argument is split into six paragraphs, each with a summary heading representing a chief point of the argument. The paragraphs expand upon these points with further claims but little evidence. The argument's structure makes a good impression in that it is short and decisive.

Fallacies

1. Ambiguous or Prejudicial Words

The use of the the word "alien" in the first sentence creates a prejudicial tone. This is followed by the phrase "flagrantly violate our nation's laws by unlawfully crossing U.S. borders." The next paragraph uses the expression "sneaking into the country," implying that this is the fact, as opposed to the legal expression, "entry without inspection."

2. Poisoning the Well

With the use of the word "alien," the authors open the argument with language that inspires fear and makes the reader feel as distant from undocumented workers as possible. The second paragraph also features words that poison the well of opinion; "sneak" and "violate" paint a mental picture of immigrants as criminals guilty of shameful criminal activity.

3. Appeal to Fear

By arousing fear of immigrants, it is much easier to criminalize them. Fear could also be incited by linking terrorists to immigrants in paragraph 7. The use of the term "alien" suggests that illegal immigrants are an inhuman mass that is slowly but surely taking over our country by causing "enormous" strain on our resources—both natural and man made. Yet no solid empirical data (besides the statistic on their half million a year increase) is offered to show in what ways these "endless numbers of poor, unskilled" people are impacting our communities.

4. Red Herring

When the authors attempt to link illegal immigration and terrorism, they do so in a vague and ambiguous statement saying that illegal immigration allows terrorists to "blend into the same shadows [as illegal immigrants] while they target the American public for their terrorist crimes." This statement in no way explains how illegal immigrants and terrorists are linked; such assumptions are left up to the reader. The author's mentioning of terrorists in an argument about immigration distracts the reader from the lack of evidence and re-focuses them on the issue of terrorism.

5. Hasty Generalization

The authors of this article make some generalizations that are not supported. For instance, it is stated that "illegal immigration causes an *enormous drain* on public funds. . . . the taxes paid by immigrants *do not begin to* cover the cost of services received by them." These are generalizations that might well be validated with supporting statistics, but in this argument only vague phrases appear.

6. False Cause

The authors of this argument are basing it on the assumption that illegal immigrants cause the social problems they describe in the article. The authors greatly oversimplify the immigration problem, never mentioning the employers who entice immigrants to cross the borders with offers of work, the policies of the U.S. government that protect such employers, or the policies of the Mexican government that facilitate immigrants in their departure.

7. Misleading Euphemisms

The use of the words "deterrence," "apprehension," and "removal" in the second to last paragraph are misleading. These words mask the often times brutal and unfair reality that is behind the actions described by these terms, thus making these ideas seem more acceptable and distant or removed from their real-world counterparts.

Hidden Assumptions

The leading hidden assumption that underlies this argument is that the only cause of illegal immigration is the criminality of the immigrants. If the authors wanted to prove this claim, they would have to consider all the complexities that make this problem so persistent.

Missing Information

1. The complex causes of illegal immigration, its ramifications, and nuances.
2. The multiple contradictions in U.S. policies regarding illegal immigration, such as the recruitment of immigrants through employment and higher wages in the United States and the allowance of amnesty to illegal immigrants in the late 1980s.
3. Employers who hire workers without papers are also committing a crime according to the 1986 Immigration Reform and Control Act.
4. The high social costs of illegal immigrants to taxpayers might have something to do with their low wages and lack of worker benefits.
5. Missing statistics in the section called "Illegal Immigration Is Not a Victimless Crime."
6. Missing statistics about other costs. If millions of workers are deported, what will happen to the employers dependent upon the services of these millions of workers?

Part II: Con Argument

Title: "Mayday for Undocumented Workers" by David Bacon
Publication: *San Francisco Chronicle*, May 1, 2008
Form: Argument
Viewpoint: Liberal

Conclusion:

"Instead of making work a crime and treating immigrants as criminals, we need equality, security jobs and rights for everyone."

Reasons:

1. Undocumented workers are contributors to the society they live in.
2. Some state and local communities, taking the green light from Homeland Security, are passing measures that go too far in an effort to criminalize undocumented workers.
3. The massive numbers of firings that would result from a proposed rule requiring employers to fire any worker who could not correct a mismatched SSN would bring many industries to a halt.

4. Regulations requiring actions based on information from an often-inaccurate SSN database would affect citizens and legal immigrants as well.
5. Undocumented workers with false Social Security numbers do no harm: they deposit money into the social security system and will never benefit from their contributions.
6. Arizona and Mississippi have recently passed stringent new laws that can also be unfair to undocumented workers.
7. For most illegal immigrants there are no jobs to return to in their home countries. When Congress passed NAFTA, it created economic hardships in Mexico that resulted in six million displaced people coming to the United States.
8. "The government is really after giving cheap labor to employers. Deportations, firings and guest worker programs all make labor cheaper and union organizing harder. They contribute to a climate of fear and insecurity for everyone."

Structure

David Bacon sets a sympathetic tone as he opens his argument with imagery of an immigrant May Day march, describing the participants as ordinary workers with "calloused hands." In the second paragraph he states his theme that they all are contributors to society and have meant it no harm. He refers to them as "undocumented workers." Bacon then spends the rest of his argument criticizing recent legal actions taken at the state, federal, and local levels that would further criminalize undocumented workers. He also explains the systemic causes for the dramatic increase in illegal immigration from Mexico since the 1980s. He concludes with three paragraphs to back up his claim that the intensified harassment of illegal immigrants makes them more vulnerable so as to benefit the employers with cheaper, unorganized labor.

Fallacies
1. Word Ambiguity

Bacon uses ambiguous language to distract attention from the fact that the entry of so many thousands of these workers is illegal. Bacon glosses over this point saying only that "some have come with visas, and others without them." He downplays the situation.

2. Misleading Euphemisms

Bacon describes illegal immigrants as "contributors to the society they've found here." A contributor can contribute many things, good and bad; thus this statement is also a hasty generalization. In addition, it ignores the impact of an untold number of illegal persons' "contributions" to the public and natural resources of this country.

3. Emotional Appeals to Fear or Pity

Bacon uses statements that inspire pity in the readers. He writes a tale of signs held in the "calloused hands" of men and women who had "come from work in a factory, cleaning an office building, or picking grapes." These mental pictures serve to create sympathy for the illegal immigrants gathered on May Day to protest for their right to work in this country; they provide no concrete data to support his argument. He goes on to speak of children living in fear of their parents being picked up in raids, which is a very real consequence of illegal immigration. However, its purpose seems mainly to tug on the reader's heartstrings.

4. Pointing to Another Wrong

Bacon's entire argument is based on the wrongs of the government—a bad SSN database, bad motives, and bad legislation—all causing problems for undocumented workers. It ignores the fact that immigrants coming to this country without papers or inspection are in fact breaking the law.

5. Red Herring

Bacon argues that because actions taken by our government forced workers in Mexico to come the United States to work, now that they are here the government needs to provide for them. However, he does not take into account what the Mexican government should be doing to help its own workers. Instead, he claims that because the U.S. government created the situation, it must help and protect people who are knowingly and willingly breaking its laws.

Hidden Assumptions

1. That the United States is unilaterally responsible for the effects of NAFTA on Mexico.
2. That the United States can keep an open-door, open-arms policy for illegal immigration indefinitely.
3. That legal immigration is not an option for these workers.

Missing Information

Except for the factor of the Mexican government in this equation, I could not find any crucial missing information.

Part III: Final Summary Comparing the Two Arguments

I believe that neither of these articles are the best representatives of those I have read on the issue of illegal immigration. My beliefs follow Bacon's argument and I agree with everything he says; however, the loose structure of the argument and the lack of consideration for other viewpoints make this argument weaker in some ways than the FAIR argument.

The FAIR argument is more successful in conveying its message. This is due to its explicit organization and explanations (though they are shallow explanations) of the argument's main points. I believe that this argument is aimed at people looking for a simple answer to a very complex question, and in that respect, it succeeds. I do not agree with the FAIR authors' viewpoint, but I do acknowledge that the way they structure their argument is more successful than the organization of Bacon's argument.

Media Literacy:

How Can I Become Well-Informed?

On Being Well-Informed

You might call the hero of this cartoon a creative thinker. But is he a critical thinker? Like so many, he keeps his attention on day-to-day survival. There seems to be no time to ask: How did pollution get to be this bad?

Who is responsible for this problem? Can I do anything about it? Sadly for us all, he remains the proverbial poor sucker.

Ideally in a democracy, a citizen always retains sovereignty together with the power to act and make a difference. Yet acting on poor information can be worse than taking no action at all. Thus it is crucial to become an *informed* citizen. But then that raises the question of how to become well-informed. How much information is enough? How does one know if the information is reliable? Where does one begin?

Although it may take some time to find answers to these questions, the act of formulating them is a significant step forward. Many students, in particular those who must also work and support families, say that they have little time to follow the news. At most they read newspaper headlines, listen to their car radios on the way to work, catch perhaps the 6:00 TV news, or watch late evening political satire on Comedy Central. Some might give up trying altogether: "I don't believe anything I hear on the news" or "You can't do anything anyway."

We live in a world that provides us with a glut of information about a world more and more difficult to comprehend. The complex causes of the growth of air pollution provide only one example taken from hundreds of unprecedented problems that affect our planetary health and survival. At the same time that our technological resources interconnect us, we are unclear about our responsibilities to one another. Yet our planetary survival remains a collective matter.

By the time you have worked your way through this text, you will already have acquired many of the skills needed for gaining information and evaluating its reliability. As you already must know, such skills will help you academically, personally, and professionally. What now remains is this mini-chapter for those of you who want to better understand the world and participate more actively therein. These skills involve media literacy, specifically as they apply to following the daily news.

Media Literacy Skills for Assessing News Reliability

Media Literacy

Media Literacy . . . provides a framework to access, analyze, evaluate and create messages in a variety of forms — from print to video to the Internet. Media literacy builds an understanding of the role of media in society as well as essential skills of inquiry and self-expression necessary for citizens of a democracy. *Center for Media Literacy*

The idea of teaching media literacy is a relatively new one, having first made headway in public education during the 1980s. Basically, it teaches students how to think critically about the media that surround and influence their whole lives.

In this short appendix we are going to focus only on two practical issues:

1. How do we know that any piece of news information is reliable?
2. What steps might lead us most quickly to that determination?

Assessing the reliability of information begins not with the reading of **content** but with giving close initial attention to the **sources** that prepared this information. When applied to the daily print news, sources range from the newspapers themselves, such as the *Los Angeles Times* or *Boston Globe*, to the news services they employ such as Reuters and Associated Press, to individual reporters, columnists, op-ed writers, public relations releases, government releases, editorials, and to excerpts taken from other newspapers such as the *New York Times* and *Washington Post*. Thus a skilled reader always begins by looking for a source designation under the article's headline or, in an op-ed piece, by jumping to the end of the article to note the author's name and credentials. Such a habit allows a provisional assessment of the work's authenticity, its potential bias, and its accountability to standards.

Some Guiding Principles

If you want to become a well-informed reader there are five useful things to know about news information and news sources. A well-informed reader, aside from having critical thinking skills, is a person who knows how to assess news significance, assess news sources and news information for reliability, keep current on significant world events, and connect these events to past events. This is a tall order, but the time involved can be significantly reduced when one gains confidence in the skills of news discrimination, and source and information assessment. Most time loss occurs from filling the mind with junk news, with false or unreliable information, or with confusion about missing information. Thus, since most of us need to budget our time, these five guiding principles offer the attraction of avoiding such pitfalls while increasing efficiency and competence.

1. **There is no one single central reliable source of information.** Some of us may have formed the habit of reading one newspaper regularly or hearing the news on one radio station or seeing it on one television station. Yet no single source lacks limitations and biases. No one single news source can claim that it always gets the truth, even though most claim they strive for accuracy and some claim to be "fair and balanced."

2. **The most accessible sources of news information are not necessarily the most reliable.** As you will see in the discussion of the mass media that follows, your local newspaper, radio, and television stations either no longer exist or lack the independence they had in the more recent past. Today, unless you find the Internet to be your most accessible source, you are left, for the most part, with sound bite news. Even though you can see and hear more depth and range of news coverage on NPR and PBS, such stations continue to struggle to retain their independence.

3. **Reliability can best be determined by comparing multiple news sources.** People who try to be well informed make it a regular habit to read, hear, or view multiple news sources. By comparing the treatment of any one story, they are able to pick up corroborations or contradictions. They also see how different sources can offer different facts, different emphases, and different interpretations. Over time, through regular reading or viewing, the well informed might hope to discover some constants that might approach truth, especially if the topic has stimulated a lot of public debate.

4. **Obviously, you can't keep up with everything.** Election time asks us to follow a lot of issues closely. However, on an ongoing basis, you may have to choose a few issues you will have the time to follow closely. Decide how much time you can give and stick to that, even if it means allotting only one hour a week.

5. **Learning how to evaluate sources takes knowledge of their background, history, values, biases, qualifications, and reputations.** It also requires knowledge of the journalistic standards that they are expected to adhere to. This is admittedly a lot to learn. And unless you have studied journalism, you probably will not gain this knowledge in college. The purpose of the remainder of this Appendix is to give you a head start in that direction.

Journalism in the Role of the Fourth Estate

Fourth Estate

The fourth estate refers to the press as an unofficial balance to the three branches of government: the executive, legislative, and judicial. Ideally, the role of the press is to serve as a guardian of democracy and defender of public interest and welfare. Essential for accomplishing such purposes are a strict code of ethics together with the rights of free speech and freedom of the press.

The concept of the press in the balancing role of a Fourth Estate that defends truth and public interest goes back to mid-nineteenth century Europe. This novel idea, adopted in our country, has influenced many events in U.S. history and contributed to our health and vibrancy as a nation. There have been times when the power of this role has been clearly prominent, as in the case of the Watergate investigations that were initiated by two *Washington Post* reporters, resulting eventually in the resignation of President Nixon.

An important adjunct to the Fourth Estate role is the Journalists' Code of Ethics, a code first developed in the 1920s. It offered journalists a clearly stated code to clarify their values, help them make ethical decisions, and enable them to deserve public trust. In 1996 the Society of Professional Journalists spent some months reformulating the Code. That code is not presented here in its entirety. Three principles stated therein are: (1) to seek truth and report it; (2) act independently ("free of obligation to any interest other than the public's right to know"), and (3) "avoid conflicts of interest, real or perceived." You can read many more of their standards following. These standards have significance for us as critical readers, because it is by them that we judge news report writing. They are also standards that we might feel inspired to emulate in our writing as well.

Journalists Should:

1. Test the accuracy of information from all sources and exercise care to avoid inadvertent error. Deliberate distortion is never permissible.
2. Diligently seek out subjects of news stories to give them the opportunity to respond to allegations of wrongdoing.
3. Identify sources whenever feasible. The public is entitled to as much information as possible on sources' reliability.
4. Always question sources' motives before promising anonymity. Clarify conditions attached to any promise made in exchange for information. Keep promises.
5. Make certain that headlines, news teases and promotional material, photos, video, audio, graphics, sound bites and quotations do not misrepresent. They should not oversimplify or highlight incidents out of context.
6. Never distort the content of news photos or video. Image enhancement for technical clarity is always permissible. Label montages and photo illustrations.
7. Avoid misleading re-enactments or staged news events. If re-enactment is necessary to tell a story, label it.
8. Avoid undercover or other surreptitious methods of gathering information except when traditional open methods will not yield information vital to the public. Use of such methods should be explained as part of the story.
9. Never plagiarize.

10. Tell the story of the diversity and magnitude of the human experience boldly, even when it is unpopular to do so.
11. Examine their own cultural values and avoid imposing those values on others.
12. Avoid stereotyping by race, gender, age, religion, ethnicity, geography, sexual orientation, disability, physical appearance or social status.
13. Support the open exchange of views, even views they find repugnant.
14. Give voice to the voiceless; official and unofficial sources of information can be equally valid.
15. Distinguish between advocacy and news reporting. Analysis and commentary should be labeled and not misrepresent fact or context.
16. Distinguish news from advertising and shun hybrids that blur the lines between the two.
17. Recognize a special obligation to ensure that the public's business is conducted openly and that government records are open to inspection.

In the last few decades, the trend toward media consolidation has raised many new ethical challenges for reporters. In 1983, Ben Bagdikian, University of California journalism professor and media critic, expressed alarm that the vast number of independent U.S. newspapers, book publishers, and radio and television stations had come under the control of only 50 corporations (*Media Monopoly*). Yet by the year 2005 that number was down to five mass media corporations: News Corporation, NBC/General Electric, Viacom, Time-Warner, and Walt Disney. By the year 2008 that number was down to *three* mega corporations controlling most of the major U.S. television and cable networks. They include News Corporation, Time-Warner (HBO and CNN), and Walt Disney (ESPN and ABC), with NBC now split off from General Electric and CBS from Viacom. All have additional holdings in newspapers, radio stations, book publishing, magazines, film, record, and music companies. In addition, all are tied to one another through interlocking directorates that include most major corporations in addition to banking, insurance, and finance corporations.

A number of media critics (as featured in the attached reading list) have claimed that the quality, freedom, and diversity of journalism have suffered because of this consolidation. Some have argued that Fourth Estate purposes have little meaning in an environment where corporate values, profit motives, and vested interests predominate, where the objective is not to inform or educate the public but to entice customers into buying their own products. Moreover, they say that the corporate media tend to prefer to avoid criticism of the government in power if the criticism might affect their business association with the government.

Yet the strength and power of the journalists' professional code of ethics can be seen in a number of events that occurred in 2004–2005. These events included the use of anonymous sources, admitted fabrications by journalists, and the government's hiring of journalists to promote unpopular government programs in their columns and radio programs. In all of these cases, journalist behavior was measured against this code.

Hopefully the future will bring even more freedom of expression and more depth of information to the news media landscape. According to the Newspaper Association of America, online newspaper readership continues to rise. Should the Internet remain a forum for free speech without censorship, it may continue to allow access to a growing wide array of news sources. The present vacuum in local news could be filled by enterprising independents or by podcasting. The changeover from analog to digital television, with the opportunity for multicasting, could result in far more in-depth community and public service information.

Becoming a well-informed citizen is not easy; it does take some research effort, education, and time, but the resulting feeling of empowerment can make the effort worthwhile. What follows is a brief outline of information designed to encourage you to explore, compare, and assess multiple media sources. This exploration can be done either through class study or self-study. If you find this study to be rewarding, you might find yourself selecting a few news sources to consult on a regular basis. Gradually such a habit may lead you to feel able to make better informed decisions and act accordingly for the benefit of yourself and others.

Suggestions for Further Study

Some Recent Books on the Media

Bagdikian, Ben. *The New Media Monopoly.* Beacon Press. 2004. A revision of a ground-breaking book first published in the 1980s by a long-time journalist and professor of journalism.

Jamieson, Kathleen Hall and Joseph N. Capella. *Echo Chamber: Rush Limbaugh and the Conservative Media.* Oxford University Press, 2008. The lead author is a communications professor at the University of Pennsylvania and director of the Annenberg Public Policy Center there.

Kovach, Bill and Tom Rosenstiel. *The Elements of Journalism: What Newspeople Should Know and the Public Should Expect.* Crown. 2001. This book includes an appraisal of journalism ethics.

Mathison, David. *Be the Media.* Natural E Creative Group, 2008. This book offers tools and instruction for creating your own independent

Steps for Assessing Information Reliability

What Is the Source of the Information?

Does the publication have a known bias?
Is the author of the article identified?
Are the person's credentials and affiliations provided?
What more would you like to know about this source?

Is This Information Current?

Is the date of its writing or publication given?

How Is the Information Framed?

How is it framed visually in terms of photos, page, and size selections?
How is it framed verbally in terms of headlines, lead lines, and relative
   dominance?
What information is emphasized?
Is any crucial information downplayed or omitted?

How Is the Information Organized?

Is this clearly a report, an argument, or a hybrid?
What is the ratio of facts to inferences?
Is this one person's opinion or are multiple views considered?
Are the sources used cited and identified?

How Is Language Used in This Information?

Is it mainly neutral or slanted?
Are any words ambiguous or prejudicial?

How Is Reasoning Used?

Is it logically coherent?
Is it free of contradictions?
Is it free of fallacies?

Comparison to Other Sources

Are they largely in agreement or not?
Does this comparison reveal inaccuracies?
Does this comparison reveal signs of bias?
Does the comparison reveal missing information?
Does the comparison reveal distortions due to oversimplifications?

media. The author is a media reform activist and former vice-president of Reuters News Agency.

McChesney, Robert. *The Political Economy of Media: Enduring Issues, Emerging Dilemmas.* Monthly Review Press. 2008. The author is a professor of journalism at the University of Illinois and author of numerous books on the media and politics.

Phillips, Peter and Project Censored. *Censored 2009.* Seven Stories Press, 2008. This annual publication involves 200 people and originates from Sonoma State University.

Postman, Neil. *Amusing Ourselves to Death: Public Discourse in the Age of Show Business.* Penguin. 2005. This is a classic text first written in 1985. The author was a media critic and professor at New York University.

Schor, Juliet. *Born to Buy: The Commercialized Child and the New Consumer Culture.* Scribner, 2004. The author is a professor of sociology at Boston College.

Zuniga, Markos Moulitsas. *Taking on the System: Rules for Radical Change in a Digital Age.* Celebra. 2008. Primer for activists by the founder of the leftist blog, *Daily Kos.*

Sample Websites for Studying the News

Current News Services Online

Here are a few sites that offer quick updates of the news, offering articles taken from a wide variety of independent sources, both U.S. and international.

> Google News
> World News
> Yahoo News

Online International News in English

> BBC News
> EINNews.com global news service
> Global Voices
> Watching America (translations of articles about the United States.)

Online Foreign News in English

> Aljazeera (Arab News)
> AllAfrica

Globe and Mail (Canada)

Haaretz.com (Israel and Palestine)

The Independent (U.K. and world news)

Xinhuanet.com (China)

Some U.S. Newspaper Sites

Some of these sites are free; some require subscriptions (which may be paid by your library). A few offer to send free daily news to your email address.

Left-Leaning Editorials	Right-Leaning Editorials
Boston Globe	Chicago Tribune
Los Angeles Times	New York Post
San Francisco Chronicle	Wall Street Journal
The New York Times	Washington Times
The Washington Post	

Some U.S. Think Tanks

Listed below are some of the more prominent U.S. think tanks. Some have reputations for being truly independent research centers seeking to influence the government and public for the common good. Others have been accused of functioning more as lobbyists for certain political, social, and economic ideas. These think tanks affect the news in that their findings are often cited in the media, their hired authors write newspaper op-ed pieces, and their "experts" appear on television programs. In the chart below their political leanings have been culled from evaluations made by InfoUSA and Wikipedia. Also consulted was a chart that appeared in the May/June 2005 edition of *Extra!* (a progressive magazine sponsored by the organization FAIR).

Progressive	Centrist	Conservative	Libertarian
Center for Public Integrity	Brookings Institution	Heritage Foundation	Cato Institute
Economic Policy Institute	Council on Foreign Relations	Hoover Institution	
Center on Budget and Policy Priorities	Carnegie Endowment	RAND	
		American Enterprise Institute	

Progressive	Centrist	Conservative Libertarian
Democracy Alliance	The Carter Center	Hudson Institute
	Worldwatch Institute	Manhattan Institute for Policy Research

Media Critique Sites

Left Wing	Right Wing	Independent
Fair.org	Accuracy in Media	Cjr.org(Columbia Journalism Review)
Freepress.net	Media Research Center	
Medialiteracy.org		Factcheck.org
Mediamatters.org		Stats
Sourcewatch		
Spin@prwatch.com (The Weekly Spin sent to your email address)		

Non-Partisan Voter Information Sites

Politics1.com

Project Vote Smart

Voter Information Services

Some Political Activism Sites

Progressive	Conservative	Independent
Biogems	Christian Coalition	Congress.org: Issues & Action: Action Alert Search
Moving Ideas: The Electronic Policy Network	Concerned Women of America	
	Family Research Council	WWW Virtual Library: International Affairs Resources
Moveon.org	National Rifle Association	
True Majority	The Club for Growth	
20/20 Vision		

INDEX